Free Speech in the Good War

Free Speech in the Good War

Richard W. Steele

St. Martin's Press
New York

FREE SPEECH IN THE GOOD WAR

ISBN 0-312-17336-9

Library of Congress Cataloging-in-Publication Data

Steele, Richard W.
  Free speech in the good war
Richard W. Steele.
    p. cm.
  Includes bibliographical references and index.
  ISBN 0–312–17336–9
  1. Freedom of speech—United States—History. 2. War and emergency powers—United States—History. 3. World War, 1939–1945—United States. I. Title.
KF4772.S74 1999
342.73'0853—dc21   98–32166
                                             CIP

Design by Letra Libre

First edition: April, 1999
10 9 8 7 6 5 4 3 2 1

For Elaine

Contents

Acknowledgments

A great many people contributed to the making of this project. I am, of course, indebted to the score or more archivists and librarians at the National Archives, the Library of Congress, and the many other research institutions whose records I drew upon. Kelley Martin, who directs the Interlibrary Loan office at San Diego State's Love Library, and the members of her staff were unfailingly obliging and deserve special mention. I appreciate as well the efforts of Keith Dyson and the other Justice Department and FBI personnel who responded to my Freedom of Information Act requests with the stacks of documents upon which much of the following is based. They were courteous and helpful. The system, however, produced delays of more than two years and I hope that some way might be found to expedite the clearance of documents more than 50 years old.

I am grateful to the San Diego State Foundation and to the National Endowment for the Humanities for grants in aid that helped offset the costs of my research, and to a number of colleagues and former students who surveyed archival collections and supplied me with materials. These include Joyce Appleby, Lyn Frankenberg, Margaret Grimshaw, Serena Kobayashi, and Jane Steele. Patrick Washburn graciously shared copies of documents he had secured under the Freedom of Information Act.

My colleague, the late Richard T. Ruetten, stimulated my enterprise in its early stages. Important assistance also came from Theodore Kornweibel and Jacob Vander Muelen, each of whom read chapters and provided me with valuable suggestions. Francis N. Stites not only spared me a trip to a relatively remote archive, but helped sharpen my thinking on free speech issues through innumerable conversations. My gratitude goes as well to Norman Rosenberg, who read the entire work while it was in progress and made numerous trenchant observations and recommendations couched in tones that encouraged refinement rather than abandonment. Without his counsel, this would have been a different, and inferior, piece.

My thanks also to Karen Wolny, Rick Delaney, and Amy Reading, my editors at St. Martin's press, for shepherding this project to completion.

I benefited most of all from the personal support and professional skills of my wife, Elaine, who critiqued and edited the manuscript more times than we care to remember and ultimately put this work into publishable form. In gratitude, I have dedicated this work to her.

Del Mar, California
RWS

A Legacy of Restraint

The Second World War may have been the "good war" for most Americans, but many did not see it that way. In the months before the Pearl Harbor attack thrust the United States into war, and for some time after, a small but noisy minority fought American involvement, condemned the president, disparaged the military effort, and praised the nation's enemies. Some of the dissident voices came from the Left—Stalinists (for a time) and Trotskyites. A few were those of black nationalists. Most emanated from what we might now call the "Radical Right." But whatever the critics' ideological orientation, many Americans, in government and out, found their sentiments intolerable, and as war approached and then engulfed the United States, pressure mounted to end the dissonance.

The Roosevelt administration investigated suspects for their "un-American" associations, and employed a variety of legal devices to harass the dissenters and suppress the dissent. The dozens victimized for their utterances and associations during World War II did not approach the thousands prosecuted for sedition during World War I. But the comparison does not fully gauge the seriousness of the repressive undertaking. If one looks at the paucity of opposition to the war and the extraordinary efforts to suppress what little radical dissent there was, the administration's record is less restrained than the figures suggest. The ambiguous results, as well as philosophical differences concerning the meaning of free speech, have left historians seriously divided in their assessment of civil liberties in World War II.[1] This study, without presuming to resolve such differences, seeks to explain both the intensity of the campaign to silence extremist views, and its meager tangible consequences. Its focus is the deliberations and actions of those, chiefly officials of the Department of Justice, who administered the effort.

"Free speech," much praised in American political discourse and raised to the status of holy writ in the 20 years since the end of World War I, in fact remained ill defined on the eve of American involvement. As a practical matter, what the phrase meant would be established by federal prosecutors and their superiors in the Department of Justice, subject only to belated review by the Supreme Court. Long before that tribunal would be called upon to judge the legitimacy of their actions, department officials were obliged to decide what suspicious activity would be investigated, and what apparent violations of the anti-sedition statutes would be punished (or tolerated). This was never merely a process of matching suspect speech against the letter of the law. Determining which words would be ignored and which suppressed was a political undertaking involving the interaction of the values the attorney general and his staff brought to the task, their predictions of how the courts would view their efforts, and the political pressures that inevitably surrounded each decision.

Justice Department policy was shaped by several major imperatives. As custodians of a branch of the legal system, the lawyers who ran the agency wanted to act in consonance with American legal principles as they understood them. Aware that their conduct reflected on them personally and professionally, they were conscious of the need to succeed in court, avoid rebukes from their peers, and leave a record of which they might be proud. As public servants in a democratic political system, they were obliged to be sensitive to the Congress and conscious of the public's demands. Most importantly, as political appointees of the president, they were loyal to Franklin D. Roosevelt and responsive to his wishes. These factors were sorted out, weighed, and converted to public policy by the three attorney generals and the other officers of the agency that was at once the guardian of the nation's internal security and the protector of its people's constitutional rights.

As the nation drew closer to and then entered the Second World War, officials repeatedly looked to American experience in World War I for instruction. Over and over, particularly in the early months of World War II, department lawyers were reminded of the mistakes the department had made earlier and recalled the damage done to the department's reputation by its association with the repressive excesses of the previous generation. The institutional memory of the World War I era disposed department leaders to proceed cautiously as the public again demanded the repression of unpopular expression.

The relevant wartime experience may be outlined briefly. By the end of 1916, the war that began among the European powers two years earlier had bogged down into a bloody stalemate. President Woodrow Wilson, who had urged Americans to remain neutral in thought and deed, nevertheless concluded that a German victory over Great Britain and her allies would undermine democracy worldwide and destroy the international rule of law. In April 1917, moved by a series of German provocations, the president asked Congress for a declaration of war, arguing that intervention was not merely an act of national self-interest, but the beginning of a great crusade for the vindication of civilized intercourse among nations. The implications this religious fervor held for dissenters were soon apparent.[2]

In the months that followed, chauvinistic citizens set about punishing those they thought failed to demonstrate sufficient devotion to the holy cause. Coerced affirmations of loyalty frequently sufficed, but on scores of occasions in communities throughout the nation the nonconforming and the unlucky were tarred and feathered, painted yellow, dunked, ridden out of town, beaten, whipped, hung to unconsciousness, and occasionally murdered by mobs acting in the name of patriotism. The foreign born, particularly those from Germany, suffered, as did radicals and even recalcitrant workers, as patriotism provided a cover for a stepped-up war on radicalism and unionism. State and local authorities, acting under pre-existing and newly enacted anti-sedition legislation, nicely complemented the work of the vigilantes.[3]

Although Wilson and other federal officials were troubled by these acts, which they regarded as "excesses," they were determined to ensure what they saw as a fragile national unity. In mid-June 1917 the administration secured passage of the Espionage Act, which would provide the legal basis for most of the prosecutions for sedition both in this war and in World War II.[4] The law provided for fines and imprisonment for anyone convicted of making false statements intended to interfere with the military, promote disloyalty among the nation's soldiers or sailors, or obstruct military recruitment. It also authorized the nation's postmasters to withdraw second-class mailing privileges from any publication that they decided carried material inimical to the war effort.

The Justice Department, under Attorney General Thomas Gregory, enforced the law to the fullest.[5] Federal agents spied on dissidents and sought evidence with little regard to due process of law except, as historian William Preston notes, in "its narrow procedural sense."[6] To increase the government's capacity to monitor dissent, the attorney general authorized creation of the American Protective League (APL), whose two hundred thousand members reported suspicious activities to the department.

Thanks in part to their activities, the department's efforts, according to Gregory, "put the fear of God in the hearts" of the potentially disloyal.[7]

The character of the acts prosecuted varied with the prejudices of the various United States attorneys who, taking their cue from the concerns of local populations, used the law to cow the few who challenged the officially proclaimed and generally accepted version of the war.[8] Prosecutors diligently pursued cases against persons whose speech making and pamphleteering posed only the remotest challenge to the war effort. Government propaganda was offered to the courts as fact against which the truthfulness of criticism was measured, and defendants were charged with making "false" statements because they contradicted the version of events propounded by the president.[9] With few exceptions, judges upheld the government's contention that utterances might be punished if they merely tended, however remotely, to encourage unlawful activities, making it unnecessary for prosecutors to show that actual harm resulted.[10] The defendants (many of them radicals) were usually, by definition, "outsiders" who found little sympathy among the middle-class jurors who heard their cases.[11] The appellate courts, in line with the then current limited view of First Amendment freedoms,[12] generally ratified the convictions, and long prison sentences were the rule.

Even so, the Espionage Act did not quite reach every dissenting utterance,[13] and to extend its reach the department secured an amendment, called the Sedition Act of 1918,[14] that provided for fines and imprisonment for anyone convicted of uttering *any* disloyal statement (true or not, regardless of intent); or expressing contempt or scorn for the government; or using profane, scurrilous, or abusive language about its agencies or officials. The stage was set for an expansion of the orgy of repression when the end of the war mercifully forestalled it.

A reaction against these repressive excesses, muted during the war for obvious reasons, began to surface as the conflict neared its conclusion.[15] For a number of years members of the growing urban intelligentsia had become increasingly disturbed over the ability of the unenlightened and reactionary members of their communities to use the law and extralegal means to undermine organized labor and stifle radical political agitation. They worried that depriving workers of a voice to protest well-known injustices promised to perpetuate intolerable conditions and turn the disaffected into anarchistic mobs. These fears commingled with concerns that those seeking to prevent economic justice were also bent on imposing their provincial tastes on the small universe of thinking people. Those who valued art and culture found common cause with economic and social reformers.[16]

The wholesale repression that accompanied the war transformed this rather inchoate discontent into a national issue. Most criticism centered on the activities of the patriotic zealots, but early on a few critics identified the government's complicity. Philosopher-educator John Dewey gave carefully worded expression to growing anxieties in an article that appeared in the *New Republic* two days before the guns fell silent. Every sensible American was "willing to sacrifice something of his ordinary freedom of speech," he wrote, but the government's spying on and persecution of Americans went far beyond the state's legitimate concerns. Although he carefully avoided naming those responsible, Dewey suggested that the administration, in an ill-disguised conspiracy to serve the interests of business, had helped create the irrational concerns that it then used as an excuse for silencing criticism.[17] The most distinguished intellectual in America had identified the Department of Justice with wartime repression, and responsible officials took note.

Dewey's general attack on the wartime administration of justice was made more explicit in a series of works by Zechariah Chafee. A Harvard law professor who had recently taken an interest in free speech issues, Chafee argued that the government's wartime record marked a shameful break with the "great tradition of freedom in English and American law." "We have made a mistake," Chafee insisted, and "we should admit it frankly before intolerance becomes a habit in our law."[18] Although he couched his criticism in temperate terms that spoke of collective responsibility, Chafee charged Justice Department and post office officials with "chief responsibility" for turning the Espionage Act into a dragnet for pacifists and other dissenters. Repression, he wrote, began at the point the government decided to punish speech that was "far from direct and dangerous interference with the conduct of the war."[19]

Even as the world war was ending, criticism of the department prompted former Department of Justice officials to counter unwarranted allegations of repression and seek reforms designed to prevent repetition of those acts justly charged against the government.[20] Leading the effort was John Lord O'Brian, a progressive Republican active in civic reform who, in 1917, found himself in charge of the department's newly created War Emergency Division.[21] His office was responsible for enforcing the anti-sedition statutes and was thus a prime target of criticism directed at federally sponsored repression. O'Brian, while chagrined by some of the violations of civil liberty with which the department was associated and hurt by the criticism, was by and large proud of the work he had done and determined that the informed public understand the pressures and constraints under which the department had been obliged to operate. O'Brian believed that speech that genuinely threatened the conduct of the war had to be suppressed, and he had no regrets about having ordered the arrest of popular Socialist Party leader Eugene Debs and others whose serious criticism suggested resistance to the war effort. On the other hand, he had decided early on that the department should tolerate the "crackpots and the ignorant" unless they were really deterring men from the draft. The issue for him was not a choice between total repression or absolute freedom, but a carefully drawn line between the two.[22]

O'Brian undertook not only to set the record straight but to counsel future department officials on how they might draw the line and mitigate anticipated public pressures. In April 1919, as he and his assistant, Cincinnati attorney Alfred Bettman, wound up the affairs of the War Emergency Division, they produced "Regulation of Free Speech," which they intended as a guide for the incoming attorney general and his successors. In it they argued that wartime repression was chiefly the product of mass hysteria, and that official abuses of civil liberties came largely in response to public demands. O'Brian urged officials to head off such pressures by publicly and emphatically dedicating the department to the proposition that "no man shall be officially discriminated against or deprived of his civil liberties by reason of his opinions or affiliations so long as he does not violate law." This would presumably ward off those who might be tempted to make repressive demands of the government, and provide officials with an answer to those who did.

Tolerance of this sort carried no penalty, he noted, because order and social progress had little to fear from dissenting voices. The irresponsible stifling of dissident opinions, on the other hand, was apt to heighten discontents and quicken seditious conspiracies, creating the very problems repression was meant to stifle, and he counseled officials to take the initiative in fighting the local sources of repression. The department, O'Brian argued, must fulfill its "peculiar function" of protecting civil liberties by curbing the vigilante, and he suggested that the attorney general seek legislation authorizing federal prosecution of private citizens and state officials who violated civil rights.[23] The Justice Department would ensure obedience to law by actively protecting the lawful airing of grievances.

O'Brian's principal public statement of his position came in a speech he gave to the New York State Bar Association, which was later reprinted by the United States Senate and made available in pamphlet form.[24] His first convert was one of the department's most important critics. In a November 1918 *New Republic* article and June 1919 *Harvard Law Review* essay,

Zechariah Chafee had laid much of the blame for repression at the door of the Department of Justice. O'Brian and Bettman succeeded in convincing Chafee that his criticism had missed the mark,[25] and his widely read *Freedom of Speech,* published in 1920,[26] reflected the O'Brian/Bettman take on the wartime Justice Department. Indeed, one of the lawyers who served in the War Emergency Division assisted Chafee in preparing the book's treatment of the department.[27] Thus, while Chafee's influential (if historically inaccurate) brief on behalf of political tolerance[28] repeated his earlier condemnation of wartime violations of what he offered as civil libertarian norms, he argued that community prejudices, not the embattled leaders of the department, were responsible. Political repression, he suggested, was principally a popular phenomenon, requiring the protection of minorities from majority demands, rather than the protection of the individual from the state.

O'Brian's message was lost on A. Mitchell Palmer, who succeeded Gregory as attorney general. Chaos and revolution in Europe in the aftermath of the war were matched by labor unrest and radical agitation in the United States. Soon the country was gripped by a Red Scare, to which Palmer responded decisively, inappropriately, and illegally. In June 1919, frightened by a bombing attempt on his own home and determined to make a reputation for himself by catering to antiradical concerns, the attorney general ordered a nationwide roundup of radical aliens. Literature confiscated in the raids was submitted to an eager press as proof of smoldering conspiracy and the need for further efforts to smother an incipient conflagration.

At first the raids drew praise from "responsible" sources. But criticism very quickly mounted. It centered on Justice Department tactics that included the indiscriminate ("dragnet") arrests that became known as the "Palmer raids," and the incarceration of the victims under abysmal conditions while they awaited deportation. In proceedings before a district court in Boston, Judge George Anderson, significantly selecting a metaphor commonly used to explain intolerance and repression, called federal agents "a mob," not "of criminals, loafers and vicious classes," but no less a mob for that.[29] A group of prominent lawyers, including Chafee, investigated, and their *Report Upon the Illegal Practices of the United States Department of Justice* detailed the unreasonable searches and seizures, warrantless arrests, cruel and unusual punishments, and other unconscionable and unconstitutional activities employed by department agents.[30] At the end of the year, the Senate Judiciary Committee investigated the charges and castigated the department for its brutal and illegal behavior.[31]

In the early 1920s, new scandals involving the department finally produced reform. Hard on the heels of the Palmer raids came charges of impropriety and corruption directed at officials of the ill-starred administration of President Warren G. Harding, including Attorney General Harry Daugherty. William J. Burns, the former private investigator who headed the Justice Department's investigations unit, came to his boss's aid by launching a campaign of spying, intimidation, and other acts aimed at discrediting those involved in exposing department corruption. In March 1924, a Senate committee discovered that bureau agents had not only gone through the files of various congressmen critical of the attorney general, but had investigated thousands of "radicals" and other suspect Americans.[32]

Responding to criticism, President Calvin Coolidge, who succeeded Harding upon the latter's untimely death, appointed Harlan Fiske Stone, a prominent attorney and former dean of the Columbia University Law School, to replace Daugherty.[33] Stone set about to professionalize the department and to see to it that its actions were henceforth above legitimate reproach.[34] His efforts focused on the Bureau of Investigation, the agency that had been the object of most of the criticism. In May 1924, Stone issued regulations aimed at ensuring that the department would no longer menace "free government and free institutions," declaring that henceforth investigations would be conducted only in conjunction with anticipated federal prosecution. The Bureau of Investigation, he told the press, would not be "concerned with political or other opinions of individuals . . . only with their conduct and then only with such conduct as is forbidden by the laws of the United States."[35] Agents were to be held strictly accountable to the law, and the bureau kept to a size commensurate with its legitimate activities.[36] In his first report to Congress, Stone assured the legislature and the department's critics that agents would no longer investigate people because of their opinions, and would abandon the practice of encouraging and collaborating with state officials in the prosecution of radicals. None of this meant a dramatic new acceptance of radicalism. Rather it reflected a feeling that the immediate threat to order posed by radical agitation was less than that implicit in the lawless and wanton pursuit of dissidents.

Stone's choice for director of the newly created Bureau of Investigation, which at the time seemed unexceptional, turned out to be an appointment of some significance. After first offering the post to John Lord O'Brian, the man who had suggested the reforms he was seeking to implement, Stone appointed a career department bureaucrat, John Edgar Hoover, who had succeeded in concealing the full extent of his involvement in the Palmer raids. O'Brian was among those impressed by Hoover's work and may have suggested his appointment.[37] Accepting Stone's offer, Hoover proceeded to rebuild the investigative office, later called the Federal Bureau of Investigation (FBI). He hired educated agents to replace the snoops that had staffed the old investigative apparatus, inculcated them with professionalism, ruled them with a tight hand, and, in line with Stone's edict, kept them from engaging in some of the more notorious practices of the past. Above all, Hoover concentrated on shaping a positive image for the FBI, even meeting with a representative of the American Civil Liberties Union (ACLU) to ask for any information implicating his agents in untoward behavior and promising swift action against any he found culpable. The civil liberties organization responded by lauding Hoover and the "new" department that he served.[38]

Nevertheless, lingering suspicions concerning the department's record in World War I prompted former attorney general Thomas Gregory to urge O'Brian to write a full account of the War Emergency Division's activities. It would be most unfortunate, he warned, if the wartime administration of justice was tainted by the reputation earned by Palmer's "senseless attacks on what he called radicalism."[39] O'Brian did not write the history of wartime justice that Gregory suggested, but for more than two decades those who wanted the inside story and the "lessons" of events in 1917–18 turned to O'Brian,[40] and his influence was apparent in the standard history of the department, *Federal Justice,* published in 1937.[41] In 1940, when the department was again faced with war and "un-American" agitation, officials called on O'Brian to share his experiences, and his counsels of restraint would be reflected in the department's attitude toward political expression during the Second World War.

Interest in curbing the Department of Justice was part of a larger appreciation of free speech that flourished in the decades between the world wars. Recent developments, including Prohibition, the suppression of information on contraception, the movement to outlaw the teaching of biological evolution, the rise of the Ku Klux Klan, and the bigotry and injustice clear in the prosecution of anarchists Nicola Sacco and Bartolomeo Vanzetti, were seen by "intelligent public opinion" as evidence of the public's repressive instincts.[42] The generation that included those who would serve in government during World War II, worried that personal liberties were at the mercy of the mob mentality,[43] and many of their cohort supported efforts to strengthen the meaning of "freedom of speech."[44] The educational efforts were led by the ACLU,[45] founded during the war by Roger Baldwin, Norman Thomas, John Haynes Holmes, and others. In the 1920s the organization, as part of a campaign to promote a more tolerant view, lent legal aid to defendants challenging the application of repressive laws.[46]

The ACLU's educational campaign helped establish the idea that, for anyone to enjoy free speech, the freedom must be guaranteed to *everyone*. "Free speech for everyone," although not meant literally, became the unofficial slogan of a diverse group of liberal and radical civil libertarians who associated themselves with the ACLU.[47] It was a persuasive ideal and the organization's membership multiplied. Affiliates sprang up across the country, and the ACLU was able to secure the volunteer services of bright young lawyers and established attorneys.[48] By the mid-1930s Baldwin and his associates had become a significant force[49] contributing to the spread of the gospel of free expression.

Kenneth Karst has noted that factions in society often seek validation of their faiths and causes in the opinions of the Supreme Court, and so it was for civil libertarians.[50] There was not much in the Court's treatment of free speech issues through the 1920s that lent encouragement to the movement for greater freedom, but there was one powerful statement that advocates of greater freedom could draw on. In *Abrams* v. *United States,* decided late in 1919, the Court upheld the conviction of a group of young socialists under the 1918 Sedition Act. But an eloquent dissent by Justice Oliver Wendell Holmes, Jr. set forth an evocative consideration of the meaning and limits of free speech that would inspire a generation of free speech advocates.

Ideas, Holmes declared, were important, and it was understandable that people would seek to stifle opinions with which they did not agree. But succumbing to that temptation, Holmes insisted, undermined the foundations of democracy because progress depended on airing unorthodox views, even if they were obnoxious. History has taught, he wrote, that "the ultimate good desired is better reached by free trade in ideas," and that "the best test of truth is the power of the thought to get itself accepted in the competition of the market." No absolutist, Holmes recognized a legitimate governmental interest in the suppression of destructive speech, and he offered a variation on the "clear and present danger" formula he had proposed in an earlier decision[51] to suggest where officials might legitimately draw the line between protected speech and sedition: "I think we should be eternally vigilant against attempts to check the expression of opinions that we loathe and believe to be fraught with death, unless they so imminently threaten immediate interference with the lawful and pressing purposes of the law that an immediate check is required to save the country."[52]

Holmes had provided libertarians with a pragmatic and authoritative rationale for resisting society's intolerant instincts.

Although from time to time over the next decade Holmes and Justice Louis Brandeis, who joined him in the *Abrams* dissent, had occasion to reiterate their endorsement of free speech, their views at first gained no support from their judicial brethren. Beginning in 1931, however, the Court, recently liberalized by the addition of Chief Justice Charles Evans Hughes and Associate Justice Owen J. Roberts, produced a number of decisions that shifted legal thinking away from the presumption in favor of repression and toward stricter limits on the state's authority to control speech. Although some commentators warned that the Court was going too far, constitutional lawyers and civil libertarians were generally enthusiastic.[53]

In the 1930s the defense of free speech assumed the proportions of a national cause, at least among the educated. Persons and groups not normally associated with the issue were prominent among those extolling First Amendment freedoms. Spokesmen for industry and commerce, seeking protection from New Deal–era controls, asserted their support for an expansive reading of the First Amendment.[54] So did newspaper publishers, who sought protection against regulation of their industry,[55] and radio broadcasters, vulnerable to the Federal Communications Commission.[56] Endorsements of a broad application of constitutional protections came also from mainstream attorneys. In his 1938 inaugural address, American Bar Association (ABA) president-elect Frank Hogan complained that the proponents of personal and political freedoms seemed preoccupied with the problems of the downtrodden. Without rejecting this application, he suggested that it unfairly neglected another small and harassed minority—the wealthy and privileged—and he counseled the profession to make the public understand that civil liberties were not just for society's traditional victims.[57] He was, in effect, upbraiding conservatives for leaving this popular, and potentially useful, issue to the leftist ACLU. His views were echoed by Grenville Clark, a distinguished New York corporate lawyer, characterized by Roger Baldwin as a man of conscience and conviction,[58] who urged conservatives to use the current libertarian enthusiasm to serve their perspective. He pointed out, however, that demanding constitutional protections for their interests entailed a commitment to the rights of others. "In the long run, there will be no such thing as freedom of speech and assembly for some . . . and restraint and repression for other groups. . . . Security for the civil liberties of any of us is dependent upon the firm defense of the civil liberty of all of us."[59]

In 1939, the ABA created a Bill of Rights Committee that, under Clark's chairmanship, would undertake to spread this message and give it practical expression. The move coincided with the celebration of the nation's sesquicentennial anniversary of the Bill of Rights, which lasted from 1939 through 1941.[60] The occasion was marked by a continuous round of tributes to the nation's heritage of freedoms, including principally its First Amendment guarantees. The ABA's contribution to the festivities was its establishment, with a Carnegie foundation grant, of the *Bill of Rights Review,* which, along with pamphlets and public discussions sponsored by the organization, offered scholarly and popular treatments of civil liberties issues. The committee also encouraged the establishment of a number of local Bill of Rights groups that filed amicus briefs in a handful of cases related to civil liberties. "Nothing is more certain," Clark declared, "than that our American values and institutions are dependent upon the maintenance of free discussion," adding that at no time was this more true than at present.[61]

The three attorney generals who led the department during World War II—Frank Murphy in 1939; Robert Jackson, from early 1940 through mid-1941; and Francis Biddle, from then through the eve of the war's end—were all aware of the controversy over free speech since World War I. Murphy spent much of the war in Europe with the American Expeditionary Force, but was a U.S. attorney during the Red Scare that followed the war. Jackson was an opponent of the war, and was profoundly touched by the conformist and repressive attitudes the conflict spawned. Biddle, a reluctant participant in the Great Crusade, was in military training when the war ended, had served as law clerk to Justice Oliver Wendell Holmes, Jr. and was a friend of Felix Frankfurter, both of whom played a major part in combating the repressive atmosphere of the era. All three of the future attorney generals were lawyers with a reformist bent, and all shared—as did most liberal-minded and educated people of their generation—a high regard for free expression. The lessons they drew differed. Murphy, a former big-city mayor, focused on the vigilantism of racial and religious bigots, and the repressive tactics used by businesses against discontented workers. His view of government and free speech centered on the need for the state to do more to prevent these things. Jackson and Biddle tended to see in the events of World War I and the Red Scare evidence of the need for government to tolerate dissent, and not lend itself to the repressive inclinations of overwrought members of the community.

Their attitudes reflected both the saliency and the ambiguity of the legacy they inherited. On the one hand, it was absolutely clear that capitulating to the popular enthusiasm for political conformity was a recipe for disaster—the department must discourage vigilantism and distance itself from activities smacking of political repression. On the other hand, the message was less certain as to what the department should do when faced with propaganda that seemed to threaten national security. Officials rejected the idea that they had blanket authority to harass persons for their beliefs or to suppress speech that was simply unpopular. But the question remained as to where to draw the line. At what point might a salutary reluctance to interfere with political discourse be overcome by the need to protect internal security and prevent the appearance of the vigilante? This somewhat uncertain inheritance of restraint would play a major role in shaping department policy in World War II. An understanding of past mistakes was, of course, only one factor in a complex of considerations weighed by successive attorney generals and their staffs. The chapters that follow are an account of how the free speech values and institutional instincts the officials inherited and internalized fared when confronted with the political realities of crisis times.

Part I

Frank Murphy
1939

Chapter 1

Champion of Civil Liberties

Frank Murphy was the first of Franklin Roosevelt's attorney generals to confront free speech issues similar to those the Department of Justice had grappled with in 1917–20. The problem in 1939 was how to deal with a small but vocal minority of ideologues who espoused un-American "isms" of the Right and Left. Murphy came to office a genuine civil libertarian, known for his liberal views and praised by libertarians for his political tolerance. Indeed he spent much of his time in office extolling these values. However, by the time he left the department a year later, he had witnessed the expansion of the police-state powers of the Federal Bureau of Investigation, which was nominally under his control, and had used his own office to conduct a campaign of largely symbolic prosecutions designed to give a hard edge to the administration's displeasure with political extremism. The inconsistency between Murphy's rhetoric and his record reflected, in part at least, a disjuncture between the civil libertarianism he and other Americans espoused and the issues they would confront during his time as attorney general.

When Murphy and many liberals spoke of civil liberties violations, they had in mind principally discrimination and intimidation directed at ethnic and religious minorities, particularly the plight of Southern blacks subject to mob violence and denied the equal protection of the law. They also thought of marginal workers prevented by ruthless employers and corrupt local officials from protesting or organizing. The villains were intolerant regional majorities, vigilante groups, or local governmental authorities. The solution seemed to lie in federal intervention on behalf of the victims. These were worthy sentiments and, insofar as he acted on them, Murphy contributed to the fight against

economic and racial injustice. But his sympathies were not easily transferred to the "un-American" agitators who seemed, in 1939, to be bent
on destroying the democratic and tolerant attitudes Murphy held dear.

Murphy's strong sense of tolerance and social justice were rooted in his
earliest experiences.[1] He was born in Michigan in 1893 and raised in a de-
voutly Catholic home. His mother was a strong influence, taking young
Frank to the religious services of other denominations and instilling an ec-
umenism and tolerance that abided with him throughout his life. Born and
raised in an era when racism, ethnic stereotyping, and discrimination were
commonplace, Murphy was brought up remarkably free of prejudice. He
was a multiculturalist long before the term became popular.

His mother wanted him to become a priest, but Frank chose a career
in the law. He graduated from the University of Michigan School of Law
in 1914 just as the war in Europe broke out, and after practicing for a short
time, he joined the army, was commissioned an officer, and served as a captain in France. A Democrat and a strong supporter of Wilson's crusade in
Europe, Murphy was staunchly patriotic, even chauvinistic. Yet while he
insisted that the nation had no place for hyphenated Americans, he was an
outspoken advocate of the foreign born and an opponent of the restrictive
immigration legislation popular in the 1920s. Murphy was appointed an
assistant U.S. attorney and was employed in that capacity in Detroit during the postwar Red Scare. He concluded from his experiences that communist agitators were cynically exploiting genuine grievances for their
own revolutionary purposes, and he gave no indication that he was disturbed by what others saw as the repressive excesses of the government in
the era.

Detroit between the two wars was already a city with a large foreign-
born and a rapidly growing black population. It was a blue-collar town, a
target of trade union organizers and radicals, and home to a powerful Ku
Klux Klan. An ambitious Murphy carved out a career in politics based on
cultivating a constituency that spanned the ethnic and racial spectrum. In
1924, then a lawyer in private practice, he was elected to the Detroit
Recorder's Court, where he would serve for the next six years. Here,
Murphy built a reputation for tolerance and sympathy among the mostly
poor (largely "minority") population of the city. He had a visceral sympathy with the underdog and he showed a particular affinity for African
Americans, explaining that "they are so out of luck and get the worst of
every deal."[2]

In 1925, a number of incidents in which white mobs drove blacks from
homes they had acquired in white neighborhoods, climaxed with a mur-

der. An African American doctor named Ossian Sweet had shot and killed a member of a crowd of whites laying siege to his new home. The irrepressible Clarence Darrow defended Sweet, arguing that a history of mob violence against his race justified the killing as an act of self-defense, and Murphy incorporated the argument in his instructions to the jury. Sweet was eventually acquitted. The widely publicized trial firmly established Murphy's reputation as a champion of equality, made him a hero in what we would now call the civil rights movement, and created a base of support among black voters of Detroit that would contribute to his election as mayor in 1930. Events during his tenure as mayor gave him an opportunity to build on the reputation he had earned as a judge, although the issue shifted some from racial to class justice.

The Great Depression hit Detroit hard, confronting Murphy with declining public revenues, an overburdened public welfare system, and a sullenly discontented population of unemployed and dispossessed. Communist Party rallies drew large crowds at which speakers condemned the capitalist system and labeled the mayor a tool of the interests. Murphy questioned the tactics and sincerity of the Communists, but was concerned lest police overreaction give the agitators the martyrdom he thought they were seeking. He showed admirable restraint and attempted, not always with success, to ensure that police efforts at maintaining order were kept within bounds. To a citizen who apparently preferred order to freedom, he observed that economic hardship had made people "impatient and miserable," and that it made good practical sense to let them express themselves. Speaking of the army's forceful dispersal of the Bonus Marchers in Washington, D.C. in July 1932, he noted that it was "unjust and actually dangerous" for a society to deny people work and then prevent them from protesting their destitution. His sentiments and performance earned accolades from the ACLU.[3]

Murphy's political courage and compassionate leadership marked him as a man with a future in Democratic national politics. He was a new breed of city politician: liberal, activist, and attuned to the problems of the diverse urban-industrial population. He found a kindred spirit in Franklin Roosevelt and enthusiastically supported the New York governor's presidential candidacy in 1932. When FDR won, Murphy was in line for an appointment in the new administration. Conscious, as his biographer Sidney Fine notes, of the "political advantages that could be derived from a war on crime," Murphy sought the attorney generalship, seeing it as a stepping stone to higher elected office.[4] The Byzantine political calculations that went into cabinet appointment need not detain us here. Suffice it to note that the post went to Homer Cummings, and Murphy went off to serve as governor general and then U.S. high commissioner of the Philippines (positions that served a number of men as a prelude to a cabinet appointment and higher political office).[5]

On returning to the United States three years later, Murphy won election as governor of Michigan, then tense and divided by labor upheaval centering on the state's automobile industry. In 1937 the United Auto Workers used sit-down strikes to extract concessions from the automakers. A number of employees in unrelated industries resorted to the tactic as well, and business saw the situation as verging on chaos and revolution. Governor Murphy, caught between the conflicting demands of workers and owners, rejected the business community's insistence that he end the strikes with force. The strikes were eventually settled, but they had antagonized a great many middle-class voters, and Murphy's refusal to get tough with labor was used against him by his political opponents. In 1938, a year that marked a resurgence of conservatism nationwide, he suffered a stunning defeat in his bid for a second term. His pride hurt but his ambitions undiminished, Murphy at the end of 1938 was looking for a chance to revive and advance his political career.

By this time the post of attorney general was again available. The incumbent, Homer Cummings, a prominent Connecticut Democrat who had served as FDR's floor manager at the Democratic National Convention in Chicago in 1932, was on his way out. Despite efforts to cultivate a tough law-and-order image for himself and the department, Cummings was the target of a good deal of criticism. For some years the Department of Justice had been seen as a dumping ground for incompetent lawyers who could claim the political patronage of various members of Congress. New Dealers wanted the agency cleaned up and made more responsive to the liberal agenda. His supporters in the department saw him as a courtly gentleman of the old school, but Cummings was not a reformer or New Dealer and, by the end of 1938, Roosevelt was looking for a new attorney general.[6]

Murphy took the oath of office in January 1939 and almost immediately set about publicizing himself and his ambitions for the department and the nation. He sought to project an image that was at once nonpartisan and sympathetic to the common man; hard-working and efficient, but spiritual and contemplative; compassionate and fun loving, but determined and courageous. Murphy's affiliations and friendships contributed to his emerging self-portrait as a progressive man of all the people. He was a member of the ACLU, but retained strong ties to the chauvinistic, sometimes intolerant American Legion. He was a member of the National Association for the Advancement of Colored People (NAACP), and a close friend of Father Charles Coughlin, the bigoted radio priest. His liberalism was broad enough to encompass all Americans, and he presented himself as a peacemaker, not the champion of any faction.[7] Murphy hoped to reassure conservative voters that he was a fair-minded and effective administrator who was interested in their problems as well. His effort to be all things to all people and his perpetual self-promotion antagonized officials of the Department of Justice, including his two successors in office, who thought him a cynical grandstander who deliberately cultivated an air of mystery as part of his unrelenting drive for higher office.[8]

The new attorney general sought grand objectives for his tenure. The war on crime had come and largely gone by the time he took office, and he would have to look elsewhere for themes. The air of scandal that hung about the department suggested the first of these, and Murphy announced that he intended to restore the public's faith in the federal justice system by driving the political hangers-on and incompetents from the department. To this end he quickly embarked on a thorough housecleaning, which included investigating and reorganizing the personnel and practices of the U.S. attorneys and marshals.[9] But if Murphy's first order of business was departmental reform, his driving interest and abiding concern was to give the purified institution a worthy goal. He found it in the defense of "civil liberties."

Reflecting the pressing issues of the 1930s, Murphy, and many others who spoke of civil liberties, principally had in mind protecting the efforts of workers to organize, and secondarily what we would now refer to as civil rights—the protection of racial and religious minorities against organized intolerance, whether of private groups or local authorities. The enemies of freedom in this context were unenlightened corporate managers, urban bosses, vigilantes, and tyrannical small-town governments. "Special interests" of this kind, Murphy told the *New York Times* shortly after he took office, were preventing society's dispossessed from airing their grievances, and their intolerance and injustice were creating a radical response that threatened to destroy the country. His mission would be to provide an effective guarantee of free speech that would end "social unrest" and ensure political stability.[10]

A federal role in ensuring the civil liberties of certain groups against local despots had been under consideration for at least a decade. In the 1920s the department had received letters from what one official described as the "remote isolated fringes of the nation," often "laboriously scrawled over rough paper," seeking racial and economic justice from a department whose name suggested that it was the source. But the issue was politically explosive, and federal legal authority, dubious. As a result, department officials had done little to vindicate the "childlike faith in the power of the Government" such letters suggested.[11] By the late 1930s, however, the Supreme Court had declared that certain constitutional rights were guaranteed against state interference by the Fourteenth Amendment, opening the way for federal executive intervention on their behalf.[12] In 1937, the Justice Department had taken the first tentative steps toward realizing the nationalization of civil rights recent Court decisions implied.

The labor wars of Harlan County, Kentucky, provided the occasion for the initial federal intervention. For years, coal mine operators, in collusion with public officials, had financed and organized "a virtual reign of terror" in the coal fields of the region in a successful effort to prevent union organizing activities.[13] The struggle flared in the early 1930s and attracted national attention. During a congressional inquiry one witness pleaded, "is there nothing that the Federal Government can do?" Must "this state of lawlessness, the complete abrogation of the law, of the Declaration of Independence . . . be allowed to continue?"[14] The answer, which at one time had been an unequivocal "yes," had by the mid-1930s turned to a hopeful, but uncertain, "no."

During 1937, a Senate committee headed by Robert M. La Follette, Jr. had begun investigating what it called "violations of the rights of free speech and assembly." It produced a sensational exposé of employer activities, including blacklisting, spying, and corporate employment of well-armed private armies of strike-breakers, that violated the recently enacted National Labor Relations (Wagner) Act. The report highlighted events in Harlan County and generated public support for federal intervention in that hotbed of labor unrest.[15] In September 1937, the department used material gathered by the committee to secure federal grand jury indictments against a number of county deputy sheriffs and coal company executives. The government charged that they had conspired to deny the miners the organizing rights guaranteed to them by the Wagner Act. A well-publicized trial followed that, while ending with a hung jury and a settlement, convinced federal officials of the utility of using existing federal statutes to punish local labor and civil rights violations.[16]

Shortly after he assumed office, Attorney General Frank Murphy announced that he was considering establishing a special bureau "to preserve the civil liberties of citizens."[17] The idea was very much a reflection of the civil libertarian concerns of the moment. Murphy's predecessor, Homer

Cummings, had been criticized by liberals for neglecting the victims of racial prejudice, and particularly for failing to act against local and state authorities who deprived blacks of their civil rights. The swift "justice" meted out to the Scottsboro boys in Alabama was a liberal/radical cause célèbre throughout the 1930s, and in August 1938, Roosevelt responded to African-American entreaties by promising to develop the means to investigate mob violence in the South.[18]

In early February 1939, the department announced that it had created a unit within the Criminal Division to actively prosecute instances in which "the fundamental rights inherent in a free people" (whatever these were) were infringed. Henry Schweinhaut, a department lawyer who had been involved in the Harlan prosecution, was to head the new Civil Liberties Unit. The department promised that while most of its cases would probably arise out of labor disputes, its defense of civil liberties would not be confined to such matters.[19]

Murphy's public commitment to the defense of fundamental freedoms reflected personal conviction and his recognition that this was a cause that was currently enjoying a surge in popular interest. In 1939, the sesquicentennial year of the ratification of the Bill of Rights, spokesmen for interests spanning the political spectrum proclaimed that political tolerance was a defining principle of American nationality, a canon of America's secular religion—a commitment that gave democracy its special resilience and made the United States the envy of a world wracked by totalitarian excesses. Tributes to political freedoms were a staple of patriotic oratory, and those who had fought on behalf of civil liberties for 20 years enjoyed unprecedented popularity.

Murphy was an active propagandist for "civil liberties." Over the course of his year in office he spoke often and passionately of his attachment to free speech. He participated as well in two conferences sponsored by the ACLU[20] and addressed a number of forums in which he dealt in general terms with what he called his "national program for the protection of personal rights."[21] When the president's staff arranged airtime for cabinet officers to speak about subjects of current interest, Murphy rejected the topic the White House suggested and chose to address the nation on civil liberties instead.[22] Unfortunately, it was not always clear what Murphy and other champions of freedom had in mind. As historian Norman Rosenberg points out, free speech was probably best captured as Norman Rockwell depicted it in his painting/poster *Freedom of Speech*.[23] This shows a quintessentially American fellow gazing skyward and speaking his piece at a town meeting surrounded by respectful friends and neighbors. It was this image, rather than a raucous street-corner rally harangued by a Nazi or Communist agitator, that Americans likely had in mind as they contemplated the First Amendment freedoms in 1939.

Murphy handled issues of civil liberties gingerly, recognizing, no doubt, that kept at the Rockwell level, it could be a unifying theme, but that explored in any depth, it was apt to be divisive. His words and gestures were intentionally vague and unthreatening, and his overt acts severely circumscribed. The principal beneficiaries of the liberties he spoke of presumably were sweatshop workers, sharecroppers, and other marginalized Americans protesting their exploitation. Yet Murphy preferred to speak in universal terms that suggested that the freedoms he espoused benefited all people in all circumstances. The sheltering wing of the department, he declared, would be extended to all, "without fear or favor [to] . . . the businessman and the laborer, the Jew and the Gentile and the people of all races and creeds, whatever their origin." (This was about as close as Murphy and other administration officials felt they could come to publicly acknowledging the injustices suffered by African Americans).[24] Civil liberties, he suggested, were ideologically neutral, based on the principle of "justice for all," and not limited to the struggles of the underdog. Its protections, Murphy said, shielded both the "poorest laborer" and the "wealthiest man in the land."[25]

Murphy's priorities were apparent in his opening remarks at a conference of federal prosecutors held that spring in Washington. He declared that the department must be ready to enforce the civil rights statutes "to the limit," and called upon the U.S. attorneys to make civil liberties "a reality for everyone in our midst, no matter how humble or how great." The speech earned full coverage and editorial support from the *New York Times*.[26] The federal government, he declared on another occasion, was duty-bound to defend Americans against public officials who used "oppressive" and "unjust" ordinances to violate "common rights."[27] Murphy no doubt had in mind events in Jersey City where, for the past year, that city's mayor and political "boss," Frank Hague, had been conducting a campaign to prevent union organizers and other "radicals" from speaking or even appearing in "his" city.[28]

In June, the Supreme Court censured Hague when it decided in favor of the Congress of Industrial Organizations (CIO) in a legal action the union had brought charging the mayor with depriving the union's organizers of their civil rights.[29] In a commencement address at John Marshall College in Jersey City, the attorney general condemned similar abuses by municipal officials elsewhere and alluded approvingly to the Court's decision. According to the newspaper account, Murphy departed from his prepared text and, "with an evident intensity of emotion," spoke of how the Justice Department too was trying to see to it that the rights of every group, "whether it be business, labor, industry or some other group," were preserved.[30]

Civil libertarians, focused on the same issues that stirred Murphy, had reason to be pleased. In its mid-1939 report the ACLU noted the growing national support for constitutional guarantees, the result, in part at least, of Murphy's support.[31] Roger Baldwin, the organization's director, was moved to comment that with civil liberties safely in the hands of the attorney general, he almost believed the ACLU "should begin to feel that we could go out of business."[32] *The New Republic* noted with satisfaction the irony of FBI director J. Edgar Hoover and his G-men being employed by the Justice Department on behalf of civil liberties. "To those of us who remember. . . . Palmer and his Red-hunts, it will be a novel and pleasing sight to watch federal agents tracking down anti-union employers."[33] The *New York Times* saw the creation of the Civil Liberties Unit as Murphy's "assurance that henceforth the right of citizens to meet and express opinions, however unpopular, will be consistently defended by the Federal Government."[34]

Murphy's statements, and the creation of the Civil Liberties Unit, however, while couched in universalistic terms, did not really refer to the rights of *everyone*. He had in mind the rights of the deserving and their denial at the hands of undemocratic others. But much as he avoided acknowledging the class and race implications of civil rights, he also did not see, and perhaps did not understand, that his defense of liberty for some might entail the suppression of others. Thus, for example, a major civil liberties issue of the 1930s and 1940s involved the claim by members of the Jehovah's Witnesses religious sect that they had a right to proselytize in Catholic neighborhoods, even though the preaching was hostile to Roman Catholicism and offensive to Catholics. Did Murphy's defense of free speech include protecting the "right" of Jehovah's Witnesses to be obnoxious, or suppressing the Witnesses' speech in deference to the right of Catholics to be free of offense? What of the preaching of native fascists and Nazis— were their anti-Semitic diatribes protected speech? And what of Communists whose message of class conflict threatened the wealthy? Murphy never spoke of balancing conflicting claims or of drawing the line between what the government might legitimately suppress, and what it should not. Perhaps he believed that there was no such conflict inherent in securing "justice." More likely he recognized that it was impolitic to suggest there were choices to be made.

Content to encourage and participate in the positive feelings that attached to his homilies, the attorney general offered no caveats. Affirming free speech, not defining it, was the principal concern of civil libertarians in the 1930s, and Murphy was not alone in the vagueness of his thinking or in his failure to explore the limits of toleration and liberty. Murphy's myopia was apparent in a speech he broadcast nationally soon after taking office. In it, he spoke of America's great heritage of personal and political freedoms that, he said—rather incredibly—had been marred only once, at the nation's very beginning, by the infamous repressive laws of 1798. That anomaly had been a mistake that the nation had since lived down, but in recent years, he said, intimidation by mobs (strikebreakers and vigilantes) threatened "a form of persecution without benefit of an Alien and Sedition Act." He was determined that, after 150 years of freedom and harmony, the new threat to liberty would not be permitted to succeed.[35]

Of course, it was only a speech, and such rhetoric cannot be held to scrupulous standards for historical accuracy. But Murphy's blindness to events within his memory was noteworthy. The repression-free past he evoked did not exist, and Murphy could only have believed his statement if he deliberately excluded from the meaning of "repression" recent acts of government aimed at enforcing political conformity. Thus he made no mention of the World War I prosecutions under the Espionage Act of 1917, still on the statute books, or of the Sedition Act of 1918, with which, as a federal prosecutor in Michigan in 1919–20, he was no doubt familiar. He voiced no regrets over the federal persecution of the Industrial Workers of the World, or the 20-year sentence for sedition given to socialist Eugene Debs during the war; and made no mention of the infamous postwar Palmer raids and the subsequent detention and deportation of aliens suspected of radicalism. Nor did he call attention to congressional efforts since 1935 to pass peacetime anti-sedition legislation, or to the investigations recently launched by the House Committee on Un-American Activities.

Murphy was caught up in, and sought to capitalize on, the libertarian mood. But with his civil libertarian thoughts doggedly focused on the issues of the early 1930s, the attorney general offered no guidance to officials who were even now seeking ways of determining the loyalty of accused radicals and silencing their dissent. Given his perception of civil liberties, it was perhaps understandable that during his last months in office the attorney general would, without apparent misgivings, launch a campaign against un-Americanism.

Even while Murphy preached the gospel of civil libertarianism, critics had begun to complain that the Justice Department he headed was employing practices that called to mind a police state. Beginning early in his administration, President Roosevelt had encouraged FBI director J. Edgar Hoover to revive the investigations of dissident political groups that Hoover had begun during World War I. The "un-American" individuals and groups subjected to this surveillance were not accused of any crime— there were no federal statutes (yet) that outlawed radical organization or advocacy in the absence of overt acts.

The chief targets of these investigations were the members of the Communist Party of the United States (CPUSA), which was affiliated with the international Communist movement. The American party was formed after World War I by a faction of radical socialists who, inspired by the success of the Bolsheviks in Russia, sought to bring the revolution to the United States. The party had little impact on American politics until the onset of the Great Depression, when desperation born of economic collapse gave credibility to its program and broadened its appeal. The Communists were the most active and militant of the factions critical of capitalism, and gained converts, particularly among intellectuals who thought they were witnessing the final collapse of a decadent economic system.

The party's image of strength and ubiquitous influence owed a great deal to its enemies' fears and ambitions.[36] At the height of its prewar prestige in 1939, the CPUSA had between 50,000 and 75,000 members, with approximately another 20,000 enrolled in the Young Communist League. Its members were disproportionately represented in certain areas of American life—in the union movement, particularly the recently formed CIO; and in reform groups, the film industry, and the arts. There was also a handful of Communists, some of them cooperating with Soviet intelligence, employed in the federal government.[37] Republicans, and political conservatives in general, worried by the movement, or merely cynically using the concerns it generated to further their own agendas, played up the Communist presence and its sinister implications. Thanks largely to the work of congressional investigators, anti-Communist crusaders, and the mainstream press, most Americans tended to exaggerate the party's size and revolutionary potential.[38]

The other target of government investigators was what was sometimes referred to as the "fascist movement." This shadowy phenomenon comprised a disparate collection of organizations and individuals united by their tendency to blame the nation's economic, political, and social problems on a loss of religious faith and personal morality, a degradation they linked to a worldwide Jewish conspiracy. Its putative leaders, several drawn from the ranks of Protestant fundamentalism, what Leo P. Ribbuffo has called the "Old Christian Right," presented themselves as religious visionaries, though nonbelievers were inclined to view them as cranks, crackpots, or charlatans. Their creed, apart from its rabid anti-Semitism, usually included a pathological hostility toward communism (and the New Deal), chauvinistic Americanism, and, sometimes, an admiration of strong-man rule.[39]

A particularly frightening manifestation of the "movement" was the Reverend Charles Coughlin, a Canadian-born parish priest from the Detroit suburb of Royal Oak, who at the outset of the depression had begun broadcasting weekly sermons that included discourses on current issues. His message was timely and his presentation persuasive, and in a short time he commanded an audience of millions, not confined to Roman Catholics. In seeking to expose the roots of the economic collapse, Coughlin harped on the failures of the government, which he attributed, first, to the influence of international bankers, and then to the Jews and communists.[40]

In the fall of 1936, such fears were heightened when Coughlin and Gerald L. K. Smith (representing the Old Christian Right) rallied behind the third-party presidential candidacy of Congressman William Lemke.[41] This foray into electoral politics was buried by FDR's landslide victory in 1936, and the movement associated with Coughlin and the others rapidly declined thereafter. But concerns about American fascism, and particularly about its anti-Semitic manifestations, were kept alive by the activities of a small group of German Americans who first associated themselves with the Friends of the New Germany and then with the German–American Bund, which succeeded it in 1936. The Bundists wore Nazi-style uniforms, employed the Hitler salute, held youth camps and drills, and openly bragged that their organization was America's Nazi Party.[42]

Many Americans associated these phenomena with the worst aspects of American life, and antifascist fears thrived among a troubled intelligentsia concerned since the turn of the century with the bigotry of the American masses, and the reactionary intentions and power of the capitalist few. For those who focused on the former, America's fascists were Klansmen without sheets. Others, of a more Marxist bent, emphasized the behind-the-scenes role of plutocrats. Events in Germany, where a demagogue believed to be supported by German industrialists had created a mass movement out of discontents similar to those played upon by America's fascists, lent a sense of foreboding and urgency to antifascist warnings.

Congress responded to public concerns by investigating first the Communists, then the "Nazis" (Bundists), and ultimately, both.[43] In 1935 the

House Committee on Un-American Activities issued a report documenting the propaganda efforts of German diplomats, the Nazi ties of the
Friends of the New Germany, the anti-Semitism of various other groups,
and the CPUSA's links to the Soviet Union. The findings lent support to
efforts led by the military to secure legislation that would outlaw inciting
disaffection among army and navy personnel and that would deport alien
radical agitators.[44] These measures were roundly condemned by civil libertarians, liberals, pacifists, and labor leaders, who assumed that *they* would
be its principal victims, and their adoption would have to await passage of
the Smith Act in 1940.[45]

Meanwhile, the president had initiated his own response to un-Americanism. Prompted by stories in the press, or intemperate letters from crank
correspondents, Roosevelt had, from his earliest days in the White House,
turned to the FBI for information about groups and individuals he found
troublesome. Occasionally the president sent his inquiries to the attorney
general, but more often he contacted the FBI directly. In either case, the
request for investigations would eventually land on J. Edgar Hoover's desk.

FDR's use of the bureau in this way was consistent with contemporary
thinking on the ethics of government surveillance. Although many Americans, mainly its most recent victims, condemned political spying, one
scholar has observed that "only a handful of lawyers and judges questioned
the legality of . . . sweeping general intelligence investigations or criticized
the use of particularly intrusive investigative techniques."[46] Historian
Frank Donner notes that liberals saw identification and surveillance as an
alternative to outright repression,[47] for if the government knew what its
critics were up to, the theory went, it would be less likely to interfere with
them in other ways. The First World War probably strengthened this belief
since vigilantism and other "excesses" of the era were often attributed to
the government's delay in uncovering and punishing genuine disloyalty.
Harlan Fiske Stone's reforms ran counter to such wisdom and were inconsistent with the growing power of the federal government in every aspect of American life.[48]

Nevertheless, investigation and surveillance had serious implications
that troubled civil libertarians, including those who led the ACLU. Authority to investigate implied the discretion to choose the subjects of investigation and the means of investigation. All was done in secret. How
was society to ensure that the investigators, once given the authority,
chose only those worthy of government attention, or that they limited
themselves to methods consistent with their targets' legitimate claims to
privacy? Moreover, those watched were apt to be intimidated by the

presence of government spies, and by the threat that government interest was often the pretext for harassment at the hands of ideologically motivated investigators.

Such considerations did not trouble President Roosevelt, who showed no reluctance to instigate investigations of individuals or organizations simply on the basis of his suspicions. He explained his thinking in one of the very few of his statements that dealt substantively with a civil liberties issue. Roosevelt was responding to a letter he had received in March 1936 from the ACLU complaining that military intelligence agencies were investigating pacifist and leftist organizations, and disseminating propaganda to discredit them. Targets included the Federal Council of Churches, the National Council for the Prevention of War, the Women's International League for Peace and Freedom, and the ACLU itself.

FDR flatly rejected the complaint, suggesting in the process his own reading of civil liberties and the boundaries of federal security policy. "As the head of the government," the president wrote, "I cannot for the safety of the nation, agree never to look into the affairs of any organization." Not all such groups, he explained, live up to their professed ideals. Some "disseminate false information and false teaching which are contrary to our democratic ideals and the objectives of a republican form of government."[49] This deceitful (though legal) activity on the part of some, Roosevelt thought, made all organizations fair game for government snoops. His candid statement, issued more than six years before American involvement in World War II, was reflected in the policy and practices of his administration over the next decade.

Roosevelt's earliest official inquiry into un-American activities came in the early spring of 1934 when, apparently responding to press coverage of Friends of the New Germany, he requested FBI Director Hoover to survey the "Nazi movement in this country." His brief injunction left open the question of who was to be investigated (and how).[50] The indiscriminate investigation thus begun on the political Right soon turned to the Left as Hoover, always more concerned about the threat from that direction, sought authority from the president to look into the affairs of America's Communists. In August 1936, he told the president of a Communist plot to take over several unions,[51] and Roosevelt invited him to come to the White House to discuss "the question of subversive activities." According to Hoover's account, the president said that he was interested in "obtaining a broad picture of the general [Communist] movement and its activities as may affect the economic and political life of the country as a whole." Roosevelt insisted that, because of the confidential nature (and dubious legality?) of the inquiries, no official record of his directive be made or retained in official files. Instead, according to Hoover, he pledged to write a memo in his own hand to be kept in his private safe. No such document has been found.[52] Though these investigations uncovered nothing illegal or seriously threatening security, each implicitly informed Hoover, and the various attorney generals who supervised him, of the president's attitude toward investigation and civil liberties.

One scholar has suggested that the president intended to target only foreign agents, and that the far-ranging countersubversive activities that Hoover later conducted on the basis of the 1936 meeting stretched the president's mandate beyond recognition.[53] Perhaps this is so. Roosevelt probably had no idea that Hoover would use the authority he gave him in situations and against targets only distantly related to those that gave rise to the 1936 directive. On the other hand, there is nothing in the president's behavior or words (on this or other occasions), or in his relations with the director, to suggest that he was concerned that his directive was subject to abuse, then or in the future. He made no attempt to limit or define the scope of Hoover's inquiries. Had he told Hoover explicitly that his objective was to uncover persons involved in espionage, sabotage, or other illegal activities, his mission would have been more specific and the scope of the investigation (perhaps) correspondingly circumscribed. But such specificity would not have expressed the far more general disloyalty-hunting expedition the president apparently had in mind. All indications are that FDR, who frequently used Hoover to dig up information on people or groups with no better rationale than that he was curious, was not concerned by the civil libertarian implications of investigation.[54]

With FDR's encouragement, the FBI expanded its program of compiling dossiers on potential subversives. Although the president did not keep track of this enterprise, its scope was suggested to him in November 1938, when he learned that the bureau was gathering information "dealing with various forms of activities of *either* a subversive or a so-called intelligence type [emphasis added]," and that it had already collected the names of about 2,500 individuals.[55]

The word "either" suggests that Hoover distinguished between "subversive" activities and "intelligence" activities, and believed he was authorized to collect information on both.[56] Neither Attorney General Cummings nor the president made any effort to instruct Hoover on the distinctions between the "subversion" implied by un-American (but nonetheless legal) advocacy or association, and illegal acts such as sabotage, espionage, and criminal conspiracy. This was not simply carelessness.

Roosevelt assumed that Hoover knew what he (the president) wanted, and trusted him to achieve the sought-after results. In part this was because Hoover, while suspect in leftist circles, had a solid reputation for professionalism within the Roosevelt administration, even among the progressive-minded. By the time Murphy took over the department early in 1939, the president had, in effect, a policy that called for the pursuit of broadly conceived national security needs, notwithstanding their chilling effect on freedom of association[57] and their potential for abuse.[58]

The arrangements between the president and Hoover, which gave the latter a free hand in tracking dissident political activity, continued with Murphy's tacit or explicit consent during his year in office. Although the director was not above concealing his activities from his superiors, by the summer of 1939 at the latest, Murphy knew generally what Hoover was doing. In writing to FDR in mid-June to support a Hoover request for exclusive authority in the field of domestic counterintelligence, the attorney general referred to the fact (provided by Hoover) that the FBI had "identifying data" on more than ten million persons, including many of foreign extraction. The figure indicated that the bureau had been collecting data on more than a handful of "agents of foreign countries" or spies, but had in fact been compiling a list that apparently included everyone whose beliefs, associations, actions, or ethnic origins were suspicious to Hoover or his informants.[59] Although the revelation should have acted as a red flag, neither Murphy nor the president saw fit to inquire as to just what the FBI was doing. The onset of war in Europe in the fall of 1939 would bring further requests from Hoover that his domestic intelligence authority be increased, and more endorsements from Murphy and Roosevelt.

In the late summer of 1939, Hitler demanded that the Poles surrender the Baltic port of Danzig. Britain and France, humiliated by their capitulation to similar demands made on the Czechs the year before, decided that this time they would stand firm. On August 24 the world learned that the unthinkable had happened. The Soviet Union and Nazi Germany, supposedly implacable adversaries, had signed a pact of nonaggression. The agreement cleared the way for the Nazis to destroy Poland without fear of interference from the east. On the first of September, the Germans invaded; two days later, Britain and France declared war; two weeks later, the Red Army commenced operations that helped wipe out the remnants of Polish resistance. The Second World War was underway.

The United States remained neutral, and would not become a full-fledged participant until after the Japanese attack on Pearl Harbor in December 1941. In the interim, the administration would shore up the nation's defenses—bolstering internal security was a major component of this effort. On September 2, 1939, the day before Britain and France declared war, Hoover directed FBI field offices to investigate persons suspected of Nazi, fascist, and Communist sympathies, and any others with alien loyalties, including members of groups with pronounced "nationalistic tendencies" and subscribers to foreign-language newspapers.[60] Sidney Fine, in referring to this "suspect" or "custodial detention" list, says that the director seems to have proceeded without obtaining the attorney general's approval or even consulting him.[61] This is similar to the contention that Hoover deliberately "stretched" the limited authority FDR conveyed to him in 1934 and 1936.

But what would Murphy have done had he been consulted? Did Hoover's failure to notify the attorney general indicate that he feared the attorney general's reaction, or was it a sign that he thought Murphy was irrelevant, or that he took his approval for granted? The latter is most likely. Murphy got along with Hoover. The only reservation the attorney general expressed about the director's performance was in regard to Hoover's reported snooping inside the administration family, and he may have told Solicitor General Robert Jackson that he intended to get a new director.[62] But if the attorney general did feel this way early on, the impulse apparently soon passed. Indeed, Murphy seems to have been convinced that the FBI chief was an asset to the department, the administration, and the nation, a position he made clear in remarks to the president after leaving office. In April 1942, at the end of a meeting with Roosevelt at the White House, now Associate Justice Murphy asked FDR how satisfied he was with the performance of the Department of Justice. The president said he was not happy with the department's leadership (Francis Biddle was now attorney general), but was well pleased with Hoover. This prompted Murphy, according to his notes, to remind the president that he had in Hoover one of government's "most competent administrators"; a man who commanded a "superb organization," and "gets results." He went on to suggest that the president reorganize the government's countersubversion work and place it under Hoover's direction. If he did, Murphy promised the president, he would "have few worries on that subject." Although Roosevelt demurred, the conversation suggests Hoover's high standing with both of his superiors.[63]

In fact the bureau thrived on the unreserved support Hoover enjoyed from above. Shortly after the outbreak of war in Europe in the fall of 1939, the president authorized the FBI to proceed with the program of investigation and list-making already well underway.[64] He also asked local, state, and federal authorities to refer to the FBI any information they received in regard to espionage, subversive activities, and violations of neutrality laws, and he approved the appointment of additional bureau agents.[65] Appearing before Congress in November 1939 and again two months later to justify increased funding, Hoover told the House Appropriations Committee that, acting on the authority of the president's declaration of a limited state of emergency, he was undertaking "special investigations of persons reported upon as being active in any subversive activity or in movements detrimental to the internal security." Lists of such individuals were being prepared, he said, "so that in the event of any greater emergency," such persons would be readily located.[66] Hoover's references to "subversive activities" troubled the ACLU, which noted that "any such vague phrase constitutes a warrant for activities dangerous to the civil liberties of minority political parties and others against whom popular prejudice is too readily directed."[67] If Murphy had any such reservations, they were not apparent.

When Frank Murphy took up the post of attorney general in January 1939, he identified himself as a civil libertarian, and no one could quarrel with his description. But during his last months in office the conditions that had generated his concern for civil liberties had faded, replaced by quite different ones. No longer was the Department of Justice being solicited by honest working men or "simple Negroes" (in the parlance of the era). The communications that now crossed Murphy's desk came increasingly from citizens worried about Communists, complaining about anti-Semitic propaganda, and demanding that the government do something—demands that found an echo on Capitol Hill. It was difficult for Murphy, as it was for many others, to see these "un-American" ideologues as having the same claim to be left alone as the innocent "little" people whose rights he continued to espouse. In the 1920s and 1930s, civil liberties had implied the protection of the underdogs against bigoted communities. Bigots were not seen as victims. Moreover, as a politician with ambitions for elected office, Murphy no doubt understood the politics of civil liberties: there were votes in championing minorities and labor organizers, but very few in standing up for extremists.

Nor was it clear that turning the FBI loose to spy on dissidents was wrong. Surveillance was an intrusive enterprise with implications that were hostile to free expression, and Stone for one had condemned it. But not everyone thought it a wholly evil enterprise. Most importantly, the president endorsed the practice and had confidence in the FBI. Even if Murphy had reservations, and this is far from certain, he had limited opportunity to express them. Looking into the activities of suspected un-Americans had been national policy, dictated by the president and carried out by Hoover since at least 1934. The president never asked Murphy's advice on the ethics or legality of the practice, and Murphy, who arrived on the scene late in the game, was not in the best position to object. Had he done so, he would have learned, as his successors did, that civil liberties policy (like national security policy) was made in the White House. The supremely confident president wanted no instruction from his attorney generals on the meaning of civil liberties. They might act on issues he had not decided, but where he made his will known, their job was to find a way.

Chapter 2

"Not a Soft, Pudgy Democracy"

The investigation of un-American activities proved to be merely a prelude to more direct forms of intimidation. For though nothing was uncovered suggesting that the Communists or fascists posed any immediate threat to American security, keeping track of their activities would not, as proponents sometimes suggested, serve as a substitute for hauling them, or suitable surrogates, before the bar of justice. Demonstrating that the government was doing all that needed to be done to defend the nation against the subversives required headline-making arrests and public trials, not merely the fattening of secret files. Murphy had to have public results, and during the fall and winter of 1939, responding to what he perceived to be the demands of his office and of his career, he launched a campaign against un-Americans on both the Right and the Left notable for its symbolic intent, overblown rhetoric, and absence of impact on national security.

The outbreak of war in Europe brought no sudden upsurge of subversion in the United States, but it did place concerns about loyalty into a more sinister and pressing context. The Nazi-Soviet Pact that served as a prelude to the conflict produced an outburst of public commentary suggesting that the forces of evil had united in a world alliance bent on destroying American democracy. Americans long concerned with fascism, Communism, or both now had evidence that seemed to confirm the danger they posed. Heightened public anxiety was reflected in increased awareness of Martin Dies's House Committee on Un-American Activities (HUAC). In January 1939 a poll found that 59 percent of respondents had heard of the committee's work. By the end of the year (after the onset of war), the figure had risen to 81 percent.[1]

Security concerns stimulated the attorney general's aggressiveness and political ambition. Fondly remembering the minor role he had played in World War I, Murphy was determined to play a larger part in the great events that were now unfolding. Twenty years earlier, aching to prove his mettle, Murphy had sought combat in France. Now, with a second conflict looming, the former army captain looked forward to meeting new challenges, if not at the front, at least in a position in which he might exercise leadership. He would have preferred to have headed the War Department in times like these, but he recognized that the Justice Department could also play a significant role in national defense. Murphy no doubt sensed that the voters, particularly in these crisis times, valued strength, and he recognized the political capital to be gained by demonstrating that toughness and dynamism underlay the idealism he had projected during his first nine months in office. These instincts were encouraged by pressure brought to bear by Chairman Dies, and by clear signals that the president wanted a no-nonsense approach to un-Americanism.

Murphy's militant mood was very much in evidence in a journal entry he made a few days after the outbreak of war in Europe. America, he wrote, was capable of a timely, decisive response to potential danger. "This time," as opposed to World War I, there would be "no laxity—no disorder—only action, action, and on time."[2] Vigorous suppression of disloyalty, he told the president, would put the evil elements in the world on notice that "we are not a soft, pudgy democracy that they could . . . kick around."[3] By presiding over such an effort, Murphy hoped, no doubt, to convey a similar message about himself.

The attorney general coupled his public endorsements of free speech with assertions of the need to deal with the un-Americans. He probably saw no tension between the two, and made no effort to reconcile them. There would be no witch hunt and no wrong done "to any man" in the current crisis, he declared, and although the country was prepared to run down spies, "we are just as anxious to protect the rights of our own citizens as to see to it that those who attack the United States do not go unwhipped [sic] of justice." His comments in the first weeks of the European war suggest, however, that when he thought of those in need of protection he was thinking less of the accused un-Americans than of those they had offended.[4] Some people, he told department employees, were preaching a creed (anti-Semitism) "alien to this land of the melting pot with its 'live and let live' philosophy." Others, he said, referring no doubt to Communists, had taken advantage of American tolerance "to promote . . . a system under which [American] principles themselves would be utterly destroyed." The department, he said, should be "alert and ready to cope with those whose aim or mission it may be to sabotage and undermine this greatest citadel of human freedom on earth."[5]

The compassionate attorney general in evidence earlier, had given way to the aggressive Murphy revealed here.[6] Both had always been there— the challenge of war had brought the more militant one to the fore. Politically, the "new" Murphy complemented the "old." For most of 1939, Murphy was spoken of as a likely Democratic candidate for president in 1940. His early championing of civil liberties had established his credentials for fairness and compassion. The challenge of un-Americanism now gave him an opportunity to demonstrate a practical toughness that would match the public image of expected Republican nominee Thomas E. Dewey, known as the fearless district attorney who had put New York's mobsters behind bars.[7]

Murphy's militancy owed something as well to the goading of the HUAC. After a three-year hiatus, the committee had been revived in 1938 under the chairmanship of Martin Dies, a Texas populist with a special animus toward aliens and a penchant for publicity. Although offended by the obviously alien character of the Bund and those who mimicked the Nazis, the chairman's real antagonism was reserved for the Communists, whose purportedly pervasive influence provided Dies, and many Americans, with a ready explanation for what they saw as the sinister drift of national policy. He was particularly interested in exposing the Communist influence in government.[8]

From his very first hearings in August 1938, Dies had used the committee as a sounding board for criticism of the administration.[9] Why, he asked, hadn't the government deported the notorious alien radical, Harry Bridges; why were radicals permitted to give a communist slant to the productions of the Works Projects Administration's theater project; what influence did the Communists have on a number of New Deal Democrats currently running for state office? Among those thus smeared was Governor Frank Murphy, who was seeking re-election in Michigan. The experience no doubt left Murphy determined not to let Dies do him in again with charges that he was receptive to Communist influence.

The issue was soon joined. Shortly after Murphy took over as attorney general in January 1939, Dies began pressuring him to assign FBI agents to his committee and to give his staff access to bureau files. He also asked that a number of "radical" organizations be investigated and prosecuted for violating the recently adopted Foreign Agents Registration Act (FARA), which required agents of foreign principals to register with the

State Department and detail their activities and foreign connections. His targets included the ACLU, which in Dies's intellectual universe had proven itself a tool of the Soviet Union because its position sometimes paralleled the Communist Party line, and because Roger Baldwin had at one time expressed himself as sympathetic to the Soviet experiment.[10]

Rejecting Dies's unreasonable demands would lay Murphy open to renewed charges that he was soft on subversion and not up to the job of combating un-Americanism. But acceding to them would smack of abject surrender of the department's prerogatives and functions. Justice Department lawyers resisted the bizarre and untenable application of the law pressed by the chairman, and J. Edgar Hoover had no intention of putting his special agents at Dies's disposal. Murphy hoped to outmanuever Dies by launching his own assault on the un-Americans. Exhorting his staff to take the offensive, he complained that there must be something wrong with a department that only reacted to Dies's headline-stealing initiatives, and insisted that the department stop acting as "the tail of the damned Dies Committee." The American people were convinced, Murphy declared, that Communists and Bundists were foreign agents and, he implied, it was up to the department to do something about it.[11] But producing results that would relieve the pressure would take time.

Meanwhile, FDR sought to rely on his charm and on concessions to quiet the troublesome Texan. Roosevelt distrusted Dies, but did not feel able to simply say "no" to him.[12] In early January 1939, at the first cabinet meeting attended by the recently appointed Frank Murphy, the president outlined a strategy that called for supplying the chairman with confidential information from the tax returns of people called before the committee,[13] and to order a bureau investigation of un-American activity; to wit, the Communist Party, one fascist organization, and one lesser known (Communist) "front organization" taken from a list Dies had provided.[14] The president hoped this would satisfy the Texas congressman while the White House convinced the administration's allies that his committee's irresponsible behavior warranted its termination.

But Dies's performance confounded the president. The hearings he conducted in the first half of 1939 were relatively balanced, and the committee concluded an uneventful year by issuing a judiciously worded report endorsing civil liberties. The performance drew praise from skeptics, including a surprised *New York Times,* and the House voted by a large majority to extend its life, although at a slightly diminished level of funding.[15] Whereupon Dies, despite the White House concessions, resumed badgering the administration. In October he demanded that if Communists and

Bundists were not prosecuted immediately under the FARA, he would refer the matter to a United States attorney for action.[16]

The president's quarrel with the chairman was not over the principle of attacking the un-Americans, but over who would drive the process. As long as the struggle against disloyalty was an exclusive function of the FBI, the White House could control its direction and pace. Or, at least, so he thought. Dies threatened to break that monopoly and to turn the crusade for ideological purity into a potentially fatal assault on the administration. Sparing the administration further embarrassment seemed to require prosecution, but investigations of the un-Americans having already failed to uncover serious punishable offenses, there really was not much the department could do, within the law, that promised significant results. As a stop-gap measure, Murphy agreed to assign bureau investigators to follow up on HUAC revelations, but that merely set the stage for additional demands.[17]

The law was the problem. While Dies could make charges with impunity, allegations by the department would eventually have to be proven in court. The department's standard reply to citizen complaints about un-American propaganda was that "the wide latitude of expression of opinion allowed in this country, and the absence of Federal statutes curbing such activities," ruled out legal action.[18] But forbearance left the department on the sidelines while Dies led the rising chorus of demands that the government do something about the un-Americans. Prosecutions were needed to give at least the impression that the government was alive to the problem of disloyalty, even though the inadequacies of current statutes might make government actions chiefly symbolic. The irony of the situation was that while Murphy contemplated a crackdown on extremism, the extremists' influence was receding.

By 1939, American fascism, whose presence had troubled political commentators for much of the decade, was in fact moribund. Evidence of economic recovery had lessened the discontent upon which it fed, while sensational and hostile press treatment of fascism (foreign and domestic) had discredited the movement by associating it with totalitarian regimes alien to American sensibilities. The focus of concern in recent months, the German-American Bund, had been harried to near extinction by police and local citizens, including American Legionnaires.[19] In May 1939, the organization suffered a near fatal blow when Fritz Kuhn was imprisoned by a New York court for misappropriating Bund funds.

The Communist Party too was now more suspect, isolated, and vulnerable than at any time in recent years.[20] Much of the support for Communists in the 1930s derived from the party's denunciations of fascism. The party forfeited much of this sympathy when, following the Kremlin's lead, it endorsed the Nazi-Soviet Pact and proceeded to denounce the administration's cautious program of defense preparedness as warmongering.[21] The implicit cynical subservience to Soviet national interests alienated many erstwhile supporters,[22] and from the fall of 1939 until the Nazi attack on the Soviet Union in June 1941, Communist influence in the United States suffered. Responses varied in intensity, but even the usually sympathetic liberal press now warned of the role of Communists in some unions and ridiculed the party's Moscow-dictated foreign-policy line.[23] The Popular Front, which sought to unify the Left in the face of fascism, was no more.

Nevertheless, though American Communism and "fascism" were nearly dead, politics, it seemed, dictated kicking at the remains. At the end of December 1939, the Department of Justice began a campaign against un-Americanism with a number of petty actions designed to demonstrate the government's even-handed toughness on disloyalty of all stripes. The public relations motive was unmistakable. Statements emanating from the department sought to lend drama and import to actions actual and anticipated. In the week after Christmas, a department spokesman told the press of the agency's stepped up "campaign against espionage, foreign propagandists and sabotage," and a newspaper report hinted at "startling developments in the Justice Department's drive against foreign spies and propaganda agents."[24] Headlines promised that evidence of sabotage and espionage would be presented to a Washington grand jury the following week. The story, however, described only the less-than-sensational indictment and conviction (all in a matter of hours) of two Russian book firm agents for violating the Foreign Agents Registration Act. The Soviet agents, who had admitted selling various Soviet publications, including the "Moscow *Daily News,*" were fined a total of $2,500 and promised to leave the country by "the first boat." A department spokesman declared that this was merely the first victory in "Attorney General Murphy's effort to rid the country of foreign propagandists."[25] A few days later, in announcing that it had brought its first charges of military espionage against foreign agents, the department described its action as part of its current war on "spies and propagandists."[26]

Murphy assured those who cared that his campaign was not an overture to repression. There had, he said, been no raids or indiscriminate roundups of suspects, and there would be none. "The hysteria, emotion, prejudices that ruled government operations a quarter of a century ago, are not going to rule at this time."[27] Having declared that the government's actions were not driven by public hysteria, the attorney general apparently believed he had established their legitimacy. But less than two weeks later, Murphy suggested that something like the Palmer raids and deportations would not be such a bad idea. The occasion was a press conference on December 28, 1939, at which he announced his planned attack on American Nazism. For some months, bullies, many of them associated with an organization called the Christian Front, had been harassing and beating Jews on the streets of New York City.[28] In September and October, the anti-Semitic plague was extensively covered in picture articles appearing in *Look*. The articles, which implied that the activity was part of a nationwide conspiracy traceable to the Rev. Charles Coughlin and, ultimately, to Berlin, produced calls for a swift federal response.[29]

At the December 28 press conference, Murphy announced that a special grand jury had been impaneled in Washington, D.C. to hear the findings of a six-month department investigation into sabotage, espionage, and the activities of organizations fostering "anti-Semitism and other isms." Now, he suggested, "foreign agents who are aliens and owe allegiance to another country will be foregathered and placed on a ship and started back where they were sent out from. . . ." In 1919, as an assistant U.S. attorney in Detroit, Murphy had endorsed the Palmer raids. Writing to his mother, he declared that he had "no sympathy with the foreigner who comes to this country and conspires to overthrow the government. . . . We must wipe [them] out."[30] Now, as attorney general, he was, perhaps inadvertently, recalling images of the "Red Ark"—the S.S. *Buford*, which 20 years earlier, almost to the day, had left the United States bound for revolutionary Russia carrying radicals rounded up by the Justice Department of that day. The deportations, which had once been a mark of a department shamefully overreaching its authority, were now evoked by Murphy as worthy of emulation.

A few weeks earlier, Special Assistant to the Attorney General Hugh Fisher, responding to public impatience, suggested that it was preferable that the un-Americans be "allowed unhampered exercise of their constitutional right of freedom of speech than to attempt to curb such utterances by invoking Federal statutes of doubtful application."[31] But Murphy, aware that the law did not prohibit disloyal or hateful speech, now declared that he intended to silence the anti-Semites with whatever statutes, including the tax code, he could bring to bear.[32]

Radio priest Charles Coughlin, the indisputable, if unofficial, leader of "American fascism," was an obvious target. In the months since the humiliating defeat of the Union Party in November 1936, the smooth-talking cleric's following of millions had largely evaporated, leaving a hate-filled distillate of tens of thousands inspired by his political preaching. He seemed to respond to his decline with an increasingly intemperate anti-Semitism, and in July 1938, *Social Justice,* a journal he had established two years earlier, began publishing excerpts from the notorious and provocative forgery, *Protocols of the Elders of Zion.*[33]

By the end of 1939, Coughlin had lost his access to the major radio networks, and was not the demagogue he once was. But as the nation's most notorious anti-Semite, reporters assumed that he was among those Murphy had in mind when he announced his intention to strike down anti-Semitism. Murphy bristled at the suggestion. No complaint against Coughlin, he sniffed, had ever been received by the department.[34] Coughlin, it turned out, was an anti-Semite with at least one friend in Washington.

Among the many apparent contradictions in Murphy's life was his friendship with Coughlin. The priest's parish was in Royal Oak, just outside Detroit, where Murphy had served as mayor. The relationship was partly personal and, even though Coughlin's influence had declined in recent years, partly political. Any direct attack on the priest was likely to be seen by large numbers of Catholics, even those who held no brief for Coughlin's views, as embarrassing to the church. Conflict with his own church was hardly an agreeable prospect for the devout Murphy, and this was doubly so for a loyal Democrat, particularly on the eve of an election year. Pursuing persons defined chiefly by their attitudes gave the attorney general considerable latitude in deciding who would, and who would not, feel the wrath of the government. In this case friendship and practical political considerations determined that Coughlin would be spared.

In January 1940, Murphy's promised crusade against the un-Americans produced its first significant arrests. The government's victim was the anti-Semitic Christian Front, founded in New York City in November 1938. Although the group had been created in response to Coughlin's call for a "crusade against the anti-Christian forces of Red Revolution," the priest's exact connection to the organization was murky, and the government steadfastly refused to suggest any connection. The group had several thousand members, many of them Irish-Americans, most living in and around New York. Although organized to counter communistic influences, most of the members' efforts were directed against Jews, whom they saw as the carriers of the revolutionary virus. Their activities included hawking Coughlin's *Social Justice* on street corners, sponsoring boycotts of Jewish merchants, and organizing parades and mass meetings. Fronters also hurled epithets, and more, at passersby whom they took to be "Reds" (Jews) and were involved in a number of violent incidents, including beatings and stabbings. Soon after its founding, the organization was infiltrated by New York City police, who gathered evidence of its members' systematic provocation of street assaults, and local prosecutions of Front members produced over one hundred convictions.[35]

Nevertheless, Murphy was looking for a high profile case against the anti-Semites and, at the urging of the U.S. attorney in New York, he agreed to target the Christian Front.[36] In mid-January 1940 the government arrested 17 men, most of them members of the Front, for seditious conspiracy, charging specifically that they had plotted to "overthrow, put down and destroy by force the Government of the United States," and to steal U.S. firearms and munitions to further their scheme.[37]

The government's handling of the case, which got underway shortly after Murphy left office, suggested a department anxious to exaggerate the significance of the crimes alleged and to garner whatever public relations value the prosecution promised. Anonymous officials discussed the case in the press even before an indictment was brought. But their extravagant claims about what the defendants had done failed to obscure the farcical nature of the proceedings. The defendants were a pathetic bunch and the evidence of conspiracy to overthrow the United States, which included a broken 1873 model Springfield rifle and "1 cavalry saber (old)," was incredible on its face.[38] Press doubts and the apparent weakness of the case elicited a stream of inconsistent and implausible explanations. Hoover insisted that the defendants were part of a larger network with possible collaborators in Boston and Philadelphia, and "hinted that possible 'foreign connections' should not be excluded." He also assured doubters that, fantastic as the allegations might seem, he "had evidence to support every iota of the charge that a conspiracy was indeed aimed at establishing a Hitlerite rule in this country." After all, he said, "it took only twenty-three men to overthrow Russia" in 1917.[39] But an unnamed official also told reporters that while the 17 were being charged with conspiring to overthrow the government, they were really being punished for their un-Americanism.[40] This might have pleased those who welcomed a federal crackdown on anti-Semitism except for the fact that the government's charges contained no indictment of the Christian Front, no suggestion of Coughlin's involvement, and no mention of anti-Semitism.

The trial, which began in April 1940, was anticlimactic. Crowds at the courthouse cheered the defendants, and the jury refused to convict. Hoover explained privately that nine of the jurors were Catholics and none were Jews, that all of the members of the panel sympathized with the defendants, and that the United States attorney had made a poor presentation. A year later, remaining charges were dropped.[41] Robert Jackson, who was now attorney general, later called the charge of conspiring against the government "a bit fantastic,"[42] and critics dismissed the proceedings as little more than a publicity stunt, which they tended to blame on Hoover, rather than Murphy.[43]

Even as the government sought to justify its prosecution of the Fronters, the department announced an equally dramatic, and flawed, attack, this time on the Left. In mid-January 1940, department lawyers presented evidence to a Detroit grand jury that a number of individuals had illegally recruited Americans to fight for the Spanish Republic in that nation's recently concluded civil war. It was clearly intended as a show trial to demonstrate the government's displeasure with communism.

The Spanish Civil War, which ended in March 1939 after two-and-a-half years of fighting, had divided Americans along ideological lines. The rebels, led by General Francisco Franco and backed by the Nazi and fascist regimes in Germany and Italy, enjoyed the support of the American Catholic hierarchy and the political Right in the United States. The Spanish government and its "Loyalist" supporters received aid from the Soviet Union and the passionate allegiance of the Left. From the beginning of the war, Communists in the United States recruited Americans to fight in Spain, and many of those who went were party members.[44] The activity provoked numerous complaints to the Department of Justice, mainly from Catholic and anti-Communist sources, and the department considered prosecuting the recruiters under an early-nineteenth-century statute that prohibited Americans from serving in, or recruiting others to serve in, foreign armies. But officials recognized that this selective prosecution would produce a storm of criticism on the Left.[45] Attorney General Cummings delayed, hoping that peace in Spain would bring an end to the controversy in the United States, but the conflict dragged on, and the recruitment issue was still simmering when Murphy succeeded Cummings.[46]

The war ended soon after, but Hoover reported to the attorney general that Dies and his allies were planning to use what an informant called the government's earlier appeasement of the Communists to do a "'job on the friends of that [expletive omitted] in the White House.'"[47] Although urged by senior department officials to secure the president's approval, Murphy, apparently acting on his own, in May ordered criminal proceedings instituted against the recruiters.[48] During the rest of the year, preparations for the prosecution proceeded by fits and starts as the attorney general gingerly circled the politically explosive issue.

In the fall, while waiting for the Spanish recruiter case to jell, Murphy launched his campaign against Communism with a couple of minor assaults. It began when officials sought the denaturalization (and eventual deportation) of William Schneiderman, the leader of the Communist party in California, on the grounds that he had hidden his Communist affiliation at the time he secured his citizenship 12 years earlier.[49] He followed this up with the announcement of the arrest of the Soviet booksellers, mentioned above. At the end of the year he was ready to deliver his most serious blow. During Christmas week 1939, Murphy was quoted extensively in the press as alleging that espionage and subversion were a serious problem in the defense industry in Detroit, and on December 28, the same day that Murphy announced a crackdown on un-Americans of all types, the Criminal Division asked the U.S. attorney in Detroit whether he could immediately present the case against the recruiters to a grand jury.[50]

The machinery of federal justice, which had been sputtering along for more than two years, went into high gear. By now the bloody conflict in Spain had been over for ten months. The only remaining link between the war and its American survivors was the emotion-laden memories that would forever tie them to what most on the Left thought of as democracy's lost cause. Nevertheless, the department secured indictments against 16 persons for conspiring to enlist Americans in the Spanish Civil War. In early morning raids in Detroit and Milwaukee, 12 of those named were seized along with evidence of their activities. As predicted, protest from the Left followed and, according to his biographer, "no event in Murphy's public career was more damaging to his reputation as a civil libertarian" than his pursuit of the Loyalist recruiters.[51]

By the time the storm of criticism struck, Murphy had moved from the Justice Department to a seat on the Supreme Court. His successor, Robert Jackson, felt no obligation to pursue what he considered an abuse of government power by a man for whom he had little respect. Cleaning up the legal rubble Murphy had left, the new attorney general ordered the cases dismissed, explaining that it seemed "inappropriate to begin prosecution for activities so long known to the government," particularly inasmuch as they seemed to have done "no public injury."[52]

The abortive Christian Front and Loyalist recruiter cases climaxed and epitomized Murphy's response to the problems of civil liberties as they related to the un-Americans. Earlier, the president, with Murphy's tacit approval, had initiated the investigation of groups and individuals thought guilty of harboring un-American beliefs and intentions. Now Murphy had extended the government's reach by using the law to punish those associated with "alien" isms. One may argue that in each case the government had evidence of criminal activity, and the attorney general was merely enforcing the law. But as a former prosecutor and judge, Murphy was fully aware that he commanded enormous discretionary authority and that a decision to seek an indictment was never merely a mechanical response to a detected crime.

Murphy brought to his responsibilities a practical attitude toward statecraft, one he shared with the president. In their view, when a political leader identified a problem, whether of suspected subversion or the administration's vulnerability to its political enemies, *he* (I use the gender-specific pronoun deliberately) responded boldly without undue concern that his actions might offend abstract, and much debated, principle. Their attitude was suggested by an episode involving a proposal to fingerprint newly arrived aliens (mostly Jewish refugees) as a national security measure.[53] In January 1940, the president raised the issue with the cabinet and, as Murphy had predicted, Secretary of Labor Frances Perkins passionately denounced the idea for its police-state implications. Murphy, who prided himself on his manliness, probably attributed Perkins's sensitivity to her sex and, in any event, dismissed her concerns, noting that "if you are afraid of anything because it is the first step in any direction you will never get anywhere."[54] Most of the cabinet agreed to the fingerprint proposal, and the president, as if to validate Perkins's slippery-slope fears, went on to discuss the propriety of fingerprinting *all* Americans. This was too much for the president's advisers, and a decision on this project was put off until after the fall election.[55]

Murphy wanted to be president. He knew that in the political culture of the era, following Perkins's lead, had he been so disposed, would have disqualified him, certainly in FDR's eyes. Not that Murphy was clear on the civil libertarian implications of FBI spying or the campaign against the un-Americans. When the attorney general spoke of the need to protect constitutional rights, he thought of selected episodes of intolerance—the night-riding of the Klan and the police-state tactics of the mine owners and their allies. He gave no sign that he recognized the dangers inherent in the department's campaign against un-Americanism. Indeed, confident of his civil libertarianism (certified by Baldwin), he saw his campaign against the anti-Semites in particular as an affirmative government effort to secure the liberal society he sought.

Murphy's year at the head of the Department of Justice demonstrated the tenuousness of the civil libertarian "tradition" that had developed in the years since the end of World War I. The ideas would face even graver challenges in the months ahead, and would fare somewhat differently under the very different man who took Murphy's place as head of the department.

Part II

Robert H. Jackson
January 1940–June 1941

Chapter 3

A "Lawyerly Way"

On January 18, 1940, President Roosevelt held an unusual swearing-in ceremony at the White House that brought together the three men who would serve as attorney general during the war years. Attorney General Frank Murphy took the oath of office that elevated him to the Supreme Court; Robert H. Jackson was sworn in to succeed Murphy as head of the Justice Department; and Judge Francis Biddle assumed Jackson's post as solicitor general. The gathering suggested continuity, and the record would eventually reveal much that justified that image. But the months ahead would also reveal a significant shift in the department's stand on civil liberties that reflected both the changing nature of the issues and the civil libertarian outlook Jackson brought to the Department of Justice. Thus while Murphy thought of the Civil Liberties Unit as his proudest achievement, Jackson allowed it to languish.[1] Where Murphy had urged his subordinates to greater efforts in the war on un-Americanism, Jackson counseled restraint, and while Murphy demanded a vigor suggesting ruthlessness, Jackson spoke of integrity, circumspection, and adherence to the strictures of the law—a package of virtues he called "the lawyerly way."

Jackson's identification of civil liberties with governmental self-discipline proceeded from his concern for legal professionalism. His high regard for the law and the canons of legal ethics dictated that ideological or political considerations had no place in investigations or prosecutions of wrongdoing. Operating within these boundaries, the legal system provided the foundation of the good society. Overstepping them produced tyranny. His efforts to make these ideals part of the departmental culture would form the central motif of his tenure at Justice.

Jackson, 48 years old when he became attorney general, was born in upstate New York, where he practiced law and was active in local politics.[2] Drawn to the Democratic Party by family tradition and a Jeffersonian dislike of concentrated wealth and power, he was an enthusiastic supporter of New York governor Franklin D. Roosevelt, and when FDR was elected president, he invited Jackson to join the new administration as general counsel for the Bureau of Internal Revenue. Jackson went on to serve as special counsel for the Securities and Exchange Commission, and later as assistant attorney general for antitrust matters, where he won a number of important New Deal cases, including the conviction for tax evasion of industrial-banking magnate Andrew Mellon.[3] He became known as a vocal New Dealer, finding favor particularly among the party's anti–big business wing. His wit and down-to-earth charm earned the friendship and support of a number of political figures, including the influential Thomas Corcoran, and he soon gained a place in the small circle of intimates with whom the president socialized. His standing with the president was solidified by his vigorous defense of FDR's 1937 court-packing plan, and in 1938, after unsuccessfully trying to get him the Democratic nomination for governor of New York, the president appointed him solicitor general. It was, Jackson later said, "the only post I ever really coveted,"[4] and his skilled advocacy earned accolades from those who witnessed his work. Justice Louis Brandeis, no mean advocate himself, suggested facetiously that the government would be well served by making Jackson solicitor general for life.[5]

As the 1940 election campaign season approached, New Dealers, assuming, as then seemed likely, that FDR would not seek an unprecedented third term, were looking for candidates to succeed the president and Vice President John Nance Garner, and Jackson was prominent among those considered.[6] He would need, of course, greater public exposure and a record to run on. The highest legal post in the government was a natural fit for the aspiring candidate's talents and reputation, and as early as April 1939 he was being mentioned as Murphy's successor. When FDR decided to put Murphy on the Court, the way was clear, and by early December "informed circles" were reporting that the president had offered the post to his New York friend and "neighbor."[7] Jackson was reluctant to leave the joys of legal practice he was experiencing in the insularity of the solicitor general's office, but seeing the attorney generalship as a stepping stone to higher office, he accepted Roosevelt's invitation.

The president probably did not seriously consider Jackson's views on civil liberties when he made the appointment, but the issue was very much on Jackson's mind. On December 30, a few days before his appointment was announced, the solicitor general wrote the president a long note outlining his unhappiness with current department policies,[8] and reflecting the strong dislike he had developed for Murphy and his behavior. His attitude was partly the result of contrasting styles and personalities—the self-effacing, publicity-shy Jackson was clearly offended by Murphy's flamboyance—but there were substantive grounds as well.[9]

Jackson's indictment of his predecessor focused on what he saw as Murphy's lack of professionalism and penchant for self-serving publicity.[10] He referred specifically to remarks the attorney general had made on December 28 indicating he was prepared to use any law, including the tax code, to punish the anti-Semites. Jackson, who had been general counsel for the tax bureau, was incensed at Murphy's suggestion. Apart from its dubious ethicality, he noted that such use invited officials yet unknown to initiate "a similar drive against Jews or Catholics or Republicans or Democrats." Anti-Semitism, he told the president, was "a reprehensible [sic] attitude of mind . . . but it is not a crime," and he warned that if the intended victims of Murphy's political prosecutions appealed, the administration would fare badly before justices suspicious that the government's cases were "really efforts to punish opinions and attitudes which we dislike."[11] These were extraordinary times, he conceded, but the department's business should be conducted in a "lawyerly way without premature publicity, with prosecutions based on criminal acts, not merely on reprehensible attitudes or opinions, and without yielding to or cultivating hysteria among our people."[12]

Jackson's critique of Murphy's regime suggests the influence of Justice Holmes and recalls the guidelines suggested by John Lord O'Brian in 1919 and Attorney General Harlan Fiske Stone in 1925. The values they expressed came naturally to Jackson, reflecting the particular cast of his personality and experience. He was motivated by a sense of the unfairness and impropriety of government imposing society's prejudices on its dissidents. Biographers have noted that in Jackson's very first case he represented workers arrested during a Buffalo streetcar strike, and that he had once defended a communist arrested for selling radical publications on the public square.[13] Jackson was not drawn by his clients' "radicalism" or by his conviction that airing their grievances would better society, but by the opportunity to exercise his budding legal skills on behalf of those who seemed to stand little chance of prevailing. It was the challenge of balancing the scales of justice that engaged him.

Jackson's suspicion of government and insistence that society's pariahs be allowed their say reflected his own experience as a wartime dissenter and victim of postwar intolerance. While Murphy had been a vigorous supporter of Wilson's Crusade for Democracy and chafed to play a part, Jackson hated war ("none of my people or I ever soldiered . . . my grandfather bought his way out of the draft in the Civil War and I was never ashamed of it"),[14] and opposed American involvement in the European conflict. His attitudes earned him a reputation in some quarters as "pro-German." Nevertheless, once the United States entered the conflict he dropped his active opposition and, in what was no doubt a concession to ambition, joined the American Protective League "in self-defense." Like many of his contemporaries, he was troubled by the public's hysterical demands for conformity, by the reckless accusations of disloyalty, and by the easy recourse of government officials to repression. A personal brush with the mob mentality made him wary of those who would take advantage of public anxieties to advance their own agendas.

Two months before the end of hostilities, Jackson was appointed acting corporation counsel for his hometown of Jamestown, New York, a position he used to resist public demands that the city act against alleged pro-Germans, aliens, and "slackers." Concerned by how easily an overwrought public opinion could shape government policy, he was critical, among associates at least, of the postwar Palmer raids and contemptuous of New York State's radical-hunting Lusk Committee. Reports to this effect prompted a newly formed local American Legion post to invite Jackson to answer charges of un-Americanism. He responded by taking out a newspaper advertisement inviting all the townspeople to the local armory to hear his accusers and his defense. The police chief, fearing a riot, prevented the confrontation.[15] The episode reinforced Jackson's distrust of efforts to impose orthodoxy on the nonconformist.

The ill-conceived prosecutions, and attendant publicity, that made up Murphy's campaign against un-Americanism were, from Jackson's perspective, very much like the sordid pandering to popular prejudice that had given rise to Palmer's anti-Red crusade—an offense against liberty of conscience, contrary to the growing body of law enunciated by the Court, and beneath the dignity of government. It was the work of the kind of "cheap people" who had exploited public fears in World War I and had sought his scalp in the Red Scare that followed. It exemplified the unwholesome, ungentlemanly conduct with which respectable members of the bar should not be associated.

Unlike Murphy, whose civil libertarianism was rooted in a genuine empathy for workers and ethnic and racial minorities, Jackson brought to the struggle for justice, as he later said, "no great emotion . . . and no conviction that the underdog is always right. . . . I was never a crusader. I just liked a good fight."[16] This retrospective view suggests an important difference between his sense of justice and Murphy's. What Jackson wanted, as he said, was a fair chance, a day in court for everyone. Murphy seemed more interested in a righteous result. The difference, certainly as it bore on the issue of free speech for anti-Semites, was important. Murphy, guided by what he instinctively felt was right, was apt to see civil libertarianism as a defense of those libeled. Jackson, given the value he placed on fairness and legal process, was likely to insist on government tolerance of the loathsome libelers. It was a difference that continues to divide the advocates of civil rights and civil liberties to this day.

Even before entering office, Jackson had clearly informed the president of his position on civil liberties and his rejection of Murphy's tactics. While the president's exact response to his lecture on legal ethics has not been preserved, Jackson recalled that "all and all" what Roosevelt said made him "feel a little contemptible and cowardly about it."[17] From what we have seen of the president's views on personal freedoms and state prerogatives, and what we will learn as the narrative unfolds, it is fair to say that Jackson's remarks struck FDR as politically naive. Roosevelt appointed him anyway, perhaps confident that the new attorney general's theoretical reservations would melt in the heat of practical demands. In taking the post despite FDR's rejection of his concerns, Jackson indicated that the president had probably not misjudged his man.

Jackson's ideals were more easily expressed than achieved. Their realization was compromised from the outset by the nature of the office and the path Jackson had traveled to get to it. The duties of the nation's first lawyer were concerned less with the practice of law, ethical or otherwise, than with the management of a succession of bureaucratic and political issues. Jackson, who prided himself on his legal acumen and professionalism, would have little opportunity to exercise his advocacy skills in a position he later described as that of "managing clerk."[18] And despite the detachment he associated with the appropriate administration of the law, his tenure was firmly situated in a matrix of political obligations and concerns that would shape his response to issues bearing on civil liberties.

Such problems affected all public officials to a degree, but they were salient for the attorney general. Writing about the office, historian Nancy V. Baker notes that attorney generals have ranged from advocates preoccupied with their role as the president's legal tool, to those who carried out their duties with minimal reference to the chief executive's political requirements or the public's desires.[19] The latter, somewhat exceptional, model was well represented by Harlan Fiske Stone, who served briefly under President Coolidge. While Jackson may have hoped to emulate Stone, circumstances dictated otherwise. Stone was an outsider brought in by a weak president to give credibility to a badly wounded department. Jackson's public career, for all his reputation for integrity, was very much the creation of his friend and political patron. Jackson was Roosevelt's man. Ultimately, his policies, if politically significant enough to draw the president's attention, would reflect FDR's judgment. But Roosevelt had interests and concerns far beyond those of the Justice Department, and it is safe to say that the issue of civil liberties was not very high on the president's agenda. This left the new attorney general with leeway to pursue his civil libertarianism up to the point at which it interfered with political necessities, as Roosevelt perceived them.

In the months following his appointment, Jackson reversed Murphy's parting initiatives. In mid-February he dropped the indictments Murphy had recently obtained against the Spanish Loyalist recruiters, explaining that the acts alleged had occurred years ago, that similar violations had been ignored in the past, and that it appeared unfair to prosecute some groups and not others.[20] Privately he noted that the case was weak and had been brought principally to satisfy elements in the Catholic Church.[21] Analogous reasoning dictated a similar resolution to Murphy's other major attack on un-Americanism—the prosecution of the Christian Fronters. Concerned that the charge of sedition was likely to "boomerang," Jackson later noted that the government at most should have charged some of the defendants with "stealing ammunition."[22] But the prosecution was already underway and he allowed it to proceed to its conclusion. In late June, a jury deadlocked in the case of one defendant and found the others not guilty. Jackson later dismissed the remaining charges.[23]

Clearly disturbed by the direction the department had taken in the last weeks of Murphy's tenure, Jackson sought to chart a new course. He set forth his objectives in an address to a meeting of United States attorneys in April. Although the prosecutors needed no instruction on this point, he reminded them that law enforcement was neither "automatic" nor "blind," and that they commanded the weighty prerogative of discretion. No prosecutor, he noted, could inquire into all the cases that come to his attention, any more than a policeman could arrest all violators of the traffic laws. Nor could the prosecutor seek to avoid responsibility for an ill-considered prosecution by leaving it to the courts to decide the defendant's guilt or innocence. Long before a case reached trial, an innocent individual, he noted, on the prosecutor's initiative, would be subjected to investigation, indicted by a usually compliant grand jury, detained, and probably convicted in the court of public opinion on the basis of leaks to the press. Should the prosecutor then dismiss a case he should never have initiated, the victim would be denied the opportunity to clear his reputation. If the case went to trial, he would be obliged to defend himself in what was apt to be a lengthy and expensive legal ordeal. Even if justice ultimately prevailed, the innocent victim would likely have been embarrassed, harassed, impoverished, and incarcerated on the road to vindication.

The preventative lay, Jackson insisted, not in changing the system—the powers subject to abuse were necessary to effective law enforcement—but in the character and integrity of the officials charged with its administration. Nowhere was this professionalism needed more than in the handling of alleged political crimes. With Murphy's misconduct very much in his thoughts, Jackson noted his disdain for anyone who used the system to harass or punish someone or some group he disliked or that is "unpopular with the predominant or governing group."[24]

He warned the prosecutors that, in the months ahead, various groups, insisting on the need to curb "so-called 'subversive activity,'" would demand the "scalps of individuals or groups because they do not like their views." The words he chose are significant, for while Congress, Murphy, and the president had casually employed the word "subversive," Jackson prefixed the term with "so-called." For him, "subversive" had no (legal) meaning and should entail no legal consequence since "the prosecutor has no definite standards to determine what constitutes a 'subversive activity,' such as we have for murder or larceny." Stay clear of cases involving the mere expression of opinion, he warned, and carefully confine your efforts to sustainable allegations of overt criminal acts.

Jackson no doubt hoped his admonitions would serve to protect free speech and association, but his arguments were based more on the demands of legal ethics and professional propriety than on libertarian principle. He did not try to impress on the prosecutors the natural right of citizens to speak their minds. Nor did he argue the social utility of a free "marketplace of ideas" or the practical value of providing the alienated with a safety valve for their discontents. Instead, he presented official tolerance as a function of professional pride—a lawyerly obligation necessary to maintain what he called "the prestige of federal law." Warning the prosecutors that the pressures to indict and convict would be great, Jackson insisted that resistance had its rewards. A record of prosecutorial successes was an attractive goal, Jackson acknowledged, but the (better) members of the legal profession will look at more than an imposing list of convictions. The "quality" of their performance in office, Jackson hinted, would have an important bearing on how federal attorneys fared after they left government.[25] Perhaps he thought that this emphasis on standards and professional expectations would be more compelling than a discussion of the value of free speech, but the emphasis on process rather than outcome was unmistakable and significant.

While Jackson spoke of honor and professionalism, he was unwilling to leave the prosecutor's performance purely to personal integrity and peer pressure. He recognized that there were bound to be at least a few who were not the gentlemanly sort. Experience, he said, referring to 1917–18, "had demonstrated that some measure of centralized control [was] necessary" to ensure that prosecutions were efficiently handled and free from prejudice. With this in mind, he announced that henceforth the planning and preparation of national security cases would be done in Washington. The purpose was to "promote uniformity of policy and action, to establish standards of performance, and to make available [to the U.S. attorneys] specialized help." What he did not say, as he later told Zechariah Chafee, was that the scheme was also designed to "supervise the activities of United States Attorneys . . . and to profit by the lesson of the World War."[26]

In April 1940, soon after the attorney general addressed the conference of federal prosecutors, the department announced creation of the Neutrality Laws Division.[27] The new agency would be directed by Lawrence M. C. Smith, a 37-year-old graduate of the University of Pennsylvania Law School who had come to government in 1932 after a short period of private practice. Although he had investigatory experience from service on the Securities and Exchange Commission, there was nothing in Smith's career suggesting a special interest in either countersubversion or civil liberties. Jackson gave Smith, who would be remembered as an "idea man" and a planner, considerable latitude, telling him only to survey the situation in regard to sedition and foreign propaganda and do what was necessary to establish department policy to deal with the problems.[28] The unit would review cases brought to its attention by the FBI, survey the statutes, and recommend to the attorney general—and through him to the 85 United States attorneys and the FBI—the appropriate courses of action. It would also compile, from files supplied by the FBI, a list of potentially dangerous persons who might be seized in case of national emergency. Over the next several years Smith would build the Neutrality Laws Division and successor operations into a large and important component of the department's national defense apparatus.[29]

The specter of department excesses in World War I hung over the undertaking. Jackson set aside a room in the Justice Department building in which documentation related to the department's antiradical and countersubversion operations in 1917–20 was gathered for ready reference. The official who collected the data also gave Smith a study, based on these and other records of the era, that provided lessons concerning the things, as he put it, that "good government in time of crisis or war should seek to avoid."[30] Similar warnings were conveyed to Smith in interviews with O'Brian (twice), and Carl McFarland, coauthor of *Federal Justice,* the 1937 study of the department's handling of national crises.[31] These encounters strengthened Smith's determination to prevent "excessive zeal against suspects by over enthusiastic United States Attorneys," and to ensure a relatively disinterested balancing of national security and personal rights.[32]

The new office significantly changed the way the department would deal with persons suspected of disloyalty. The procedure until now was for the FBI to refer evidence of possible criminal activity to the United States attorney in the district in which the crime was alleged to have occurred. The attorney, on his own authority or after consulting the department, would secure search and arrest warrants, which were then executed by the FBI's locally based "special agents." Henceforth no one was to be arrested on charges stemming from suspected internal security violations without prior approval of the Neutrality Laws Division.[33] By inserting Washington into the close cooperative relationship that hitherto existed between U.S. attorneys and the FBI agents in their districts, Jackson had undercut the power of both and greatly diminished the role of local political pressure in arrests and prosecutions for "un-American activities." Of course, citizens and local politicians could still make their concerns felt in Washington, but the new arrangement meant that the effect of any such pressure would be indirect. This was no mean achievement, but, as we will see, it was far from knave-proof.

Although a spokesman for the department took care to indicate that the new unit would not supersede or overlap the functions of the FBI, the timing of the decision seemed to some a rebuke to the bureau. The sub-headline of a *New York Times* story on the new unit declared "Civil Liberties In Mind, FBI's Findings Face Scrutiny Before Any Authority for Prosecution Given."[34] Hoover immediately took exception to the implied criticism. Hurried consultations among officials produced a White House announcement insisting that Smith's operation was intended to "help" the FBI and "not [to] overlap or subtract from anything the FBI's doing." Furthermore, the president's press secretary told reporters, the new unit had been created with the director's approval.[35]

The decisive step in Jackson's efforts to centralize control over the prosecution of political crimes came on June 7, 1940, when the attorney general announced that he reserved to himself (acting on the advice of the Neutrality Laws Division) the final decision on what cases involving national security matters would be pursued.[36] With the United States still at peace, Zechariah Chafee exulted, Jackson had achieved the control that Attorney General Gregory had not secured until the final weeks of World War I.[37]

Virtually everything Jackson did and said in his first six weeks in office evidenced a policy of restraint. In a piece that appeared in the inaugural issue of the *Bill of Rights Review,* Jackson attempted to steer readers away from the issue of vigilantism currently preoccupying the civil liberties community, toward what he believed was the more pressing issue of publicly driven, politically motivated federal prosecution.[38] While Murphy had spoken expansively on local denials of civil rights and exaggerated the achievements of the Civil Liberties Unit, Jackson warned the civil liberties community that staff and jurisdictional constraints limited what the department could realistically accomplish.[39] Jackson implied that his greatest contribution to the protection of free speech would be to ensure that the Department of Justice did not become part of the problem of repression. Under his direction, he insisted, the agency would not exceed the "proper bounds" of its authority, nor go "beyond the realm of criminal acts into that of unpopular opinion." Officials would not be issuing "statements tending to prejudge the accused" in criminal cases. His department, he indicated clearly, would be known for its restraint and obedience to the law.[40]

Jackson thought that his chief contribution to the protection of free speech lay in the area of prosecutorial restraint. But investigations could also inhibit free expression, and the department's reputation among civil libertarians would rest, as well, on the performance of the FBI. Dissidents, and ordinary citizens, had legitimate concerns that an overly intrusive government might be listening in on their phone conversations and compiling dossiers of rumor. Aliens from potential enemy nations had reason to believe that in the event of a "national emergency" they could expect heavy knocking at their door, followed perhaps by detention *without* prosecution. These fears grew in early 1940, fed by FBI activities that, taken against the backdrop of contemporary Nazi and Soviet secret police tactics, revived memories of the "old" Justice Department.

The problems associated with federal investigative practices had been addressed, but not laid to rest, by the reforms Attorney General Stone had promulgated in 1924. In declaring that "the FBI shall investigate only where it has credible information or reasonable suspicion that a crime has been or may be committed," he had, in the words of one commentator, "provided little guidance for those discretionary decisions at the heart of the power of a law enforcement agency."[41] Operating in secrecy and with a plausible justification for maintaining it, agents charged with the investigation of political matters had developed an administrative culture that desensitized them to the repressive effects of their efforts. Information illicitly obtained might be excluded by a trial judge, but this provided little check on such activities since the vast majority of those subjected to surveillance or investigation in regard to radical or seditious activities had not violated any law. The material in their dossiers and the methods by which it was obtained were, therefore, unlikely to be subject to judicial scrutiny. In this hothouse atmosphere, "security" investigations proliferated, driven by Hoover's wish to catalog all those whose loyalty was suspect, and limited only by his fear of being caught and embarrassed by his enemies.

When Jackson assumed direction of the department, he knew little of FBI operations. He had been warned by Murphy that Hoover had "gone too far" in investigating government officials, including Jackson. But when Hoover told him that he had looked into Jackson's war record only at Murphy's instigation, Jackson, perhaps willing to believe the worst of Murphy and not in a position to do much about Hoover, did not pursue the issue.[42] But the FBI's potential for wrongdoing would be forced on him by a spate of criticism directed at the bureau in the early months of 1940. The attack came at a time when worries about internal security were somewhat relieved by the lull in fighting that settled over Europe in the winter of 1939–40. This period of "phony war" raised hopes for peace, and for a short time the conflict seemed safely distant. Civil libertarians and liberals unhappy with the growth of FBI authority following the president's September declaration of a state of limited national emergency, were worried that reactionaries, including Hoover, were seeking to turn the European crisis into an excuse for an assault on aliens and radicals. Allegations of agent wrongdoing in the arrests of the recruiters for the Spanish Loyalists provided a convenient starting point for the counterattack.

In early February 1940, FBI agents had raided homes and offices in Detroit and Milwaukee, taking 12 accused recruiters into custody. Although Jackson announced a week later that the case against them would not be pursued, those arrested complained of their treatment at the hands of federal agents. The liberal *New Republic,* charging that the episode was reminiscent of the operations of the secret police of Soviet Russia and Nazi Germany, called on the attorney general not only for an investigation of the Detroit arrests, but for a study of the "whole record of the lawlessness of Hoover's bureau."[43] When Jackson asked him for an explanation, Hoover responded with a detailed refutation of each of the specific charges: the raids were at 5 A.M., not at 4; the shackling of prisoners was done by federal marshals, not his special agents; the accused were presented with warrants and allowed to consult attorneys, etc.[44]

Jackson accepted this explanation, but the attacks continued. In late February, in the midst of a Senate discussion of government appropriations, Senator George Norris, a one-time progressive Republican, now an independent from Nebraska, who had survived his opposition to United States entry into World War I to lead a handful of congressional liberals through the postwar conservative ascendancy,[45] called attention to what he viewed as the vast and dangerous expansion of the FBI's budget over the past ten years, and in this context raised the issue of the agents' alleged misconduct in Detroit.[46]

In early March, the founder and current director of the American Civil Liberties Union, Roger Baldwin, wrote to Jackson to complain of the ill-defined and troubling mission the director had set forth for the FBI in recent public statements. For the first time in 20 years, Baldwin noted, the bureau apparently had carte blanche to target almost anyone that the FBI believed to be unpatriotic, including pacifists, religious groups, labor unions, and unpopular political factions.[47] The clamor against Hoover was joined by others not normally aligned with Norris, Baldwin, or the *New Republic.* A number of journals and journalists, including the *New York Daily News,* the Scripps-Howard syndicate, and columnist Westbrook Pegler, suggested that the director's bureaucratic empire-building had gone too far and that Hoover was taking on imperial airs. They took particular exception to Hoover's hobnobbing with the rich in Florida while presumably more pressing issues went unattended at the office.[48] After a number of years of virtual immunity, Hoover was now the focus of serious criticism on a number of fronts.[49]

The director, who could boast of a remarkable record of survival, was not without resources, and he fought back vigorously, telling his allies in the press and his sympathizers in the Washington establishment that the attacks on him were part of a politically motivated conspiracy. In a long and unctuous letter to Associate Justice Harlan F. Stone, Hoover wrote of his continuing dedication to Stone's reforms and "principles of decency and fairness and tolerance," contrasting the agency's current professionalism with the undisciplined gumshoe tactics of an earlier era. Stone, a respected figure who commanded enormous respect in legal circles, responded cordially with words of encouragement.[50]

In his message to Stone and in observations he shared with other potential supporters, Hoover suggested that his problems stemmed from an alliance of Communists and Washington fellow-travelers,[51] and the followers of presidential confidant Thomas G. "Tommy" Corcoran. The latter, according to the director, was seeking Hoover's removal so that he could extend his control of appointments into the bureau, thus increasing the patronage at his disposal.[52] Smearing his critics was Hoover's typical response to criticism.[53] His countercharges, however, were more plausible at the time than they may appear to be in retrospect. Communist intrigue was well known and exaggerated in Washington, and Corcoran, who was currently serving as a special assistant to the attorney general, was responsible for the appointment of a number of persons to important posts in the New Deal government and was indeed thought of as an inveterate schemer.[54]

While Jackson tried to decide what, if anything, should be done about the criticism of the FBI, the assault on bureau practices came to focus on allegations of illegal wiretapping. The new turn began when Democrat Theodore Green of Rhode Island told the Senate that officials in Pennsylvania, Massachusetts, and his own state had been subjected to wiretapping by unidentified persons apparently seeking political intelligence.[55] Although Green made no mention of the FBI, the sensational charges, coming against the background of accusations against the bureau, triggered demands for a full inquiry that would cover not only these incidents, but all wiretapping, including the bureau's investigative practices.

Green's charges rekindled a national controversy over telephone interceptions and other kinds of electronic spying that had been smoldering for more than a decade. Labor and the Left had historically been targeted by the practice and were particularly sensitive to its use. Legislators, who sensed their own vulnerability to blackmail, were also concerned, and though the *Olmstead* decision in 1928 had approved the practice by police, the 1934 Federal Communications Act contained a provision that seemed to categorically prohibit it. Nevertheless the practice continued to be widespread.[56]

With the threat of a serious inquiry into FBI surveillance practices looming, Hoover struck back, putting the administration on notice that it had better stand by him. In late March, he reviewed the wiretapping issue with former Brain Truster and current Assistant Secretary of State Adolf

Berle, who headed counterespionage activities for the State Department. According to Berle's account, Hoover acknowledged that the FBI for years had been tapping phones at the request of various senior federal officials, including specifically the cabinet's most outspoken liberal, Secretary of the Interior Harold Ickes. What is more, Hoover declared, the scale of FBI tapping was dwarfed by that done by Treasury and other federal agencies. These and other allegations led Berle to note in his diary that "if anyone ever learns of some of the wilder activities of Corcoran and his friends, there will be trouble on all fronts."[57] This, no doubt, was the message Hoover intended to convey. The director was in a position to tell all (which may well have included stories of investigations done at White House instigation) and, if pushed to the wall, he would.

The charges against the FBI posed a serious problem for Jackson. He entered office determined to strengthen the department's reputation for professionalism and respect for civil liberties. Criticism of Hoover's expanding suspect list and allegations of wrongdoing in the Detroit raids had raised doubts about the FBI's operations and the attorney general's ability to control them. If suggestions that the bureau was involved in extensive illegal wiretapping were proven or even merely believed, the image of red-eyed operatives huddled over their listening devices would be added to the recently revived specter of faceless federal clerks pouring through dossiers and arrogant agents bursting in on sleeping citizens in the wee hours of the morning. Public familiarity with the Nazi and Soviet secret police provided critics with a model for what could not be allowed to happen here. A decade-and-a-half of work building public confidence in the Justice Department was in jeopardy.

The Hoover problem, however, was not easily resolved. Whatever the attorney general's views of the director, and these appeared to have been a mixture of respect and concern, any effort to curb or remove him would have involved an unwelcome and uneven political struggle. Jackson had been in office only a few months; if he received his party's call, he would not serve out the year. Hoover had already been director for 15 years, and had been associated with the federal investigative bureaucracy for longer than that. He had fashioned a successful operation made to look even better by his public relations skills, and appeared to enjoy the president's complete confidence and support.

Jackson may also have come to accept the proposition that an agency charged with counterespionage and national security functions necessarily cloaked in secrecy was likely to press the boundaries of civil libertarian propriety regardless of who led it. Challenged by Baldwin to curb FBI dossier collecting, the attorney general had intimated that the practice was not sufficiently troubling to offset the nation's interest in having the information. Jackson rejected (as had Murphy) the ACLU director's claim that persons had a right *not* to be investigated, and patiently explained that in times like these, prudence required the collection and collation of information on individuals suspected of subversive views. Such investigations posed little danger to personal liberties, in his view, since any prosecutions arising out of the bureau's list-making would be initiated only by the department's lawyers, not by Hoover, and only for specific violations of law.[58] Jackson, partly out of political necessity, insisted that prosecutorial restraint was the point at which the line could best be drawn in ensuring civil liberties.

In early May, Jackson endorsed both the agents' actions in the Detroit arrests and the FBI's overall record in the treatment of suspects.[59] Conceding that mistakes may have been made, as they often were in such cases, he insisted that "wide discretion" must be left to officers in the field who face danger without the benefit of time for calm decision making. The bureau's record was good, he wrote to Senator Norris, noting that since Hoover had become its head, not one government case had been reversed by an appellate court because of the improper actions of an arresting agent. All in all, he concluded, to the extent that "traditional civil liberties" were endangered in this country, the FBI was not the culprit.[60] He later dismissed Norris's complaints as traceable to the effects of the octogenarian's age.[61]

Jackson wanted very much to ensure that the administration of federal justice was orderly, restrained, and within the letter of the law. At the same time, he was not certain that serious restraints on the FBI were either needed or wise. He told critics on occasion that he understood and even sympathized with their concern that the FBI was going too far, and confessed that if he were in their shoes, he might join in their criticism. But he insisted that his responsibilities compelled him to take a less liberal view, and asked critics to imagine what they would do if they were in his place.[62] Nevertheless, he was convinced that he had to do something about the bureau's use of wiretapping. He would later say that he was uncomfortable with the widespread use of tapping under his predecessor, and that he was glad that, as he believed, the 1934 Communications Act outlawed the practice.[63] He was a stickler for observing the letter of the law, and on this issue the law seemed settled.

In mid-March 1940, Jackson announced a new department policy. He assured critics that Hoover had never sought wiretapping authority (which was true), and had only occasionally used the tactic in connection with very serious crimes like kidnapping (which was not true), and he insisted that the eavesdropping never involved congressmen or other government officials—a statement Hoover had contradicted in his discussions with Berle. The attorney general nevertheless pledged that henceforth there would be no wiretapping by agents of the Department of Justice, until Congress specifically authorized the practice.[64] Having announced a ban on tapping, Jackson embraced Hoover and the work the bureau was doing. Nothing, he declared, warranted the suggestion "that police activities in the United States resemble those of an Ogpu or a Gestapo."[65]

Jackson had taken steps that curtailed Hoover's autonomy, but the success of the effort depended ultimately on the attitude of the president. FDR, who liked and trusted both men, accepted Jackson's initiatives because Congress and elements in the press seemed concerned. His support for Jackson, however, was not premised on the belief that personal liberties were seriously endangered by Hoover's wiretapping or his agents' relations with the U.S. attorneys, and he never evinced any sense that the bureau needed to be reined in. Quite the contrary, he stood solidly with the director. Asked at a press conference at the beginning of March to comment on Senator Green's proposed Senate investigation of government surveillance activities, he said he had "never heard of it," frequently his way of suggesting issues were not worthy of his attention. And in mid-March, with the furor over the FBI at its height, he went out of his way at a White House Press Club dinner to conspicuously indicate his support for the director and his disdain for the inquiry.[66]

Hoover, unhappy with Jackson's ban on the use of electronic surveillance and confident that he could count on the president's support, was soon agitating for a change. In mid-April, he told the attorney general that he found it impossible to live with his no tapping rule and implied that unless the ban was lifted, Jackson would be responsible for the resultant investigative and prosecutorial failures.[67] The attorney general ordered a thorough investigation and decided to ask for legislation permitting tapping in limited circumstances, with his prior approval.[68] Hoover, who did not want a congressional inquiry, rejected this idea and took his case to the White House. A changed international situation guaranteed him a favorable reception.

Chapter 4

Changing Concepts of Civil Liberties

Jackson's resistance to Murphy's campaign against the un-Americans drew heavily on the commitment of the American elite to the free speech ideals enunciated in the Holmes/Brandeis dissents and popularized by the ACLU, the Bill of Rights Committee, and others. The attachment to free speech for everyone was widespread (Murphy's frequent invocations of the ideal attested to that), but its depth had yet to be tested. How strongly Americans were committed to tolerating groups espousing ideas that seemed inimical to American security was not certain. How "clear" and how "present" did the danger posed by radical and obnoxious advocacy have to be before the situation demanded repressive remedies? Murphy's abortive campaign against the un-Americans seemed to suggest that the ideal was weak or at least poorly understood. But Jackson's response indicated that it had considerable strength, at least at the Department of Justice. The first serious test would not come until the late spring of 1940, when the nation learned that recent German military successes against France and other democracies was attributable, so the story went, to the insidious workings of a so-called fifth column—Nazi and Communist agents working behind the defenders' backs. Convinced that a similar phenomenon could undermine American defenses and turn the nation over to the forces of totalitarianism, erstwhile supporters of American freedoms came to conclude that the application of these ideals was far more limited than the rhetoric of the Bill of Rights celebrations suggested.

Although the fifth-column scare emanating from Europe in the late spring and summer of 1940 would become the occasion for wholesale departures from the earlier preoccupation with tolerance, these frightening events merely exposed a debate over the limits of free speech that had been going on among liberal intellectuals since at least the mid-1930s. The conditions that had given rise to the civil liberties movement had changed dramatically in recent years. In the decade after World War I, a fledgling intelligentsia, struggling to free itself from the grip of cultural and political orthodoxy, had welcomed the liberating aphorisms of Holmes, Chafee, and the ACLU. Threatened by the enforced conformity and reaction of wartime and postwar America, intellectuals and progressives had championed the rights of radical others (with whom they often sympathized) in order to secure their own freedoms. But by the mid-30s liberals, the natural constituency for libertarian values, were more confident than they had been, and the alienation and fear that had given rise to civil libertarian enthusiasms were largely absent in the New Deal era. Liberalism, including a belief in unfettered political discourse, if not triumphant, at least commanded a respectable presence, and while there was still uncertainty about the meaning of "free speech," the ideal had assumed the authority of political holy writ. In these circumstances liberals felt free to examine the principles they had helped popularize, to make distinctions among the claimants of free expression, and to deny its universal application.

Unhappy with newspaper coverage of New Deal measures and chagrined at what they saw as the hypocritical use to which reactionary press moguls like Robert R. McCormick had put First Amendment freedom, liberals had made attacks on the press (and freedom of the press) a staple of their political commentary.[1] Those who cast their lot with the interventionist New Deal, and most liberals did, sought to counter the threat of a completely autonomous (and largely conservative) newspaper business by reminding the public of the pragmatic origins of the rights they claimed. Writing in 1934, eminent historian Carl Becker, in a clear repudiation of the assumptions mistakenly associated with Holmes, noted that "society is something more than a debating club of reasonable men in search of the truth."[2] This and similar comments suggested a questioning of free expression's universal application that would become even more insistent when liberals confronted the danger to democracy posed by the growing strength and apparent popularity of totalitarianism.

Liberals were united in their concern over Nazi Germany's challenge to their values and America's institutions, but divided as to how to respond. Non-interventionists of the Left, sensing a movement to stampede the nation into another war, clung fast to both isolationism and toleration, no doubt anticipating that their own freedom was in jeopardy. But an increasing number of liberal intellectuals, having decided that United States intervention was necessary to stop the spread of Hitler's fascism, challenged the wisdom of an undiscriminating tolerance of political expression, particularly fascistic propaganda.[3] The new militant liberalism, led by literary lights Lewis Mumford, Waldo Frank, Van Wyck Brooks, and Archibald MacLeish,[4] was an amalgam of democratic idealism and what they thought of as hardheaded, give-no-quarter realism. In contrast to what they saw as the effete timidity of the "old liberalism," they offered an aggressive defense of American nationalism, unreserved condemnation of totalitarianism, forthright advocacy of United States involvement in the struggle against Hitlerism, and, ultimately, a somewhat deflated view of free speech. The attitude was manifest in the formation of a number of organizations dedicated to exposing and discrediting fascist propaganda; raising and sustaining American morale; promoting democracy; and, later, urging in subtle and not-so-subtle ways, all-out aid to Great Britain.[5] Believing in the malleability of popular opinion, the militants sought national salvation through mass education. But what of the propaganda for evil that simultaneously attempted to negate their effort?

The militants' fear and hatred of Nazism and their commitment to the affirmative defense of democracy made the idea of "free speech for everyone" troubling. Was tolerance and the free exchange of ideas the essence of democratic thought and process, or the anachronistic legacy of the old, pragmatic liberalism's relativistic inability to distinguish right from wrong? Could believers in democracy remain indifferent to its enemies here at home—tolerant of loathsome expression that denigrated fundamental truths?[6] Those who thought not could draw on the conclusions of an influential series of articles published in 1937–38. Karl Loewenstein, an émigré political scientist teaching at Amherst College, had examined the laws and administrative practices adopted by a number of European countries in response to fascist and Communist agitation. He concluded that those governments, like the Weimar regime in Germany, that had scrupulously tolerated political dissent and agitation had lost their nations to totalitarianism. Only those, including Czechoslovakia (he wrote before the German occupation) and Great Britain, that had abandoned "the customary complacency of traditional liberalism" had survived. In these countries, Loewenstein wrote, "liberal democracy, style 1900," including "instrumentalities and constitutional rights" too long held in awe by "democratic fundamentalists," had given way to "'disciplined' or even 'authoritarian' democracy.'" Unless his adopted country learned from these experiences, he warned, it would share the fate of fascism's European victims.[7]

Yet militant liberals at this point shrank from all-out war on the purveyors of totalitarian propaganda. Their reticence stemmed in part from a fear of supplying the Dies Committee and the Right with support for their already repressive proclivities. Intolerance was a two-edged sword, and although the 1939 Nazi-Soviet Pact had destroyed the special affinity many liberals had for Communism, most continued to defend American Communists against the Red-baiters whom they associated with reaction and even fascism. They could not avoid the nagging fear that the kind of repressive authority Loewenstein appeared to countenance would ultimately victimize the Communists, and then the Left in general.[8]

Fear was one restraint, habit was another. The American Civil Liberties Union and others had so firmly established the idea of free speech for everyone as an inviolable Americanism that liberals could not quite bring themselves to openly deny it. At this point at least, most seemed prepared to take chances to preserve the freedoms that had served them well in the recent past. Nevertheless, if there was no precipitous abandonment of free speech for everyone, compromise and confusion were in the air. The uncertainty in civil libertarian thinking was reflected in the actions of two of the institutions most responsible for free speech orthodoxy—the ACLU and the Supreme Court.

Although civil libertarians had often made common cause with the Communists, some ACLU leaders, like liberals in other organizations, had become convinced that the party faithful had used their joint efforts principally to further the CPUSA's agenda. Distaste for the Communists increased dramatically with the signing of the Nazi-Soviet Pact, when distrust and the desire to appear impartial and responsible led Roger Baldwin and others to conclude that it was time to free the organization of the taint of Communist involvement.[9] In February 1940, the ACLU's board of directors adopted a resolution that banned from its governing committees persons who were members of organizations, including specifically the American Communist Party and the German-American Bund, that supported totalitarian regimes or by their public statements indicated support for totalitarian principles. The chairman of the National Committee, Harry F. Ward, who had been identified as a fellow traveler, resigned; Elizabeth Gurley Flynn, a board member and long-time avowed member of the CPUSA, was expelled.[10]

The message conveyed by the purge was not lost on Attorney General Jackson. In March, when Baldwin complained about the FBI's publicly announced policy of spying on Americans, Jackson drafted a response in which he pointedly reminded Baldwin of the board's action. If the Civil Liberties Union felt obliged to take cognizance of the nature of the totalitarian parties and to assume that affiliation with such parties was a legitimate predictor of an individual's views and actions, could the government do any less? Should the Justice Department, in seeking out the potentially disloyal, ignore past and current political affiliations? Does the "proper requirement that the government remain tolerant," Jackson asked pointedly, "also require it to remain ignorant?"[11]

A few weeks later the Supreme Court ratified the idea that the state had a legitimate interest in the political allegiances of its citizens by declaring that government officials had a right to demand affirmations of loyalty from school children. In April 1940, with only Justice Stone dissenting, the Court upheld the action of authorities who had expelled Jehovah's Witnesses from a Pennsylvania school because they refused to participate in a mandated pledge of allegiance.[12] Justice Felix Frankfurter, who as a Harvard law professor had been an active exponent of civil liberties, now suggested that the times dictated a new look at political tolerance. The conflict currently raging in Europe, he would later say, was "a war to save civilization itself,"[13] and in such a struggle personal freedoms sometimes had to be sacrificed. Writing for a majority that included liberal justices Hugo Black, William O. Douglas, and Frank Murphy, Frankfurter suggested that mandating a ritual of allegiance was an act of national defense. The flag was the nation's quintessential patriotic symbol and the public school the primary agency for making a single community out of the country's disparate elements. "National unity is the basis of national security," he wrote, and the state's responsibility to ensure it overcame the students' right to follow their consciences.[14]

The *Gobitis* decision was roundly condemned by legal scholars and newspaper editorial writers,[15] indicating that a substantial portion of the civil libertarian elite was not yet convinced that the time had come to repudiate principles whose value had only recently been affirmed. Nevertheless, the decision was bound to complicate Jackson's efforts to limit the department's response to un-American activities. With the once apparently solid consensus on civil liberties revealed as an illusion, the attorney general sought guidance and support for the controversial decisions he would be called on to make.

Jackson turned naturally to Grenville Clark, the distinguished New York attorney who had founded the American Bar Association's Bill of Rights Committee and then served as the committee's first chairman. In April 1940, Jackson told Clark that he was "searching for a sensible and balanced solution" to the problem of reconciling the legitimate rights of political dissenters with the demands of domestic security. On the one hand, as Clark understood him, Jackson recognized there were such things as "real sedition, espionage and sabotage which had to be paid attention to." At the same time, the attorney general said, he was "not going to stand for hysteria or red-baiting or persecution or anything remotely resembling the Mitchell Palmer days." Jackson had in mind creating something like the officially appointed Royal Commissions employed in Great Britain and the Commonwealth to produce official findings on difficult civil liberties issues confronting the government. Discussions with other distinguished members of the bar produced similar recommendations for committees of wise men to whom Jackson could turn for advice and support in "holding the line for civil liberties at a decent point."[16]

Jackson's efforts to secure support for a policy of restraint came to nothing. Even as he sought guidance, a hurricane of events would loosen the philosophical moorings of most conservative and interventionist civil libertarians. The dramatic change was brought on by the jarring experience of witnessing France succumb to the Nazi blitzkrieg in a matter of weeks. The fear precipitated by this event and attendant rumors was comparable to the Red Scare that followed World War I, and the impact on civil libertarian thinking was profound. While those associated with the ACLU stood firm, Grenville Clark and the *Bill of Rights Review* would begin writing about "changing concepts of civil liberties" and the need for a new understanding of constitutional liberties. Over the course of the summer of 1940, the ideal of free speech for everyone, which the ACLU continued to espouse as a practical way of ensuring orderly discourse, was redefined by frightened militants as unrealistic and utopian. Some of those who now emphasized the limits of free speech found ample justification in the well-known exception Holmes attached to his classic definition of free speech. The current world situation constituted, they suggested, the "clear and present danger" of which he had spoken. True or not, the crisis produced a massive shift in libertarian thinking and rhetoric.

Following the Nazi victory in Poland in September 1939, the European conflict settled into a "phony war" characterized by military deployments and diplomatic maneuver, but little combat except at sea. In late April, however, the "sitzkrieg" came to a sudden and dramatic end when Nazi forces descended on Norway. The invasion was unconventional, with some troops emerging from the holds of freighters docked at Norwegian ports and others landing in transport planes or dropping from the sky by parachute. On May 10, with the conquest of Norway almost complete, Germany turned west.

A substantial force, including airborne units, invaded Belgium and Holland, and in a full-scale display of the blitzkrieg techniques they had only hinted at in Poland, German tanks and motorized infantry rushed through the supposedly impenetrable Ardennes forest and turned north to come up behind the main Anglo-French force. The Wehrmacht advanced with breathtaking speed, bypassing or routing the defenders, many of whom fell back on the channel ports. These stunning events culminated in the dramatic forced evacuation of 300,000 Allied troops from the beaches at Dunkirk in early June. The fate of France was sealed. A conflict that most observers had thought would drag on indecisively for months had been decided in a matter of days. On the tenth, Mussolini's Italy declared war; four days later, German troops entered Paris. Six weeks after the war began, the French government, now at Vichy, accepted Hitler's surrender terms. The fuehrer made a triumphant tour of the French capital, and his generals prepared for an invasion of the British Isles that fall. For the remainder of the summer the British battled to stave off a *Luftwaffe* assault and grimly prepared to meet the anticipated cross-channel attack.[17]

Americans were shocked by the magnitude and swiftness of the German victory and worried by the threat Hitler now posed to Great Britain and the rest of Europe, and beyond. It was not, however, the efficiency of the German military that was most disturbing. Rather, it was the sense that there was more at work here than force of arms. The French, it was thought, had actually been laid low by internal subversion, and this led some Americans to question their reliance on the nation's oceans (or even on its armed forces) for security.

While the concept of betrayal from within was ancient, the term "fifth column," now used to describe it, came from the recently fought civil war in Spain. A rebel general, in describing his coming assault on Madrid in 1936, had declared that he had four columns of troops converging on the capital, and the equivalent of a fifth column, made up of anti-Republican elements, operating within the Spanish capital. In the summer of 1940 the concept was freely used to explain everything that went wrong for Hitler's victims—the panic and despair among the populace, the indecisiveness among national leaders, and the lack of discipline and ill-preparedness of the Allied armed forces.[18]

There was some truth in this version of events, but it was grossly exaggerated by people who found in it a serviceable alternative to a realistic appreciation of the debacle. In France, the military used it to excuse their failure,[19] and politicians used it as a stick with which to beat their opponents. For the Right, lack of preparedness was laid to Communist-inspired slowdowns and sabotage in defense industries. For the Left, it was the indifference to a Nazi victory of fascist-minded industrialists and anti-Semitic officials. Journalists could impartially give credence to all the self-serving explanations. American reporters had plenty of anecdotal evidence—some of it events they had witnessed; most based on rumor or second-hand reports. It was a particularly frightening tale, readily illustrated, that explained developments that were otherwise complex and confusing. Just the stuff to fill news stories, and with a lesson for Americans.

The warnings implicit in the European tale reverberated through the popular media in the United States. In mid-June, *Life* ran a pictorial account of "Signs of Nazi Fifth Column Everywhere," which included a "sneaked" photo of young "American Nazis" at the Bund's Camp Siegfried on New York's Long Island.[20] A popular publicist, writing in the *Saturday Evening Post,*[21] warned that no one, not even the FBI, knew how many "alien propagandists, professional culture carriers, spies and agents provocateurs" were loose in the United States. George Britt, a reporter for the *New York World-Telegram,* who had specialized in exposing city corruption, turned out *The Fifth Column is Here,*[22] which his publisher predicted would be "an eye-opener" to those unaware of the "dangers of total destruction that are lurking on almost every hand."[23] Patriotic organizations helped enliven public awareness—the Veterans of Foreign Wars produced a long pamphlet of "Fifth Column Facts."[24] Fifth-column talk had become, as *Time* characterized it, a "national phenomenon."[25]

American officials proved remarkably credulous. It was an article of faith among the American elite that while their kind of people might manipulate mass fears, they were themselves immune to hysteria. The response of various government officials to fifth-column stories suggested otherwise. Many were genuinely frightened and willingly passed along the fifth-column story to colleagues and the general public.[26] The befuddled response was suggested by Assistant Secretary of State Adolf Berle's reaction to what he described as "a rather shattering" encounter with Norman Alley, a news photographer working for the Hearst newspapers who had just returned from Holland.[27] According to Berle, Alley told an elaborate tale of German agents "already in control of New York," and of plans for utilizing the fifth column to take over the country. His story was so graphic that the one-time member of FDR's "Brain Trust" and putative expert on counterintelligence confessed, "it frightened me completely." In assessing what he had heard, Berle applied the logic that helped sustain and spread the fear. Thus, it first occurred to him that Alley (who in 1943 would land with U.S. troops in the invasion of Sicily) was "probably a Nazi agent" and was exaggerating in a (successful) effort to panic him. On reflection, however, he mused that what Alley had told him about Nazi operations in New York might well be true. After all, "more fantastic things have happened."[28] In either case—whether the subversion consisted of the vast conspiracy he described, or was merely manifest in Alley's effort to sow distrust—the episode helped confirm Berle's impression that the plotting against the nation was well underway.

Many officials found the fifth-column stories useful, whether they totally believed them or not. J. Edgar Hoover, the object of considerable criticism in the early spring, needed only to allude to the evidence of the American fifth column to justify the bureau's continued expansion and autonomy.[29] Martin Dies, the now apparently prescient chairman of the House Committee on Un-American Activities, produced *The Trojan Horse in America,* as an "I told you so" warning of worse things to come.[30] The purported Nazi use of foreigners, including Jewish refugees, lent authority to the longstanding efforts of nativists to control the influx of those seeking asylum in the United States and to deport alien troublemakers. Liberals quickly adapted the fifth-column rubric for use against their current and traditional enemies: the "Dieses" and "Hearsts," the Red baiter, the "union buster," and the "racist of anti-Semitic or any other complexion."[31] Commissioner of Indian Affairs John Collier, hoping perhaps to gain support for his efforts to help Native Americans, warned officials, the public, and Congress of Axis efforts to incite "the New World's Indians to revolution."[32]

The president tended to credit reports of internal subversion, but whether he believed them or not, he used them and the resultant apprehension to further his foreign-policy agenda. Determined to dispel what he believed was the dangerous delusion of America's invulnerability, the president found an emotionally powerful tool in the images of the fifth column and the Trojan horse. In a mid-May message to Congress asking for additional defense appropriations, President Roosevelt spoke of the new "treacherous use of the Fifth Column," mentioning in particular the danger posed by refugees recruited as enemy agents. In accepting the Democratic presidential nomination for a third time, FDR explained that he felt duty bound to lead the nation in these times of ideological upheaval and the threat of "unbelievable types of espionage and national treachery."[33] In January 1941, alluding to the non-interventionists who continued to frustrate his policy, he would charge that those encouraging skepticism, promoting disunity, or preaching appeasement were fifth columnists.[34] Just as he had earlier used the term "subversive" to describe radical dissenters, he now employed "fifth columnist" to identify not only willing Nazi agents and intimidated Jewish refugees, but anyone who actively resisted intervention. He no doubt hoped that cultivating popular fears of the enemy within would help discredit those who emphasized America's insularity.

Americans heard Roosevelt's text but missed the larger message. Polls revealed that the increased consciousness of the internal threat failed to translate into increased support for military intervention.[35] Indeed, a focus on internal security was compatible with the fortress-America mentality. On the other hand, while the fifth-column warnings did little to advance interventionism, they did encourage demands for a crackdown on suspicious elements (including refugee Jews and Jehovah's Witnesses) as the country sought security not in an American expeditionary force, but in heightened vigilance and greater repression at home. On the day after the president's May 26 Fireside Chat, FBI offices throughout the United States were deluged with stories of espionage, sabotage, and "other violations of a national defense nature," and although there was no real upsurge of espionage, the year witnessed a fifteen-fold increase of such reports.[36] The fifth-column phenomenon seems to have hastened the retreat from tolerance.

Fearing foreign-inspired subversion, Americans began to organize to meet the danger and to pressure local, state, and federal authorities for repressive measures. Although much had changed since the closing of the frontier at the turn of the century, citizens in many areas were apparently still ready to use the law, or operate outside of it, to defend their community and its values.[37] Many fondly recalled their contribution to security on the home front in 1917–18 and looked forward to this new opportunity to express their love of country.

Evidence of incipient vigilantism abounded in the summer of 1940. *Time* reported that "defense organizations," like fifth-column talk, had become "a national phenomenon." The defense corps and rifle clubs popping up all over the country were, the story explained, the result of a combination of "hysteria, an itch for publicity, a deep-seated fear that official defense measures might be botched or a resurgence of the old backwoods instinct that nothing so calms a man's nerves as polishing a rifle."[38] Many prepared to act on their own, but others offered their services to local, state, and federal authorities.[39] It seemed to one official that "literally millions" of Americans were eager to do their bit.[40]

Local and state officials needed little encouragement. The anti-sedition and anti-syndicalism laws adopted by most states in the World War I era were still on the statute books, and new ones were being introduced in state legislatures across the nation.[41] Some of the anti-alien measures [42] were unlikely to survive judicial scrutiny, but local initiatives were driven by fear and politics, not by need or the logic of the law. In early August, Governor George Aiken of Vermont predicted that unless the federal government could somehow prevent it, "there will be the biggest lot of 'crackpot' [alien control] legislation that the country ever saw."[43]

By the end of May 1940, federal officials had become concerned by what the ACLU called "the present wild and unreasoning eagerness to defend the country."[44] Justice Department officials were particularly sensitive to reports of vigilantism and local anti–fifth column preparations. To avoid a repetition of the "excesses" of World War I, Jackson had asserted control of the locally based federal prosecutors.[45] Now, in the summer of 1940, with volunteers besieging Washington, he moved quickly to forestall the threat from the grassroots. Urging calm and faith in federal authority, Jackson insisted that American liberties were endangered more by "our own excitement" than by enemy conspiracies,[46] and he instructed federal officials, including the United States attorneys and Immigration and Naturalization Service personnel, to discourage private citizens from taking the law into their own hands.[47] Editorial writers picked up on the theme. Leave the "squelching of subversion to the Department of Justice," said one; "Vigilantes are criminals," opined another.[48]

While J. Edgar Hoover and the attorney general had their differences, on this point they were in complete agreement. There should be no mob justice, quasi-official security groups, or more-than-minimal involvement by the states in countersubversion efforts.[49] The director wanted no interference from local patriots and pronounced himself "diametrically opposed to anything suggesting vigilante activities" or a reconstitution of the American Protective League.[50] Hoover was moved by personal as well as professional concerns. He was aware of threats to his security preserve from super-patriot pretenders, including Martin Dies,[51] and recognized in Jackson's determination to centralize the control of disloyalty an opportunity to eliminate contenders for his own role as America's number-one policeman-patriot.

Jackson supported Hoover's quest for a monopoly on repression and increased resources for the FBI, seeing a strong bureau and a happy director as a counter to accusations, heard often during World War I, that the department was not up to the task of combating the threat of disloyalty. For Jackson, there was a critical distinction between the operations of the FBI and the activities he anticipated from the American Legion, municipal "Red" squads, or even military intelligence. At least, he thought, the FBI was subject to the attorney general's influence, and its repressive effects circumscribed by rules of criminal procedure and judicial scrutiny. The FBI occasionally did distasteful things, he admitted, but in his view it remained "the most restrained and careful organization in the field of law enforcement today."[52] Posing Hoover as the alternative to chaos may now seem a bit contrived, but Jackson was sincere. As he later put it, the FBI, whatever its faults and dangers, was "infinitely preferable" to the "local snoops" who had plagued the administration of justice during World War I.[53]

The first fruit of the Jackson/Hoover alliance was the taming of the American Legion. Since its founding at the end of World War I, the powerful veterans' group had given expression to the nation's obsession with "Americanism."[54] In the fifth-column spring of 1940, Legion officials issued a number of bombastic statements[55] suggesting the organization's determination to play a larger role in internal defense and, in early June 1940, Hoover turned away a Legion delegation seeking approval of its offer to supply the government with various internal security services. The disgruntled legionnaires left promising to present their scheme to military intelligence officials.[56] In late June, the attorney general, who had had an unhappy encounter with the organization 20 years earlier, sought to placate Legion leaders without surrendering any part of the anti-subversion effort to them. In an ironic twist, given the organization's history, Jackson sought to enlist the Legion in a war on intolerance and vigilantism.[57] Legion officials agreed, and although they would not entirely surrender their "intelligence-gathering" activities, in October the organization, which had been the principal source of anti-radical terrorism since the decline of the Klan in the mid-1920s, formally renounced vigilantism.[58]

Having domesticated the American Legion, Jackson turned to the threat posed by the states. In mid-June, he initiated a series of conferences between senior department officials and representatives of the state attorney generals and other state functionaries to coordinate countersubversion efforts.[59] The conferees agreed that states' home defense efforts would be kept within the bounds of "law and order" and consonant with the generally understood dictates of civil libertarian principle—a significant, if vague, commitment. Using the state attorney generals as the points of contact, federal authorities continued over the following months to eradicate "uncoordinated, undirected, voluntary actions," in effect subordinating local countersubversion activities to federal efforts. The result was that even after the United States entered the war, there would be nothing like the local- and state-originated terror associated with World War I.[60]

With local and state capacity for repression greatly diminished, Congress now threatened to fill the vacuum left by the retreating states. Since the mid-1930s, federal lawmakers had been considering legislation aimed at controlling sedition and curtailing the rights of aliens. In 1939, with war in Europe likely and concern about Nazis and Communists very much on the minds of legislators, many of the extant proposals were incorporated into a single measure, HR 5138 ("Crime to Promote the Overthrow of Government"), which offered a smorgasbord of legislation designed to outlaw disloyalty. In late May 1940, the omnibus anti-alien/anti-radical bill, which had been left for dead in the last session, emerged from the Senate Judiciary Committee as the "Alien Registration Act of 1940" (or Smith Act, after its principal author, Virginia Democrat Howard W. Smith).[61] The act provided for the mandatory registration and fingerprinting of all resident aliens—hence its name—along with a list of familiar devices for political purification. There was a provision aimed at facilitating the deportation of the accused Communist labor leader Harry Bridges, and another punishing those who spread disaffection among military personnel or attempted to discourage enlistment in the armed forces. Duplicating the wording of state anti-syndicalism and anti-sedition laws, the Smith Act also outlawed teaching or advocating the overthrow of the government, and membership in organizations that did.[62]

Passage was never in doubt. The intelligence community and the military favored it, and the Justice Department, which had been involved in drafting the legislation, posed no major objection.[63] The president, who shared many of the current fears about aliens and radicals, was silent. With the White House and Justice Department behind the measure, the Smith Act rushed forward with little public or official debate.[64] When the bill came to a vote in the House, the leadership had difficulty raising a quorum, and some members appeared confused about the nature of the legislation before them. There was little opposition. On June 22, 1940, the same day that the French officially ended their resistance to the Germans, the Smith bill passed the House—382 in favor, 4 against, and 45 not voting.[65] There was no recorded vote in the Senate. FDR, disregarding protests from the ACLU, signed the measure into law, commenting only on its alien registration provisions, and then only to emphasize the protection they would give to the foreign-born.[66] Zechariah Chafee later noted, with bitter irony, that the legislature had put into the statute books the peacetime anti-sedition act that A. Mitchell Palmer had sought in vain.[67]

Although ACLU general counsel Arthur Garfield Hays tactfully put Jackson on notice that the organization intended to test the law's constitutionality at the first opportunity,[68] Roger Baldwin observed that ultimately "the preservation of civil liberty in this crisis will depend largely upon the attitude of the Department of Justice." In Jackson's hands, he thought, the Smith Act posed little threat to free expression.[69] Chafee agreed. Writing in 1941, he noted that the act was like a loaded revolver. If it was handed over to the U.S. attorneys, "some of them may start sniping at soapbox orators by the front gate," but if the attorney general kept it in his desk lest a "burglar ever shows up," it was unlikely to be misused.[70]

With the Smith Act and alien registration a reality, Jackson moved to gain the states' official acceptance of their diminished role in internal security. For three days in mid-August, senior state and federal officials met in Washington at a conference on the Law Enforcement Problems of National Defense. Officially it was sponsored by the Interstate Commission on Crime, the Governor's Conference, and the Association of State Attorney Generals (which, ironically, a few years earlier had condemned encroaching federal power). In fact, the meeting was conceived of and directed by the Department of Justice,[71] and while its stated purpose was to ensure cooperation in the war against the fifth column, a large portion of the agenda was aimed at limiting local efforts to ensure patriotic conformity. The tone was set in an introductory message from President Roosevelt (drafted by Solicitor General Francis Biddle) in which he condemned the "prejudice and emotional haste" and the "cruel stupidities of the vigilante in the last world war," and emphasized that there was no place in the home defense effort for the "amateur detective" or "the untrained policeman."[72] Speeches by J. Edgar Hoover, who was a prominent presence at the affair, John Lord O'Brian, Jackson, and others echoed the theme.[73] The states' role in the current crisis would be confined, as Jackson put it, chiefly to stopping the "ruffians and self-constituted groups who seek to take the law into their own hands."[74]

The meeting was a triumph for the attorney general. State officials agreed to discourage counterespionage activities by individuals and private groups, and to accept primary responsibility for the prevention of "mob violence" and the protection of aliens. In line with the reversal of traditional roles implicit in these actions, the conferees also turned aside proposed model state legislation providing for the regulation of subversive groups and the deputizing of private guards to protect the defense industry (a device used in the past for strike-breaking), and conceded to the federal government sole authority to register noncitizens. Such self-denial by state and local authorities was a tribute to the respect state officials had for Jackson, the department, and particularly Hoover and the FBI.[75] It also owed something to the timely passage of the Smith Act. By vesting vast peacetime anti-sedition powers in federal hands, the act provided a strong argument for leaving the fifth column to the FBI and the Justice Department.

In the event, there would no repetition of the hysterical overreaction experienced during World War I—no lynching, no tar and feathering, almost none of the marks of mob justice that had characterized the reaction to subversion jitters 20 years earlier. Nor would the state and local governments mobilize to enforce conformity and root out disloyalty. The subdued reaction reflected changes in attitudes and expectations over the past 23 years. Americans were one more generation removed from the frontier experience than they had been in 1917, and American society was altogether more orderly and bureaucratized than it had been then. The shift of authority on the disloyalty issue was part of a larger transfer of power that had been developing for at least a generation. The federal government, a minor presence in the lives of most Americans in 1914, had since made itself felt at the grassroots.[76] The New Deal, by demonstrating that Washington could do what the states had been unable to do, whether in regard to economic relief or natural disasters, had furthered the development. In particular, the once unknown or reviled gumshoes of the Bureau of Investigation had metamorphosed, under Hoover's guiding genius, into the "special agents" of the FBI, an agency now well known and respected by most Americans. The populace, having become accustomed to G-men successfully tracking down bank robbers, seemed willing to leave the hunting of public enemies, including the "fifth columnists," to Hoover's bureau.

The near-total eclipse of local loyalty-enforcement tradition evoked little public comment. A national commitment to order through law, the determination of local elites to reject mob rule, and the nation's increasing homogeneity and integration all combined with growing faith in federal law enforcement to put the vigilante well on the road to extinction. A year after the state-federal conference, Roger Baldwin concluded from reports from local ACLU branches[77] and from his own observations while traveling throughout the nation, that there was no spirit of vigilantism anywhere—not even on the Pacific Coast, where anti-labor vigilantes had recently been quite active. Outbreaks of violence against African Americans, particularly in the South, would come to be a significant exception to Baldwin's otherwise valid generalization,[78] but the vigilantism traditionally directed at aliens and radicals was all but dead. Nor did state and local government expand to fill the repressive void. In May 1941, a Justice Department report noted that the many repressive bills introduced in the state legislatures in 1940 had produced few laws, and that the attempts to bar aliens from employment had failed completely.[79]

While Jackson's efforts hastened the demise of the major local threats to constitutional guarantees, free expression was far from secure. The Smith Act was problematic. It gave the department extraordinary powers to inquire into the lives of citizens and aliens alike, and to severely punish expressions or associations deemed seditious. And while many, including some department lawyers, thought the act would be found unconstitutional,[80] a good deal of suppression could (and would) be accomplished before the courts got around to ruling on the issue. Those, including Attorney General Jackson, who had worried lest the federal government become an engine of repression, had made a Faustian bargain, cultivating the vast expansion of federal repressive power as a way of forestalling repression threatening from a far more dangerous quarter. The cost of combating the fifth column, without stirring up grassroots hysteria, was to increase the Justice Department's potential for wrongdoing. Most civil libertarians seemed willing to pay the price.

Liberals, speaking through the *Nation,* while reaffirming the "classic" Holmes doctrine that only a "clear and present danger" could justify interference with free speech, noted that recent experience had driven home the lesson that even traditional liberties were contingent on circumstances. Radical speech that at an earlier time might have been dismissed as the tolerable ranting of fanatics, could in the current context be more prudently treated as the destructive propaganda of the ubiquitous fifth column. The journal urged passage of group libel legislation to check anti-Semitism, and creation of a congressional watchdog committee to expose fifth-column propaganda. This, it naively declared, should be headed not by Martin Dies, but by a Robert LaFollette or a George Norris.[81] Of course, the legislature had its own views on subversion and would in fact keep Dies on as chairman of the House Committee on Un-American Activities, and increase his committee's budget.

The rush to encourage federal authorities to determine the limits of free speech was even more pronounced on the Right. In 1939, Grenville Clark had declared that a democracy required the freest possible exchange of ideas; urged toleration for America's anti-Semites, including Father Charles Coughlin; and rejected the attempts of local communities to impose the flag salute.[82] Now Clark's concern over the need to stop Hitler overwhelmed his interest in liberty at home. In mid-May, Clark made his priorities clear. In a piece appearing in the very first issue of the Bill of Rights Committee's *Bill of Rights Review,* he suggested that the principal concern of civil libertarians, and everyone else, should be stopping the Germans, since a Nazi victory would mean an end to all personal and political liberties. Compared to countering Hitler, "all other public questions . . . sink into insignificance."[83]

The "responsible" talk of temporary curtailment of rights had a judicious ring, but exactly what rights did Clark and like-minded libertarians have in mind? In the second issue of the *Bill of Rights Review,* which appeared after the adoption of the Smith Act, the newly appointed editor, in a piece he called "Changing Concepts of Civil Liberties," supported restrictions on aliens, intensified government surveillance, and outlawry of "suspect groups."[84] In January 1941 the Bill of Rights Committee appointed a five-man subcommittee to examine the issue. The panel recommended that civil libertarians be urged to accept severe limitations on academic freedom (apparently an endorsement of the current purge of Communists from teaching positions); reject the "right to strike," a "right" that Clark called a "perversion of sound concepts of civil liberty;" endorse the Dies Committee, which Clark argued was necessary to keep the public satisfied that un-American activities were not being ignored in Washington;[85] and support the temporary suspension of civil liberties in (this) time of national emergency. The proposal was only narrowly defeated by the whole committee.[86]

In "quieter and softer times," Clark would later write, it was appropriate for civil libertarians to emphasize rights rather than duties; the interests and privileges of the individual rather than the safety of the country. But in the current circumstances personal liberties and guarantees had to be "temporarily modified lest the security or very existence of the state be endangered." Roger Baldwin, who, aside from his role in expelling the Communists from the ACLU, resisted the drive toward repression, lamented that support for freedom was "more and more confined to the small circles of defenders of civil liberty on principle" and to the partisans of the movements attacked.[87]

It was difficult for Jackson to accept this new, supposedly more "realistic," stance. He had repeatedly committed himself and the department to a restrained approach, and had roundly condemned Murphy for the latter's campaign against un-Americanism. Moreover, his perception of the war in Europe was very different from Clark's, the president's, and others who urged a more radical approach to "suspected subversion." His experiences in World War I led him to discount cries that the nation was in imminent danger, and to reject repressive demands premised on the existence of emergency conditions. He had put away the pacifism of his past, understanding, as he later wrote, that "there was a wide gap between the Kaiser's Germany and Hitler's."[88] But according to Biddle, who knew him well,

Jackson was a small-town isolationist at heart ("in the best sense"), and his mind was centered more on the "monstrosity of war" than on the importance of "saving England."[89] He supported the president's foreign policy, but with rather more skepticism than others in the administration, and he seemed decidedly less easily moved by what others perceived to be the pressing need to combat dissent.

"The unhappiest man in Washington these days," one commentator wrote in June 1940, was Attorney General Robert H. Jackson, who was faced with the unenviable task of winnowing a righteous policy from the "alien-baiting and other forms of minority oppression" that now constituted the gravest threat to the Bill of Rights since 1918.[90] It was a task Jackson would have to undertake without the help of the "responsible" civil libertarians.

Chapter 5

Searches, Stealing, and Tappings

Having been granted extraordinary powers to combat subversion, Jackson was expected to use them—and more. From the fall of 1940 through the end of his tenure as attorney general the following June, Jackson was pressed by the chairman of the House Committee on Un-American Activities, the director of the FBI, and senior officials in the War Department to employ questionable means to get to the bottom of defense industry disruptions that seemed to be the work of enemy-inspired saboteurs and provocateurs. The demands threatened the right of union officials and others to conduct legitimate organizing activities free of wiretapping and other intrusive tactics associated with police-state operations. The attorney general reacted with a series of compromises that would find him backing down from the high standards he had set when he entered office, but resisting those who would have him sacrifice the department's integrity, and the rule of law.

In the two years before American involvement in the war, and probably for some time thereafter, the production of war materiel was America's principal contribution to its own defense and the defeat of the Axis. As late as the fall of 1941 shortages of the implements of war required the army to conduct training maneuvers with trucks labeled "tank," and similar ersatz arms. Any disruption in the production of the real instruments of war critically threatened the defense effort and quite rightly aroused the strongest feelings. And, indeed, there were a large number of fires and explosions of "mysterious" origins that, whatever their true origins, could with very little imagination be attributed to Nazi or Communist intrigue. This inclination was abetted by memories of German industrial sabotage in the last war,[1] and by recent allegations that Nazis and Communists had paralyzed French military production on the eve of the German assault. Some observers were so sure that the Germans were planning to disrupt American industry that they took the absence of clear evidence of sabotage as proof of the saboteur's skills at concealment.[2]

Those who worried about sabotage pointed to the fact that significant numbers of naturalized Americans of German origin were employed in defense industries, particularly as skilled tool and die makers. Radical labor leader Harry Bridges was among those who warned that Nazi sympathizers were plotting to sabotage the nation's aircraft manufacturing industry.[3] Most observers, however, were generally more concerned by the presence of suspected Communists and fellow travelers—like Bridges—in the ranks of organized labor.

Officials, including the president, were concerned by disruptions, current and anticipated, and they were partly responsible for raising public anxieties. In June 1940, FDR publicly alluded to 40 or 50 instances of sabotage;[4] J. Edgar Hoover warned that the notorious "saboteur, or 'sabcat' of World War I, was back in operation in the United States, and in force;"[5] and despite the fact that suspected sabotage was attributable in almost every instance to industrial accidents, Secretary of War Henry L. Stimson hinted to the press that recent defense industry explosions were the work of Nazi agents.[6] Jackson worried that such talk had created a situation in which "some great act of sabotage would create a mass hysteria" that would lead the public to take things into its own hands. Any such development, he recalled, could have had "serious consequences for the department," as well as for the nation.[7]

Pressure for action came chiefly from Martin Dies.[8] Long a thorn in the administration's side, the chairman of the HUAC gave notice in early August 1940 that his committee had compiled a list of potential troublemakers (aliens, Communists, and Bundists) in the defense industry, and was preparing for public hearings on the issue.[9] In September, he charged that a recent explosion at the Hercules Powder plant at Kenvil, New Jersey, which killed more than 50 people, was an act of sabotage that could have been prevented had officials taken his earlier warnings seriously.[10] When the department insisted that there was no evidence that the explosion was the result of sabotage, he called the assertion a craven coverup and warned that the "most crippling act of sabotage in American history" was going to "hit the airplane industry within 90 days." He challenged the department and the FBI to reverse their record of incompetence before it was too late. All that was required, Dies insisted, was for officials to act on the detailed information he had supplied.[11]

Countering sabotage and strikes in defense, however, was a particularly difficult and sensitive undertaking. Officials could not lawfully prosecute individuals, or have them summarily removed from their jobs, merely on the basis of the chairman's assertions.[12] Existing federal statutes were ill-adapted to preventing peacetime sabotage or politically inspired work stoppages,[13] and provided little help in keeping likely subversives out of munitions production.[14] Rooting out potential saboteurs and obstructionists meant employing techniques that industrial management had used for generations to suppress unionism, and many union leaders, unimpressed by government warnings, were suspicious of such tactics. Effective laws, even if they could pass the test of constitutionality, would be strongly opposed[15] and difficult to secure.

Nevertheless, the public charges hurt the department and angered Hoover, who suspected that Dies was after his job.[16] Under pressure from the director to do something to quiet the chairman, Roosevelt invited the obstreperous congressman to the White House. Although FDR lectured Dies on the meaning of due process of law and the imperatives of common decency,[17] he was prepared to compromise civil libertarian principle in the cause of peace with the committee. Following the White House chat, Justice officials informally agreed to supply Dies with information from its files, and to act on his allegations if a case could be established by "technically admissible evidence legally obtained." In exchange, committee representatives agreed to bring their allegations and complaints to the department before airing them in public.[18] At the same time, concluding that the Dies problem thrived on exaggerated public concerns over sabotage, for which they were largely responsible, administration officials decided that the sabotage epidemic was over—indeed, that it had never existed. In mid-December, Hoover announced that to date, thanks to his efforts, there had not been a single act of destruction in the United States attributable to a subversive conspiracy.[19]

The resultant decline in anxiety about fires and explosions coincided with rising suspicions and anger over defense industry strikes. The number of work stoppages, which had been relatively stable over the past four years, rose sharply in 1941 as workers responded to poor working conditions and unfulfilled wage expectations in the rapidly expanding defense sector. Given existing anxieties, government officials (no doubt encouraged by industry leaders), assumed that the upsurge was attributable to foreign intrigue. In his earliest warnings about hostile activities in America's munitions plants, Hoover had declared ominously that "sabotage does not always consist of actual physical damage," but included as well the "more subtle method" of politically inspired work stoppages.[20] Jackson had cautiously echoed the conclusion,[21] and in the early months of 1941 the "unnecessary strike" replaced the "unexplained explosion" as a mainstay of press discussions of defense production problems.

Concern focused on the nation's aircraft industry, which was plagued by labor discontent (and was the source of the weapon widely assumed to form the foundation of America's defenses). Largely because of niggardly government contracting practices,[22] wages in the industry were below the national average for similar work, and aircraft manufacture was an attractive target of union organizing efforts.[23] On November 15, the same day that Dies charged that the administration was indifferent to evidence of sabotage in the nation's defense industry, workers at Vultee Aircraft in Downey, California, walked off the job. There was evidence suggesting Communist influence, but it was far from conclusive.[24] Nevertheless, Jackson, having been warned by Hoover that the Communists intended to shut down critical defense industries, publicly charged that Communists were behind the walkout.[25]

The strike ended after 12 days, but suspicions of a Communist campaign to shut down the defense industry intensified in late January, when seven thousand workers struck the Allis-Chalmers plant in Milwaukee,[26] which had forty-five million dollars in defense (mainly navy) contracts. Again the strike was denounced as Communist inspired, and though settled after 75 days through the efforts of the National Defense Mediation Board,[27] the episode fed the image of Communist conspiracy and portended further, perhaps more serious, interruptions in munitions production.

Such concerns revived the wiretapping issue. Hoover saw electronic surveillance as a major weapon in the war against subversion, with particular application to labor intrigue. But in March 1940, with Congress up in arms about administration surveillance practices, Jackson had publicly pledged to end wiretapping unless and until Congress specifically authorized it. Congress would debate the issue for months, without result, but Hoover had no intention of waiting for the legislature to decide. In April he warned Jackson that his order seriously threatened national security and, receiving no satisfaction, the director took the matter to the president. On May 21, 1940, FDR sent the attorney general an apparently hastily drawn confidential memorandum prompted, Jackson believed, by Hoover's intervention.[28] Under "ordinary and normal circumstances," FDR wrote, "wire tapping by Government agents should not be carried on for the excellent reason that it is almost bound to lead to abuse of civil rights." But, he went on, he was convinced that the Court, in ruling against tapping, had never intended its decisions to "apply to grave matters involving the defense of the nation." Writing in the midst of the fifth-column scare, the president observed that the government could not sit by while foreign agents busily organized propaganda in the United States and prepared to commit acts of sabotage. He therefore "authorized and directed" Jackson to investigate cases of "suspected . . . subversive activities . . . including [though inferentially not limited to] suspected spies," and to authorize tapping, as needed, on a case by case basis. FDR concluded by requesting that Jackson keep these investigations to a "minimum," and suggesting that he "limit them insofar as possible to aliens."[29]

Here, in line with other presidential directives on such matters, was a vaguely worded license for questionable police practices. It differed from similar presidential directives to the FBI and the Justice Department only in that the president, recognizing Jackson's sensibilities, offered some weak cautionary caveats. Despite the suggested limitations, the directive ultimately gave the FBI enormous discretion. It left open the possibility that agents, once authorized to spy on a given individual, could place as many taps on him as they saw fit and could, under the single authorization, tap the phones of an indefinite number of unnamed individuals implicated in the case. Involvement of the attorney general provided little control over the process, since he was not likely to have the time to examine tap requests on a case-by-case basis, and because he, or more likely his designated subordinate, was ultimately dependent upon the information and assessment of need provided by the director. The discretion the president's guidelines left to the attorney general and the FBI was an invitation to abuse.[30]

The attorney general was uncomfortable with the order, which obliged him to violate his public no-tap pledge, and he redoubled his efforts to secure legislation that would ratify the president's secret policy and honor the attorney general's public commitment. Early in 1941, the attorney general urged Congress to specifically approve of wiretapping on the authority of the head of *any* executive agency.[31] In August, the House adopted a department approved proposal, now sponsored by Alabama Representative Sam Hobbs, and referred it to Senator Burton K. Wheeler's Committee on Interstate Commerce. Opposition, led by labor, was strong.[32] Wheeler, who had been a victim of government snooping in the 1920s, was now a leader of the isolationist bloc in the Congress. Suspicious of the administration on both accounts, he delayed Senate action while resistance mounted.

Liberals were worried about the terms of the bill, and in early February, with passage in doubt, FDR sought to reassure them.[33] The White

House arranged for freshman New Deal congressman Thomas Eliot, a member of the Judiciary Committee who opposed the Hobbs bill, to publicly solicit the president's views on the legislation. In his open letter to Eliot, the president asserted both the value of wiretapping as a law enforcement tool, and the importance of protecting Americans against "unwarranted snooping." In giving the authority to authorize tapping to the head of *any* executive department, FDR said, the Hobbs bill went "entirely too far." He proposed instead to limit the objects of wiretapping to those persons who are "not citizens of the United States, and those few citizens who are traitors to their country, who today are engaged in espionage or sabotage against the United States," and to confer on the attorney general alone the authority to determine in each instance that a wiretap was necessary.[34]

The president's statements, if taken as a policy directive, would have reduced the targets of national security taps from "persons suspected of subversive activities" (the phrase used in FDR's May 21 order), to aliens and those engaged in espionage or sabotage. It would also have required the attorney general to certify the necessity in each case in writing. But the letter to Eliot was not intended to provide instructions to Hoover and Jackson. Designed to disassociate the administration from the overly broad Hobbs bill, it failed to reassure some liberals, who wondered whether the FBI could be trusted with such potentially intrusive powers. Jackson, the *Nation* patronizingly conceded, "was certainly a man of liberal views and good intentions," but his involvement with the Hobbs bill suggested that Hoover, not he, made department policy on internal security matters.[35] Even though liberals were prone to concede considerable discretionary authority to the federal government in the pursuit of the fifth column, there were limits, particularly in matters touching on labor's prerogatives.

The Hobbs bill was revised,[36] but the revision failed to satisfy many liberals, including Congressman Eliot, and the resistance to tapping remained strong. In April 1941, James Lawrence Fly, the outspoken liberal lawyer who served as chairman of the Federal Communications Commission and head of the Defense Communications Board, told an executive session of the House Judiciary Committee that he opposed tapping and rejected the Hobbs bill, even as amended. News of what the chairman said in committee reached the president while he was on a fishing trip with Jackson, and an unhappy FDR demanded that Fly provide him with a transcript of his testimony and an explanation.[37] Fly confessed that he had told the committee that in tapping phones, agents were bound to violate the privacy of innocent people as they followed their natural tendency "to spread the tapping process into a dragnet. . . ." He characterized the Hobbs bill as "both unrealistic and unlawyer-like." (The latter, ironically, a term prominent in the attorney general's lexicon of denunciations.)

Roosevelt curtly dismissed the chairman's objections. The issue for him was loyalty to the president, not civil liberties. "I do not think that any of us should be in a position of hampering legislation . . . by going too much into technicalities."[38] But the damage had been done. Fly's testimony had given opponents of the bill, an odd coalition of liberals and conservatives led by conservative Democrat Francis E. Walter, the expert support they needed.[39]

The attorney general had sought the legislation to sanction what the president had secretly made official practice, but only the president supported Jackson's frantic efforts. No one, he would later comment, wanted to stick his neck out by acknowledging complicity in the "dirty business."[40] On June 30, 1941, the same day that the Senate Judiciary Committee approved Jackson's nomination to become associate justice, the House of Representatives defeated the Hobbs wiretapping bill 154 to 146.[41] The effort to legalize (and limit) wiretapping was dead for this session of Congress, but wiretapping continued as before—without regulation outside the Justice Department, and on the authority of the attorney general, inside the department. Historian Robert Goldstein notes that 92 "bugs" were placed in 1941, including one at the Los Angeles Chamber of Commerce.[42] It is far from certain that Hoover applied for permission in every case.

Ironically, Jackson's attempts to curb (or at least legalize) the expansion of the surveillance state demanded by Hoover and FDR attracted criticism from those worried about the possible uses of the wiretapping authority. His liberal critics, unaware of the pressure exerted by the White House, saw only his endorsement of abhorrent tactics, and they wondered out loud what was happening to the attorney general's once staunch commitment to civil liberties.[43] The attorney general, in turn, was galled by what he saw as the unfairness and ingratitude of the criticism. The difference between his critics and himself, Jackson suggested, was that they answered only to their consciences and political prejudices, while he was responsible for the nation's security and obliged to enforce its laws.[44] "I suppose that different responsibilities produce different reactions," he wrote one New Deal congressman, noting that if his liberal critics in Congress "sat in my seat" and were "held responsible" for acts of sabotage and espionage, they would look at the wiretapping bill differently.[45] More important, although he did not mention it, was the fact that the attorney general, whatever his obligations to the law, served a demanding client in the president and felt obliged to placate a contumacious subordinate in Hoover.

Controlling the director became more difficult as the security crisis deepened. From the summer of 1940 forward, the attorney general would attempt to restrict FBI investigations of defense industry employees only to be repeatedly assured by Hoover that his agents were proceeding cautiously and with due sensitivity to organized labor's suspicions.[46] Indeed, Hoover was conscious of the delicacy of the issue and did move carefully. Thus, in early December, when he ordered "very discreet" inquiries into all defense industry strikes, actual or proposed, Hoover told agents that they were to conduct their inquiries in ways that left no room for claims that the bureau was interfering "in any manner" in a labor dispute.[47] Nevertheless, problems arose and labor/liberal suspicions of the FBI remained strong. Predicting "loyalty" (even defining it) was a problematic enterprise at best, and FBI agents, not bound by rules of evidence or due process, made up their own criteria for what activities, associations, or beliefs suggested "subversive" intent. FBI reports, usually based on the information supplied by undercover American Legion operatives and other such sources, often had an anti-leftist bias, and while Hoover directed his agents not to explicitly recommend firing suspect employees, managers, who were made aware of FBI suspicions, were apt to do just that.

In late March 1941, Jackson, in an effort to prevent FBI interference in labor's affairs, drafted a set of rules governing what sorts of investigations the FBI might undertake.[48] The suggested restraints were repugnant to Hoover, who rejected them and rebuked Jackson (in the backhanded manner he normally employed in such matters) for sacrificing the nation's security to the demands of "so-called liberals" who, he insisted, were either affiliated with "Communist Front organizations or [were] out-and-out Communist." France, he noted, had suffered the consequences of having failed to deal firmly with its fifth column, and he pointedly reminded Jackson of the "wisdom" of the president's September 1939 directive authorizing *him* (Hoover) to compile a list of potential subversives. This directive, he intimated, sanctioned the kinds of investigations the bureau was now conducting, including those affecting organized labor.

The attorney general, fearing he had offended the director and aware that he did not have the president's support, beat a hasty retreat. "I had no thought to restrict or alter in any manner the internal operation of the F.B.I. . . . or its *right* to proceed in all the fields in which it has been operating [emphasis in original]."[49] There were, nevertheless, limits to the attorney general's willingness to see the bureau employed as a secret police, and these were reached in the spring of 1941 in response to the army's demands for extraordinary measures to clean the subversives out of the nation's munitions industries.

The strikes at Vultee and Allis-Chalmers proved to be a prelude to a spate of disruptive job actions in the defense industry. During the first half of 1941, production of almost every military-related commodity and device, from aluminum to machine guns, was interrupted by labor disputes.[50] In early 1941, strikes and threatened stoppages in defense agitated War Department officials beyond endurance. Assistant Secretary of War John J. McCloy led the demands for an aggressive response.[51] A New York attorney, McCloy had represented U.S. Steel Corporation in the company's effort to recover the losses it had suffered in an explosion engineered by German saboteurs at the Black Tom shipping terminal in New Jersey in 1915. He was convinced that an extensive German sabotage network was again at work in the United States and favored exaggerating the problem of subversion to worry the public and politicians into sanctioning an all-out war on subversion.[52]

But McCloy's hands were tied. The Justice Department did not want to stir up public anxieties, and the army was constrained from acting against suspected provocateurs on its own by presidential directive. In 1939 Hoover, who feared army encroachments, had prevailed on the president to delegate to his bureau responsibility for all countersubversion activities within the United States. Under this arrangement, the army's own counterintelligence service, which functioned as part of the Military Intelligence Division (MID), could not involve itself in countering labor subversion. Unable to authorize a campaign himself, Stimson commissioned McCloy to approach Hoover with the military's concerns.

Accounts of the meeting between McCloy and the director on April 26, 1941—McCloy's in a letter to Stimson, and Hoover's in a memo to Jackson—agree on essentials. Both men believed that labor troubles originated in subversive activities, and that unconventional means (Hoover described them as "unethical if not actually illegal" tactics, while McCloy referred to them as "second-story methods") were now needed to combat them. Hoover's account depicts him as a passive and somewhat skeptical listener, while McCloy's suggests that the director was a willing co-conspirator.[53] There was apparently no consideration given to what would be done with any information obtained.

Two days after his discussion with Hoover, McCloy appeared in Jackson's office accompanied by Under Secretary of War Robert Patterson—

the World War I hero and successful attorney, who had recently left the U.S. Circuit Court of Appeals to serve as Stimson's chief deputy.[54] He and McCloy outlined for Jackson a proposed FBI investigation of labor disturbances by "methods more vigorous and unrestrained" than the law or rules governing the FBI currently permitted. Patterson told the attorney general that the president had approved of their scheme and that Hoover was prepared to act if the attorney general gave the go-ahead. According to Jackson, the gentlemen from the War Department insisted that it made no sense for the FBI to be kept *"within the limits of the law"* at a time when "normal methods should be abandoned [emphasis in original]." They sought Jackson's approval to create (using Hoover's phrase) a "suicide squad" to proceed as necessary.

Jackson's response, as McCloy reported it, was to insist that even in difficult times, the law must be treated as a sacred trust; not just an inconvenience to be circumvented. Moreover, he said, tactics like those the army proposed had been employed in the past and the department had yet to live down the public distrust they had engendered. Patterson, disappointed by what he called the attorney general's "peace-time attitude," assured him that the current crisis warranted wiretapping, theft, and other unsavory methods. Was Jackson concerned about what the courts might say about such goings-on? Judge Patterson advised him that, if the episode was discovered and he were on the bench and called upon to review the government's action, he would be prepared in times like these to overlook the wrongdoing. Having assured Jackson that breaking the law in defense of the nation was what a practical man would and should do, he went on to address what must have impressed him as Jackson's petty concern for the department's reputation. If Jackson authorized Hoover to assign some of his agents to do the dirty work under the War Department's direction, he said, the military was prepared to assume full responsibility for the illicit operation should it be exposed. The second-story job would entail no risk to the Department of Justice.

The entreaties of McCloy and Patterson, men who were well on their way to earning sterling reputations for integrity, clear thinking, and rectitude, were far more persuasive than the demands of the likes of Dies. These were the sober arguments of men speaking from the lofty reaches of the legal fraternity; their mission had been endorsed by the esteemed Henry Stimson and apparently sanctioned by the president. Confronted with the advice of these respected lawyers (all of them with military experience), Jackson's resolve may have weakened. McCloy and Patterson left with the understanding that the attorney general would propose the compromise to Hoover.[55] They apparently thought they had a deal.

While Hoover might have approved of the suicide squad as originally conceived (indeed the tactics were not unknown to the bureau), he had no intention of putting his men under army control. He rejected the compromise, and Jackson, bolstered by Hoover's rejection of the scheme, confidently approached the president who, he understood, had given a "green light" to the War Department's proposal. Focusing on the effects of the "extremely dangerous" proposition on those who would carry it out, he reminded the president of the lasting impact of the department's earlier lawless activities.

Jackson noted that the current "intensive drive" to use lawless methods to resolve the labor crisis had led officials to spy on each other, citing his understanding that agents of the Office of Naval Intelligence were tapping the phones of defense production officials. The administration, he concluded, could not "afford to become characterized as lawless," and unless confronted with dangers far greater than anything he could foresee, "we should adhere to the legal and ethical standards of investigation in cases dealing with subversion in the labor movement the same as any others."[56] In any event, the attorney general insisted, he was not "the type of man to run that sort of unit." The following day Jackson wrote to Patterson and McCloy that they would have to look elsewhere for the proposed "suicide squad" recruits.[57]

Stimson felt betrayed. On the basis of earlier meetings, he thought he had an understanding with the attorney general, and he was angered by what he took to be Jackson's self-serving and self-righteous letter, which the president had shown him. Convinced that the slowdowns and "imaginary [labor] grievances" had been instigated by Communist agitators, he was determined to do whatever was necessary to meet the threat they posed to the arms buildup.[58] Saboteurs and Communists in defense were discussed at length at the May 1 cabinet meeting, and cryptic notes taken by Jackson record a "demand" [probably from Stimson] for "ruthless—limitless searches, stealings- tappings—etc."[59] The president again seemed to approve in principle, leaving the details of execution to his subordinates. In any event, the issue was still open, and a few days later McCloy again urged the attorney general to get on board.[60]

Jackson would not budge. "The man who today will rifle your desk for me, tomorrow will rifle mine for someone else. I just don't want that type fellow in my outfit." He refused, he said, to compromise the honorable young men who made up the bureau, and urged the War Department to support his current efforts on behalf of legalizing some of the practices the army was pressing him to employ.[61] Stimson, worried by complaints from defense contractors that the administration had failed to purge their plants of Communist agents, spoke to the president and arranged for conferences between Justice and army officials looking for a legal way to address the problem. But he was doubtful, as he noted in his diary, "whether I can persuade a lukewarm Attorney General" to do more under existing law.[62] He was right.

More was involved in Jackson's resistance to army overtures than emerged from their discussions. In the years since the Civil War, the Justice Department had developed a wariness of possible military encroachments on civil authority. Experiences during World War I, when the army frequently interfered in labor disputes, made fears of displacement by the military in crisis times a part of the departmental culture.[63] In 1919, John Lord O'Brian had warned of the military threat to civilian rule and recommended that in any future conflict, the maintenance of domestic security "be lodged exclusively in this [Justice] Department." It was important, he argued, to ensure that the law be administered by lawyers, rather than by military officials whose functions disposed them to arbitrariness.[64] In 1940, O'Brian was still warning of "rule by military tribunals."[65]

Jackson had withstood this egregious assault on the rule of law, but by the spring of 1941, the twilight of his days in office, he seems to have despaired of holding the line across the board. Fifteen months in office had hardened Jackson's outlook. While still conscious of the need to draw the line at a decent point, he had surrendered earlier hopes that reasonable men could agree on what was right, or that they would respect sincere and well-intentioned efforts to achieve it. Convinced that he could not satisfy his critics, the attorney general wearily conceded to Biddle that "we must make up our minds in these times that the world is divided into two unreasonable camps. Each will blame us for everything it does not like and will promptly forget everything we do for it."[66]

A speech he made to the American Bar Association in early May reflected the effects of the unremitting criticism—he was beginning to sound a bit like J. Edgar Hoover. The critics of government countersubversion policy, he suggested to the assembled lawyers, were in league with the fifth column. The "enemies of America," he declared, were not idle. "They show up at congressional hearings to oppose every move to strengthen our law enforcement; they show up in court astutely to raise every legal difficulty to prevent convictions and to obstruct obtaining evidence; they propagandize endlessly against investigative officials and agencies, against prosecution policies, against law enforcement itself."[67] Jackson's fight to hold the line for civil liberties had taken its toll—on him.

Chapter 6

Harry Bridges and the War on Communism

Although Attorney General Jackson resisted efforts to use FBI agents as "second-story men," he believed that Communists were instigating strikes in defense plants and was determined to do what he could about the situation—within the law. The opportunities were limited. Obviously, organizing strikes was not a crime per se, and attempting to prove that such activities had a criminal purpose was difficult and politically dangerous. There was, however, one way to get at the provocateurs. If the government was able to establish that a strike agitator (or anybody else, for that matter) was a member of the Communist Party (CPUSA), that person might be prosecuted under the recently enacted Smith Act, which criminalized membership in organizations that advocated revolution. But any such use of the Smith Act was likely to provoke outrage from organized labor and opposition from the political Left, and Jackson was reluctant to follow this course until the non-Communist Left could be made to see the Communists, and the harm they were doing to the defense effort, as he saw them. An opportunity to provide such instruction occurred at the end of 1940, when the notorious Harry Bridges case, which already had a long and tumultuous history, was thrust into Jackson's hands.

The enigmatic Harry Bridges, though he may not have been a Communist—the issue is unresolved to this day—was a useful symbol of the alleged pernicious Communist influence in American labor.[1] Bridges, a native of Australia, had come to the United States in 1920, and for the next 14 years he toiled (and agitated) in obscurity, one of the six million or so resident foreigners in the land of opportunity. Ironically, given subsequent events, he twice filed declarations of intention to become a citizen. Had he followed through and become a naturalized American, he would have made himself less vulnerable to his enemies, and perhaps able to escape the protracted legal ordeal that was to be his fate. But, as he later explained, it took him two or three weeks to earn the $20 fee required to secure citizenship papers and, with a wife and two children to support, felt unable to make the investment.[2]

The events that would bring the whole weight of government down on Bridges began in 1934 when he played a key role in the efforts of long-shoremen and seamen to shut down U.S. Pacific coast ports. The "Big West Coast Strike,"[3] which began in May and lasted for three months, was one of several labor conflicts that erupted in 1934. The strike was violent, costly, and thoroughly frightening to business interests and government authorities on the coast. Businessmen sought to enlist public support by depicting the labor conflict centering on the San Francisco docks as an apocalyptic struggle between order, patriotism, and civilization (which they represented); and the alien-dominated, Communist-motivated, revolutionaries among the unionists. In such a scenario, it was useful to single out an individual who personified the evil. Bridges, a self-described radical and an alien to boot, was an obvious choice, and over the next few years the unkempt, fast-talking, and defiant dockworker would gain a national reputation as one of the most powerful, feared, and persecuted labor leaders in the country.

From the onset of the strike, West Coast employers and their allies, unable to dispose of Bridges through the local or federal criminal justice systems, sought to have him deported as an undesirable (radical) alien. While federal law at that time did not prohibit radical advocacy or affiliations to citizens, the Alien Act, adopted on October 16, 1918, and amended in 1920, made identical behavior by aliens punishable by deportation. This anti-radical weapon was particularly effective because it was implemented through a relatively simple and usually quick administrative hearing, and not through the criminal justice system. Officials had only to convince an examining officer appointed by the commissioner of immigration that an alien was at the time of his or her entry, or at any time thereafter, a believer in or advocate of the overthrow of the government, or a member of an organization that subscribed to this belief. Since this process was a civil proceeding, protections normally enjoyed by a defendant in a criminal case were not available to the alien, who might, however, appeal a deportation order to the federal courts. The government's action might be reversed on the grounds that the action was not authorized by statute, the government had not fairly applied its own rules of procedure, or the evidence could not sustain the finding. Until the passage of the Smith Act in 1940, the 1918 statute remained the federal government's most effective tool for the suppression of radical speech.[4]

From 1934 through the end of the decade, conservative elements, particularly on the West Coast, continually sought to force Secretary of Labor Frances Perkins to institute deportation proceedings against Bridges. Department investigations, however, failed to satisfy the secretary that Bridges was subject to deportation, and the president at first supported her in resisting the pressure.[5] But as the political strength of the New Deal ebbed in the late 1930s, so too did the administration's resistance to demands for Bridges's scalp. In 1937 a severe downturn in the economy and a resumption of violent labor disputes, which included use of the controversial sit-down strike tactic, undermined public confidence in the New Deal's recovery and reform program and gave a boost to its right-wing critics.[6] Much of the criticism of labor's "radical excesses" was directed at Perkins, whose cautious (and correct) handling of the Bridges case had fed her detractors' ire.[7] The attacks were as dastardly as they were unrelenting.

In late January 1939, Representative J. Parnell Thomas, a Republican member of the Dies Committee, introduced a resolution calling for the impeachment of the secretary of labor, her chief legal advisor, and the commissioner of immigration. The charge—conspiring to avoid enforcing the law against Harry Bridges, "an alien who [in the phraseology of the 1918 statute] advises, advocates, or teaches the overthrow by force or violence of the Government of the United States." In April, Howard W. Smith, the chairman of the House Judiciary Committee, introduced a measure that provided, among other alien and radical control devices, for the deportation of noncitizens found to be members of any group that advocated "a change in the form of government . . . or engage[d] *in any way* [emphasis added] in domestic political agitation."[8] If his enemies could not secure his deportation as a Communist, they would at least be able to get rid of him for being an "agitator," which he unquestionably was.

Under considerable pressure, and aware that Congress would not rest until at least some effort was made to deport Bridges, Perkins relented, issuing a warrant ordering him to appear at a hearing to determine whether he should be deported. Ordinarily such a hearing would be conducted and decided by a district immigration officer, but given the political controversy surrounding the Bridges affair, Perkins elected to appoint a special hearing officer whose judgment and reputation were thought to be above reproach. She chose James M. Landis, a former law clerk to Justice Brandeis who was currently dean of the Harvard Law School. The appointment was well received in the press.[9]

For nine-and-a-half weeks in the summer of 1939, Bridges, Landis, and the corps of lawyers for each side made the daily round trip by ferry boat from the San Francisco embarcadero to Angel Island in the bay, accompanied from time to time by some of the more than 60 witnesses who gave testimony. The proceedings were well covered in the press. At the end of December, coincidentally on the same day that Attorney General Murphy announced his campaign against the un-Americans, Landis issued his findings. There was no doubt, he concluded, that Bridges had friends and associates who were Communists, and that he worked with them in his various labor activities. He had freely admitted as much. But the Supreme Court had recently ruled in the *Strecker* case that proof of *current* membership or affiliation with a proscribed organization was required for the government to deport an alien accused of radical beliefs or associations, and the evidence, Landis declared, "established neither that Harry R. Bridges is a member of, nor affiliated with the Communist Party of the United States of America."[10]

That should have settled the matter; it did not. Landis's high reputation failed to ensure the acceptability of his findings. Critics characterized his careful hearings as whitewash, and those who believed that Bridges was a Communist or merely wanted him silenced continued to demand his deportation.[11] In the spring of 1940, in the midst of the fear-filled and intolerant political climate engendered by the fifth-column scare, Congressman A. Leonard Allen, a freshman from Louisiana, decided to end the pussyfooting and make Congress's will unmistakable.[12] On May 14, Allen introduced a bill directing the secretary of labor "to take into custody and deport to Australia the alien, Harry Renton Bridges." The bill was unanimously endorsed by the House Immigration Committee and, in mid-June, it passed the House by a vote of 330 to 42.[13]

Attorney General Robert Jackson was outraged. For the first time, he wrote, Congress proposed to single out a named individual for deportation and, by directing that the action be taken regardless of any other provision of law, in effect deprive him of time-honored legal protections. Bridges, Jackson pointed out, had been "investigated and tried at great length, and found not guilty." What, he asked, "becomes of equality before the law, of the impersonal and impartial character of our government, if it is to select unpopular persons to suffer disadvantage or punishment?" Jackson concluded by observing that there was no condition, "existing or threatened," that requires arbitrary legislation or banishment by legislative fiat. Harry Bridges, he conceded, might be all that the bill's authors suggest, but he was insignificant compared to the repressive implications of the efforts to get rid of him.[14]

Some congressional leaders agreed that a law mandating the punishment of a named individual (and hence akin to a constitutionally prohibited bill of attainder) was beyond the bounds of legislative propriety. Nevertheless, convinced that the longshoreman had to go, they devised a compromise that would circumvent the *Strecker* decision and, without naming Bridges, provide a legal basis for securing his deportation. A provision was inserted into HR 5138, the omnibus anti-alien/radical bill that would later become the Smith Act, which provided for the deportation of any alien who *at any time* after entry had expressed revolutionary sentiments or affiliated with a proscribed organization (which it did not name) as defined in the 1918 legislation. Congressman Sam Hobbs, a "moderate" in the current controversy, joyously informed his colleagues that the Smith Act would accomplish Allen's objectives "in a perfectly legal and constitutional manner," since the Department of Justice "should now have little trouble in deporting Harry Bridges and all of the others of a similar ilk."[15]

FDR signed the Alien Registration Act of 1940 (Smith Act) into law in June. At the same time he transferred jurisdiction over immigration and naturalization matters from the Labor Department to the Justice Department. The move, which Perkins welcomed, and Jackson strongly resisted, met the demands of anti-alien forces who had long complained that the Labor Department was sympathetic toward radicals. Bridges's fate was now largely in Jackson's hands.

But the attorney general was in no hurry to apply the Smith Act to Bridges, or anyone else.[16] He would later say that the idea that the country could be made safer by deporting radicals was a fraud that served only to make martyrs of the intended victims.[17] Many department officials shared this view.[18] But senior INS lawyers, disappointed at Landis's decision, welcomed another go at Bridges, and some Democrats in Congress warned that if the attorney general failed to act under the Smith Act, the failure would be used against the party.[19] "Redness," Hobbs told Assistant Attorney General Alexander Holtzhoff, was the most serious charge the Democratic Party had to confront, and the best way to counter it was for the attorney general to immediately bring another proceeding to deport Bridges.[20] Senator Richard Russell of Georgia, who engineered the defeat of the Allen Bill in the Senate, joined Hobbs in lobbying Justice officials for action.[21]

In mid-August, Holtzhoff advised the attorney general that regardless of the merits of the case, Congress, having acted to deal with Bridges, was "entitled to some action under the new law." Moreover, he pointed out, if the administration did nothing, the despised Allen bill was likely to pass, and be brought to the president for his signature just before the fall election. Holtzhoff recommended that the attorney general announce that he was reviewing the Bridges case in light of the Smith Act provision.[22] Such an announcement, as Jackson recalled it, had the president's tacit approval. Political concerns no doubt played a role in his thinking, but more than that, FDR was by this point concerned about Communist opposition to defense preparations and the sympathy he had once exhibited for Bridges had dissipated. According to Jackson, FDR was "fed up with Bridges and with all those people," and had become militantly anti-Communist.[23]

Bowing to pressure from Congress (while denying it), and accommodating the administration's own anti-Communist feelings, the attorney general announced on August 24, 1940, that he had instructed J. Edgar Hoover to determine whether there was new evidence that would warrant reinstituting the deportation proceedings against Bridges.[24]

This may have been a ploy designed to delay dealing with the issue at least until after the election. Despite the administration's anti-Communist feelings, Jackson was understandably reluctant to take on the Bridges case. Whatever the outcome of a new effort to punish the longshoreman, his heroic status among militant elements in organized labor and on the Left was likely to assume mythic proportions should the government try him again. Moreover, the effort would seem to twice put Bridges in jeopardy for violating the same law. Though this was technically not a violation of the constitutional prohibition since he had not been, and was not being, charged with a criminal offense, an odor of impropriety hung about the case, and Jackson probably preferred to let the whole thing blow over.

But Hoover had other ideas. He not only wanted Bridges deported, but saw in the reopening of the case an opportunity to establish authoritatively that the CPUSA was a revolutionary party as defined by both the 1918 immigration statute and the recently passed Smith Act. Upon receiving Jackson's order, the director secured approval from Assistant to the Attorney General Matthew McGuire, his immediate superior in the department, to reinvestigate the CPUSA as well.[25] At the end of November, Hoover presented Jackson with a report, probably consisting largely of evidence he had been gathering for 20 years, documenting both Bridges's CPUSA affiliations and the party's revolutionary intent. In transmitting the material to the attorney general, the director made a point of recommending that the department use his findings as the basis for the prosecution of party leaders under the Smith Act.[26] Jackson received Hoover's suggestion without comment, but he did refer the proposed use of the Smith Act to the Neutrality Laws Unit, whose director, L. M. C. Smith, first endorsed the idea in principle and then recommended it as the most efficacious legal device for ridding the defense industry of its subversive elements.[27] An open government attack on the CPUSA was beginning to take form.

The next move was up to Jackson. Delay remained an option, but only so long as Hoover's voluminous report remained secret. The director decided to force Jackson's hand. In mid-December, speaking to newspapermen at Miami Beach, he said that he had uncovered "secret new evidence" establishing that Bridges was a member of the Communist Party and that the party advocated the overthrow of the government.[28] When the story appeared in the press, Hoover hastened to assure the attorney general that he had not urged Bridges's deportation or the prosecution of party leaders, but had merely indicated what he had found. He had made it clear, he said, that it was up to the attorney general to decide what to do about his discovery.[29] These tactics were typical of Hoover[30] who, once again, got his way. In February 1941, Jackson announced that Bridges would be served with a deportation warrant ordering him to appear before a trial examiner at a public hearing to be held in San Francisco beginning at the end of March.[31]

Jackson, acting on the hope that "good" men made unassailable decisions, appointed his friend Charles B. Sears as special examiner to listen to the evidence. Sears was a distinguished New York attorney and, until his recent retirement, had been a judge in the New York State judicial system. His credentials were not unlike those of the distinguished lawyers from whom Jackson had hoped to draw a panel of disinterested experts to advise him on civil liberties. The attorney general would later describe him as "liberal,"[32] but Bridges's lawyers found him conservative both politically and in his judicial rulings.

Although the hearing closely resembled the one held a year earlier, it was markedly different in tone. The defense team, led by Carol King, the veteran defender of accused radicals, was the same. The government sent a strong contingent that included Judge Clarence N. Goodwin, who had been appointed to present the government's legal arguments. The informality of Angel Island, however, was replaced by what a reporter called the "judicial atmosphere" of the high-ceilinged courtroom in the San Francisco federal building where the second inquisition took place.[33] The hearing, open to the public, was crowded with an audience made up largely of longshoremen. The ideologically charged atmosphere was palpable.[34]

This latest round in the Bridges saga, though it had begun as an effort to placate the anti-Bridges forces, had by the time it commenced become a serious department effort to expose the true face of the Communist Party and its meddling in labor disputes bearing on the nation's security. Reports of Communist-inspired sabotage and work stoppages in defense, many of them originating with Hoover, circulated freely in Washington,[35] and the attorney general, who had condemned the Vultee strike as Communist inspired, shared the anti-Communist feelings that suffused the administration and shaped the prosecution's case.

As the case against Bridges was being developed in San Francisco, another defense industry shutdown loomed in Southern California. Bridges would briefly involve himself in that struggle, and the government would seek to make this episode an element in its case against him. The scene for the latest and most confrontational in the series of suspicious defense industry job actions was the North American Aviation plant in Inglewood, California, just outside of Los Angeles. Workers at the facility, which turned out about 20 percent of the nation's military aircraft, among them the army's most advanced fighter plane, had genuine grievances growing out of economic issues very much like those that had precipitated stoppages elsewhere. Wyndam Mortimer, a United Auto Workers (UAW) organizer strongly suspected of Communist ties, led workers demanding a better contract. The company resisted and, in late May 1941, negotiations between North American Aviation and the United Auto Workers local deadlocked. A strike seemed imminent. The recently created National Defense Mediation Board summoned the parties to Washington in an effort to settle the dispute, but on June 5, without waiting for the outcome of the mediation effort, the union local put up a massive picket line that closed the plant.

The administration saw Red. Secretary of War Henry L. Stimson privately characterized the wildcat strike as flagrantly contrived—the latest in a series of stoppages engineered by a "band of subversive agitators who are suspected to be in pay of the Germans."[36] Senior officials concerned most directly with the strike, including John Lord O'Brian in his capacity as general counsel for the Office of Production Management (OPM), urged the president to take over the plant. The cabinet agreed. Roosevelt first personally directed the workers to return to their jobs. His appeal had the support of national union officials including Richard T. Frankensteen, national director of the aviation division of the UAW, who condemned the walkout as the "irresponsible, inexperienced and impulsive action of local leaders."[37] At this point Harry Bridges stepped in. Earlier, he had gone out of his way to encourage his International Longshoremen's and Warehousemen's Union (ILWU) to denounce, in insulting terms, a friendly request from the president that asked unspecified sacrifices from labor as its contribution to the national defense effort. Now, in the midst of his deportation hearing in San Francisco, he urged the North American workers to reject the efforts of the government and of their union's leaders to get them back to work. The strikers defied the government and the national union leadership, and the strike continued. On June 9 federal troops, on orders from the president, dispersed the strikers and re-opened the plant.[38]

The press linked the strike to Communist influence,[39] and polls showed public opinion running strongly against defense industry strikers.[40] Most of the nation's union leadership now supported drastic action against subversive influences in defense, and labor leader Sidney Hillman, now co-director of OPM, pressed for creation of a special board to investigate Communist activities in defense. Even the *Nation* was convinced that there was more to the North American strike than the legitimate demands of militant unionists. Strikes on the West Coast may or may not have been directed from the Kremlin, wrote editor Freda Kirchwey, but they served Communist interests, helped sabotage the defense effort, and stirred up repression. Supporting the government's suppression of the North American strike, she characterized it as a "revolutionary challenge" that the president could not ignore.[41] Encouraged by these attitudes the Department of Justice let it be known that Jackson had ordered the formulation of plans for ridding defense industries of potential subversives.[42]

Meanwhile, in San Francisco, the government laid out its case against Harry Bridges. Much of the effort was designed to discredit radical unionism by demonstrating that Bridges's activity typified the undercover efforts of unacknowledged Communists in the labor movement. Bridges was well suited for this role in the government's scenario. He was a militant and well-known organizer who opposed the war effort. If it could be shown, despite his consistent denials, that he was also a hidden Communist, suspicion would be cast on all unionists who refused to compromise worker demands to national defense requirements.

In his opening statement for the government, Goodwin said that the case he would present would demonstrate that the Communist Party was not an innocuous debating society, as some "well-disposed and intelligent people" might have it, but a ruthless conspiracy that rejected the nation's "present economic organization" and sought its overthrow. The party's hostile intent, foreign connections, and discipline commanded over members (like Bridges) meant that the government could not look with equanimity on the organization or its members. Bridges, Goodwin declared, had violated the law by affiliating with a group that was currently involved in a dangerous subversive conspiracy. His deportation was a necessary act of national self-defense.[43]

The defense helped make the case against the party by refusing to offer evidence contradicting the government's assertions. Taking the position that since (as he claimed) Bridges had never been a member or otherwise affiliated with the Communist Party, its doctrines, intentions, and tactics had no bearing on his case. Defense lawyers confined themselves to exposing the unreliability of the government's witnesses and the manifest unfairness of the government's continued persecution of their client. King, his principal attorney, noted with some justification that Bridges was again faced with deportation because officials, indifferent to the abuse of governmental authority their actions represented, were intent on pursuing a politically motivated and apparently unending vendetta. "'Is Mr. Bridges to be retried,'" she asked, "'each time his enemies dig up some new witnesses against the CIO?'"[44] In referring to the CIO, the national union with which Bridges's ILWU was affiliated, the defense was telling the proceedings' larger audience that the case was about far more than Bridges or even Communism. It was, King's remark suggested, part of the continuing campaign of reactionary bosses and their government allies to discredit the militant, worker-oriented, industrial unionism that the CIO (and Bridges) represented.

The proceedings lasted more than ten weeks. Shortly after the government rested its case, Goodwin briefed the attorney general on what he thought the government had accomplished. Calmly and judiciously, Goodwin wrote, he and his associates had sought to discredit Bridges's alleged achievements and to strip him and other Communist-led agitators of their "progressive" unionist masks. He predicted that the government's strategy, together with the fairness and clarity with which Sears presided over the exposure of Bridges, was bound to have a "most wholesome influence in trade union organizations here [San Francisco] and throughout the country, and bring about a better understanding of the problem which Communist control creates for the trade unions themselves."[45]

In the trial's closing days, the attorney general was moved to suggest a bold new tactic that he hoped would seal the government's case and make the administration's larger political point. Seizing on Bridges's message urging the striking North American workers to reject mediation, Jackson telephoned INS director Lemuel Schofield, the senior government lawyer in the Bridges case, urging him to call Richard Frankensteen, head of the UAW's aircraft division, as a last minute witness. His object was to use the testimony of this committed unionist, who had opposed the North American strike, to discredit Bridges's claims that he (Bridges) was simply a good union man who resorted to strikes only when all else failed. By inference, the opposing roles the two men played in the North American dispute would support the government's contention that those, like Bridges, who sought to shut down defense plants in defiance of their president were Communists who could be counted on to subordinate the national interest to the party line.

Frankensteen testified fully and as the government anticipated. He also insisted, over the government's objections, on reading a statement in which he condemned the persecution of Bridges and warned that his deportation would antagonize many workers. Initially chagrined, Schofield later concluded that the statement had actually increased Frankensteen's credibility, and that his testimony, together with the government's close final-day questioning of Bridges concerning the strike and his attitudes toward national defense policies, constituted "one of the strongest points in the entire case."[46]

On June 12, Special Examiner Charles B. Sears concluded the hearings and retired to consider his decision. Whatever the outcome for Bridges, federal officials believed they had succeeded in laying the basis for the contemplated war on domestic Communism. Hoover in particular was optimistic and determined to capitalize on what he saw as the government's triumph. On the day the inquiry ended, the FBI director met with Secretary of War Stimson to discuss the Communists-in-defense problem. He urged Stimson to take advantage of the victory at Inglewood by enlisting the attorney general in a campaign to clean the Communists out of the North American plant. Under Secretary Patterson wrote to the president in the same vein.[47] The Bridges hearings, Hoover noted, had effectively established the party's revolutionary objectives, and the FBI could now begin to collect evidence to establish that the North American strike leaders were, like Bridges, party members and prosecutable under the Smith Act. The bureau, Hoover said, had been restrained to this point by the attorney general's policy of keeping hands off radicals in the labor movement. But the Communists had overstepped themselves at North American and that, together with the educational effect of what had transpired in San Francisco, made this a propitious time to break with that policy. Hoover urged Stimson to bring the issue to Jackson's attention. The secretary of war, who for months had been encouraging the Department of Justice to take a more vigorous stance, immediately telephoned the attorney general, who promptly gave the director the investigative license he sought.[48] Zechariah

Chafee had described the Smith Act as a revolver to be kept in the attorney general's desk for use if a burglar ever showed up—kept in reserve should a genuine crisis arise. Within a short time of the law's enactment, that crisis seemed to be at hand and Jackson, egged on by others and caught up in the fears himself, reached for his gun.

At this moment, Jackson left the department to take a seat on the Supreme Court and Solicitor General Francis Biddle took over the department as acting attorney general. Ten days later, Biddle, who would later claim he had been dubious about the constitutionality of the Smith Act, endorsed its use to rid the defense industry of its Communist elements. Cases brought under this law, he wrote in a memo to the president, might be difficult to prove, but bringing them might "have some salutary effect." Perhaps he thought that instituting criminal prosecutions would immobilize those forced to defend themselves, and intimidate others. In any case, falling back on "the law is the law" argument, he concluded that "the Department of Justice has responsibility for the enforcement of this statute and must proceed whenever practicable." Biddle told the president that the investigation now underway would produce sufficient evidence for submission to a grand jury in the near future.[49]

By the time Biddle's June 23 recommendation reached the White House, it had, as the expression goes, been overtaken by events. The day before, three million German troops launched an assault along the 900-mile Soviet western frontier. The Soviet alliance with Hitler had come to an ignominious end, and with its demise came a reorientation of Communist Party policies. The CPUSA would quickly drop its opposition to the American arms buildup and to the administration's efforts to aid Great Britain. In August, the beleaguered Soviet Union itself became a beneficiary of U.S. arms production when the administration formally extended aid to Moscow.[50]

Presidential assistant James Rowe, who delivered Biddle's recommendation to the president, noted that "from the moment Hitler started toward the Pripet marshes," the problem of Communist interference with defense production had become "academic."[51] Strikes in the defense industry did not end, but officials could no longer blame them on Communist agitation. Indeed, Communists who followed the new party position lined up behind the administration and enthusiastically supported an all-out defense effort and intervention. As a result, the CPUSA's attachment to Soviet interests, which once supplied the chief rationale for an attack on the American party, was now cited as a principal reason for keeping hands off the party and its followers. Ironically, some of the West Coast employers and politicians who had recently demanded his deportation now saw Harry Bridges as essential to ensuring labor passivity. In any event, the decision in his case was still months off.

During his 18 months as head of the Department of Justice, Jackson had done a creditable job of anticipating the threat to civil liberties from local officials, potential vigilantes, overzealous federal prosecutors, and even the FBI. But his time in office had also made him more receptive to greater federal activism. He had concluded, as Hoover had contended all along, that the department could not afford to sit by while the nation's enemies plotted against it; that there would be few, if any, overt acts before a conspiracy was carried out; and that in the absence of overt acts the strongest clues to the identity of conspirators and enemy agents were their expressed beliefs and affiliations. Jackson had come to accept the need, if not the desirability, of investigating and even prosecuting people suspected of subversive beliefs and associations as a preventative measure, so long as the law permitted it. Having given up on finding what was "right," he was guided in the end only by what was legal. The approach had the appeal of relative certitude and simplicity. From a civil liberties standpoint, it promised at least that harassment of dissident minorities would be orderly and relatively restrained. On the other hand, his abandonment of prosecutorial discretion left liberty vulnerable to the acts of an overwrought Congress, which in many respects was no better informed, motivated, or restrained than the oft-reviled mob.

When the Smith Act was under consideration, Zechariah Chafee noted that the key to preventing the suppression of free speech was keeping repressive laws off the statute books because, once there, "patriotic judges and panic-stricken juries" would ensure that they were enforced to the limit.[52] Later, bowing to the event, he identified the attorney general as a competent and trustworthy custodian of the act. What Chafee missed, or perhaps did not wish to contemplate, was that it took extraordinary independence, more than that commanded by Jackson, to resist the temptations and pressures that possession of the weapon would generate. The attorney general acted cautiously and reluctantly, but in the end he opened the door to the use of the Smith Act not only against Communists, but against other presumptively dangerous agitators. Events would validate Chafee's doleful warning that "once we taste blood in this way, I do not know where we shall stop."[53]

Nevertheless, while Jackson had come closer to FDR's position, the president still found his protégé too scrupulous. The president saw civil liberties as one relatively small issue among the many with which he had to deal, and he certainly never worried that his political future or his place in history rested on the assessment of civil libertarians. He shared neither Jackson's concern with the department's reputation nor his reverence for the law. FDR was a lawyer by training, but he was a politician by choice and a leader by instinct. He wanted an attorney general who understood and would respond to the demands of practical politics and statecraft. From this perspective, Jackson, despite his compromises, proved parochial and inflexible.

These feelings, implicit in his dealings with the attorney general, were transparent in a conversation FDR had with Justice Frank Murphy at the White House just before Jackson left office. Roosevelt, anticipating Jackson's departure, asked Murphy if he would take his place. It was an entreaty he would repeat in the weeks to come. Murphy's earlier performance as attorney general, which many of his colleagues in the department had despised, had for the president set the standard for the office, and he told the justice so. The department, FDR told Murphy, had just not been what it was under his skilled direction. Jackson had not handled Hoover correctly, and it was clear that "Bob" was not much of an administrator. Moreover, Jackson did not have a proper sense of the balance between civil liberties and national security. It seemed to Roosevelt, as Murphy recorded the president's remarks, that civil liberties could be protected without sacrificing the national interest to subversive elements, as he intimated Jackson had been prone to do.[54]

Jackson went on to serve with Murphy on the Supreme Court, where Murphy, ironically, turned out to be the leader of the liberal wing on cases bearing on civil liberties, while Jackson, more often than not, was found in opposition.[55] The president would continue for some months to search for an attorney general that met his needs. In Francis Biddle he did not quite get the man he wanted, but FDR's preferences were clear and would help shape the office during the remainder of the Roosevelt years.

Part III

Francis Biddle
June 1941–June 1945

Chapter 7

Attorney General by Default

Robert Jackson had not wanted to be attorney general, and he had become increasingly unhappy in the post. The president, who liked Jackson, but was none too pleased with his performance, welcomed an opportunity to move him along. A seat on the Supreme Court seemed an appropriate destination. With Justice James C. McReynolds retiring in January 1941 and Chief Justice Charles Evans Hughes, now approaching his eightieth birthday, departing in early June, FDR had two vacancies to fill. Jackson and others thought that he would be named chief justice, but the president nominated Associate Justice Harlan Fiske Stone to the post vacated by Hughes, and appointed Jackson and Senator James F. Byrnes associate justices. Jackson's elevation to the Supreme Court left Roosevelt looking for someone to take over the leadership of the Department of Justice. He eventually settled for Francis Biddle.

Biddle was not Roosevelt's first choice. Aware of the circumstances of his selection, Biddle struggled to establish a positive identity for himself and to win his boss's approval. The undertakings were incompatible, and he never succeeded in either. Like his predecessors, Biddle understood his tenure as something of a test. For them, the goal was higher elected office; for Biddle, it was to prove his worth to FDR, doubting peers, and himself. It was a confusing quest. On the one hand, it required him to demonstrate unwavering loyalty—falling on his sword, if need be, for a leader he revered. On the other hand, it required a willingness to exhibit the courage and independence of someone who was indubitably "his own man." His efforts produced a number of controversial decisions.

The sources of his personal conflicts are not elusive—Biddle wallowed in his perceived shortcomings, and his own account of his life makes it clear that he expected much of himself, and was almost always disappointed. His restless preoccupation with achievement and recognition provides the major theme of his two-volume memoir which, if it does not quite "tell all" in the manner of contemporary autobiography, is nevertheless a candid and revealing account of his personal longings and his persistent sense that he never quite measured up to his progenitors or his peers.[1]

Illustrious forebears and a distinguished name were part of Biddle's problem. Inside the front cover of each volume of his recollections is a sketch of his maternal family tree proudly displaying his descent from the Randolphs, one of the first families of Virginia, and the source of the nation's very first attorney general. The end papers reflect his Biddle lineage—a long line of Philadelphia merchants and lawyers who had been among that city's commercial elite since the early eighteenth century. The Biddles of yore, he tells us proudly, had been "men of action": statesmen, bankers, soldiers, and sailors, "all vigorous and resolute." He had a sense, however, that the time of the Randolphs and Biddles had passed, and he was troubled by the fact that in recent generations the name Biddle had become synonymous with the effete, self-absorbed life. Just as Philadelphia was no longer the great city it once was, Biddle was no longer a name that commanded respect. He hoped to do better, but could he?

The wealth and social standing into which he was born provided young Francis with advantages in his struggle. He was raised in an upper class environment that was a good deal like FDR's. Born in Paris during one of his family's frequent travels abroad, he was raised in comfort surrounded by the accouterments of upper-class wealth and achievement. In 1899, at the age of 12, he almost literally followed in FDR's footsteps by entering the exclusive Groton School. The future president, four-and-a-half years older, was then already a senior, a fact with which FDR would later "good-naturedly" tease his attorney general. The central idea of Head Master Endicott Peabody's establishment was to take boys from their overly soft, upper-class backgrounds and mold them through competition and physical (as opposed to intellectual) activity into the late-nineteenth-century idea of a "man." Life at Groton was Spartan and demanding, and its emphasis on conformity was sometimes cruel. Peabody saw it as preparation for leadership—his ideal was Theodore Roosevelt, who was already well on his way to the personification of the selfless, vigorous, courageous, and public-spirited American.

Biddle found his time at Groton a dark and unpleasant experience. This was not unusual—even the famously irrepressible Franklin Roosevelt was brought low by the academy. The difference was that FDR later looked back fondly on his years there and went out of his way to heap praise on Peabody and his institution,[2] while Biddle forever despised both. It was, he said of life at the boarding school, "a man's world, a rather bleak world," run by a narrow-minded, unapproachable anachronism. The Groton experience contrasted starkly with the family life to which Biddle retreated between school terms. In that more hospitable environment created by his mother and maiden aunts (his father died when Francis was five), he found a "female world," as he characterized it, which valued culture, aesthetics, and romance. Both of his worlds demanded that he excel. Groton and Harvard insisted he become a man of affairs, substance, and achievement; his Victorian and Southern mother urged him to live gallantly and heroically. Throughout his memoir he writes of his attempts to succeed in both worlds and his sense of inadequacy and fear of failure, concerns accentuated by the robust imperatives of Mr. Peabody's academy and his adoration of his mother.

Held back at the end of what should have been his last year at Groton because Peabody thought him immature, Biddle made a small place for himself competing in intramural boxing. Although he confesses that he made no friends and found little joy in school, this achievement made this the most satisfying year he spent at the place. On to Harvard where, while he was not chosen for any of the college's exclusive social clubs, he found a niche as a member of two literary groups. He wrote stories and what he later described as "some thin sentimental poetry," but was twice rejected for a place on the Harvard *Crimson*. His tendency to mark his life story by recording his failures and near successes is worth noting.

He graduated cum laude, and then, "brought up in the tradition of my father's devotion to law" and feeling the need to emulate his success in the profession, he entered Harvard Law School. Again he graduated with honors, which, he notes, failed to impress the members of the Philadelphia bar. In 1911 he spent a singularly influential year in Washington as secretary to Justice Oliver Wendell Holmes, Jr. His service with Holmes, which consisted largely of listening to the Justice's musings, left him with a lifetime admiration for the great jurist and his pragmatic view of the law and life. From encounters with the young progressives, including future Supreme Court Justice Felix Frankfurter, with whom he socialized during his sojourn in the nation's capital, he gained a broader outlook on American life, an awareness of its problems, and a brief enthusiasm for effecting change. He enlisted in the army in World War I, saw no service overseas, and, on his discharge, returned to the comfortable, if uninspiring, life of a Philadelphia lawyer. By the 1930s he had built a successful law practice serving corporate clients that included the Pennsylvania Railroad.

While Biddle remained interested in reshaping the nation, the failure of Theodore Roosevelt's 1912 bid for the presidency left him disillusioned and skeptical of the ability of right-minded people to make a difference. His pessimism was reflected in a novel (*The Llanfear Pattern*) he wrote in 1927 about a young man bent on changing the world "but afraid to go through with anything tough, and timorous of acting on his instincts. . . ." In the end the hero surrenders to his fears and accepts a job from the political machine he had hoped to destroy. A mixed message. Go boldly whence the spirit directs—but don't expect to get there.

Biddle's outlook brightened with the advent of the New Deal. Although at first he evinced no enthusiasm for FDR's bid for the presidency, FDR's election suddenly seemed to make great things possible. Looking for a progressive-minded person with the proper conservative credentials, Roosevelt appointed Biddle to head the recently established National Labor Relations Board (NLRB). Biddle acquitted himself well, displaying what political scientist Peter Irons describes as a "core of toughness" in his dealings with hardened and contentious representatives of business and labor. Although he had earlier been attracted to the progressive era critique of politics, his interest had been cerebral. Now this close-up involvement in the conflicts of industrial society, and the chance to make a practical difference, committed him to public service. He had found a sphere in which he could make a difference and a leader he could happily follow.[3]

FDR was just the kind of man Biddle aspired to be, and his admiration grew as his contacts with him increased. Here was the happy warrior: sure of himself, ruthless in achieving his purpose, unmoved by intellectual ambiguity. He was a pragmatic liberal, not one of those effete "principled unpolitical prigs" masquerading as reformers, who, according to Biddle, Roosevelt delighted in deflating.[4] He was cruel as well as witty, but that was a "man's way," and though Biddle would more than once be the butt of his jokes, he would look back on their association with unabashed hero worship. FDR remained, as he had been at Groton, "a magnificent but distant deity,"[5] and Biddle never lost the sense that he was still the insignificant new boy.

A return to private practice and a brief but successful stint as legal counsel for a congressional committee followed the controversy-filled months at the NLRB. In 1939, Roosevelt appointed him to the circuit court of appeals, but Judge Biddle found work on the bench dull and detached from the real life of public service. In early 1940, when Murphy was replaced by Robert Jackson, Roosevelt appointed Biddle to take Jackson's place as solicitor general.

He enjoyed his period as the nation's advocate and was particularly proud of his success in getting the Court to affirm the constitutionality of the Wages and Hours Act, which contained a provision that, in effect, outlawed child labor.[6] Twenty-five years earlier, in *Hammer* v. *Dagenhart*,[7] with Holmes dissenting, the Court had struck down a statute that presumed to regulate child labor. In 1941, in describing his effort to overturn that precedent, Biddle spoke of dedicating his victory "to the Old Man [Holmes], as a matador dedicates a bull."[8]

By this point Biddle, like Frank Murphy, had earned a reputation for being sympathetic with the "little people" and a defender of their civil rights. He was a member of the National Association for the Advancement of Colored People and the American Civil Liberties Union. His wife, the former Katherine Chapin, was an accomplished artist and a member of an avant-guard (and leftist) literary set, and her associations and work contributed to the perception of Francis as someone who, in unfriendly circles, might be labeled a "flaming liberal." His outlook on race was liberal for the era,[9] and as attorney general he would revive the Civil Liberties Unit that had languished under his predecessor. The unit, despite its shortcomings, would bring at least two important civil rights cases before the Supreme Court.[10]

Biddle's known sympathies for the foreign born led Jackson to ask him to take on an assignment far removed from the normal work of the solicitor general's office—administering the alien registration portions of the Smith Act. It was a happy choice, as he efficiently ran the controversial program without offending the millions of people concerned with its outcome. It also introduced Biddle to the attorney general's countersubversion efforts, and to the problems of drawing the line for civil liberties "at a decent point."

When FDR had an opportunity to move Jackson to the Supreme Court, many observers assumed that Biddle would become attorney general. Indeed he was Jackson's own candidate. But while Biddle would take over immediately as acting attorney general in early June 1941, he was left in this tenuous and increasingly embarrassing position for two-and-a-half months as the president, without speaking to him about it, searched for someone else to replace Jackson. During this crucial period Biddle, who wanted the post and thought he deserved it, sought to demonstrate to the president that he was the man for the job. Meanwhile, supporters, led by Justice Felix Frankfurter, a man of considerable influence in the administration, "bombarded" the White House with endorsements of Biddle. The president was unmoved,[11] and many Washington insiders shared his doubts. It is quite clear that Biddle's candidacy generated little enthusiasm.

Almost everyone who assessed him (including himself) expressed reservations about his temperament or character. Biddle's memoirs characteristically set forth his shortcomings as he saw them: impulsive, inclined to be too easily convinced by the last comer, and excessively concerned with public approval.[12] His contemporaries were no less critical. Jackson, who urged his appointment, saw Biddle as "something of a dilettante,"[13] an assessment with which Secretary of the Interior Harold Ickes agreed. Jackson would later say that he thought Biddle "generally right in things that really mattered," but suggested that his potential was shadowed by "temperamental defects."[14] Roger Baldwin, who considered Biddle an old friend, found him indecisive, "constantly debating with himself the right course of action."[15] Friend and adviser James Rowe, who knew him well, described him to FDR as a man of "strengths and weaknesses," adding that he had "considerable of both."[16] The venerable Charles Burlingham, whom Biddle described as a dear friend, and the respected circuit court judge William Clark registered their objections to Biddle's candidacy. Clark did not explain his reasons; Burlingham noted simply that Biddle "doesn't have enough sense" to be attorney general.[17]

Even his appearance seems to have been a source of trouble, and he confessed to having been less than pleased by the way the newspapers described him.[18] Contemporary photos reveal a neat, balding little man with a round, sad face dominated by large plaintive eyes. An associate found "something very birdlike" about him.[19] The nation in mid-1941 seemed to demand an aggressive and tough chief law enforcement officer, an image Biddle failed to convey.

FDR's reticence may have been encouraged by some of Biddle's views on freedom of speech. In September and December 1940, at a time when the nation's initial intense preoccupation with the fifth column had subsided some, Solicitor General Biddle gave two major addresses on civil liberties and contemporary events. In them he observed that the nation seemed restless, impatient with talk and on the verge of demanding shortcuts to national security. He cautioned against an overreaction, suggesting that it was the task of responsible people to resist demands born of the public's natural penchant for hysteria and excess.

The need to control the irrational beast, thought by Biddle and many of his cohort to dwell in the breast of their countrymen, was of the essence of his (and their) civil libertarianism. As a boy at Groton he was shocked and frightened by the group punishment meted out to the students who failed to conform. He was himself involved in "pumping" a boy or two, and years later recalled with distaste not only the events, but the fact that "far from experiencing shame or regret," he reveled in "the thrill of exercising mob justice." Reflecting on mass psychology, he recalled with revulsion his "excitement . . . as I struggled to be in the center of the crowd that was handling its victim."[20]

In his public speeches Biddle counseled restraint and reminded his audiences that since World War I, the nation had established a legal tradition of rejecting demands for political conformity. The Court, he said, had ruled in cases arising out of Espionage Act prosecutions that the state had the authority to suppress utterances that threatened the nation, but it had also affirmed (quoting Holmes) that "we do not lose our right to condemn either measures or men because the Country is at war." Biddle understood the free-speech decisions of the era to mean that while the state might appropriately suppress speech that contemporary circumstances made a genuine menace, it could not simply use its repressive powers to satisfy public demands for the elimination of dissent. Until seditious propaganda became a serious and *immediate* threat to the national security, officials must stay the repressive hand of government, relying on the "market place of ideas" to ensure the rejection of unsound thinking.

Whatever relationship this interpretation bore to the judicial record, these sentiments represented Biddle's thinking in the fall of 1940. He endorsed the right of isolationists to speak freely: "Why shouldn't [Charles] Lindbergh say 'England is defeated; we must keep out', if he wants to? Isn't that part of our theory of freedom of speech? Isn't that the thing that we must fight back with other ideas?" Certainly anti-Semitic speech was obnoxious and pernicious, he declared, but it must be tolerated so long as it "doesn't incite to violence" and does not give rise to a "clear and present danger." He noted with approval the opinion in the *Herndon* case, decided only three years before, which cited Holmes's "clear and present danger" formula in striking down a state conviction for seditious incitement. He quoted Justice Owen Roberts's declaration that "the limitation upon individual liberty must have an appropriate relationship to the safety of the state."[21]

The way to counter un-American speech, Biddle insisted, was with truth. He favored exposing the foreign or other un-American sources of evil propaganda (like anti-Semitism), while counterpoising an educational effort that would extol the aims and ideals of American democracy. Biddle's views were very close to those espoused by the ACLU and may well have given FDR reason to question whether he was "tough enough" to deal with the subversive element. The president, who warned privately that he thought Lindbergh a "Nazi," was ill-disposed to rely solely on a strategy of exposure and truth to counter the isolationist aviator/hero and his ilk.[22]

But while the solicitor general's 1940 thinking was suspect, by the following June his rhetoric suggested that he had fallen into line with the president's views. On the eve of taking over as acting attorney general, Biddle spoke again of political exigencies, but where earlier he had used this relationship to resist demands for repression, he now emphasized the latitude this gave the government. The new cast to Biddle's rhetoric was apparent in a speech he made before the liberal-minded National Conference of Social Work a week before Jackson left office and at a time when Biddle was pushing his candidacy for attorney general.[23] Speaking to an audience likely to harbor libertarian convictions,[24] Biddle insisted that the times called for flexibility. It was true, he said, that not all constitutional rights disappear in wartime, but he noted, the government was obligated in crisis times to exercise broad authority under the law to deal severely with elements it deemed dangerous. Naturally, he conceded, Holmes had not believed that a "'silly leaflet by an unknown man,'" misquoting the *Abrams* dissent, should be severely punished. A mindless and pointless suppression of obnoxious views was not within the government's prerogative or the nation's interest. But, Biddle pointed out, Holmes had reiterated his belief that "the government in time of war had power to punish speech that was, as [Holmes] phrased it, 'intended to produce a clear and imminent danger.'" Addressing the awkward fact that the United States was not currently at war, the solicitor general suggested that Nazi military tactics, which included psychological warfare, had placed the United States in a "curious twilight zone" between war and peace that dissolved the distinction.

Wrapping himself in the cloak of pragmatism, Biddle addressed those who worried that the government's struggle against un-Americanism was going too far. The operations of the law, he suggested, must be fluid and realistic, not bound by formulas or slogans.[25] Like Lewis Mumford and other militant democrats, he demanded that liberals put aside their fears and habitual fecklessness and support a more active national defense posture including, as necessary, limitations on "traditional" civil liberties. Don't allow yourselves, he cautioned, to become "confused and timorous . . . encumbered by all those sterile doubts and overwrought warnings with which the isolationists summon the liberals to their distorted view." There was a danger, he told liberals, that their faith was becoming "timorous [twice he used the word] and defeatist," and he obliquely warned labor leaders of the likely hostile public reaction should they continue to resist modest restraints "because of an impalpable fear of how they may be construed or enforced."[26] In retrospect, much of this sounds like self-admonition.

Biddle's sobering warnings came amid frightening news of German successes in the Balkans, the Middle East, and at sea, and rising tensions with the Japanese. On the other hand, FDR had been reelected in November 1940 and isolationism, if not vanquished, was at least in retreat; the Luftwaffe blitz had failed to cow the English, and the Lend Lease Act adopted in March 1941 committed the United States to Britain's continued survival. American military mobilization was proceeding (albeit slowly), and the "arsenal of democracy" was beginning to turn out the material needed to stop the Nazi war machine. The only development that might have justified a major shift in civil libertarian outlook was the current concern that Communist intrigue among industrial workers threatened to undermine defense production. Perhaps Biddle was genuinely worried by this. Certainly he was aware that the problem was high on the president's agenda, and he may have intended his speech to the Conference on Social Work as notice to FDR that he was prepared to do what the situation demanded.

One speech was not enough to convince the president that Biddle was his man. FDR met with Justice Murphy at the White House at least four times between the beginning of June and mid-July 1941, fueling speculation that lasted into early August that the president was actively courting the former attorney general for the job tenuously in Biddle's care.[27] Insiders reported that the president thought that Biddle was "too strict [about civil liberties] at a time like this when . . . we ought to have an attorney general who can close his eyes on occasion."[28] This is confirmed by notes that Murphy made following a conversation he had with the president at a mid-June White House luncheon. On this occasion, according to Murphy, Roosevelt declared that while "Francis was a fine fellow," he just was not right for the job of attorney general. Biddle, FDR reportedly said, had not the least notion of how to "get tough with the subversive element," adding that he "would sleep better" if Murphy would take up the job he had left in early 1940.[29] Murphy said he would do whatever "the boss" wanted, but he coveted a post closer to the center of unfolding military events, and the issue was left unresolved.

Meanwhile, Biddle went about compiling a record as acting attorney general that suggested, perhaps by design, that he had the right stuff. Almost everything Biddle did for his first six months as head of the Justice Department seemed calculated to prove that he had modeled himself more on the aggressive Murphy than on the cautious Jackson. Jackson told the president as much at a July or early August luncheon meeting when the issue of who would succeed him on a permanent basis was still undecided. The recently departed attorney general referred to two incidents. On June 16, four days after FDR nominated Jackson for the Supreme Court, the State Department had ordered the closing of all German consulates, and the arrest of suspected spies was to follow. Two of the suspects, both American citizens, were reported to be planning to leave the country the next day. Their immediate arrest seemed called for, but if they were seized, others would be alerted and might flee. According to Jackson, the issue was put to the acting attorney general at noon. "Within ten minutes" Biddle had ordered the arrest and "incommunicado" detention of the pair. Noting that Biddle did not tell him about this until after the arrests had been made, Jackson confessed that if it had been up to him, "I rather think I would have gone courtish"—meaning (I assume) that he would have felt bound by the norms of arrest procedure. Jackson recommended Biddle to the president on the ground that the acting attorney general had moved quickly and decisively and had not been deterred by the excess of legal scruples that FDR associated with Jackson.

The second incident Jackson cited was Biddle's authorization of the prosecution of the "Minneapolis reds."[30] He was referring to members of the Trotskyite Socialist Workers Party recently arrested on charges that they had openly advocated and secretly plotted the overthrow of the government. The latter charge, involving the first use of anti-sedition portions of the feared Smith Act, was condemned by civil libertarians and virtually the entire non-Communist Left. Jackson offered the prosecution, discussed in chapter 8, as additional evidence of Biddle's willingness to approach security issues without excessive sensitivity to civil libertarian concerns. Biddle would later claim that he intended the episode as a demonstration of firmness.[31]

The ultimate test of Biddle's "flexibility" was how well he got on with FBI director J. Edgar Hoover. Murphy seems to have been very comfortable with Hoover; Jackson more than once narrowly backed away from confrontations with him. For Biddle there was no question of taming the director; the issue was whether he could make himself acceptable to Hoover. He may well have understood that winning over the director was a condition of his employment and in his ten-week trial period as acting attorney general, Biddle demonstrated that he would do just fine in this regard.

As the national crisis deepened in 1941, Hoover's political power grew. Aware that Biddle enjoyed little support in or out of government, the director sensed an opportunity to strengthen his own position in the Department of Justice. Since 1933, supervision of the FBI had been assigned to the assistant to the attorney general (not to be confused with the several assistant attorney generals), the third-ranking official in the department. Since 1940 this post had been held by Matthew McGuire, who maintained good relations with the bureau. Nevertheless, Hoover did not want *any* official between him and the attorney general, and when the president nominated McGuire for a district court judgeship in July, Hoover set about to end the role McGuire had played as intermediary between the director and the attorney general. Using McGuire himself as a friendly go-between, Hoover secured Biddle's assurance that if Biddle were appointed attorney general, he would establish regular direct contact with the director. Biddle also assured Hoover that he would appoint Hoover-partisan Alexander Holtzhoff to handle routine dealings with the FBI.[32]

Shortly before McGuire left the department he took up with Biddle another problem that had been troubling Hoover—L. M. C. Smith's Special Defense Unit. The unit, created as the Neutrality Laws Division in April 1940 to provide departmental oversight of federal prosecutions of internal security-related crimes, had been depicted in the press as designed to curb the FBI. Hoover had not been pleased. Now, as a parting service to the director, McGuire attempted to put Smith in his place by telling the acting attorney general that he opposed the budget Smith had proposed for the unit, and calling into question its entire raison d´être. Smith survived, but his Special Defense Unit played little of the supervisory function originally intended for it.[33]

On August 25, FDR nominated Biddle to be attorney general. Rumors immediately circulated (as they had when Biddle's predecessors had been nominated) that the attorney general designate would, if confirmed, fire Hoover. Those who genuinely thought that Biddle's liberal reputation meant the end of Hoover apparently knew little of the political dynamics of the situation. Nevertheless, the director left nothing to chance and immediately set out to determine where Biddle stood, possibly intending by his inquiries to let it be known that if the candidate gave him reason to doubt his loyalty, Hoover would use his much-feared influence in Congress and the press to undermine Biddle's nomination. On September 3, the day the Senate Judiciary Committee held hearings on his nomination, Biddle met with the director's assistant, E. A. Tamm, to deny rumors that he was in any way dissatisfied with Hoover or intended to remove him. The attorney general designate assured Tamm that he would make a statement attesting to his "close personal friendship" with, and confidence in, his boss.[34] At his first press conference after becoming attorney general, Biddle responded to a reporter's question, probably planted, that Hoover "certainly will stay,"[35] and one department official notes that relations between Hoover and his nominal superior turned out to be "very good."[36]

The issue of who would take McGuire's place as Biddle's senior assistant was still to be resolved, and it became all the more pressing because Biddle had not yet announced, as Hoover wished, that the assistant to the attorney general would no longer supervise the bureau. With this issue hanging fire, Biddle selected Presidential Assistant James Rowe to replace McGuire. For Biddle, it was an excellent appointment. Rowe was friendly, loyal, politically savvy, and well connected on Capitol Hill. Moreover, he enjoyed the president's confidence. The president may have felt that Rowe, who claimed that Biddle would listen to him when he "won't listen to anyone else," would act as a voice of reason with the man the president still regarded as a Groton School second former.

Nevertheless, the nomination posed problems for Hoover. Having identified the liberal and talented young Rowe as an enemy, the director sought to secure a guarantee of good behavior before he would agree not to work against the appointment. Rowe pledged his fealty, and although a Hoover aide suspected that Rowe's obeisance was hypocritically "intended to prevent any open [FBI] opposition" to Rowe's appointment, McGuire apparently succeeded in convincing him that a wiser and more responsible Rowe was determined to "make amends" for having sometimes questioned Hoover's conduct. The director was assured that Rowe intended to follow the same general policy as his predecessors, that is, "allowing the Bureau complete latitude" in the administration of its affairs.[37] Rowe's appointment was approved without further incident, and Biddle ordered that henceforth the director would report directly to him.[38]

Biddle's support for Hoover, as well as his (new) realistic attitude toward civil liberties issues were reflected in his response to a sensational public disclosure of FBI wiretapping activities in circumstances that suggested abuse of the government's dubious authority in that area.[39] The target, Harry Bridges. In June 1941, Charles B. Sears, the special investigator selected by Jackson to determine whether Bridges was deportable, had concluded more than two months of hearings. While Sears deliberated Bridges's fate, the leader of the West Coast longshoremen spent some time in New York City conferring with other labor officials. In late August, just about the time the president announced Biddle's nomination, lawyers for Bridges revealed they had irrefutable evidence that for three weeks earlier in the month, FBI agents had been tapping the phone in Bridges's New York hotel room.[40]

Following the incident's exposure, Hoover and Biddle, at the acting attorney general's suggestion, went to the White House to explain. When they told their story, according to Biddle's recollection, FDR grinned, slapped Hoover on the back and exclaimed "by God, Edgar, that's the first time you've been caught with your pants down!"[41] FDR's cavalier acceptance of the realities of FBI activities suggests the response of a practical political leader who kept his principles and his statecraft nicely compartmentalized. What must be done, would be done, civil libertarian scruples notwithstanding. He assumed that subordinates would absorb whatever embarrassment exposure entailed.

The assumption may have been misplaced. Bridges's lawyers attempted to have Judge Sears reopen the case on the basis of what they contended was the government's improper behavior. He refused, but Hoover confided to another department official at the time, that if he were called by Sears to testify on the matter, "he would frankly state that he was authorized to tap the wires by the President, himself." The official, a staunch FDR partisan, was shocked—not by the revelation, but by Hoover's lack of loyalty to the president.[42] In any event, the president had made his position on the issue clear to the would-be attorney general.

The incident was raised at Biddle's confirmation hearings. The nominee had been briefed on the judicial rulings on tapping by Assistant Solicitor General Charles Fahy (soon to succeed Biddle as solicitor general), who concluded that, apart from the non-admissibility of tapping evidence in court, the courts had not decided what the 1934 statute meant by its prohibition on the "divulgence of an intercepted message."[43] When members of the Senate Judiciary Committee asked what the acting attorney general knew about the Bridges affair, and how he felt about government wiretapping, Biddle replied that he first learned of the alleged tapping when he read about it in the newspapers and claimed that he had not authorized tapping in this or in any other case. Nevertheless, he insisted that it was within the administration's legal authority to use the practice. Biddle said he agreed with Justice Holmes that tapping was a "dirty business," and thought that "ordinarily" it should not be permitted. But in line with his mentor's thinking (and FDR's), he insisted that "all rights . . . must bow to the greater rights of the community," and that these are "bad times." Taking the position set forth in the Fahy brief and put forward by Jackson earlier in the year, Biddle endorsed controlled government tapping. The editors of the *Nation* accused him of "splitting hairs" and of dancing to Hoover's tune,[44] and the committee asked whether under the flexible principles he had enunciated, the interception of the conversations of congressmen or labor leaders (the chief concerns of the anti-tapping lobby) might not be justified. Biddle denied that he would authorize such taps. His assurances rang hollow given his admission that the tap on Bridges had been placed entirely without his knowledge. Nevertheless, accepting his professions at face value, the committee ratified his appointment.

In 1942 the administration, though continuing to insist that it had legal authority to tap, again sought legislation ratifying this view. Congress refused, and the department stopped asking. Two months after Pearl Harbor the president asked Biddle if he was tapping. "Yes, whenever necessary," was his answer.[45]

Biddle, like his immediate predecessors, was strongly influenced by the civil-libertarian rhetoric and free-speech experiences of the past 20 years. He saw himself as a "civil libertarian attorney general." But it was clear from the outset that his inclination to prove his worth and personal toughness would encourage him to find considerable latitude under that rubric. In his hands the ordinarily difficult task of doing the right thing on matters impinging on civil liberties was further complicated by personal uncertainties and the constant need to prove himself, and Biddle turned out to be an unpredictable, occasionally eccentric custodian of free speech and other civil liberties.

Chapter 8

The "Minneapolis Reds": A "Clear and Present Danger"?

In early October 1941, with United States involvement in the European war two months away, Harvard University Press issued an updated version of Zechariah Chafee's 1920 classic, *Freedom of Speech*. In the thoroughly revised work, which he called *Free Speech in the United States*, Chafee warned that, historically, when the advocacy of force and violence had been criminalized, the law had been "stretched in practice to imprison people who do not resemble at all the desperate revolutionists of whom one naturally thinks on reading these words." The evil effects of the Smith Act, he argued, lay not in the words of the statute or in the interpretation that would eventually be given them by the Supreme Court, but in the attitude adopted by those who would apply it. "Can we rely on the present administration," he asked rhetorically, "to construe it narrowly and use it only against really dangerous men?"[1] Even before the book appeared in print, Attorney General Francis Biddle had provided a preliminary answer.

The Smith Act's first victims were a group of radicals, typical of a fading era in American labor politics, who led the tiny Socialist Workers Party (SWP). Their leader, and the principal defendant in the Smith Act prosecution, was Vincent Raymond Dunne. Born in rural Minnesota, Dunne had worked in mining, construction, and lumber camps, and as an express wagon driver and messenger for Wells Fargo and other express companies in the West. He was among the early members of the Industrial Workers of the World (IWW), and from 1905 to 1908 participated in strikes and demonstrations in Missoula, Spokane, Seattle, Fresno, and San Francisco. When the IWW was virtually destroyed during World War I, he signed on with the Communist Party of the United States (CPUSA).[2] In 1928 the

CPUSA split. Most of the membership followed the lead of the Russian Communist leader Joseph Stalin, who had recently prevailed in a struggle for control of the Soviet Union and the international movement. Dunne and two of his brothers, however, were part of a small minority who identified themselves instead with Stalin's soon-to-be-exiled rival, Leon Trotsky. They went on to form the Trotskyite SWP, a group that, at its strongest, commanded the allegiance of no more than two thousand members in 30 branches scattered about the country. According to the FBI, only the Minneapolis branch had any real influence within the labor movement.[3]

That city provided fertile ground for radical labor organizing efforts.[4] Although Minneapolis was once the hub of thriving commerce, by the early 1930s many of its inhabitants were struggling to hold on. Displaced workers from throughout the region flocked to Minneapolis and its twin city, St. Paul, and in 1934 a third of their work force was unemployed. Much of the work available was in trucking, though even here hours were long and labor discontent rife. In the early Depression years, the Dunne brothers[5] and other Trotskyites managed to gain control of a small local affiliated with the International Brotherhood of Teamsters (IBT), and they launched an organizing drive that increased membership (drawn from a number of industries) more than tenfold.[6] In May 1934, they led a strike against Minneapolis truck owners in which the strikers fought pitched battles with vigilantes and police. Attempts by federal mediators to settle the conflict failed, and for a time the well-organized workers controlled the streets of Minneapolis. Conservatives charged that the strike leaders were Communists bent on sovietizing the Twin Cities and, after further confrontations produced two dead and dozens wounded, Governor Floyd B. Olson declared martial law. The struggle and settlement, which infuriated the city's establishment, raised the prestige of the Dunne-led Local 544 and its leaders among the city's workers.

Over the next four years Local 544's power grew, and so did the concerns of government officials. In the late 1930s the Dunne brothers organized and secured contracts covering a quarter of a million workers in an 11-state area in and around Minnesota.[7] Among those organized were federal relief workers, and in 1939, FDR ordered Attorney General Murphy to prosecute Works Progress Administration (WPA) employees who participated in a strike led by Local 544. One hundred and sixty were charged with criminal conspiracy. Thirty-three were tried, convicted, and sentenced to prison terms ranging from three to eight months. Jackson later dismissed the charges against the remainder.[8]

As the likelihood of another European war increased at the end of the decade, government concerns about Local 544 grew. The Trotskyites were on record as totally rejecting United States participation in another war, and refusing to cooperate with any program of military preparedness. "Not one iota of support to the armaments program for war!" an SWP manifesto proclaimed. "We have a war of our own to fight [against injustice and inequality at home] . . . and that war can be won only if it is fought against the capitalist class and its chief executive in Washington."[9] Local 544's open hostility to the administration's mobilization plans made its leaders vulnerable to criticism from the national teamsters union, and from dissident members of the local itself, who charged that the Dunne brothers were intent on sabotaging the nation's defense.

In March 1941, a disgruntled faction calling itself the "Committee of 100" lodged a protest against the leadership of the local with the IBT. In June 1941 the Executive Board of the international classified the SWP as a "subversive, revolutionary party" from which all union officers and members were obliged to disassociate themselves. The local's membership thereupon voted to secede from the AFL-affiliated teamster's international and join the CIO rather than abandon their Trotskyite leaders. Organizers flocked to Minneapolis, which now became the center of the CIO's drive to enlist workers throughout the region.[10] IBT president Daniel Tobin released a statement to the press complaining that a radical clique in Local 544 had engineered the move to further its efforts to undermine American capitalism and obstruct the defense effort. "Some remedy," Tobin continued, "should be procured by the Government to prevent this serious boring from within" by what he suggested were undercover agents of Germany and Russia.[11]

Tobin, a staunch supporter of FDR's foreign and defense policies, and a valued political ally, sent a copy of his statement to the White House. FDR responded by declaring that this was "no time . . . for labor unions, local or national, to begin raiding one another for the purpose of getting memberships or for similar reasons."[12] This mild condemnation of internecine union warfare did not allude to Tobin's charges of subversion or radicalism. But critics became convinced of presidential involvement in the dispute when Press Secretary Stephen Early sent copies of Tobin's telegram to Acting Attorney General Francis Biddle, and two weeks later federal agents raided the offices of the Socialist Workers Party in the Twin Cities and Biddle announced that the government would seek criminal indictments against the soapbox radicals.[13]

Critics attributed the government's attack to the president's desire to help Tobin in his struggles with the rebellious local. Why else, they asked, would the Justice Department attack the "tiny Trotskyist" faction, this "obscure sect," while it ignored the activities of the overtly anti-Semitic Christian Front flourishing in New England?[14] Historians, beginning with Thomas L. Pahl, who examined the episode in the mid-1960s, have followed the critics' lead, and the Tobin-related conspiracy interpretation has reappeared wherever the episode has been discussed.[15] Department documents now make it clear that the assault on the Trotskyites was rooted in developments that pre-date the Tobin request, and that it is better understood as the culmination of a government drive to end Communist obstructionism in the defense industry.

Dunne and his colleagues had been under investigation by the FBI since the early 1920s. Bureau reports since that time, focusing on the origins of the group in the Communist Party and on the occasional collaboration between members of the two factions, tended to depict the Trotskyites as a Communist Party faction, rather than as a separate and rival entity.[16] This thinking persisted despite Trotskyite efforts, culminating in their creation of the SWP, to establish a clearly independent identity. By the end of 1940, with administration concerns about politically inspired work slowdowns and stoppages on the rise, J. Edgar Hoover had concluded that Local 544 was bent on controlling transportation in the nation's midsection. The director, emphasizing the considerable importance he attached to the inquiry, ordered the FBI regional office in St. Paul to recruit confidential informants to gather evidence of the SWP's use of the teamster's local to "obtain control of interstate trucking."[17]

In early 1941, Hoover repeatedly warned officials, including President Roosevelt, that the Trotskyites and Communists, acting in concert through Local 544, were in a position to obtain "complete control of all labor in the state of Minnesota."[18] Plans were afoot, he claimed, for a strike that would shut down more than 30 defense contractors. Amid rumors that the Trotskyites were about to tie up the defense industry,[19] and warnings from Minnesota governor Harold Stassen that the situation posed a "real threat to the state,"[20] the department's Criminal Division asked the FBI and Victor Anderson, the U.S. attorney in St. Paul, to intensify their efforts to build a case against Local 544's leadership.[21]

Biddle had been aware for some time that department lawyers were interested in prosecuting the Trotskyites under the Smith Act and, although he would later question the propriety of the prosecution, he raised no objections at the time. In an early June report to the president on ways in which the government might deal with "Communistic and subversive activities" among defense plant workers, Biddle had predicted that prosecution of the Minneapolis Trotskyites would have "some salutary effect," presumably in establishing a precedent for future use and as a warning to other subversives. The only reservation he expressed did not involve the constitutionality or desirability of prosecuting people for advocacy, but the difficulty of proving criminal cases.[22] As the new head of the department and an uncertain applicant for a permanent appointment, an already insecure Biddle was prone to favor action rather than indulge any personal reservations he may have had.

At staff conferences on June 16 and 17, the acting attorney general was thoroughly briefed on the case, and on June 17 he authorized the prosecution recommended by department lawyers. They in turn predicted swift results of "outstanding importance," referring perhaps to the case's potential value as a model for future Smith Act prosecutions. The decision was kept secret while warrants were secured and preparations laid for the raid on the SWP.[23] On June 27, 1941, Biddle announced that the government intended to prosecute the leaders of the Socialist Workers Party, which he described, significantly, as the "Trotskyite branch of the Communist movement." This description, which in part reflected Hoover's thinking, may have been calculated to attach more significance and greater sinister import to the group than its size and isolation would seem to warrant, and to suggest that the action was somehow directed at the well-known and much-feared Red menace. Despite the antagonism between the Trotskyites and Stalinists, the daily press picked up on the suggestion and treated the government's effort "as a drive against the Communists."[24]

In mid-July a federal grand jury in St. Paul returned indictments against 29 Trotskyites, charging them with (1) conspiring to "destroy by force the Government of the United States;" and (2) committing acts intended to interfere with the discipline of the armed forces, and organizing and becoming members of groups "whose purpose it was to teach, advocate, and encourage" the overthrow of the government of the United States.[25] They pled "not guilty," and trial was set for early October.

Liberals were troubled by his prosecution of the Trotskyites,[26] and criticism of the action dogged the attorney general from his announcement of the indictment in June through the end of the trial six months later.[27] American Civil Liberties Union director Roger Baldwin, warning that "we're up against the first big tough wartime case," began preparing to support a legal challenge even before an indictment was handed down.[28] A Civil Rights Defense Committee, whose supporters included an impressive list of well-known leftists, libertarians, and literary figures,[29] was formed with ACLU backing to publicize the case and raise money for the defendants.[30] Some of these liberals and literati no doubt found that the Trotskyite defendants projected the romantic aura that had always drawn intellectuals to radical causes.

A beleaguered Biddle repeatedly defended the department's initiative, often contending that he had no choice.[31] At his first news conference as attorney general, he took complete responsibility for the Twin Cities prosecution, contending that no constitutional protections were involved: "Opinion stopped when an individual started to incite insurrection and violence," he said, and he would prosecute anybody who crossed the line.[32] His job, he insisted, was only to enforce the laws, not to determine whether they were constitutional, but he declared that he would welcome an appeal to the Supreme Court.[33] When Bruce Bliven, editor of the *New Republic,* demanded that all branches of government adhere to the limits imposed by Holmes's "clear and present danger" formula, Biddle replied that the Smith Act, as written, had built into it cognizance of that principle since the Congress had acted in full awareness of both the standard and the world situation. He made no comment on Bliven's suggestion that the department was obliged to apply the standard in choosing who it would prosecute, saying only that given the actions of the SWP he "had no choice, consistent with my duties."[34] Congress had defined certain words and activities as criminal. The department, having satisfied itself as to existence of a violation and the identity of the violators, was simply discharging its responsibility. It was, he suggested, a mechanical process.

Chafee's soon-to-be-released *Free Speech in the United States* addressed Biddle's discretion-denying defense. Historically, Chafee noted, everyone involved in the criminal justice system excused their indifference to the Constitution by declaring that its requirements were determined solely by the Supreme Court and that until an issue had been so adjudicated, officials were not responsible for assessing the constitutionality of their actions. The principle of judicial review had thus been treated by officials as a license for the suppression of dissent, with the result that repressive laws could accomplish much of their intent well before and regardless of how the Supreme Court ruled.[35]

Chafee's point was not unknown to Biddle. The need for prosecutorial restraint had been much discussed in recent years and was a favorite topic of Jackson's. Biddle's friend, the brilliant Frankfurter protégé Edward Prichard, Jr., now special assistant to the attorney general, repeatedly complained to him about the prosecution, dismissing the argument that the attorney general was bound to enforce the laws to the "limit of their literal application," telling his friend (and boss) that this smacked of the "disingenuous" to one "sophisticated in the ways of prosecutors." Prichard, who had earlier protested Jackson's actions in the Bridges case,[36] bluntly condemned Biddle's refusal to be bound by "clear and present danger," which he characterized as an "accepted . . . classic statement of the liberal position."[37]

The critics' frequent invocation of the "clear and present danger" formula reflected the attachment to the slogan that had developed since it was first enunciated by Justice Holmes in 1919. In the 20 years since, liberals had "fought and bled," in the hyperbolic description of one of their number,[38] to gain official acceptance of the idea that this now familiar formula should guide the determination of whether specific utterances were criminally seditious. "The question in every case," Holmes had written, "was whether the words used are used in such circumstances and are of such a nature as to create a clear and present danger that they will bring about the substantive evils that Congress has a right to prevent."[39]

First offered by Holmes in early 1919 in the *Schenck* case to uphold a conviction under the Espionage Act, he used the standard a few months later in *Abrams* to condemn the government's prosecution of some young socialists convicted under the Sedition Act for distributing pamphlets critical of the government's intervention in the Russian civil war.[40] Holmes, joined by Justice Louis Brandeis, now argued that the First Amendment imposed significant limits on the government's authority to regulate political speech, and he used the clear and present danger test to suggest that wide latitude be given to political expression hostile to the state and its activities. Only speech that produced or was intended to produce "a clear and imminent danger," he wrote, fell outside the First Amendment's protections, explaining that this tolerant view of speech was necessitated by society's interest in the free exchange of ideas from which, he intimated, political truths would emerge.[41]

In *Freedom of Speech,* Chafee presented "a brief for the danger test" in its *Abrams* incarnation.[42] Although the Court recognized the formulation only once in the next 20 years,[43] and then only to reject Holmes's broad reinterpretation of *Schenck,* Chafee's advocacy, bolstered by occasional pronouncements by Holmes and Brandeis, kept the doctrine alive. In 1937, in the *Herndon* case, for the first time since *Schenck,* it was employed by a Court majority,[44] and after 1941, according to First Amendment scholar Harry Kalven, the test, all but ignored for a generation, rapidly emerged "as the touchstone of First Amendment policy." "Having lost each of the battles," Kalven noted, Holmes had "won the war."[45]

But not in St. Paul, where district court judge Matthew M. Joyce emphasized the common sense limits on free speech and, with a fine sense of irony, quoted Max Eastman in his support. Eastman was the legendary radical and founding father of Trotskyism in America whose journal the *Masses* had been suppressed during World War I.[46] No longer the enfant terrible, in 1941 he had published an article castigating what he saw as the dangerous impracticality of the ACLU's defense of free speech for fascists and Communists.[47] "The simple fact," he wrote, "is that criminal power-fiends are ganging up against human civilization. . . . Their chief weapon is [propaganda]. . . . Are those who understand this fact going to let civilization be destroyed because its further progress depends upon the free discussion of ideas?"

The "power-fiends" in Eastman's article did not include Dunne and company. What Eastman wanted was freedom for righteous or harmless orators and prison for genuine subversives. This was no doubt what most people wanted, but the goal left open the question of who would decide which orators were which, and on what basis. Joyce quoted Eastman in support of the suppression of the Trotskyites, leaving a chagrined Eastman to protest that this was not the application he had in mind.[48] The affair illustrated a problem entailed in giving the courts discretion, guided only by "remote bad tendency," to determine what speech was suppressible.

The Trotskyite prosecution forced department officials to confront the implications of clear and present danger, and to take a stand on the issue. For despite his hostility to the defendant's invocation of Holmes, Judge Joyce refused to deny a defense pre-trial motion that he instruct the jury to weigh the evidence against the "clear and present danger" standard, calling it premature.[49] His refusal to foreclose the issue obliged the government attorneys to seek instructions from Washington as to what position they should take on "clear and present danger."

Assistant Attorney General Wendell Berge, although subscribing to the doctrine in the abstract, refused to apply it to the SWP prosecution. In an address to the Foreign Policy Association Forum in late October, he condemned as "irresponsible and reckless" charges (mostly from isolationists) that the government was undermining freedom of speech and assembly, and lauded what he said was the department's restraint in enforcing federal statutes: "We believe with Mr. Justice Holmes," Berge said, that freedom of speech "must always include [paraphrasing the *Abrams* dissent] 'freedom for the thought that we hate.'" This, he said (paraphrasing *Schenck*), should be the policy unless the government was faced with words that created "a clear and present danger" of bringing about substantive evils the government had a right to prevent.[50] But Berge had decided, as he later said, that the doctrine did not apply to the Trotskyites since in "actually advocating" revolution and counseling "direct action by members of the armed forces," their words were a "far cry . . . from the futile murmuring of some of the frustrated people who were prosecuted during the first World War."[51]

But Berge was not willing to leave that judgment up to the Trotskyites' peers, and on October 9 he responded to the prosecutors' request for instructions by ruling that no precedent made it necessary for a jury to find a clear and present danger before it could convict a person for doing what Congress had made unlawful. Noting that Judge Joyce in denying the defendants' pre-trial motions had already ruled that Congress had legitimately and reasonably exercised its authority to make certain "definite and specific acts [words] offenses in and of themselves," he concluded that it was unnecessary to leave room for the "play of the imagination of the court and the jury. . . ." From the government's perspective there was nothing for the jury to decide except "whether the defendants did conspire to advocate the overthrow of the government by force and violence."[52] The possible consequences of the advocacy, present or infinitely far removed, were not at issue.

Twenty years after the event, Biddle admitted that the Trotskyites could by "no conceivable stretch of a liberal imagination" have been said to have constituted a clear and present danger to the government.[53] But at the time, the attorney general, having decided that ensuring maximum freedom of expression was not his responsibility, looked on as department lawyers not only dismissed the prosecutorial self-restraint implicit in Holmes's idea, but fought efforts by the Trotskyites to have it applied to their case. Sensitive to criticism, he sought to assure libertarians that the prosecution was intended to strike a blow for free speech! Ten days before the trial was to begin he told ACLU officials and the press that he had instructed the prosecution team to "try the case in low key," not to play to popular prejudices, to seek modest sentences should the defendants be convicted, and "to assist the court in exploring the freedom of speech issues raised by the case." Biddle managed to leave Baldwin believing that the attorney general was embarrassed by the whole affair and would have been "glad to dismiss the case if there were a face-saving way out."[54]

Testimony in the trial began at the end of October and lasted almost a month. The prosecution was optimistic from the outset, and grew more so as the case unfolded. The government had little trouble demonstrating that Local 544 had created a Defense Guard, amassed an arsenal (consisting of a few pistols and .22 caliber rifles), and conducted target practices and drills. The defendants insisted that these were for self-defense—the local concededly had many enemies. Prosecutors argued that these acts, together with the defendants' revolutionary rhetoric and the fact that some of them had met with Leon Trotsky in Mexico, left no reasonable doubt that the Trotskyites were conspiring to overthrow the United States as charged in count one. Prospects for obtaining convictions on count two were even better. The Trotskyites had made plain their belief in revolution, and there was no shortage of creditable witnesses to tie the defendants to the revolutionary advocacy punishable under the Smith Act. As long as Judge Joyce did not require the government to demonstrate that these acts and words were clearly and proximately tied to some illegal outcome, convictions seemed certain.

After hearing a month of testimony, the judge directed a verdict of "not guilty" for five of the original defendants. In rejecting a motion for the acquittal of the rest, Judge Joyce told the defendants, with the jury out of the room, that he was unable to find any "constitutional right to circulate seditious and revolutionary material" and suggested it was hypocritical for the accused, "when confronted with the consequences of such conduct," to "rush to the protection of the Constitution they would not amend but would absolutely destroy." Addressing the apparently inconsequential size of the alleged conspiracy, he noted that it was "well to remember on this point that Hitler went around in a greasy raincoat in his early days and was belittled for his efforts."[55]

Lawyers for the remaining defendants renewed their request that Joyce include in his instructions to the jury on count two that it was necessary for the government to have proven beyond a reasonable doubt that the defendants' "writings or statements or utterances created a clear and present danger of the overthrow of the Government of the United States [etc.]." The defendants asked the court to define "clear and present danger" to mean that it was "certain, obvious, or easily apparent that the Government . . . might at the present time, be overthrown or destroyed. . . ." Prosecutors countered that since the Supreme Court had not consistently endorsed this standard, such an instruction would be improper.[56] The judge rejected the defendants' motion, and his instructions to the jury made no reference to the clear and present danger doctrine.[57]

On December 1, after two-and-a-half days of deliberation, the jury of "farmers, workingmen, merchants and one woman,"[58] returned a verdict of "not guilty" as to each of the defendants on the first count (seditious conspiracy), and acquitted five of them as well on the second (advocacy). The 18 remaining defendants (one committed suicide during the trial) were found guilty on count two, although there was no indication as to whether the jury had found the defendants guilty of inciting disaffection in the military, conspiring to advocate revolution, or both. The jury recommended leniency, and 12 of the defendants were sentenced to 16 months imprisonment. The remainder received a year and a day. The defendants notified the court that they would appeal.

Some observers were amused by the government's effort. *Time* ridiculed the whole affair, calling its conclusion a triumphant snagging of "a nestful of mice."[59] Others were incensed. The *New Republic* castigated the department's success as a "disturbing and unfortunate" precedent.[60] The Communist Party self-righteously endorsed the outcome. Although quarreling with the government's attempt to depict the defendants as "radicals," Carl Winter, writing for the *Daily Worker,* was pleased that the crimes of the "pro-Nazi [the Trotskyites, unlike the Stalinists, still opposed American intervention] servants of reaction" had been justly punished. There was no danger, he added, that the case might serve as a precedent to be used "against genuine progressive individuals and organizations" like the CPUSA.[61] In fact, the party's time was not far off.

The ACLU leadership also chose to deny the case's ominous implications. In a statement intended principally for the libertarian faithful, the organization declared that the prosecution was "evidently an isolated case brought under rather unusual circumstances" (apparently a reference to the allegations that the prosecution was FDR's payoff to a loyal and unhappy Dan Tobin). The ACLU preferred to treat it as an anomaly forced on Biddle by the president, and accepted the attorney general's assurances that the Trotskyite case was not "a precedent for bringing similar prosecutions" under the new anti-sedition statute.[62]

Determined to use the case to test the Smith Act, ACLU officials urged the defendants to bypass the circuit court of appeals and appeal directly to the Supreme Court on the ground that the case raised important constitutional issues. The ACLU in effect wanted them to concede that they advocated the overthrow of government by force and violence to set up an appeal that would vindicate the right of persons to do so. The defendants, who were concerned less with discrediting the Smith Act than with winning their freedom, insisted that the SWP had not advocated forceful revolution[63] and sought to have the case heard by the court of appeals, which, they thought, might (without referring to the constitutionality of the Smith Act, or the relevance of "clear and present danger") reverse the conviction on grounds that the indictment was defective or that the evidence failed to show a violation of the statute.[64]

The appeal of the 18 remaining defendants was heard by the Eighth Circuit Court of Appeals in September 1943—about midway through the war. The appellants urged both the invalidity of the Smith Act and the insufficiency of the indictment and of the evidence. A unanimous three-judge panel rejected their appeal and went on to discount "clear and present danger." On the constitutionality of the Smith Act, it found the decision in *Gitlow* v. *New York* (1925) controlling. In that case, Justice Edward T. Sanford, writing for the Court in what Harry Kalven has called an "unusually luminous holding as to the precise boundaries of permissible speech," declared that "utterances of a certain kind involve such danger of substantive evil that they may be punished, [and] the question whether any specific utterances coming within the prohibited class is likely, in and of itself, to bring about the substantive evil, is not open to consideration."[65] That is, uttering certain words might itself be made criminal without reference to "clear and present danger" or any other measure of their likely effect. Holmes and Brandeis had dissented. Following the reasoning of the majority in *Gitlow,* the circuit court in *Dunne* held that Congress had every right to define and punish seditious speech. The Smith Act, modeled on the New York statute upheld in *Gitlow,* was clear enough for this purpose. As for "clear and present danger," the court insisted that, while the doctrine enunciated in the *Schenck* case had been of practical guidance in some free speech cases, the *Gitlow* decision "definitely determines" that it was not applicable in "situations where the legislative body had outlawed certain utterances." This ruling, the court concluded, had not been weakened by later decisions.[66]

Although Biddle had intimated that he looked on the case as a test of the law, the government opposed a petition for a hearing by the Supreme Court, and the Court refused certiorari. The attorney general suggested at the time (and reiterated 20 years later), that the defendants were guilty of no more than rhetorical excesses, but he refused, on the advice of his staff, to recommend a pardon to the president. His inconsistent and ultimately repressive behavior earned him Baldwin's lasting enmity. After the war, when the ACLU's board considered Biddle for chairman of the organization's National Committee, Baldwin opposed the nomination citing the Trotskyite affair.[67]

In his 1962 memoirs, Biddle observed that history had shown that laws like the Smith Act, "addressed to what men said," were "unnecessary and harmful" and had invariably been used "to prevent and punish criticism of the government." He wrote that he doubted whether "any speech or writing should be made criminal," and dolefully admitted that he had come to regret authorizing the Minneapolis prosecution, conceding that "there had been no substantial overt act outside of talk and threats, openly expressed in the time-honored Marxist lingo." He had done it, Biddle recalled, because as a new man on the job, anxious to make an impression on his colleagues and boss, he had surrendered to an "instinct to display firmness on appropriate occasions."[68]

Biddle's retrospective critique of his actions bore the imprint of the time in which it was written. In 1962 the nation had just come through a second Red Scare. As concerns about internal security receded, faith in free speech re-emerged. American Communists and their assumed conspiratorial designs now seemed less threatening and public fears the work of reactionary politicians. A series of Supreme Court decisions had recently gutted the Smith Act, and the Trotskyite case no doubt seemed sillier in retrospect than it had at the time. In these circumstances Biddle preferred to present his actions in 1941 as the product of momentary weakness, rather than of calculated policy.

There was much to Biddle's candid explanation—his desire to impress doubters with his toughness surely played a large part in the story. But the prosecution of the Trotskyites grew out of genuine (though perhaps misplaced) administration concerns about Communist interference in defense production, and it was the consensus within the department that the Smith Act should be used against Communist functionaries. Biddle, who shared these feelings, probably did have reservations about the Smith Act and was attracted to the *Abrams* reading of "clear and present danger," but there was enough doubt about these matters among the legal experts that he could comfortably subordinate them to the need to strike at "Communism." Once the prosecutorial machine had been set in motion, the goal of winning this case, and strengthening the government's hand against other accused seditionists, overcame any misgivings Biddle and the others may have felt about the merits of "clear and present danger," or the dangers of the Smith Act. In short, conflicting impulses—an intellectual commitment to tolerance of loathsome (but harmless) expression, and the need to act forcefully to save the nation and assert himself—were at war in Biddle's mind as he took over the duties of attorney general. The struggle would continue for the remainder of the Second World War.

Chapter 9

Free Speech for Fascists?

On December 7, 1941, Japanese forces attacked the American naval base at Pearl Harbor in the Hawaiian Islands. A few days later, Germany and Italy declared war on the United States. After months of tension and undeclared hostilities, the Axis had thrust the country into war. While there was little of the crusading spirit that animated the nation in 1917–18, the earlier missionary zeal was replaced by the grim determination of a people whose nation had been attacked. This was a war for survival, the president suggested, and most Americans agreed.

Nevertheless, a small minority challenged the war's righteousness, denigrated the nation's military efforts, castigated the president, criticized America's allies, and sympathized with its enemies. The dissidents, most of whom had long been alienated from American society, saw the war as the inevitable consequence of the immoral and perverted course the nation had been steering for more than a decade. For them, the conflict served no legitimate American interests, and they believed it should be promptly ended through negotiations.

Some of those who expressed these views were unreconstructed prewar isolationists, but most were more generally disaffected Americans who believed that national affairs were controlled by a vast international conspiracy of Jews, Communists, (international) bankers, and British. For weeks, even after the Pearl Harbor attack, their strident, hate-filled ranting filled the pages of dozens of low-circulation sheets and resounded in small auditoriums across the nation. Soon, concerned Americans, led by liberal publicists, were demanding that Attorney General Biddle suppress the antiwar agitation—and punish the dissenters, whom they commonly referred to as "fascists" or "seditionists." Biddle held back, convinced that the war's critics were protected by the First Amendment. It was a position that would be denounced by antifascists, most of them liberals, and ultimately earn him a rebuke from the president. By the spring of 1942 the Justice Department had embarked on a campaign of suppression aimed at the fascists and designed primarily to satisfy the attorney general's critics.

The fascist phenomenon was far past its prime and declining as the United States entered the war.[1] Extremist dissent came mostly from the same persons, most of them mere curiosities who had gained a measure of notoriety in the early 1930s—Charles Coughlin, Gerald Winrod, William Dudley Pelley, et al. But the economic discontent and social upheaval on which they thrived in the Depression decade had subsided during the defense-generated boom of the 1940s, and their extremist rhetoric and association with Nazi ideology had gained them few converts in recent years.[2] There seemed little likelihood that the fascist menagerie would regain even its earlier modest popularity.

The signs of its defeat were everywhere in 1941. German-American Bund fuehrer Fritz Kuhn was in jail, and in January the Dies Committee released what purported to be a confidential German government document "proving" that the organization was a puppet of the Nazi government.[3] Coughlin, the "radio priest," was off the air. James True (known mostly for his "kike killer" club) and pioneering anti-Semitic pamphleteer Robert Edmondson had discontinued their publications. Silver Shirt mystic William Dudley Pelley had disbanded his organization and would spend most of the year attempting to avoid being jailed on charges brought against him in North Carolina.[4] Even so, almost anyone who could command a printing press or commandeer a soapbox could still count on an audience—and a reaction from worried antifascists.

Concerns prospered on sensational and irritating reports from the fascistic subculture. American fascists were closely watched and repeatedly exposed. Here was no underground conspiracy, but a well examined and publicized phenomenon. Its propaganda was analyzed by the scholarly Institute for Propaganda Analysis[5] and denigrated by a number of other organizations that promoted democratic values or espoused intervention.[6] Fascist groups were infiltrated and their leaders' speeches recorded by freelance journalists and investigators. John Roy Carlson was the most successful such infiltrator. Engaged in 1939 by Russell W. Davenport, the managing editor of *Fortune* magazine, to survey the New York fascist scene, and later paid by the FBI for the same service, Carlson began an odyssey through the fascist underground that led to the publication in 1943 of the sensational and enormously popular *Under Cover.*[7] Carlson and others interested in exposing the fascist network received help from the Reverend Leon Birkhead's Friends of Democracy, which tracked the un-Americans nationally, kept extensive files documenting their activity, and produced and distributed counter-propaganda.[8] Birkhead's efforts were supplemented by the *Hour,* a newsletter established in 1939 by the American Council Against Nazi Propaganda, which enjoyed great success in placing antifascist material in the mainstream press and into the hands of government officials.[9] Jewish defense groups, especially the Anti-Defamation League of B'nai Brith (ADL), helped finance and otherwise assist these and similar activities.[10] British officials, who were convinced that Americans did not take domestic fascism seriously enough, also provided the government and the media with information.[11] Anti-fascist accounts were often picked up and repeated by the liberal weeklies and, increasingly, by national journals and daily newspapers. The publication and republication of these exposés had the ironic effect of feeding the egos of the fascists while stoking the ire of the antifascists. An American Jewish Committee official, commenting on that organization's contribution to the exposure, noted that he had decided to ration the information he gave to the press because "the crackpots" so loved publicity.[12]

Motives for active antifascism varied. Jews, aware of the palpable and potential consequences of anti-Semitic agitation, had an obvious interest in its destruction, as did liberals who saw anti-Semitism as a mainstay of the irrational forces threatening the nation and an oft-employed tool of reactionary movements. Ellen Herman has written of the influence of social psychologists like Gordon Allport and Harold Lasswell who, seeking the sources and cures for what they saw as a national malaise, concluded that racism (as anti-Semitism was seen) was "'unquestionably the weakest spot in our national character' and 'a moral cancer that must be controlled before it kills.'"[13] Historian John Higham has noted that in the 1930s, "anti-Semitism became the 'classic prejudice'; a sure indicator of the authoritarian personality, and a litmus-paper test of the racial nationalism that liberals were fighting."[14]

The inevitable anti-Semitic component of fascistic propaganda naturally raised concerns in some quarters that such talk would increase anti-Jewish sentiment. This does not seem to have been the case. Asked in March 1944 if anti-Semitism was on the rise, Roger Baldwin commented that "it would be more accurate to say that the awareness of anti-Semitism and its dangers have increased, but not the evidences of it."[15] He went on the declare that the fascistic agitators were not to be taken seriously. "They have never had any influence except in very limited circles and attracted no support by the powerful interests which, in the event of a crisis, might lead the country towards fascism."[16]

Liberals, while angered, and perhaps worried, by the fascist phenomenon, also saw it as offering an opportunity to discredit their more respectable and dangerous enemies on the Right. Liberals depicted the Second World War as an apocalyptic struggle "against the whole [fascistic] future society" that threatened both America and the world.[17] With the war polarizing and delineating the forces of progress and those of reaction, it was now possible to reveal America's powerful reactionaries as aligned with world fascism. A crackdown on domestic fascism, liberals seemed to believe, would rid the country of hate-filled and divisive rhetoric. In the process it promised to discredit the political Right by convincing the public that America's racial bigots, political reactionaries, and narrow-minded chauvinists were somehow in league with the Axis enemy.[18]

Regardless of its political or ideological utility, a campaign against fascism was bound to be emotionally satisfying. Fascistic rhetoric was loathsome and often directed at the much revered president. Simple decency demanded not only that it be stopped, but that the purveyors of the filth be punished. Three pamphlets that circulated in the Detroit area in the fall of 1940 were typical of the rhetoric that evoked such feelings: "The British an Inferior Breed," "The Jew Makes a Sacrifice," and "The Diseased Spinal Cord."[19] The last of these suggests the tone of the "criticism."

> "Crush my enemies" screams Jewry; "be bold, take the offensive; we'll back you up." "We're fighting for freedom," says our leader, with his sick body coiled around the brain as with a snake prepared to strike. "We are fighting to save Poland" say the British hysterically; "we hate other peoples aggression." . . .
>
> "I dare you to hit me" said our leader to the "bad" dictators. He now twists on his weak spine as . . . many are beginning to recoil with horror from a proposed invasion of Americans who, as before, would only accentuate world revolution.

Before the war, such material had to be tolerated. As Attorney General Jackson explained to the president in regard to a similar opus, the only way to get at such writings was through a prosecution for criminal libel. But, he noted, this was most unlikely to succeed. There was, in fact, nothing practical that could be done,[20] and the author of the "Diseased Spinal Cord" and those of similar offerings continued to distribute their work with impunity.[21] The frustrating inability of the government to respond to such exercises of free expression encouraged FDR and his supporters to welcome the opportunity afforded by the war to use the anti-sedition statutes against the purveyors of fascistic invective.

The antifascist agenda notwithstanding, the Justice Department entered the war committed to a policy of restraint. There were no plans for an assault on fascistic expression. Remembering the overreaction of World War I, the department projected a carefully limited response. For more than a year before the war, the FBI had been identifying persons suspected of being a danger to national security in the event of an outbreak of hostilities. The Neutrality Laws Division had classified these people according to the degree of threat they were thought to pose, and, should hostilities break out, aliens in the most dangerous category would be rounded up immediately. Others on the "suspect list," including citizens identified as potentially threatening, would be dealt with by appropriate administrative action (denial of defense employment, etc.), and watched until their activities brought them clearly across the line of legality. The list, taken together with Jackson's order requiring the FBI and the U.S. attorneys to secure the attorney general's authorization of any action against persons suspected of disloyalty or sedition,[22] was meant to ensure that there would be no dragnet, excessive detentions, or unwarranted prosecutions.[23] There would be no persecution of dissidents based solely on their views or associations. At least that was the intention.

When the Japanese struck at Pearl Harbor, however, the plan was abandoned as officials frantically sought to cope with the sudden crisis. Hours after the attack, Hoover asked Solicitor General Charles Fahy, who was the senior member of the Justice Department committee that oversaw the emergency detention program, whether arrests were to be limited to those suspects whose dangerousness had been assessed and classified. Fahy, aware that the process (and list) were not complete, and wishing, as he later said, to avoid the hysteria and vigilante activity that an incomplete roundup might produce, told the director to use his own judgment.[24] FBI agents began taking people into custody without regard to the suspect list and without securing any further authority from the Department of Justice. Blank warrants, provided by the department under a presidential proclamation issued on December 8, were used to effect most arrests, but in some instances, suspects were seized without any warrant. Within two weeks, federal agents had arrested about three thousand persons. The overwhelming majority were citizens of Japan, Germany, or Italy, and thus technically "enemy aliens." But non-enemy aliens and citizens (at least 46, according to an FBI report) were also taken in and detained.[25]

Among those seized were Robert Noble and Ellis Jones, a pair who represented a major strain of American fascism. Noble was a longtime peddler of political nostrums of the kind for which California was justly famous. He had supported socialist Upton Sinclair's bid for governor in 1934 and worked for Huey Long's Share Our Wealth project, the California Technocrats, and the Ham and Eggs movements.[26] His collaborator, Ellis Jones, was a pacifist who had been aboard Henry Ford's "Peace Ark" in 1915, and opposed American involvement in the First World War. A socialist as well, he had been arrested for allegedly seditious remarks made after the armistice.[27] In 1941 he was a member of the Executive Committee of the southern California branch of the American Civil Liberties Union, and had in recent years been beaten by vigilantes for his part in defending the rights of farm workers in California's Imperial Valley. An ACLU official who knew both men described Noble as a "racketeer and demagogue and probably a little 'cracked'," and Jones as "apparently honest," but "more 'cracked' than Noble."[28]

Shortly after the Japanese attacked Pearl Harbor, Noble and Jones had conducted a meeting of Friends of Progress at which Jones reportedly declared that the Japanese had a right to Hawaii ("There are more of them there than there are Americans"), and announced that he would "rather be on the side of Germany than on the side of the British." Noble praised Hitler and the "good job" Japan had done in the Pacific."[29] Acting on the authority of the U.S. attorney in Los Angeles, federal agents arrested the two men and several associates, charging them with uttering false statements with "intent to interfere with the success of the military or naval forces of the United States"—violations of the Espionage Act of 1917.

The arrest of Noble and Jones was a clear sign of the failure of months of effort to ensure a measured response to crisis. For while their utterances were obnoxious, they were threatening only to those who had little confidence in the American people's loyalty or common sense. Joseph Prendergast, deputy director of L. M. C. Smith's Neutrality Laws Division (now called the Special War Policy Unit), angrily submitted his resignation in protest. The attorney general hastily responded by ordering the release of those seized by "mistake,"[30] and he cautioned officials against unnecessarily interfering with free speech. The following day a department press release explained that "free speech as such ought not to be restricted by punishment unless it clearly appears that such speech will cause direct and dangerous interference with the conduct of the war."[31] "Direct and dangerous," somewhat more demanding than the "clear and present" standard, had first been proposed by Chafee in 1918.[32]

Biddle often referred to these slogans and Holmes's dissent in the *Abrams* case to suggest the limited circumstances in which speech might legitimately be suppressed. In his reverential 1942 biography of Justice Oliver Wendell Holmes, Jr., he wrote that he hoped that a general acceptance of the wisdom of the great dissenter's eloquent defense of freedom might help the nation avoid a recurrence of the public hysteria that had sent too many Americans off to prison in the last war.[33]

For Biddle, the words of the West Coast fascists did not constitute a danger that demanded government suppression. His correspondence reveals no sense of outrage at fascist activities, no fear that they could harm national interests.[34] Noble and Jones, he told a newspaper interviewer, had committed no crimes and could not be arrested simply because they were "s.o.b.s."[35] It was "better in most instances," he said on another occasion, "to ignore the senseless hissings of the human safety-valve [a Holmes metaphor] than to invoke the dangerous procedures of too hasty prosecution. . . . Hysteria must gain no foothold in the execution of our purpose."[36] Worried about local or vigilante efforts, Biddle instructed the U.S. attorneys to prevent and punish violations of federally secured civil rights.[37]

The attorney general's attitude proved to be an invitation to crackpot bravado. A pamphlet distributed by Noble after Biddle had ordered his release proclaimed that "the U.S. Attorney General says we have a perfect right to talk—and we will."[38] And they did. Extremist agitators were soon thumping their podiums and turning their presses as if they had nothing to fear. Every Sunday night a "World Events Forum"—sponsored by what was unsympathetically described as a combination of "ex–America Firsters, Bundists, Ham and Eggers, and three or four other types of group joiners"—met in the Embassy Auditorium in Los Angeles in late December and early January to expatiate on: "No business in this war; Roosevelt got us into this; International Bankers; conditions in India [a slap at the British, not intended as endorsement of the Indians]; Jewish Marxism, etc., etc."[39] Noble and Jones also presided over mock hangings of the president and ridiculed General Douglas MacArthur and his efforts to defend the Philippines.

Military developments in the early months of the war made this kind of talk particularly difficult to tolerate. The Japanese "sneak attack" on Pearl Harbor had been followed by an unbroken series of setbacks for the United States and its allies. A few days after Noble and Jones were released, Wake Island and Guam fell to the Japanese. On Christmas day, the British surrendered Hong Kong. In February, Singapore, the "Gibraltar of the

East," surrendered and sixty-two thousand Allied troops ignominiously marched into Japanese captivity. In early April, seventy-six thousand American and Filipino troops capitulated, and what remained of America's Far Eastern empire was confined to Corregidor Island, whose defenders awaited their fate. American morale and tolerance were low. In the midst of catastrophe, Biddle's courageous restraint looked like stupidity or worse.

With Noble and Jones now back on the rostrum in California, complaints from that state were soon echoing throughout the media. Thanks to the national press services and the work of antifascists who made a point of tracking and publicizing such utterances, almost any disloyal statement, though delivered in the most obscure forum, was apt to capture national attention. Soon, columnist Dorothy Thompson, well known for her acerbic wit and antifascist convictions, was pointing a finger, first at the seditionists, and then at Biddle. Thompson wrote of a vast "Fascio-Nazi organization network" openly and secretly collaborating on the West Coast with "the Japs," while the Justice Department sought to deal with the problem by picking up a leader here and there. "I'm no hysteric," she began an overwrought syndicated column published at the end of February, but the current procedure for dealing with the "internal enemy" is as outmoded as "cavalry against a Blitz." Biddle, she wrote, in the patronizing tone in which criticism of the attorney general was frequently couched, was a "humane man," but he was oblivious to the new face of subversion. "The whole world," she declared, is "honeycombed with a gigantic conspiracy" (just what the "fascists" contended), and the situation demanded the wholesale roundup of the conspiracy's American leaders, the blacklisting of its members, and surveillance of its fellow travelers. While denying that she advocated vigilantism, she insisted that in the absence of government action "the organized people" had to do the job.[40] Her sentiments were echoed by respected columnist Roscoe Drummond and America's premier political pundit, Walter Lippmann.[41]

By mid-January the problem of fascist agitators on the West Coast was swallowed up in demands, to which the president was sympathetic, for the removal of the Japanese Americans and for stringent controls on the coast's alien population. An overwhelmed Biddle was soon in retreat. Although he rejected the massive roundups that the army wanted, he was prepared to "wink at" the probable cause requirement that requests for search warrants usually demanded. He was apparently willing to see the rights of the Nisei violated so long as the Justice Department was not directly involved.[42]

It was in the context of a crackdown on the West Coast "fifth column" that the president raised the issue of fascistic agitation that Biddle thought he had put to rest. Three weeks into the new year Roosevelt wrote a short note to Hoover asking what was being done about William Dudley Pelley, the Hitler-hailing, anti-Semitic mystic who was free on bail pending appeal of his conviction for fraud in North Carolina. FDR's note was very likely provoked by a piece in the *Hour,* the antifascist newsletter that was a principal source of information on fascistic doings. A few days after receiving an issue that featured Pelley's recent activities, the president wrote Hoover noting that he had learned that Pelley had "started a new publication called 'The Galilean' and that some of the stuff appearing therein comes pretty close to being seditious. Now that we are in the war," he concluded, "it looks like a good chance to clean up a number of these vile publications."[43]

The phrasing of the note is suggestive. The president did not say that national security demanded the suppression of fascistic rhetoric, but rather that the war offered an opportunity to accomplish a little (overdue) housecleaning. Significantly, he characterized Pelley's remarks as "pretty close to being seditious." "Pretty close" was not close enough for the law and may explain why the president approached Hoover rather than his attorney general. He wanted "something" done. What that something was, he left to the director. FDR may have had in mind the earlier arbitrary arrest of Noble and Jones.

But the director refused to act. An FBI report that Hoover submitted to the president in late January explained that the bureau's attempts to intimidate the antiwar fringe elements by arresting Noble, Jones, and a few others had been frustrated by the attorney general.[44] In March, when the president again urged the bureau to do something about seditious agitation, the director insisted that his hands were tied and that if the president wanted something done, he would have to tell the attorney general himself.[45] FDR confronted Biddle at the weekly Friday cabinet meeting that same day, demanding to know what was being done about the publications of Pelley and his ilk, thus initiating a none-to-subtle process of intimidation. As Biddle later described it, FDR first let him know by his manner that he considered him "out of step," then "he began to go for me in the Cabinet." When it was the attorney general's turn to report, FDR dropped his "habitual affability . . . looked at me, his face pulled tightly together . . . 'when are you going to indict the seditionists?'"[46] The cabinet members supported the president.

Biddle was not convinced that the fascists posed a threat to the war effort, and he was concerned that prosecuting them raised serious questions of principle and law. But these issues were not thrashed out at the cabinet meetings, which ordinarily were more ceremonial than deliberative.[47] There seems to have been no debate of the issues that had shaped the civil liberties controversy over the past 25 years. Rather than quoting Holmes to FDR, Biddle sought to justify his failure to act by pointing to the inadequacy of existing law. It was not an absence of will or a matter of principle, but a lack of authority.

Biddle's reputation and his job were on the line. In a friendly note, James Rowe, his principal assistant and political advisor, noted that the attorney general and the department were being talked of as "civil liberties boys" and "softies." A number of people, Rowe wrote, including the gossip columnist/broadcaster Walter Winchell, persons close to the president, and senior military officials, were apparently determined to hound Biddle out of office and replace him with someone "tougher."[48] The military's dissatisfaction, brought to the president's attention by Army Chief of Staff George C. Marshall, focused on the situation on the West Coast where the Justice Department's insistence on time-consuming hearings before it would approve the removal of individual suspect aliens had left that potentially dangerous element at large.[49] Shades of Groton, Biddle may well have thought. A friend had warned him—the big boys had it in for him and he had better mend his ways quickly or suffer the consequences. But there was no easy way out for the attorney general—not, at least, under the law.

The statutes, as potentially repressive as they were, were not easily applied to fascist agitation. The Smith Act's provisions outlawing the advocacy of the overthrow of the government by force were not applicable to the native fascist groups or to the Bundists since a call to revolution formed no part of their doctrine or message.[50] The only portion of the law that might be made to apply to the likes of Noble and Jones was the section that punished efforts to undermine the morale, discipline, or loyalty of members of the armed forces. Here the difficulty for the government lay in establishing that their words were in fact addressed to members of the military. The 1917 Espionage Act, which had come into effect with the declarations of war against the Axis powers, outlawed making false statements with intent to interfere with the war effort; willfully attempting to cause insubordination in the military, or obstructing recruiting or enlistment. But even in World War I, when free-speech doctrine was in its infancy and the government's right to suppress expression was generally accepted, the department had found the act's scope limited. The courts had held that the government was required to prove actual obstruction, not mere attempts, and officials concluded that they would be obliged to prove that the defendant's remarks were not only addressed to persons who were in the military, subject to the draft, or eligible to enlist, but were *willfully intended* to dissuade them from loyal service. Department officials also worried that the Court would hold them to a libertarian interpretation of the "clear and present danger" standard.[51]

Biddle, like Jackson before him, seems to have been willing to put aside his free-speech scruples if he could find the appropriate legal authority. What he needed, he told the cabinet, was reenactment of the 1918 Sedition Act (which had expired at the end of the war)—the statute under which Abrams had been convicted. The Act, an amendment to the 1917 Espionage Act, had been secured by Attorney General Gregory to remedy the difficulty he was having in punishing statements hostile to the war or the government where these were "made from good motives, or . . . [where] traitorous motives were not provable." The amendment outlawed *any* "disloyal, profane, scurrilous, or abusive language intended to cause contempt, scorn, contumely or disrepute as regards the form of government . . . the flag . . . [as well as any] words or acts supporting or favoring the cause of any country . . . opposing the cause of the United States. . . ."[52] No doubt a revival of this law would have put an end to seditious speech in the United States.

In January 1942, Representative Herman Eberhardter of Pennsylvania introduced a bill intended to reinstitute the 1918 law, but passage was unlikely. With Communist agitation no longer a major issue, there was little support among Republicans and conservative Democrats for legislation that would extend the administration's reach. Despite public-spirited pledges, partisanship had not been suspended for the duration, and the isolationist contingent in Congress in particular was suspicious that the president was looking for an opportunity to get even with or intimidate his foreign-policy critics.[53]

Administration words and initiatives fed the suspicions. In February, Biddle responded to the *Chicago Tribune's* publication, on the eve of the Pearl Harbor attack, of the War Department's super-secret "Victory Program" by proposing a war-secrets bill that would have imposed severe penalties on anyone who published any information the government labeled "secret." The effort was immediately condemned in some responsible quarters as an "assault on democratic practices."[54] At about the same time, FDR suggested that there was an American "Cliveden Set," alluding to the group of anti-Communist, fascist-minded Britons who had supposedly met at Lady Nancy Astor's estate to plot appeasement policy before the war, and in March, Roosevelt spoke of a "sixth column" of defeatist journalists and others who spread rumors emanating from the fifth column.[55]

Suspicions of the administration's supposed vindictive and repressive instincts were encouraged by the difficulties experienced by Representative Hamilton Fish, the isolationist, anti-Communist New York Republican who had collaborated with the prewar anti-interventionist America First movement. His troubles with the administration dated back to October 1941, when a special grand jury in Washington, D.C., that had been investigating foreign propaganda activities indicted George Sylvester Viereck, a paid propagandist for the German government, for failing to register as an agent of a foreign government. Later in the month, Fish's secretary, George Hill, was indicted for perjury for lying about his involvement with Viereck in an elaborate scheme whereby German propaganda was distributed from congressional offices using the postage-free franking privileges of various isolationist congressmen, including Fish. Two days before Pearl Harbor, the grand jury had called the congressman, and a gleeful liberal press sought to depict him as part of the nation's fascist conspiracy. Leaks of evidence submitted to the grand jury suggested that a number of right-wing and isolationist congressmen had distributed material supplied by individuals linked to Axis propaganda agents. Hill and Viereck were convicted[56] and Fish feared that he would be indicted.[57] Liberal journalists closely followed the Capitol Hill saga[58] and presumably would have liked nothing better than an official exposé of Fish and other congressional isolationists focusing on their alleged Axis ties.

It did not happen, but the threat, together with other reports suggesting the president's hostility to the loyal opposition, made it unlikely that the Congress would agree to expand the administration's repressive authority. Indeed, despite suggestions that restrictions on wiretapping had contributed to the surprise at Pearl Harbor, a bill and several joint resolutions aimed at authorizing tapping by the attorney general were defeated in 1942.[59] Not unexpectedly, the Eberhardter bill never emerged from the House Judiciary Committee.

But with or without the law, Biddle was determined to satisfy his critics.[60] At a press conference on March 25, he set forth the rationale for the reversal of the tolerant policy toward antiwar dissent he had lately affirmed. Just as his biography of Holmes, praising the great jurist's free speech strictures, appeared in bookstores, Biddle declared his mentor's words dated and inapplicable. Conditions had changed. Propaganda was a weapon of war and certain utterances might have to be considered equivalent to seditious acts. Action was called for, and the attorney general promised it would be forthcoming. "We are now ready to shoot and we are going to shoot very quickly."[61]

Two days later, the department announced that the FBI had arrested Rudolph Fahl, a former Denver high school physical education instructor, and Tennessean George W. Christians, the leader of the Crusader White Shirts. Fahl was charged with having told army officers they were suckers for serving and for believing that they were fighting for democracy.[62] Christians, characterized by one-time Roosevelt braintruster Raymond Moley as a "harmless lunatic," wore a little mustache and his forelock down over his forehead, á la Hitler.[63] He was accused of violating the Smith Act by "communicating to soldiers statements designed to impair their morale." On March 31, Noble and Jones, who had been released on Biddle's orders in December, were once again taken into custody,[64] and four days later, FBI agents seized Pelley. Each was charged with violation of the Espionage Act for encouraging insubordination in the military.[65]

The department's announcement that it had bagged this pathetic handful met with general approval, but did not totally satisfy the demand for repression. *Time,* in an article entitled "Milquetoast Gets Muscles," welcomed the news that the "bald, bantam-beaked" attorney general was "cracking down at last on U.S. citizens who love the Axis."[66] But most of the press, led by a relatively small but influential group of liberal journalists, demanded more. Most Americans remained ignorant of what liberals identified as the fascist conspiracy in the United States.[67] A well-publicized government investigation and prosecution of the culprits could do what the antifascist press could not.[68] Just as conservatives had made, and would continue to make, political capital out of the overlapping of liberal and Communist positions, so liberals now hoped to score political points against conservatives, non-interventionists, and Republicans by identifying them with the Nazis.[69]

Roger Baldwin and a few others, including John Haynes Holmes, Arthur Garfield Hays, and Norman Thomas, keeping what Baldwin called the "traditional" ACLU perspective on events, challenged the logic of using government repression to further democratic goals. Given that "the propaganda of the more or less Fascist-minded crackpots cannot be distinguished from the more subtle propaganda of considerable sections of the American press," where, Baldwin asked, would militant liberals end their attempt to purge the nation of its fascist influences?[70] Would they silence all "fascistic" newspapers, including the *Chicago Tribune?* And what about African-American publications that "protest against democratic pretenses" and the pacifist organizations that support a negotiated peace? Starting down the road of repression, Baldwin warned, would take the United States to extremes greater than those witnessed in World War I. And to what end? Repression, he predicted, would spread the message of the "crackpot fringe" while leaving the powerful large-circulation dailies untouched. The answer to anti-democratic propaganda, he argued, was exposure and counter-propaganda, and no more.

Although Baldwin was reluctant to publicly oppose the essentially friendly and liberal authorities in Washington, at his instigation the ACLU rebuked the attorney general for his "disturbing reversion to the sorry tactics of World War I."[71] Privately, in commenting on the department's announced anti-sedition plans, Baldwin pointed Biddle to the British experience which, he suggested, demonstrated that draconian measures were unnecessary, even in a nation far more vulnerable to Axis attack. In its first two-and-a-half years at war, he wrote, Great Britain had not instituted a single anti-sedition prosecution.[72] Baldwin was off the mark. Although the British prosecuted few for seditious utterances, they were guilty of a great deal of arbitrary and unjustified suppression of persons suspected of opposing the government and its war policies. What misled Baldwin was the fact that repression was carried out not by prosecution, but through the more egregious process of "executive detention," which involved no trial and little publicity.[73]

Baldwin asked the organization's counsel, Arthur Garfield Hays, to write Biddle, who he said, "is evidently being pushed around as he has been so many times."[74] Hays would oblige, but his efforts to get longtime allies to join him in petitioning the attorney general were rebuffed. One friend, in turning down Hays's request, replied that today's anti-Semitic rabble-rousers could not be considered akin to the "innocent martyrs to popular war passion," whose rights civil libertarians had championed in the last war.[75] The *Nation's* Freda Kirchwey insisted that misplaced fears of indiscriminate repression had led some libertarians to "underestimate the capacity of a liberal government—with a liberal Attorney General—to distinguish between enemies and traitors on the one hand and loyal critics on the other." The "treason press in the United States, small or large," she insisted, was "an integral part of the fascist offensive" and "should be exterminated exactly as if they were enemy machine-gun nests in the Bataan jungle."[76] Liberals distanced themselves from Baldwin's civil libertarianism. Kirchwey resigned her ACLU membership as did the indefatigable champion of minority rights, Carey McWilliams. Baldwin gave up trying to convince them to hold fast to his view of civil liberties. "It is hopeless to argue the case with our so-called liberal friends who labor under the obsession that civil rights in wartime exist only for their friends."[77]

Emphasizing the limits on free speech rather than its value required calling upon new historical lessons. For years, liberals had looked to the repressive horrors of World War I as a warning of the evils that would befall the nation should it again betray its heritage of freedom. Those lessons were now forgotten as liberals looked past the Great Crusade to the Civil War to speak approvingly of Abraham Lincoln's stern treatment of Southern sympathizers. Essayist Bernard DeVoto insisted that the current situation was much closer to that faced by Lincoln than it was to the imagined domestic crisis of World War I, and *PM,* the daily tabloid established in 1940 as an outlet for militant liberalism in New York, found in Lincoln's treatment of "the Coughlin problems of his day," the appropriate model for FDR and Biddle.[78]

The reorientation of civil libertarian thinking that had begun in 1939 reached its intellectual apogee with the appearance in 1942 of a long article by David Riesman called "Civil Liberties in Transition." It was one of a series of pieces he wrote during the war under a special research fellowship from the Columbia University Law School.[79] In them, Riesman, then a law professor, later renowned for *The Lonely Crowd,* called for a rethinking of what he described as the uncertain goals and unrealistic principles of current thought on free speech. "The negativism and 'objectivity' of a certain group of influential liberals [referring, no doubt, to Baldwin, Hays, and company] who wish to protect freedom of speech without any exploration of what free speech is for,"[80] he suggested, made as much sense as denying government a responsibility to police the economy. If public discourse was to serve its legitimate function of promoting social and political progress, then society, operating through government, must play a "selective and discriminating" role in seeing to it that deserving groups had (exclusive?) access to the public.[81]

Riesman was primarily interested in serving reform goals by breaking the virtual monopoly the wealthy had on the mass media. He was less clear on how the government should respond to the dozens of fascistic sheets that currently claimed the public's interest. Although he rejected the slogan of "no tolerance for the intolerant" sometimes heard in liberal circles, noting that it would probably wind up being used by the reactionaries "to harass unpopular or weak minorities,"[82] his observations seemed to imply the suppression of fascist speech. For if the government was assumed to be capable of discriminating between positive and negative speech, then surely it had as much responsibility to suppress the latter as it had to promote the former.

Baldwin, recognizing the importance of what historian Norman Rosenberg has described as Riesman's call for "reconstructing civil liberties discourse,"[83] distributed copies of "Civil Liberties in Transition" to members of the ACLU Board and announced a special conference to debate the article. Riesman declined Baldwin's invitation to participate, and the debate never took place. Riesman's explanation, which he supplied years later, is instructive. He had written the attack on civil libertarian assumptions, he declared, for those already committed to civil liberties, "not for the unenlightened . . . [and] I felt that before a large lay audience [that would witness the debate], I would prefer to support Baldwin on certain major issues rather than attack him on minor ones."[84] The issues he raised were hardly minor, but Riesman's alternatives to Baldwin's orthodoxy were not nearly as clear or compelling as was his criticism and its implications. No doubt he was concerned that his work would provide ammunition to those who would destroy the flawed and beleaguered free-speech culture that Holmes, Chafee, Baldwin, and others had painfully shaped, without ensuring the adoption of the positive civil libertarianism he espoused.

Riesman's dilemma was reflected in the controversy that split the ACLU leadership.[85] Samuel Walker notes in his outstanding history of the organization that during the war the Civil Liberties Union came to be dominated by an alliance of conservatives, militant liberals, and leftists who were inclined to support the government's efforts against the fifth column.[86] The coalition succeeded in limiting the organization's response to the removal of the West Coast Japanese Americans, and at the end of April blocked the efforts of Baldwin and Hays to provide legal assistance to accused fascists Christians and Fahl.[87] In July, after reaffirming its attachment to the "clear and present danger" test, the Board concluded that it would not "participate in any way in the defense" of the nine persons who had thus far been charged with sedition. The defendants, it reasoned, were adequately represented, and the atmosphere surrounding the trials did not suggest "unfair procedure or undue pressure." The ACLU would only monitor the trials to determine whether intervention on appeal was called for.[88]

For more than 20 years, liberals had extolled the generous meaning Holmes had given to free speech in *Abrams*. Now, confronted with the pernicious activities of American fascists and a chance to strike a blow against the American Right, they resurrected the restrictive spin Holmes had put on "clear and present danger" in the earlier *Schenck* decision. In four months of war, the free-speech ideals Chafee, Baldwin, and others had constructed out of the Holmes/Brandeis dissents lost the support of the group most closely associated with free speech. Yet the ideal retained a certain cachet, and the courts had yet to be heard from. What remained to be seen was how far Biddle and the government would go to carry out the demands of liberal pundits and the White House that fascistic speech be stamped out.

Chapter 10

Nazi Themes and "Dirty Little Sheets": Postal Censorship

Attorney General Biddle's commitment to do something about fascistic agitation ran into the poor fit between the actions of accused seditionists and the acts prohibited by existing anti-sedition law. Biddle sought to expand his repressive authority by turning to Congress, but with prospects for the passage of more draconian legislation low, the attorney general felt obliged to press his staff to seek creative approaches under existing law that would meet political demands. The effort drew officials to tactics they knew were questionable. Putting aside their doubts, department officials did their duty.

The circulation of obnoxious antiwar and anti-Semitic publications was a chief source of irritation to antifascists. Fortunately for them, the way in which most such publications were distributed happened to make this form of propaganda vulnerable to a controversial provision of the Espionage Act of 1917 that authorized postal authorities to refuse to accept for delivery any second- or third-class mail whose content was, in their judgment, seditious. The act also gave them the authority to ban in advance any issue of a periodically appearing publication that had appeared consistently disloyal. First-class mail, which under law could not be opened and could not be evaluated, was unaffected. The law provided for quick summary judgments—the accused publisher had no right to a trial, and the only issue appealable was whether postal authorities had acted in accord with the rules they themselves had created. In this respect the authority of the postmaster general was analogous to that of the attorney general in deportation cases. It was assumed that use of the mails was a privilege extended at the government's sufferance (akin to the residence granted aliens) that could be withdrawn at the government's discretion.[1]

Refusal to mail was not exactly censorship, but it was close. Rejection at the post office did not prevent publishers from printing the material and distributing it through privately owned means. Those who wished to broadcast their ideas could throw leaflets out of windows (as the defendants in the *Abrams* case did), or mail them first class at great expense. But second-class mail enabled wide distribution at low cost, and the success of most periodicals, radical and otherwise, depended on this subsidized form of postal delivery. Withdrawing the "privilege" was an effective way of putting all but the most determined, or well endowed, publisher or pamphleteer out of business.

When the Espionage Act came into effect with the declaration of a state of war between the United States and Japan, local postmasters were immediately empowered to refuse to accept for delivery material that they believed conveyed false reports intended to interfere with the military, promote the nation's enemies, encourage disloyalty in the military, or obstruct recruitment. Although some local officials acted under the law, there was at first no systematic effort to curb the fascist press.[2] This changed in the third week of March 1942 when, in response to the president's demands, Biddle and senior department officials worked out with the postmaster general a plan by which they would cooperate in the identification of publications that would be denied the reduced mailing rates.[3] The prime target was to be Father Charles Coughlin's *Social Justice.*

Although Coughlin's radio days were over and his influence significantly diminished, his journal, *Social Justice,* with an estimated circulation of two hundred thousand, was far and away the most widely read of the virulently anti-administration/antiwar publications.[4] Its appeal was populist, and its style, in contrast to the diatribes often found in the rest of the fascistic press, relatively subdued. Some issues, which ran about 14 pages, were sold on street corners and at the rallies of isolationist and fascist factions, but most were distributed by second-class mail.

The administration had long been troubled by Coughlin, and even before the war FDR had worked behind the scenes with the American Catholic hierarchy and Vatican representatives to silence the priest. But all Coughlin's ecclesiastical superiors had been able to achieve was the severance of his *formal* ties to *Social Justice.*[5] Control remained, unofficially, in Coughlin's hands, and he used it chiefly to fight the administration's interventionist foreign policy. When the United States entered the war, the editor suggested that *Social Justice* would support the common effort, but issues were soon featuring pieces critical of the sacrifices asked in the name of the war effort, magnifying administration mistakes, belittling military training and equipment, and citing Allied setbacks as signs of impending collapse. Few opportunities were missed to suggest the duplicitous nature of Great Britain and the Soviet Union and to remind readers that the war had been thrust upon the Axis by British and American actions. Immediate peace, the journal insisted, was the way to stop the impending slaughter.[6]

Early in January an article in the *New Republic* entitled "The Same Old Coughlin,"[7] prompted the attorney general to suggest to his staff that it was time to silence the troublesome cleric.[8] Biddle apparently hoped to uncover sufficient incriminating information concerning Coughlin's activities to intimidate the priest into silence or provide grounds for his prosecution under the anti-sedition statutes, should that prove necessary. A discrete investigation was initiated,[9] aimed at establishing that *Social Justice* had been distributed to members of the armed forces or men of draft age, that Coughlin controlled the editorial content of the journal, and that it was linked to Axis propagandists.[10]

Early results were disappointing. After examining copies of *Social Justice* through January 12, 1942, Special Assistant to the Attorney General James McInerney concluded that while the issues contained a number of statements that fit the category of "false reports" (as required by the Espionage Act), there was no evidence outside of the statements themselves to establish that they were made, as the law also stipulated, "with intent to interfere with the operation or success of the military . . . or to promote the success of its enemies." Nor could it be shown that the journal actually caused disloyalty in the armed forces or obstructed recruiting or that there was any "clear and present danger" that it would produce such results.[11] These deficiencies, McInerney suggested, would have to be remedied before Coughlin could be successfully prosecuted. In late January, Hoover, with Biddle's approval, authorized "special types of surveillance [wiretaps and electronic bugging]."[12] But even this failed to produce the hoped for evidence that Coughlin had willfully circulated *Social Justice* among military personnel, received foreign funding,[13] or was in fact linked to Axis agents.[14]

Officials were still hoping to secure evidence of Coughlin's criminal behavior when they felt obliged to act without it. In early April a *Life* magazine spread vividly depicted the seditious work of what the popular picture magazine called the nation's "Voices of Defeat." Coughlin was among those depicted. The article sent shock waves of embarrassment through the department and lent urgency to its efforts to deal promptly with *Social Justice* and other defeatist publications.[15]

Biddle decided to resort to mail censorship, at least until adequate sedition cases could be developed. On April 14, after consulting Hoover and the president,[16] the attorney general recommended that Postmaster General Frank Walker withhold delivery of the next issue of *Social Justice* pending a determination of its mailability, and that he move to revoke the journal's second-class mailing privilege. Walker immediately announced that a hearing would be held at the end of the month, at which the journal's publisher (not Coughlin, who was legally divorced from the sheet)[17] would be called upon to show why *Social Justice's* mailing privilege should not be revoked.[18]

In his public letter to Walker, Biddle justified his recommendation at length. He pointed out that in the related World War I *Milwaukee Leader* case, the Supreme Court had upheld the authority of postal officials to refuse to carry matter that they believed violated the Espionage Act. He went on to say that since statements drawn from *Social Justice,* which he listed, were very much like those ruled seditious in the earlier case, there was sufficient precedent to act against Coughlin's journal.

The attorney general revealed no awareness of the irony of citing as justification one of the most egregious incidents of World War I repression. The censorship procedure Biddle invoked had been ruthlessly employed during that war by Postmaster General Albert Burleson, who publicly announced that no one would use the mails to "impugn the motives of the Government," or claim that "this Government is the tool of Wall Street or the munitions-makers." That kind of thing, he continued, "makes for insubordination in the Army and Navy and breeds a spirit of disloyalty throughout the country. It is a false statement, a lie, and it will not be permitted."[19] That dictum sealed the fate of radical papers for the duration. The most celebrated victim was Max Eastman's leftist monthly, *Masses.* Burleson first ruled the August 1917 issue of the journal unmailable, and then refused to accept any issue irrespective of the content.

The post office actions, in this and similar cases, were roundly criticized, then and since.[20] In October 1917, Walter Lippmann, then a principal voice of progressivism, wrote privately that while he was no doctrinaire believer in free speech, he was concerned that the arbitrary suppression of dissident publications, like *Masses,* was undermining liberal support for the war and tending to divide "articulate opinion into fanatical jingoism and fanatical pacifism." Liberals, he told presidential confidante Colonel Edward M. House, could not understand why Burleson was apparently so apprehensive about criticism appearing in some "obscure and discredited little sheet," while former president Theodore Roosevelt was free to go about denigrating the quality of the American army. The inconsistent suppression, he wrote, gave insignificant papers "an importance that intrinsically they would never have."[21] John Lord O'Brian, in his end-of-the-war critique of the Justice Department's anti-sedition effort, noted that of all the criticism leveled at the department during the war, the only one he thought was seriously justified was that which pointed to the department's failure to limit the post office's censorship program.[22]

Despite criticism of his efforts, including a rebuke from President Wilson, Burleson was determined to vindicate his wartime rulings.[23] During the war the postmaster general had banned the *Milwaukee Leader,* a Socialist weekly with a circulation of about nine thousand. When its publisher, Victor Berger, sought to reclaim its second-class mailing status after the war, Burleson refused, and the Supreme Court was asked to decide whether his interpretation of the law was constitutional.[24] In 1921 the Court ratified Burleson's actions. The majority, in line with existing precedents, held that second-class mail rates were a special favor to publishers that could be granted or withdrawn in accord with postal regulations. But Justices Brandeis and Holmes, who had by then parted company with their brethren on the meaning of First Amendment guarantees, dissented here as well. The United States, Holmes noted, "may give up the post office when it sees fit, but while it carries it on, the use of the mails is almost as much a part of free speech as the right to use our tongues."[25] Political necessity blinded Biddle to his mentor's admonition.

The attorney general followed up his postal censorship initiative by announcing that the department had asked the special grand jury in Washington that had been investigating Axis propaganda activities in the United States to take a look at Coughlin.[26] The announcement was probably part of the government's psychological warfare against Coughlin, since department lawyers had yet to build a solid case against him.[27] In any event his status as a priest raised serious policy and public-relations concerns that seemed to rule out prosecution on anything less than the most compelling grounds. After talking to several politically astute persons familiar with the case, Biddle, alluding to Catholic suspicions of "Jewish power," concluded that "it would be very unwise" to indict Coughlin since this might "stir up the old anti-Semitic, anti-Administration fight between the Catholics and the Jews." If Catholics concluded that a prosecution of Father Coughlin was in effect a "crucifixion" engineered by the Jews, as some were apt to do, the administration, the war effort, and both religious groups were apt to suffer. The matter, Biddle concluded, and the president agreed, "had to be handled carefully."[28] Mail censorship seemed just right. It would secure the quick suppression of the journal without the need to prove that the priest was an enemy agent. Although the *New York Times* wondered how far the government should be permitted to go "in the direction of the suppression of opinion," the government's announced strategy was widely applauded in the press—the nation's dailies did not use the second-class privilege.[29]

The announced second-class mail hearing and the threatened grand jury investigation produced the intended result. In April administration officials concluded an arrangement with representatives of the Roman Catholic archbishop of Detroit whereby the department would not press for an indictment of Coughlin, in exchange for the archbishop's assurances that the priest never "opened his mouth again."[30] In early May 1942, *Social Justice* voluntarily surrendered its second-class mail permit.

Quieting Coughlin was a significant accomplishment, but the White House was after bigger game. In a fireside chat on April 28, FDR had spoken of a handful of "noisy traitors" and "bogus patriots who use the sacred freedom of press to echo the sentiments of the propagandists of Tokyo and Berlin."[31] He was apparently referring not to the crackpot fascists, but to the slightly less eccentric, isolationist, Roosevelt-hating, "divisionist" publishers—William Randolph Hearst, Col. Robert R. McCormick (*Chicago Tribune*), Joseph Patterson (*New York Daily News*), and his sister Eleanor (Cissy) Patterson (*Washington Times-Herald*). (The last two were McCormick's cousins.)

The antagonism between the president and Hearst and McCormick was traceable to the early New Deal years when the press moguls had let it be known that they considered Roosevelt a communist and his reforms an ill-disguised effort to regiment the American people. When international affairs came to dominate the administration's interest in 1940, their criticism turned to foreign policy and they, together with the Pattersons, became the chief source of isolationist attacks on the government. Although all four incurred the president's wrath from time to time, as did Roy Howard of the Scripps Howard chain, FDR's annoyance focused on McCormick, who was particularly adept at getting under the president's skin.[32]

The onset of war found FDR's critics in the press as unrepentant and obstreperous as ever. "Voices of Defeat," *Life*'s guide to America's defeatists, included the *Chicago Tribune,* which it noted was an inspiration to "pro-Nazi and defeatist groups throughout the country." The divisionist press no doubt had a greater negative effect on the war effort than the more extremist publications. Hearst, McCormick, Patterson, et al. reached a readership more than ten times larger than that of the extremists. And while the readers of the overtly disloyal papers were likely attracted to them by the extremist slant they knew they would find there, those who picked up the *Chicago Tribune* or the *New York Daily News* were drawn principally by their features, advertising, sports, and local coverage, and came to the papers with a relatively open mind on public issues.[33]

But the influence commanded by the large isolationist newspapers was probably not the salient issue for FDR. The president appears to have had confidence in the good sense of the American people and was not unduly concerned that the public would turn against the war. But he was profoundly annoyed by McCormick and company, whose criticism he took personally. The best comment on his antiwar critics, Roosevelt said, had come from columnist Elmer Davis, who quipped that "some people want the United States to win so long as England loses. Some want the United States to win so long as Russia loses. And some people want the United States to win so long as Roosevelt loses."[34] Although the carping criticism of the Hearst-McCormick-Patterson axis was not new, episodes on the eve of the war, and again six months later, in which the *Tribune* revealed military matters that the administration, for valid security reasons, wanted kept secret,[35] convinced FDR that "Bertie" McCormick and the others deserved a serious public rebuke. The war had made them insufferable and seemed to offer an opportunity to censure them. He made it clear to his subordinates that they should do *something*. The burden fell principally on Biddle.

Roosevelt discussed what might be done at a cabinet meeting on April 11,[36] and on April 22 he spoke with Biddle about the "subversive mind of Cissy Patterson." He suggested that the FBI "put a surveillance on her and on Col. Patterson," and Biddle assured him that this had already been done.[37] Biddle's chief assistant and political advisor James Rowe, pointing to the president's remarks and "the beating" that Postmaster General Frank Walker took from the president at a recent cabinet meeting, warned Biddle that the president wanted immediate action against the divisionist/seditionist press. There was nothing more important for the department to do at this point, he wrote, "than to get on top of, and perhaps a little ahead" of the president in this regard.[38]

In early May, Roosevelt sent Biddle an anonymous study, one of several being circulated by various antifascist sources,[39] that pointed to the presence of Nazi propaganda themes in the divisionist press. The "tie in between the attitude of these papers and the Rome-Berlin broadcasts," the president concluded, was "something far greater than mere coincidence," and he suggested that the attorney general use the information to prosecute the divisionist publishers, or at least to publicly expose and discredit their newspapers.[40] Accompanying the note was a set of folders containing articles appearing in the *Tribune,* Hearst's *New York Journal American,* Joseph Patterson's *Daily News,* and *Social Justice.* The study concluded that these journals, in attempting to discredit America's allies; encourage a defensive posture for the United States; and promote disunity between races, classes, and groups, were following the Axis propaganda line. While at times FDR judged the publishers as only terribly wrong-headed,[41] he now seemed prepared to accuse them of sedition.

Administration officials did their best to uncover the necessary evidence. Beginning in May 1942, the contents of the *Tribune* and its allies were surveyed first by the Office of Facts and Figures (the agency, led by Archibald MacLeish, charged with monitoring antiwar propaganda), and then repeatedly by the Department of Justice in an attempt to produce conclusive evidence of the suspected link with the Axis.[42] Finally, in November, L. M. C. Smith, whose Special War Policies Unit was chiefly responsible for the department's investigation of the divisionist press, reported to Biddle that repeated sampling and analysis had revealed that the newspapers consistently reflected only four of sixteen Nazi propaganda themes—not enough to warrant charging their publishers with sedition.[43] Barring the journals from the mails was still possible, but this would have been an empty provocative gesture since none of the daily newspapers relied on the mails. Moreover, all were in a position to fight the government's attempt and would no doubt point to the effort as further evidence of the administration's dictatorial proclivities. The post office continued to monitor the divisionist press, but no issue was kept from the mails.[44] The widely talked about comparisons may have chastened Roosevelt's tormentors some, but the success of the U.S. war effort was the most effective response to their criticism.

Unable to silence the powerful and potentially most harmful of the administration's critics, Biddle still hoped to use postal censorship as a quick and easy way of satisfying the president's demand that he silence the handful (sometimes estimated by antifascists to be many hundreds) of "dirty little sheets" that continued to circulate.[45] Monitoring was increased after *Life*'s exposé appeared, with particular emphasis on the publications featured in the article.[46] Issues containing material identified by local postmasters as problematic were sent to the solicitor of the post office, who would ask the Justice Department for a final determination as to their mailability.[47]

One of the first targets of the program was *X-Ray,* described by antifascist muckraker John Roy Carlson as "a half-literate sheet" whose "pathological nonsense" might be ignored if it "did not fit so snugly into the larger pattern of the [fascist] psychological offensive."[48] Published by Court Asher in Muncie, Indiana, *X-Ray's* principal claim to government attention was that it had been among the score of such publications featured in the *Life* exposé. The divisive content of the paper was blatant and typical of the species. It was, of course, crudely anti-Semitic and anti-British, and emphasized the cost of the conflict, delineating, for example, the horrors of poison gas, which Asher predicted would be used against American (but not British) troops.[49]

In April the attorney general ruled that the journal was in violation of the Espionage Act. On May 1, postal officials refused to deliver its current issue and advised Asher that a hearing would be held in two weeks, at which time he would have an opportunity to show cause why his second-class mail privilege should not be revoked.[50] But at Asher's hearing, held before postal officials in Washington in mid-May, the misgivings of Justice Department officials concerning the program were apparent. L. M. C. Smith, who was advising the post office on censorship, was not inclined to withhold postal privileges except in instances where a strong case for willful collaboration with the enemy could be made against the publishers.[51] Thus, rather than simply allowing postal authorities to cite *X-Ray's* offensive passages and indicate why they thought these were in violation of the Espionage Act (no more was required), Justice Department officials insisted on demonstrating that the utterances fit a pattern of Nazi propaganda that indicated the publisher's intent to serve the enemy's cause. They called on the eminent political scientist Harold D. Lasswell, director of the War Communications Research Project at the Library of Congress, to supply the proof.[52] Lasswell testified that Nazi propaganda habitually argued that: the U.S. was "economically corrupt"; "the Administration's foreign policy or conduct of the war" was misguided; the president was morally or ethically reprehensible; Great Britain and other Allies were unworthy; and "Washington is run by Communists, plutocrats, Jews or crooks." Lasswell gave *X-Ray* a 65 percent agreement rating, enough, he asserted, to warrant the conclusion that the journal deliberately followed the Nazi propaganda line. No one challenged the validity of Lasswell's methodology or the dubious conclusions the government drew from his results. It was possible, for example, that Asher's ideas were homegrown and that the similarity between his views and German propaganda was the result of Nazi propagandists drawing on the same populist themes (long current in American political discourse), that Asher echoed.[53] This was not an adversarial proceeding, and such arguments were not considered. The post office suspended Asher's second-class permit.

But Smith came away from the hearing uncertain that in Asher he had encountered the Enemy, and more dubious than ever about using postal censorship except as a prelude to (not as a substitute for) prosecution. The *X-Ray's* founder and editor was a World War I veteran, classified by the Veterans Administration as "a psychopathic case," who had been granted a government disability allowance. A bootlegger in the 1920s, he had a record of Prohibition Act violations so long that the FBI declined to list them all in its report to the post office.[54] At his hearing Asher passionately insisted that he was "a 100 per cent American," and pointed out, with some justification, that he had seen "worse stuff [than his] in the *Congressional Record.*" Moreover, he professed to be offended by magazine reports that characterized him as a "petty bootlegger," protesting that he had only sold by the case.[55] Asher appeared less a vicious Nazi agent than a possibly unbalanced, patriotic scamp with a disarming sense of humor.

Smith was having second thoughts about the whole process. By mid-1942 the post office had kept about 30 publications from the mails on grounds that they were seditious, and revoked the second-class mailing privileges of 6 journals (*Philadelphia Herold, Galilean, X-Ray, Publicity,* the *Boise Valley Herald,* and *Social Justice*).[56] But the cases submitted to the department, Smith now observed, were becoming "thinner and thinner," and he told Deputy Solicitor of the post office Calvin Hassell that he was concerned lest an opinion from the department indicating that a given publication was seditious embarrass the attorney general should he subsequently decide that the publisher could not be prosecuted. Critics were bound to ask why persons whose writings were found to be seditious were not punished under the anti-sedition statutes. And if the reason was that the government could not prove its case in court, was it right to suppress their expression by administrative fiat?[57] The postal censorship invoked by the department to counter accusations that it was not doing enough about the seditious sheets, Smith thought, was now threatening to humiliate the department by committing it to cases that officials thought they could not, or should not, win.

Four days after the Asher hearing, Smith notified the post office that the Department of Justice would no longer assume responsibility for declaring published materials (like *X-Ray*) "seditious," preferring instead to offer only advisory opinions. The change, Smith apparently hoped, would distance the department from post office censorship and avoid any implication that the department was prepared to indict publishers like Asher for sedition. The department's refusal to assume responsibility for post office findings of non-mailability exacerbated tensions between the two agencies, and by the end of the year officials who were supposed to be cooperating, were barely speaking.[58]

Department uneasiness over post office suppression was increased by a public controversy over a recent dramatic upsurge in post office censorship of obscenity. The ACLU reported that during 1942, when a total of six publications had their second-class mail privileges revoked on grounds of seditious content, over fifty others had suffered revocation on the grounds that they were obscene.[59]

In the spring the ACLU had begun pressuring both the post office and the Justice Department to change the censorship procedure. Postmaster General Frank Walker, a genial man and an FDR favorite, appears to have taken little interest in the issue,[60] but Baldwin did succeed in getting Biddle to champion changes in post office practices. Postal censorship became even more controversial in September 1943, when Walker served a show cause order on *Esquire,* a popular "man's" magazine noted for its sexual innuendo. The post office's action produced protest from the artistic community,[61] derisive criticism from liberals, and the threat of legislation that would have transferred obscenity rulings from the post office to the courts.[62]

Meanwhile, more determined than ever not to be associated with post office censorship, the Justice Department continued to quarrel with postal authorities over the dwindling pool of allegedly seditious journals. The contest between the agencies now centered not on overtly "fascist" sheets, but on a miscellany of other "subversive" publications. These included issues of the *Saturday Evening Post;*[63] the *Progressive;*[64] a number of religious pacifist publications including the *Christian Century;*[65] and the *Militant,* the journal of the Socialist Workers Party whose second-class mailing privileges had been revoked in early 1943 on grounds that it had criticized the war effort and stirred up disunity by reporting recent racial incidents and attributing them to American racism.

To many Americans, a nation at war for its life could legitimately silence those who questioned the integrity of the nation's leadership and the justice of the cause, or who otherwise undermined national cohesion and purpose. In 1942 postal censorship offered a way of suppressing obnoxious expression that could not be reached easily or surely under the anti-sedition statutes. Under pressure from the president, Biddle embraced the device. But department lawyers were uncomfortable with the arbitrary authority it entailed, and insisted on proceeding on firmer ground than was provided by the commonsense judgment that any caustic criticism that inadvertently served the enemy's cause, should be suppressed.

In fact, much of what the seditionists wrote derived from the anti-Semitic, anti-establishmentarian Anglophobia that characterized American populist discourse. When officials sought to come to grips with the "internal enemy," they found that he or she was hard to isolate from significant segments of the population at large. Antifascist John Roy Carlson inadvertently made the point. In an *American Mercury* article exposing *X-Ray* and similar journals, he noted that the sheet might be ignored by the government and concerned Americans "were it not that so many Middletown businessmen actually advertise in the publication."[66] Middle-American businessmen, he was suggesting, had fascistic proclivities that had to be rebuked and silenced by government before they spread. But another way to look at *X-Ray's* advertising was that the townspeople, and hence advertisers, saw Asher's ideas as only a little eccentric and not grossly un-American.[67] Department officials came to recognize that it would be embarrassingly inconsistent and politically untenable to suppress *X-Ray* and others simply for printing what could be found, as Asher pointed out, in the extended remarks of American congressmen. In the end, thanks largely to the restraining influence of mid-level department officials, postal censorship failed to provide a way around the First Amendment and the inadequacy of anti-sedition statutes, and despite the experiment, the administration was left with the problem of how to suppress obnoxious printed matter that was not clearly seditious in intent. After seven months of war, officials were reconciled to the fact that whatever the solution to this problem, it would not be speedy or certain.

Chapter 11

"Where Sedition Begins and Ends Among Negroes"

Biddle's deliberations on sedition were dogged by the issue of prosecutorial discretion. Legal commentators had long argued that public policy, in some instances, dictated official indifference to alleged crimes. This was particularly so in regard to utterances viewed as seditious, and those disposed to protect the principle of free speech urged the attorney general on occasion to turn a blind eye to inconsequential words that in another context might legitimately demand a government response. Of course, defendants in such cases were free to invoke the "clear and present danger" defense. But early in the war this seemed unlikely to be accepted by the courts, and in any event the relief that it might provide would come only well after the defendants had been incarcerated and deprived of their right to speak.

The appeal to prosecutorial restraint was particularly appropriate in regard to African-American antiwar agitators, whose expressions of disaffection, some argued, were of doubtful consequence and best understood as a blowing-off of steam generated by the frustrating realities of black life in America. Biddle, faced with a number of instances of outspoken opposition to the war based on black discontent, was asked to decide what if any dispensation should be granted to agitators on the basis of the provocative circumstances thrust upon them by American racial attitudes.

Black antiwar agitation, although little noticed at the time or by scholars since, accounted for a substantial portion of the cases arising out of accusations of disloyalty during World War II.[1] The black agitators, leaders of a half dozen or so small African-American religious or fraternal associations, offered a commentary on the war and on public affairs that was comparable to that of the white fascists.[2] Their speech, mostly in the form of street-corner or meeting-hall harangues, condemned American society and institutions, celebrated Japanese military victories, and encouraged listeners to refuse to serve the nation's war effort. The agitators often insisted that blacks had everything to gain from a victory by the Japanese, whom they frequently referred to as a kindred "colored" people. Like the fascists, their racist rhetoric was unseemly at best in a nation in the midst of war.

The racial essence of black disloyalty during World War II had contradictory implications for law enforcement. On the one hand, Biddle recognized that such talk grew out of the injustices suffered by African Americans, and was prone to sympathize with advice he received that repeatedly alluded to black "sedition" as an expression of the outrage widely felt in the black community. On the other hand, the already volatile nature of American race relations suggested that the government needed to be more attentive to signs of disloyalty within the black community than to similar expressions in society at large. Thus the truths that animated the black agitators could be seen as both a mitigating factor, and as making the talk all the more dangerous.

Virtually all blacks were unhappy with the racial caste system that consigned them to a position of social and economic inferiority and limited their access to political power. Eighty years after Emancipation, rigid separation of the races in the South was maintained by law, custom, and random acts of unpunished individual and mob violence. In the North, to which many Southern blacks had fled since the turn of the century, African Americans found poverty, discrimination, and a white community that treated them as irredeemably inferior.

Some blacks and sympathetic whites sought to stop the violence, end racial discrimination, and cultivate interracial harmony. In recent years, liberals, including some members of the Roosevelt administration, and most notably Eleanor Roosevelt, had worked for racial justice. But despite the sympathetic ear the government lent to the concerns of mainstream representatives of the black community, the administration produced only modest reforms, as President Roosevelt, deterred by the scale of racial problems, the virulence of racism, and his need for southern Democratic political support, refused to take up the challenge of race relations.[3]

The insufferable quality of life in such conditions, the humiliating arrogance of whites, and the inertia that characterized the political system gave rise to a desperate separatist ideology that resonated in the black community among those who found in it explanations for their miseries, pride in themselves, and schemes for their deliverance. Since the 1920s various nationalist groups, preeminently Marcus Garvey's Universal Negro Improvement Association, extolled the achievements of colored peoples, often speaking of them as a chosen race, and offered emigration to Africa or elsewhere as an escape from white racism. Others held out the promise of deliverance for believers by supernatural or pseudo-scientific interventions of spiritual origins.[4] While most African Americans remained attached to their Christian churches, explicitly nationalistic groups attracted thousands, perhaps tens of thousands of adherents. [5]

Increasing black militancy, whatever its form, worried J. Edgar Hoover, who had what his biographer Richard Gid Powers called an "instinctive antagonism toward black protest." Justice Department investigators and military-intelligence operatives had been infiltrating and monitoring African-American groups since World War I, and despite Attorney General Harlan Fiske Stone's 1924 order banning politically motivated investigations, surveillance of the black nationalists continued. [6] In the mid-1930s, when FDR authorized sweeping investigations into subversive activities, Hoover, with the president's knowledge, included black groups among his targets, and his reports to the president on subversive activities during the war listed "Negro Organizations" along with German, Italian, and Japanese groups as potential sources of fifth-column activity.[7] Federal surveillance was not confined to "extremists," and from mid-1941 through the war years the FBI closely watched (among others) A. Philip Randolph, head of the Brotherhood of Sleeping Car Porters and a leader of the March on Washington Movement that protested discrimination in employment.[8]

Interest in black discontent increased with American involvement in World War II. One morale agency official wrote privately that he had learned that "something like nine out of eleven Negroes in Harlem have been so neglected that they don't care who wins the war. They think the Japanese would treat them better."[9] A government survey found that while blacks remained fundamentally loyal, there were signs of a "recent tendency toward identification with the Japanese as a 'dark race' warring against the white." Some of the African Americans surveyed volunteered statements like: "Negroes have not been allowed to fight against the Japanese because they [whites] know that they [Japanese] are our brothers and are afraid we would not fight."[10] In May 1942 the president's cabinet concluded, in the words of Secretary of Interior Harold Ickes, that "the Japs" were "doing a great deal of disturbing undercover work among the Negroes."[11]

Reports of African-American disaffection abounded,[12] as many blacks, not just black nationalists, described the conflict as a "white man's war."

Soon after the Pearl Harbor attack, the *Pittsburgh Courier* proclaimed a "Double-V" campaign, demanding that the administration pursue victory over racism at home with the same vigor it sought victory over the Axis. Other black newspapers followed the *Courier's* lead, and officials, troubled by their exposure of racial incidents and condemnation of the nation's race policies, threatened the black editors with prosecution and other sanctions if they did not moderate their expressions of disaffection.[13]

Nevertheless, the profoundly disaffected continued to find a reflection of their sentiments in the rhetoric of the black nationalist fringe. Significantly, from the point of view of officials, the nationalists often accompanied their criticism of white America, with praise for America's Pacific enemy. The seemingly odd attraction to Japan, an aspect of black nationalist thought since at least Garvey's time,[14] thrived on the desire of alienated black Americans to identify with a modern, powerful "colored" people, and explains why some blacks found satisfaction in Japan's successes early in the Second World War, just as they had reveled in its victory over the (white) Russian Empire in 1905.

The Japanese affinity was apparent, for example, in the early teachings of the Nation of Islam, one of a number of black nationalist groups that had adopted doctrine, ritual, and titles based more or less on Muslim forms. The leader of this sect, Elijah Muhammad, proclaimed that American blacks were the direct descendants of the original people who, in ancient times, had ruled the earth from their homeland in Asia. Condemning the evil institutions and ways of the United States, America's Black Muslims predicted the nation's imminent destruction, from which the followers of Allah would be saved by a divinely inspired and commissioned space vehicle. Significantly, Muhammad taught, this "Mother Plane" was being constructed in Japan in accordance with advanced technological expertise.[15] While the Japanese content of the Nation of Islam's teachings seems to have been confined to the story of the Nation's Asian origins and the Japanese-built spaceship, Japan figured more prominently in the messages of other groups.

The black nationalist–Japanese link grew in the early 1930s, partly as the result of the activities of Ashima Takis, a Filipino, possibly of Japanese descent, who promoted the Japanese homeland idea among African Americans. Holding himself out as a Japanese, Takis toured the United States trying to interest black groups in a scheme of emigration to Japan where, he promised, they were assured an agreeable life among a kindred dark-skinned people. He also spoke of establishing an African-American colony in Brazil.[16]

According to FBI reports (which at present seem to be our only source on these matters), Takis, possibly at the instigation of one Satokata Takahashi, purportedly an agent of the Japanese government, had a hand in the creation of several pro-Japanese black nationalist groups, including pre-eminently the Pacific Movement of the Eastern World (PMEW), which was chartered in Chicago at the end of 1932 as a non-profit, religious, civic, and educational association.[17] The group gained a number of adherents throughout the Midwest and was particularly popular in East St. Louis, Illinois, and Kansas City, Missouri. Its message of black pride and deliverance from white oppression stressed the "worldwide unity of the colored races under the leadership of Japan."[18] Takis was busy on the East Coast as well. In 1935 he had joined with black nationalist Robert O. Jordan to found the Ethiopian Pacific Movement, which from the mid-1930s gained adherents among New York City's African-American population. Jordan's message also promised black salvation through the intercession of Japan.

Though repudiated by mainstream black leaders,[19] the black nationalists were taken seriously by J. Edgar Hoover, who thought he detected in their attraction to Japan a national security issue. Soon after the Pearl Harbor attack, Hoover alerted the attorney general to alleged Japanese-inspired activities in Harlem. Biddle, who had only recently released "fascists" Robert Noble and Ellis Jones for making statements in Los Angeles very similar to those charged against Jordan, declined to act.[20] Nevertheless, in February 1942, Jordan, a West Indian by birth and a British subject, was picked up by federal agents and incarcerated for a short time for failing to notify immigration authorities of a change of address.[21] The arrest was likely intended as a warning, but on his release, Jordan immediately returned to his objectionable preaching.

Serious interest in prosecuting black nationalists seems to have grown not out of Jordan's activities, but from the discovery of black-nationalist agitation in southeastern Missouri. This in turn developed, in a circuitous way, out of a tragic incident that occurred in Sikeston, Missouri. In January 1942, a mob of whites had taken a black mill worker named Cleo Wright from his cell in the local jail, where he was being held on charges he had attempted to rape a local white woman, and brutally murdered him. Although the perpetrators had been identified, a local grand jury refused to indict anyone for the crime. Biddle, who was more sensitive to racial injustice than most, was shocked by the lynching and ordered the department's Civil Rights Division to make an all-out effort to bring Wright's murderers to justice.

During the course of a thorough FBI investigation, which officials hoped would lead to federal indictments against the mob members and local officials for violating or failing to protect Wright's civil rights,[22] agents uncovered evidence of black-nationalist activities in the area around Sikeston that Hoover believed warranted further department action. His attention focused on the Pacific Movement of the Eastern World (PMEW), which had been preaching nationalist and pro-Japanese ideas in the area.[23] In March 1942, in what appears to have been an effort by Hoover to move the department toward prosecution, many of the details of the FBI's investigation appeared in a front-page story carried by the *St. Louis Post Dispatch* under headlines proclaiming the existence of a "Pro-Japanese Negro Fifth Column" in Missouri.[24] The article described at great length the activities of Takis and Takahashi (identified as a former Japanese army officer), their alleged plans for black emigration to Japan, and their supposed success in spreading the word throughout southeast Missouri, southern Illinois, and Arkansas. The newspaper explained how what at first seemed to be "just another Negro fraternal organization," had been transformed over the past ten years into a secret organization whose "subversive teachings" now alarmed some of its former leaders. According to the account, the group's doctrines had recently become intensely pro-Japanese and appeared aimed at spreading "confusion and dissension" and disrupting the war effort.[25]

The "conspiracy" uncovered by the FBI was led by David D. Erwin and his principal associate, General [his name, not a rank] Lee Butler. Erwin, according to testimony he later gave authorities, had been entrusted with the organization by Takis in the fall of 1939, and the group now had branches in several states. Even after the Japanese attack on Pearl Harbor, its speakers lauded Japan as the champion of the colored peoples and suggested that when Japan conquered the United States, members of the PMEW would be assured favorable treatment by America's new masters. More importantly from the standpoint of their vulnerability to the anti-sedition statutes, Erwin and Butler urged African Americans not to participate in the war effort, and claimed that persons who were ordained ministers of the Triumph Church of the New Age, which Butler had founded in 1939, were exempt from the draft.[26]

As the FBI compiled evidence looking toward the prosecution of the leaders of PMEW and similar groups, the attorney general decided to assign a major role in the preparation of the cases to the department's Civil Rights Division, which was currently working on the Cleo Wright lynching. Perhaps he wanted to ensure that the case was handled with the racial sensitivity assumed to prevail in the civil rights unit. There was, of course, no question of assigning a black department lawyer to the case. In early April, taking note of African-American protests about being shut out of government employment, Biddle urged his division heads to hire Negro attorneys. The suggestion was resisted by the department's staff[27] and, while there were some blacks in the department, none were of sufficient rank to assume a prominent role in this case.

Victor Rotnem, who headed the Civil Rights Division, decided that a grand jury probe into pro-Japanese activities would have a "salutary effect . . . on all negroes who might be susceptible to Japanese influence."[28] His strategy was to time the hearings on PMEW to coincide with the expected indictment of suspects in the Wright lynching. This would suggest the government's even-handed administration of justice and presumably head off adverse reactions from either the black or white communities. But this plan exploded when the federal grand jury in the Wright case failed to return an indictment.[29] Undeterred, officials proceeded with the investigation of the black nationalists, and at the end of the summer, the government asked a federal grand jury in St. Louis to look into pro-Japanese movements in Missouri, Illinois, Indiana, and surrounding states.[30] What had begun as an effort to bring the members of a white racist mob to justice, ended with an investigation of unrest in the black community.

Rotnem seemed disposed to move ahead to a series of grand jury investigations and prosecutions in several states, as was being done in regard to the fascist seditionists. But the prospects of uncovering evidence of black disloyalty, particularly in racially tense areas, posed a dilemma. On the one hand, a thorough exposure of black nationalist agitation was likely to stir up white resentments and inflame racial antagonisms. On the other hand, ignoring potentially seditious speech was apt to provoke hostile local responses, including, perhaps, vigilantism. In April the dangerous implications of inaction were driven home to federal authorities when they learned of the arrest in Lexington, Mississippi of Jim Barnes, a Moorish Science Temple organizer. Members of this group, which was one of the oldest and most popular of the black nationalist sects, had been telling local blacks that when the Japanese won the war, they would gain equality with whites. Moreover, they advised listeners that, as members of an alien nation, to wit, the "Moorish race," blacks were not obligated to serve the United States and did not have to register for the draft.[31] Barnes had gone further—he had refused to ride in the back section of the bus provided for "colored" passengers. An altercation ensued, and he was arrested and charged by local authorities under Mississippi's anti-sedition law.[32]

The episode was reminiscent of the kind of local repression that had plagued the department during World War I. With this in mind, senior department officials, seeking to maintain order and the department's preeminence in the control of disloyalty,[33] rejected the idea of a series of potentially provocative general grand jury probes. Nevertheless, Biddle apparently believed that selected prosecutions of pro-Japanese agitators were unavoidable.[34]

By the end of 1942, the likelihood of a Japanese invasion and occupation of the United States, never very great, had been interred on the battlefields of distant Pacific islands. Nevertheless, in January 1943, Erwin, Butler, and an unnamed co-conspirator (identified only as a Japanese agent) were indicted in East St. Louis for violating the Espionage and Selective Service Acts by conspiring to promote disloyalty in the armed forces and hinder compliance with the draft law.[35] Biddle, commenting on the indictments, emphasized the role of Takis and Takahashi and referred to alleged Japanese promises of arms and ammunition that would enable the defendants to "stage an uprising to assist the Japanese when they invade the United States."[36] These allegations were not part of the charges leveled against the defendants, and the statement was apparently designed to give the public, black and white, an impression that the defendants were more threatening than they actually were.

Officials were probably less certain that prosecution was warranted than their pronouncements suggested. Rotnem, Berge, and Biddle, who were in frequent contact with officials of the ACLU and the National Association for the Advancement of Colored People (NAACP), had been told by Walter White, executive secretary of the NAACP, that there was no evidence that black nationalist preaching had "any [seditious] effect on any number of Negroes." White warned that prosecution, by exaggerating the incidence of disloyalty among blacks, would divert attention from the victims of racial discrimination and make "martyrs of these nondescript and unimportant persons."[37]

Both Roger Baldwin and NAACP special counsel Thurgood Marshall joined White in questioning the wisdom of prosecuting the black nationalists. Baldwin, complaining that he had been unable to learn much about the black nationalists or their activities, approached journalist Louis Martin seeking enlightenment. Martin, who wrote for the *Michigan Chronicle,* the most widely read black journal in Detroit, told Baldwin that while he assumed that a few of those indicted "had some connections with enemy agents," he was convinced that most of them were "confidence men" who were "exploiting Negro grievances for personal profit." Black nationalism and attraction to Japan, ideas pioneered by Garvey, had been given a "new lease on life," he wrote, by a war in which blacks "were again being asked to fight and die for democracy" despite lynching and other injustices. Martin aptly observed that it was "very difficult to determine where sedition begins and ends among Negroes."[38]

Baldwin's skepticism was strengthened by an interview with Erwin's lawyer, who assured him that the defendants were the victims of the false testimony of Takis (the alleged "Japanese" agent) who, he suggested, was seeking revenge for an earlier falling out that had put Takis in jail for misappropriating organization funds.[39] In pressing Rotnem and Berge not to act until the facts of the alleged Japanese connection could be sorted out, Baldwin argued that while the defendants had expressed pro-Japanese sentiments, such sentiments were not uncommon among African Americans and that any effort to prosecute because of such attitudes would "rouse instant sympathy among Negroes everywhere."[40] Berge agreed to drop the Espionage Act counts against Erwin and Butler if they would plead guilty to counseling draft evasion.[41] The PMEW leaders declined the offer and asked for a trial without a jury.

Baldwin succeeded in getting Thurgood Marshall to join him in requesting department reconsideration of the looming prosecutions, but a decision to assist in their defense hinged not on the issue of the effect of the alleged seditious agitation, but on the possibility that the nationalists were somehow connected to Axis agents. In response to the early fascist sedition cases, the ACLU's board had adopted a policy of not participating in any case in which there was evidence of a tie between the defendants and a nation with whom the United States was at war. An exception would be made only if there was a clear denial of due process.[42] Berge and Rotnem insisted that they had evidence of Japanese influence, and neither the ACLU nor the NAACP could say differently. There would be no intervention.[43]

During the summer of 1942, as investigators gathered evidence against a number of black nationalist groups, Biddle considered whether to prosecute. He was probably convinced that the black nationalists posed little threat to the war effort, and this worked in their favor. On the other hand, the attorney general, already under fire for his weakness, could not afford to ignore disloyalty (in any quarter) that was, or was likely to become, notorious. Exposé in wider (white) circles was in the offing. Early in 1942 the antifascist *Hour* had called attention to "Axis" (black nationalist) propaganda in Harlem. In March the *St. Louis Post Dispatch* had exposed the PMEW's Japanese connections, and Hoover, who was likely behind those revelations, was capable of others. John Roy Carlson was planning to devote considerable coverage to Jordan (the "Harlem Hitler) in *Under Cover,* his sensational exposé of the American fifth column that would appear early the following year.[44]

In August, Biddle authorized the United States attorney in New York to move against the leaders of the Ethiopian Pacific Movement[45] and, in the fall of 1942, a grand jury charged Robert O. Jordan, his principal lieutenant Lester Holness, and three others with conspiring to promote insubordination in the military and obstruct recruiting and enlistment.[46] The government alleged that they had held meetings and given speeches designed, in the words of the indictment, "to mislead and to corrupt the patriotic, loyal and law-abiding colored population of Greater New York and particularly of the community known as Harlem." The government referred to a long list of the defendants' statements supporting the government charges. Jordan reportedly declared that, if drafted, "I would wave my handkerchief as a sign of surrender and go over to join the Axis Powers and I expect my followers to guide themselves accordingly." He also asserted that he was praying for an Axis victory and urged military personnel to "go back to your outfit and start the whispering campaign. When they tell you to remember Pearl Harbor, you reply, 'Remember Africa'. When you boys get over there, turn your guns on the English speaking countries." Addressing the black servicemen's mothers, he advised them to "tell your sons to throw down their guns and put their arms around the little brown man's shoulder."[47]

The case against Jordan and company was probably the strongest the government presented against any of the black nationalists. Holness's lawyer had advised him that the group's statements might land them in jail, but as late as July 1942, he and Jordan and the others were still tempting the government to act.[48] When the indictment was handed down in mid-September, the prosecutor told reporters that the defendants had made "so many enemies among the Negro population that there will be plenty of witnesses to testify against them at their trial."[49] The infamous Takis himself was the government's star witness, but there were many more, including investigative reporter John Roy Carlson.[50]

Jordan seemed to enjoy making outrageous comments, and the government had no difficulty in securing evidence suggesting his alleged Japanese associations. While awaiting trial, he told two fellow inmates that when the Japanese put him in "charge over here," he intended to "cut off a lot of colored people's heads," referring to various civil rights leaders. The conversation was entered as evidence at his trial—the press relished the story.[51] In the course of Jordan's month-long trial, the jury, which included three African Americans,[52] had an opportunity to hear the defendant in action when the prosecution, in a surprise move, introduced recordings of his speeches.[53] It found Jordan and three others guilty on all counts. A fifth defendant had pleaded guilty before trial. Jordan was sentenced to ten years and fined. His co-defendants received prison terms ranging from four to eight years.

Meanwhile, the FBI in Chicago had arrested 84 persons involved in what a government spokesmen told the wire services was a nationwide "Japanese-inspired race hatred and disobedience campaign . . . based on the gullibility and superstition of the American Negro." The defendants were members of three groups—the Nation of Islam, the Peace Movement of Ethiopia, and the Colored American National Organization—which the FBI claimed were an "outgrowth of the Black Dragon Society founded in 1930 by Major Satokata Takahashi of the Japanese Imperial Intelligence." Although the government reported that the leaders of the "cults" claimed between four and six million adherents in 46 states, the federal prosecutor assured the public that the vast majority of "America's negroes were fervently patriotic."[54] Newspaper readers may have reconciled the extravagant membership claims with the assertions of black loyalty by recalling the supposed gullibility of blacks to which officials and newspaper accounts often alluded. In October 1942, 12 of the Chicago black activists were indicted for sedition; the others with failing to register for the draft.[55]

Trying to make the strongest case they could for the disloyal and seditious intent of the various defendants, department officials repeatedly suggested that they had evidence of Japanese involvement in antiwar dissent. In the Erwin/Butler case, they indicted an unnamed Japanese co-conspirator, and in statements to the press, the government suggested that Takis and Takahashi were responsible for the pro-Japanese (and anti-American) element in black-nationalist rhetoric. Officials even succeeded in convincing Thurgood Marshall. [56]

There was a good deal of evidence, of questionable probity, suggesting that the black nationalists had drawn their inspiration, and more, from Japanese agents. The principals, when interviewed by federal agents, testified that Takis and Takahashi had been involved in the formation of their groups, and had suggested they serve as Japanese agents. But Takis and Takahashi denied they had any official standing, and there was very little beyond their earlier boasting to establish that they were in fact Japanese agents. It seemed more likely that Takis passed himself off as Japanese to lend credibility to his organizing among blacks and to his emigration schemes. The even more shadowy Takahashi also appears to have been a fraud.

In fact, the department found no conclusive evidence of the much-talked-about black nationalist ties to Japan, and the allegations played no role in the prosecutions. The failure was not for want of trying. For 15 months FBI offices all over the country searched for information concerning the alien connections of various African-American organizations and spokesmen as part of a massive survey of Racial Conditions in the United States (RACON) ordered by Hoover in June 1942. The report contained some evidence that was suggestive of the elusive link Hoover was anxious to establish, but the FBI produced nothing approaching proof that the black nationalists acted on behalf of Japan or were subsidized by the Japanese government. There was nothing, the bureau report concluded, to indicate any connection between Takahashi and the Black Dragon except the "unsubstantiated claim" he made to black nationalist groups.[57] The RACON report concluded that the black nationalist organizations appeared to have "only an abstract connection with the Japanese government or Japanese aims," and that few of the organizations or individuals "had Japanese affiliations or contacts of any consequence. . . ." All the talk about ties to Japan had apparently been designed by the two Asians and their African-American contacts "to suggest that the authority of the Japanese government was behind them."[58] Had Baldwin and Marshall known what emerged from the RACON report, which was completed in September 1943, their organizations might have offered legal assistance to the black nationalists.

The fact that the accused were African American and that officials decided to proceed in less than compelling circumstances, raises the possibility that racial prejudice played a role. The suggestion does not seem to have been aired by the national black leadership, but Frederick Harold Robb, a graduate of Howard University and the Northwestern University Law School, and one of those indicted in Chicago,[59] accused the government of trying to prevent "Negroes from expressing the injustices to which they are constantly subjected."[60] Indeed, the race of the defendants, and more importantly of those to whom they addressed their remarks, certainly had a bearing on the government's action. It was also true that unflattering stereotypes pervaded the thinking of federal officials, as it did most white Americans. The assumption that the African-American population was particularly susceptible to disaffecting agitation probably played a role in the decision to silence the agitators. But beyond this, can the government's actions fairly be ascribed to white racism?

While officials no doubt harbored racial prejudices, these do not appear to have decisively shaped their actions. There was enough in what the accused were saying and doing to draw the attention of federal authorities. If any remarks made in wartime, short of direct incitement to acts against the government, could be deemed seditious, certainly those of Robb and others indicted in Chicago could. Testimony revealed that, in August 1942, Robb had repeatedly declared that the Japanese victory, which he predicted and hoped for, would benefit African Americans. "Negroes," he said, "owed no allegiance to the American Flag" and had no obligation to register for or respond to the draft.[61] Mittie Maude Lena Gordon and three of her associates[62] in the Peace Movement of Ethiopia, who faced the same charges in a separate indictment handed down in Chicago at the same time, expressed similar sentiments. According to witnesses, Gordon told a group at the end of May 1942 that the Japanese attack on Pearl Harbor was a blow for the freedom of the world's one billion black people, and that the Japanese were going to "redeem the Negroes from the white men in this country." On other occasions she announced that American blacks were citizens of Liberia and that they owed no allegiance to, and should not fight for, the United States.[63] Such sentiments testified to the tragic state of race relations in the United States and the extreme views to which it had led some black people. But the core truths the statements reflected did not erase their seditious content.

The department ultimately secured indictments for sedition against two other groups of black nationalists in addition to those in Chicago, East St. Louis, and New York.[64] In October 1942, Anselm Broaster, a native of British Honduras and leader of the International Reassembly of the Church of Freedom League, was arrested in New Orleans after writing to a number of draft boards making clear his church's opposition to the draft. In December, 16 other members of the group were also taken into custody and charged, along with Broaster, with having conspired to advise others not to serve in a war involving overseas duty. Fifteen of the group were convicted, and Broaster received a 15-year sentence from a judge who appears to have been particularly harsh.

Seven members of the House of Israel in Newark, New Jersey, were arrested in January 1943 for conspiracy to undermine compliance with the Selective Service Act. During the trial several defendants announced in open court that they were Israelites not Americans, and saw no reason to fight for a nation that, in the words of one, had "Jim Crowed [us] to death." The FBI explained their opposition to the war and the draft somewhat differently, telling the press that the defendants were "formerly connected with a Japanese propaganda movement." In February, six defendants were convicted. Each was sentenced to three years in prison.[65]

Federal officials in all of the black sedition cases noted that the black community had rejected the conspirators' efforts, and the judge in the Butler/Erwin case concluded that "thanks to the intelligence of the colored race, little damage was done by the conspirators."[66] Designed no doubt to reassure white folk (and acknowledge the loyalty of most blacks), the admission inadvertently ratified Baldwin's contention that the insignificance of the agitators made prosecution unnecessary. Nevertheless, Butler and Erwin received sentences of four years each. The punishment meted out to them and the other black nationalists was less than the 20-year sentences possible under the law (and commonly applied in World War I) and comparable to those dispensed to the convicted native fascists.

Erwin and Butler, and Gordon and her associates appealed their convictions on various grounds. Two appeals courts concluded that the evidence was sufficient and the trials fairly conducted. The Seventh Circuit ruled that it was not necessary to show that Erwin and Butler in fact caused insubordination or obstructed enlistment. It was sufficient, the court said, harking back to a pre–World War I formula, to show that the words were used in such circumstances and were of such a nature that "they would have a tendency" to produce these outcomes.[67] The defendants did not appeal to the highest court; they probably could not afford the expense, and did not have the support of organizations whose intercession might have made the appeal possible.

The government's position, upheld by the courts to this point, was that words that had a dangerous tendency were punishable under the anti-sedition statutes. The degree of influence commanded by the accused was not a decisive legal issue. A recent circuit court ruling in a case involving William Dudley Pelley had held that it was not necessary for the government to show that the defendant in a sedition case had moved anyone to action. Nor was the absence of significant impact a decisive factor for the ACLU. That organization, while inclined to give wide latitude to critical political expression, drew the line at utterances that consisted of "(1) specific advice, especially to members of the armed forces, to disobey the law, and (2) propaganda specifically in favor of a military victory by the enemy; and possibly constant repetition of enemy propaganda where the motive of support of the enemy is reasonably clear."[68] The black nationalist rhetoric qualified on each count.

The government could prove that the defendants had expressed extravagant admiration for the Japanese, and wished publicly for an Axis victory.

Moreover, and this was crucial, they specifically urged draft resistance and even mutinous behavior. The difference between the ideas expressed by Erwin, Robb, Gordon, and Jordan, and those found in publications like the *Pittsburgh Courier,* was a matter of degree. But the discrepancy was decisive. Any fair account of America's racial policy had a tendency to undermine the allegiance of African Americans to the nation and the war, and in a sense any discussion of American race relations had seditious implications for black listeners. Hence the administration's efforts to get the black press to tone down its comments. But there was a crucial distinction between simply condemning America's racial policies and advising young black men to avoid the draft or turn on their officers. The boundaries of free speech were elastic, but not unbreakable. The Department of Justice had already demonstrated that one need not be black to suffer for such utterances—a number of (white) fascists had already been successfully prosecuted for statements that were no more egregious than these.

The black defendants were afforded equal justice under the law. Outside the courtroom, department spokesmen publicly exaggerated the sinister nature and influence of the various groups of defendants; inside, the cases they presented were reasonable, if ill-advised, and the trials fairly conducted. In the Chicago case, representatives of both the ACLU and the NAACP carefully monitored the proceedings, and lawyers from the Chicago branch of the Civil Liberties Union interviewed Robb and his attorney as soon as the indictments were handed down.[69] Neither the branch, nor the national board, nor the NAACP found grounds to support an appeal.[70]

Even if the prosecutions were soundly based on truly seditious utterances and the process fair and relatively free of prejudice, the question remains whether they should have been brought at all. Were the activities of the black nationalists, even if demonstrably illegal, sufficiently grave to warrant trial and punishment? Baldwin thought not,[71] and he believed he detected misgivings among the Justice Department officials with whom he spoke.[72] But policy was shaped by public perceptions as well as public needs. Ignoring grossly disloyal utterances, regardless of their influence, was likely at least to earn the attorney general severe censure in the press and a rebuke from the president. In this instance it might also have produced "justice" at the hands of the vigilante or local government. Ultimately Biddle acted because what the black nationalists were saying was seditious; because what they were saying was on the verge of becoming notorious; and because (despite warnings) they showed no sign of changing their tune. In these circumstances it would have taken more courage and independence than Biddle had to stay the hand of repression.

Chapter 12

The Denaturalization Strategy

The Justice Department's successful campaign against the black nationalists did nothing to relieve demands for the extirpation of seditious propaganda. Critics, most of them liberal antifascists, were not interested in the activities or fate of Robert O. Jordan, General Lee Butler, and the other black agitators, and took little notice of their prosecution. What they wanted, and the president concurred, was the destruction of American fascism, and although their demands had produced the arrest of a few extremists and the first tentative steps in the department's program of denying second-class mailing privileges to suspect journals, they continued to complain that hundreds of fascistic propagandists remained free to spread their corrosive notions. Biddle concluded that something more had to be done immediately to placate the critics—but what?

The leaders of the now defunct German-American Bund offered a target that satisfied the attorney general's political needs. The Bundists were well known (their antics had been in the news for years), they were numerous, and above all their status as naturalized Americans meant that they could be punished for their beliefs or associations without the protracted and uncertain process of prosecution under the anti-sedition statutes. The means was denaturalization, a civil process by which persons who had fraudulently acquired their citizenship might be stripped of their American nationality. A successful action of this kind against a naturalized American of German nativity would result in the victim's again becoming a citizen of Germany, and subject, as a result, to internment at the government's convenience. The process offered a relatively quick and simple way of punishing large numbers of well-known "Nazis." The only problem it posed was that the arbitrariness of the process raised the issue of fairness and, like the revocation of the second-class mailing privilege, some department officials expressed reservations concerning its wholesale use as an anti-sedition device. Nevertheless, Biddle, overcoming such scruples, approved of a denaturalization project that would target about one thousand German-Americans, most of them former Bundists.

Unlike the native fascists, who were hardly known outside of antifascist circles, the Bund had long been notorious for its contempt for American institutions and values. Bund rallies and youth camps made excellent copy, and this Nazi presence in America had become a staple of American journalism. While William Dudley Pelley and others of his ilk might be dismissed as cranks or misguided (Christian) superpatriots, the Bundists, like the Communists, had been pictured in the press as the sinister agents of a foreign power. Their accented speech and prewar parading in foreign uniforms emphasized their alien allegiance and dubious loyalty to their adopted country. Although the Bund had disbanded shortly after Pearl Harbor and posed no threat to American security, its prewar image lingered in the public's imagination. An attack on the ex-Bundists seemed to be an excellent way for Biddle to demonstrate his intolerance of disloyalty.

The *Amerika-Deutscher Volksbund,* or German-American Bund, had led a troubled existence. Founded by Fritz Kuhn in 1936, the organization had branches in a number of states, but was most active in the New York metropolitan area. Most of its members were recent German immigrants who found in the organization's rituals and social-cultural activities a sense of community, "racial" identity, and pride. Bund leaders defended the German-American population against charges of disloyalty (for which Bund activities were largely responsible), opposed anti-Nazi measures (such as the late 1930s boycott of German goods), and criticized the purported excessive influence of Jews and Communists in making national policy. The message, and the stridently anti-democratic tone in which it was delivered, repulsed most German Americans, who either were, or sought to be, fully integrated into American society. Thus, while there were tens of millions of Americans of German extraction and over a million recent immigrants from Germany, the Bund only attracted between ten and twenty-five thousand members.[1] Even the German government repudiated the group. Troubled by the Bund's success in antagonizing the American public, the German foreign office in 1938 decreed that German nationals would no longer be permitted to associate themselves with the organization. Kuhn went to Berlin to protest and, although German officials re-affirmed the order, the American fuehrer (and his enemies) continued to talk of the close ties between the Bund and the Nazi regime.

The group's reputation reached its nadir following a rally it held in New York's Madison Square Garden in February 1939. Newspapers reported the anti-Semitic diatribes while newsreels and photos revealed what must have struck many as the offensive incongruity of the Nazis using a huge portrait of George Washington flanked by American banners and swastikas as the backdrop for the Bundist dignitaries arrayed on the speaker's platform.[2]

From this point on, the Bund rapidly slid into oblivion. In May, Kuhn was indicted for embezzling organization funds, and the onset of World War II would find him in New York's Sing Sing prison. Gerhard Wilhelm Kunze assumed the leadership and presided over an organization riven with internal feuding and beset by active public hostility. By the summer of 1941, attacked by veterans groups and harassed by antifascist elements and local authorities, the group could no longer hold public meetings. In November, Kunze, anticipating federal prosecution, fled to Mexico. Soon after, the remaining Bund leaders dissolved the organization.[3] Their troubles with the federal government, however, had hardly begun.

America's Nazis had been an object of federal scrutiny since 1934, when President Roosevelt ordered the FBI to look into the "movement's" activities. Protests from private citizens and demands from the House Committee on Un-American Activities, which had conducted its own investigation of the Bund, had by 1937 produced a considerable body of information from which officials concluded that, despite the obvious disloyalty implicit in Bundist activities, neither the organization nor its leaders had broken the law.[4] In September 1940, the Criminal Division gave Attorney General Jackson a list of ways in which the government might harass the Bund and other fascist organizations. It recommended, for "publicity and educational" purposes, "frequent presentments" to grand juries. These would presumably show the public that the department was alive to the problem, and notify Bund leaders and members that the government was after them. The problem with this tactic was that it could not get around the fact that federal statutes did not outlaw the activities charged against the Nazi imitators. Jackson rejected the grand jury harassment scheme on the grounds that it would oblige the government to reveal the inadequacy of its evidence of criminal activity, thus undercutting "the integrity of the Department" and subjecting it to criticism that it was employing "Star Chamber tactics."[5]

The fact that the Bundists were mostly foreign born suggested denaturalization, a process long used to rid the United States of Communists.[6] All that this procedure required was for Justice Department lawyers to petition a federal judge to void a Bundist's certificate of naturalization on grounds that his words and associations impeached the authenticity of the oath of allegiance he had taken. If the judge agreed, Citizen Kuhn, for example, would become Alien Kuhn. Should Germany and the United States go to war, Kuhn would then be subject to detention as an enemy alien.

Officials recognized from the outset that the idea of using denaturalization in this way was legally and ethically questionable.[7] Although its use during World War I had been upheld by the courts, the rulings had been ambiguous. On one hand, the courts affirmed that naturalization conferred upon the new citizen all the rights enjoyed by other citizens, save the privilege of serving as president. They had also ruled, however, that citizenship thus granted could be revoked if the government could prove it had been fraudulently obtained.[8] Evidence of such fraud naturally included actions that the court may not have known about *before* granting naturalization, but actions taken by the defendant for a reasonable period *after* naturalization might also be considered. There were questions, however, as to what was a *reasonable* time and what later actions constituted evidence of the citizen's state of mind at the time he or she had applied for naturalization. This issue was sufficient to suggest that denaturalization based principally on subsequent behavior might no longer be sustained by a Supreme Court that was plainly a good deal more sensitive to civil libertarian concerns than its predecessors of 15 or 20 years earlier.

With this in mind, department officials were at first reluctant to take advantage of denaturalization. The misgivings were apparent in an article published in 1941 by Forrest Black, who was then serving as special assistant to the attorney general. A law professor and an authority on constitutional rights, Black reviewed the case law on denaturalization and noted that, in many instances, it had been employed in cases that placed "too great a strain on the fiction of relation-back" and "made a mockery of the presumption of a 'reasonable time.'" Use of the procedure, he suggested, smacked of the unethical or at least the unseemly, and he insisted that if the administration wished to attack persons suspected of disloyalty in this way, it should seek a new law that made the process indubitably legal. "If the American people believe that it is a sound national policy to denaturalize on the ground of disloyalty, Congress should so declare" and thus remove the temptation from the courts and the Justice Department to resort to legal "chicanery." He recognized the possibility that such a law might not successfully run the "gauntlet of constitutionality."[9]

In late 1941 the Justice Department, following Black's advice, sponsored a change in the law. The proposed amendment to the naturalization statutes was introduced by Representative Samuel Dickstein, whose January 1934 resolution proposing an investigation of Nazi activities in the United States had earned him the dubious honor of having fathered the now notorious House Committee on Un-American Activities. Dickstein had been impressed by the fact that many of the Nazis called to testify before the committee were either naturalized citizens, or in the process of obtaining their naturalization, and he had raised the question of whether Bund membership was compatible with American citizenship.[10] Passage of his bill would mean that the Justice Department would no longer be obliged to ask the courts to infer from later actions the applicant's state of mind at the time of naturalization. Henceforth it could use evidence of subsequent disloyalty as prima facie grounds for denaturalization.

The Dickstein bill, which had the support of the military as well as the Justice Department, was unanimously endorsed by the House Immigration Committee and submitted to the House in early January 1942. During floor debate members pointed to the galling inadequacy of current law, which made it possible, as one put it, for "Fritz Kuhn and all his ilk," although convicted of the "most heinous crimes known to our law," (embezzlement?), to emerge from prison with his American citizenship intact. Although Representative Hamilton Fish, the conservative and isolationist patrician from FDR's home district in Dutchess County, New York, worried about the power the legislation would confer upon U.S. attorneys and federal judges to decide what constituted "disloyalty,"[11] the House voted to expand the repressive potential of the Dickstein bill by adding subsequent "utterances, writings, [and] actions" to "conduct," as grounds for denaturalization. In this form, the anti-seditious speech amendment to the naturalization law was sent on to the Senate Immigration Committee.[12]

The measure generated considerable opposition. The ACLU quickly assembled a group of distinguished constitutional lawyers who signed a brief opposing the legislation. The bill, which clearly threatened naturalized citizens who had become Communists, was also opposed by the leftist Lawyer's Guild and by the Communist-dominated American Committee for Protection of Foreign Born.[13] L. M. C. Smith testified in favor of the measure for the Justice Department, although some department officials reportedly thought the House had gone too far. The House bill was reported favorably by the Senate Immigration Committee in October, but was not brought to a vote, and at the end of the year the issue was dead.[14]

Long before then, the Justice Department decided to go ahead without waiting. The decision was not dictated by concern for the Bund's subversive potential. Although officials would later publicly claim, rather implausibly, that the organization continued to form the nucleus of a fifth column,[15] there is no evidence that this view was taken seriously by senior officials. In any event, Bundists could be—as some were—prosecuted under anti-espionage and other statutes that applied to all residents. In fact, a number of Bundists so charged either were, or would shortly be, imprisoned on such charges.[16] Nor was the government responding to a public demand for Bundist blood. On New Year's Day 1942, the chauvinistic and sharp-tongued columnist Westbrook Pegler had written demanding that all the former Bundists be locked up, but this seemed to be his favored response to all signs of un-Americanism,[17] and few commentators endorsed his suggestion. Although fears of industrial sabotage generated by the sinking of the *Normandie* in February raised some concern about German Americans, press attention and public interest in the winter and spring of that year were first preoccupied with the assumed threat Japanese Americans posed to West Coast defenses, and then with the outrageous speeches and writings of Coughlin, Pelley, and the native fascists.

Yet public opinion had everything to do with the department's decision. In the winter and spring of 1942, antifascists, supported by the president, were insisting that fascistic agitators be silenced and punished. Suitable targets among the native fascists proved to be scarce, but the naturalized German Americans who made up the leadership of the once notorious Bund were numerous and it would take very little to offer their denaturalization as proof that the department was effectively punishing disloyalty. In early March, James Rowe, the attorney general's principal assistant and chief political advisor, discovered the political opportunity the program offered. "I have been hearing a great deal . . . about the denaturalization cases," he wrote Biddle, "and it has suddenly occurred to me, that I have been completely asleep on this matter." Once awake, he asked to be put in charge of preparations,[18] and less than a week later the Criminal Division had a plan for denaturalizing the Bundists, and possibly others, on the attorney general's desk.[19] Rowe, Criminal Division head Wendell Berge, and L.M.C. Smith of the Special War Policies unit agreed on the need to proceed quickly and to pay special attention to the accompanying public relations campaign.[20] Warning Biddle, "as a friend," that he needed to act now to dispel his reputation for softness, Rowe pressed the value of a vigorous, well-advertised pursuit of the Bundists.

Fear of military usurpation of Justice Department authority may have influenced department thinking. Such concerns, raised by events during World War I,[21] had recently been revived by the department's humiliation at the army's hands in regard to the West Coast Japanese Americans. In

February 1942 the War Department had sought authority to clear militarily sensitive areas of persons whom the military determined threatened national security. Justice Department officials opposed the mass removal on constitutional grounds, but the president supported the War Department. Biddle capitulated even before his subordinates had been able to argue their case, and President Roosevelt signed Executive Order 9066. This provided the authority for the ignominious Japanese relocation, but the order was not limited in its application to the Japanese Americans and was in fact applicable to anyone the army designated.[22] Under this authority several hundred aliens and citizens, apart from the Japanese Americans, were forced to leave the nation's coastal and other security-sensitive areas.[23] These "exclusions" were a point of serious contention between the military and the Justice Department, and Justice officials had reason to fear that if Biddle did not act to denaturalize and intern the Bundists, the army would, at least in some cases, use its authority under the executive order to secure their summary removal.[24] This would constitute not only a defeat for civil liberties, but a serious incursion of military authority into an area the Justice Department claimed as its own domain.

Determined to act against the Bundists, Rowe set out to secure the right man for the denaturalization effort, one who would deliver a "100% performance and a big press campaign." He recommended O. John Rogge, the outspoken prosecutor whom Jackson had fired as head of the Criminal Division for his excessive zeal. Anticipating Biddle's concerns, he noted that the contentious Rogge "can't do any political harm in this sort of situation and he does get results." What was important, he said, was to "emphasize that we are using our crack prosecutor to go after the Nazis."[25] When Rogge proved unavailable (or unacceptable) for the job, Rowe urged the appointment of the colorful and aggressive U.S. attorney in New York, Mattias Correa. Denaturalization cases, Rowe pointed out, were not difficult to prepare, and Correa could do them "part-time." But departmental politics made it difficult to appoint either Rogge or Correa without offending senior staff attorneys, and the attorney general finally settled on an experienced insider, Dewey Balch, a Minnesota attorney who had been working on the denaturalization issue for the Criminal Division.

On March 26, the attorney general, claiming that the department had approximately 30 cases ready for immediate action and several hundred more in preparation, announced the denaturalization program. There was to be no indictment or jury trial.[26] A department official (usually the U.S. attorney) would present its case against the accused Bundist to a federal district judge who, on the basis of the evidence submitted by the government, to which the accused had a right to respond, would decide what the defendant's state of mind was at the time of his naturalization. This was a dubious undertaking given the fact that naturalization may have been obtained five, ten, or even forty years earlier,[27] and officials were aware that they were treading uncertain ground.[28] But driven by the public relations benefits the campaign promised, they set aside their doubts, encouraged, no doubt, by the conviction that regardless of the fairness of the proceeding, the accused Bundists deserved their fate. In the week following Biddle's initial announcement, the department would issue four more statements concerning the impending drive.[29]

Baldwin and Hays protested the denaturalization announcement and attempted to rally civil libertarian lawyers to their cause. They failed.[30] Zechariah Chafee, in turning down a Baldwin request, revealed the anomalous situation in which he found himself. He noted that under the present state of the law, no court could properly revoke a naturalization without a finding of fraud or illegality at the time citizenship was obtained, and assumed that the department would be acting in consonance with this understanding of the law. But, he wrote, his relations with Biddle were so friendly that "I like to give him the benefit of the doubt and assume that the 'several hundred' [Biddle referred to in his announcement] are all recent citizens, and that they are the sort of men who joined the Bund right after they got their citizenship papers."[31]

Chafee was on good terms with Biddle and his staff. What he said mattered to the people who made department policy. Wishing to preserve the association and his influence, Chafee and, perhaps, others were reluctant to expend their political capital on protests until "all the facts were in." So they held back, encouraging the attorney general to believe that his actions had at least the tacit acceptance of the people whose views on the subject counted a great deal. Then again, Biddle was unlikely to have been moved by entreaties from such sources, and Chafee, recognizing the futility of intercession, may have been using his relationship with Biddle as an excuse not to accede to Baldwin's request.

During the summer of 1942 the drive against the Bund gathered momentum. Rowe, who oversaw the program, reminded laggard prosecutors that the attorney general regarded the denaturalization campaign as of the "utmost importance" and insisted that they should consider it their "first matter of business."[32] There is some evidence that Rowe expected the U.S. attorneys to meet quotas in regard to Bund-related cases.[33] Although results were not nearly as dramatic as had been hoped, the publicity that attached to what had been accomplished, what was in progress, and what was planned, created the impression that a massive German-American fifth column was being vigorously and successfully attacked. This was particularly so because announcements of denaturalizations were frequently coupled with criminal prosecutions of a handful of Bund leaders, the roundup and detention of German aliens, and even the recent capture and trial of German saboteurs.

A prime target of the collateral campaign was the Kyffhaeuser Bund (League of German War Veterans in the USA),[34] an organization of German and Austrian veterans of World War I that, since 1939, had been soliciting contributions from German-American groups for transmittal to Germany. Although the Kyffhaeuser Bund officially disbanded in January 1942, the department decided in mid-March to prosecute the organization and its officers for prewar violations of the Neutrality Act and the Foreign Agents Registration Act (FARA). The FBI raided a number of Kyffhaeuser Bund sites in April, seizing evidence of the group's fund-raising and German connections. Sixty-four people were arrested and faced internment as dangerous enemy aliens. In addition, about thirty American citizens were reportedly added to the list of those to be denaturalized.[35] The FBI made no mention of the charges—failure to register under FARA—emphasizing instead that the raids had uncovered evidence of the organization's clandestine fifth-column activities. A cache of seized arms, ammunition, and Nazi paraphernalia was put on display in the Federal Building in New York for the public's edification.

This coup was followed in early July by Biddle's announcement that a federal grand jury in New York had returned indictments charging 26 German-American Bund leaders in eight states with conspiring to subvert compliance with the Selective Service Act. A second indictment named these persons, and three more, as conspiring to encourage members to conceal their Bund affiliations in the filing of alien registration forms. The first indictment referred specifically to a 1940 Bund directive that, while encouraging members to comply with Selective Service regulations, went on to say that the leadership believed "that an induction in the military service is not justified . . . [and hoped that] every man, if he can, will refuse to do military duty" until Section 8 of the Selective Service Act, which they noted discriminated against members of the Bund, was repealed. Section 8, a non-binding piece of political chest-thumping, declared that it was the expressed policy of the Congress that job vacancies resulting from the departure of employees for military service should not be filled by members of the Communist Party or the Bund.[36] The leadership would later describe its order concerning the draft as a protest against this gratuitous slap at the membership. The government presented it to a grand jury as a counsel of draft evasion.[37]

Two days later, the front page of the *New York Times* reported that the "swift pace of the government's sudden drive to wipe out" the sinister remnants of the Bund had taken another giant stride with the roundup of 70 alien relatives and friends of those charged in the draft evasion case. They were held on Ellis Island pending hearings to determine whether they posed enough of a danger to warrant their internment for the duration.[38] Other announcements documenting the government's attack on German-American disloyalty followed in quick succession.[39]

The latest target was the *Deutsche-Americanische Berufsgemeinschaft* (DAB) or German-American Vocational League. The DAB was an association of German workers founded at the turn of the century. After Hitler came to power, the DAB became the American branch of the German Labor Front, and its members came to enjoy the privileges of membership in that association of German employer and employee groups. The DAB provided vocational training, job placement, and unemployment insurance, and had been cooperating with the Kyffhaeuser in collecting funds for Germany. In January 1942 the FBI raided DAB facilities and carted away documents on the basis of which the Criminal Division recommended that its officers be prosecuted for violation of the Foreign Agents Registration Act.[40] In July, 158 persons affiliated with DAB were taken into custody in what the *New York Times* described as the "largest single seizure of enemy aliens of one nationality." The newspaper account failed to mention that the charges involved prewar registration violations, reporting instead that those seized had been arrested on "charges that they are dangerous to the security of the United States."[41]

And so it went through the rest of July and August and into the fall of 1942.[42] The well-publicized campaign combined exaggerated charges and intimations of fifth-column plots, with confusing figures relating to rounded-up aliens and planned denaturalizations.[43] The campaign was concentrated in the New York City area, but went on across the nation. What the defendants had in common (besides their German origins) was that they had been targeted for prewar associations that allegedly made their current loyalty suspect. None were charged with wartime sedition.

Behind all the hoopla, the department was, in fact, uncertain about its undertaking, and prone to move cautiously. Presidential advisor and confidante Harry Hopkins suggested that the denaturalization campaign be widened to target all Bund members, not just the leaders, but Rowe told him that he doubted that the courts would accept membership as the sole basis for determining fraud.[44] Indeed, Roger Baldwin came away from discussions with Dewey Balch, who was running the department's denaturalization program, impressed by his apparent determination to carefully choose the cases they would pursue,[45] limiting their targets to "national and local officers, other active leaders, . . . and possibly others whose militant activity" warranted their inclusion. In fact, although the Justice Department opened about eleven thousand potential cases, it produced only a few hundred denaturalization petitions. Even so, in many of these there was little evidence of overt disloyalty apart from the suspect's connection with the Bund, and the government relied on making an overwhelming case for the subversive intentions and activities of the organization in hopes that, absent better evidence of individual culpability, the group's disloyal activities might be assigned to its active members. Balch worried that the government's theory might not be sustained on appeal.[46]

On the eve of the first anniversary of American involvement in the war, Biddle proudly reviewed the department's achievements over the past year. The government, he said, had "virtually put an end to organized sedition in the United States," and he attributed its success in part to the 42 denaturalizations the department had effected to date, and the hundreds of others in process.[47] Prospects for the year ahead looked good, as district court judges approved most of the early petitions. In November a federal judge in Missouri denaturalized Carl W. Baumgartner, who had become a citizen in September 1932. Baumgartner had repeatedly expressed his admiration for the Nazi regime, which came to power the year after he was naturalized. He told investigators that his political views in 1932 were the same as they were currently. His statement, which he intended to affirm his pre-naturalization loyalty, was presented by the government, and taken by the court, as proof that he had been as disloyal ten years ago as his post-naturalization statements appeared to suggest he was now.[48] In upholding a similar denaturalization in mid-December, the judge ruled that the defendant's words since the United States had been at war with Germany were "sufficiently lacking in Pro-Americanism" for the Court to conclude that he had never fully given up his loyalty to his mother country.[49]

With the success of the denaturalization campaign against the Bund seemingly assured, department officials turned to serious consideration of applying the technique to disloyal Italian Americans and their organizations.[50] The issue of fascistic sympathies among Italian Americans is too complex to be explored here.[51] Suffice it to say that a number of department officials were concerned about the phenomenon, and Rowe, Berge, and Smith hoped to use denaturalization proceedings against a number of suspect individuals. Their motive seemed principally visceral—an understandable pique at the spectacle of Mussolini's ardent American admirers freely going about their business even as American troops prepared to confront the Fascisti in Italy.

But satisfying this sense of justice was complicated by the fact that the public was not greatly concerned about disloyalty among Italian Americans,[52] and that, unlike the Bundists who were pariahs in the German-American community, fascist sympathizers enjoyed positions of leadership among Italian Americans. Moreover, Italian Americans, unlike German Americans, were an important Democratic Party constituency—a fact of no little consequence in producing Biddle's Columbus Day 1942 announcement that he was removing Italians from the enemy alien category. That act took the sting out of any denaturalization effort aimed at Italian Americans, for in declaring that resident Italian aliens were no longer *enemy* aliens, Biddle had ensured that should the government take away the citizenship of Italian-American fascists, it would merely be making them resident ("friendly") aliens—not the more vulnerable nationals of an enemy state.[53]

While 1943 dawned brightly for the anti-Bund campaign, developments would soon portend the collapse of the effort. At the beginning of January the government began presenting its major case in New York against a large group of Bundists, including Fritz Kuhn. It was aimed primarily at establishing the subversive character of the German-American Bund, thereby making it unnecessary for the government to argue the nature of the organization in each subsequent proceeding. In mid-March, District Judge John Bright handed down his decision agreeing with the government that the Bund's constitution and outward forms of loyalty to the United States had merely been a front for its un-American and subversive objectives. But he also said that the character of the organization did not adhere to every member, and that the government was still bound to prove that a given defendant "knew, approved of, or adopted those aims" and, further, that attachment to Bund ideas demonstrated the defendant's state of mind at the time he took the oath of allegiance. Bright was convinced that such a showing had been made in regard to Kuhn and ten of his fellows, but he refused to annul the citizenship of nine other Bundists.[54] The implications of his rulings for the anti-Bund drive were driven home by the Supreme Court when in June it decided the case of *Schneiderman* v. *U.S.*

The case of William Schneiderman began in 1927, when the 20-year-old Russian immigrant was granted U.S. citizenship. He had been involved with radical groups before his naturalization and had gone on to become the leader of the Communist Party in California, and the party's candidate for governor. His prominence brought him to the attention of immigration officials, who in 1939 petitioned the court to revoke his citizenship on grounds that during the five years prior to his securing the certificate of citizenship, he had not "behaved as a person attached to the principles of the United States." The evidence of this disloyalty was his involvement with various organizations dedicated to advancing Communist principles and goals. A federal district court in California agreed, Schneiderman appealed, and the decision was affirmed by the Ninth Circuit Court of Appeals.

Schneiderman was not the first Communist to have been treated in this manner, but now, in the midst of the war, his case and others were embarrassing for the administration. Writing of pending litigation against Stanley Nowak, a party official who had been elected to the Michigan Senate, Assistant Attorney General Wendell Berge told Biddle that he would like to dismiss the case, but could not because the Communists would brag about their ability to influence government policy. He noted, however, that if the government lost the *Schneiderman* case, which was to be heard first, it would at least have a way out of the *Nowak* case.[55] Such were the political calculations that went into these matters.

In March, the Court listened to arguments in the *Schneiderman* case— Wendell Willkie, the Wall Street lawyer and Republican candidate for president in 1940, represented the Communist. In June, a divided Court reversed the findings of the district court and the circuit court of appeals, and in so doing established a burden of proof that would affect hundreds of denaturalization cases now before the courts or being prepared in the department.[56] The five-to-three majority, formed around the liberal core of Justices Hugo Black, Frank Murphy, Wiley Rutledge, and William O. Douglas, wrote three separate opinions. Chief Justice Stone delivered a strong dissent.

Justice Murphy, writing for the Court, declared that he found the record of the case "barren of any conduct or statements . . . which indicates in the slightest that [Schneiderman] believed in . . . force and violence," and that it was not proper to assign to him the revolutionary statements issued by the organizations to which he belonged. Moreover, and significantly for the anti-Bund drive, the Court ruled that "events and writings" since Schneiderman obtained his citizenship had "little relevance" in establishing his earlier state of mind. The Court refused to venture an opinion on whether or not the Communist Party espoused revolution, noting that the issue was irrelevant since the government in any case was not entitled to impute the organization's purposes to its individual members. To strip a person of his or her citizenship, the government would have to prove by "clear, unequivocal and convincing evidence" that he had been wrongly granted it in the first place. "Were the law otherwise," Murphy wrote, "valuable rights would rest upon a slender reed, and the security of the status of our naturalized citizens might depend in considerable degree upon the political temper of majority thought and the stresses of the times."[57]

Murphy, who as attorney general had initiated a government crackdown on Communists (including Schneiderman) and Nazis, had issued a pointed affirmation of personal freedoms, and, inferentially, a rebuke to his two successors at the Justice Department. It remained to be seen, however, whether the court would apply the controversial *Schneiderman* standard to the somewhat different issues posed by the still pending Bund denaturalization cases.

Up to this point the government had enjoyed some success in its drive against the Bund. In October 1943 the ACLU reported that the Justice Department had brought 270 cases to deprive Americans of their citizenship, and had been successful in 131. In 54 instances the case had been dismissed or decided in favor of the defendant. Several cases were on appeal.[58] At the end of August, however, a district court judge, citing *Schneiderman,* dismissed a government denaturalization suit against Alexander Hartmann, whom the FBI had described as the "no. 1 Nazi" in Philadelphia.[59] The fate of the Bundist denaturalization program was now in doubt.

The Department of Justice had embarked on its denaturalization effort primarily because the process seemed to promise the dramatic and satisfying successes over Nazism that the president and segments of the public demanded. The targets of the government's campaign were in almost every instance persons who had evinced unseemly loyalty to Nazi Germany, a nation with which the United States was now at war, and who had, at best, shown themselves to be indifferently attached to American ideals. In such circumstances, taking away their citizenship, interning them, and eventually deporting them to their native land seemed eminently defensible.

Nevertheless, the process was inconsistent with Biddle's oft-expressed commitment to civil liberties and violated a basic tenet of civil libertarian principle in that it punished people for their beliefs and associations rather than their actions. The foreign-born Bundists were to be interned and exiled, while American-born citizens with similar associations and ideas would only suffer the disapproval of their neighbors. Moreover, denaturalization, as the department pursued it, validated the pernicious idea that there were two classes of citizenship—that naturalized citizens were not entitled to the same constitutional protections presumably enjoyed by other Americans.

Chapter 13

"Crackpots and Cranks from All Parts of the Nation"

While their status as naturalized citizens made the Bundists vulnerable to punishment for their disloyalty, or at least so it was thought, most of the notorious fascist agitators were not so easily disposed of. Almost all were native born and if they were to be punished, it would have to be under the criminal statutes governing sedition. However, in most instances the words and activities of the suspected seditionists did not seem sufficient to meet the law's requirements. Unlike the black nationalists, who urged disaffection in the military and resistance to the draft, and bragged of their contacts with people they took to be Japanese agents, the fascistic agitators were relatively circumspect in their rhetoric and associations. If they had any connections to the Axis, they were well hidden, and their attacks on administration leaders and the war effort were often intentionally based on material appearing in the *Congressional Record* or the *Chicago Tribune*. Indeed, their anti-Semitic, anti-administration, anti-British ideas were not far removed from the thinking of many Americans, particularly in the Midwest and southern California, where most of the seditionists operated. Local juries would be asked to decide whether the defendants' expressions of opinion went beyond the bounds of free speech guaranteed by the Constitution. Officials were far from certain how they would decide, and Biddle felt obliged to ask for a new statute broadening the definition of sedition. Congress refused to oblige. Nevertheless, under pressure from antifascists and the president, Biddle was determined to go ahead. In the early spring of 1942, the Department of Justice began working on plans to prosecute those who could plausibly be indicted under existing statutes.

The department's agenda was determined to a large extent by "Voices of Defeat," the April 1942 *Life* article that presented brief, dramatic accounts of organizations, individuals, and journals openly circulating "subversive doctrines."[1] Here were the names of America's leading defeatists and a rundown of the disloyal things they had said. There seemed to be no excuse for continued inaction. But the fact was that some of the persons in the *Life* exposé were totally unknown to the department, and officials believed that the evidence against the rest ("Voices" notwithstanding) was inadequate to sustain successful prosecutions. Seeking to placate critics until realistic cases could be constructed, the department's Criminal Division under Wendell Berge cobbled together a program of actions the government might take immediately to demonstrate its determination to deal forcefully with disloyalty. In late April, the attorney general announced the department's new program to the nation.[2] In addition to nullifying the citizenship of the leaders of the German-American Bund, Biddle declared that the department would institute a series of federal grand jury fact-finding inquiries aimed at developing evidence against various persons named in the *Life* article. These were to begin in Chicago at once, and continue at one-week intervals thereafter in the other areas in which the named seditionists operated.[3] The attorney general's most dramatic announcement, however, was that the government was ready to prosecute the notorious William Dudley Pelley. The president let Biddle know he was pleased.[4]

After Father Coughlin, Pelley was the chief target of the antifascists. His creation of the Silver Shirts in the 1930s, and his nefarious associations and long record of affection for Germany and Japan were well documented. The war produced no noticeable letup in his incendiary talk as he continued to castigate the president and freely predict an Axis victory.[5] *Time* characterized him as the "most brazen U.S. Naziphile."[6] In January 1942, a report in the *Hour* that Pelley was gloating over the reverses suffered by the United States in the Pacific had moved FDR to put an end to Biddle's policy of tolerating obnoxious dissent[7] and, in late February, postal authorities declared that an issue of his weekly *Galilean* was non-mailable. Soon after, the Post Office ended second-class mail distribution to the journal's 1,200 to 1,500 subscribers.[8] An undaunted Pelley assured his followers that he could not be silenced. His personal "esoteric experiences and adventures," he declared, assured his destiny, and he boasted that "thousands of powerful Discarnates are working in conjunction with us and they furnish us with the indisputable evidence of how the struggle is coming out."[9] In this instance, the "Discarnates" appear to have been mistaken.

Pelley was arrested in early April. Two months later, a federal grand jury in Indianapolis indicted him and two associates on 13 counts of making, and conspiring to make, false statements designed to interfere with the war effort in violation of the Espionage Act. In a move calculated to improve the government's chances with the Indiana jury, Biddle appointed Oscar Ewing, a native son and graduate of Indiana University (and the Harvard Law School), to prosecute the case. His task would be to show that Pelley's statements were not only false, but that they had been issued with intent to aid the enemy or undercut the United States war effort.

Ewing's tactics were inventive. To prove that Pelley's statements were false, he called upon various experts: a banker to refute Pelley's charge that the country was bankrupt, a traveling salesmen to disprove Pelley's assertion that the American people were not behind the war effort, and so on. Seeking to establish that Pelley intended to promote disaffection in the military, but having no evidence that he was employed by the Axis, Ewing sought to link the mystic's writings to the themes of Axis propagandists by relying on techniques developed by Professor Harold Lasswell, and employed, as we have seen, in the postal censorship cases. Ewing also introduced the contents of several boxes of Axis propaganda that the FBI had seized at the *Galilean's* offices,[10] contending that Pelley was aware of what the Axis was saying and had demonstrated his seditious intentions by parroting the enemy's words.

In his summation, Ewing countered defense suggestions that Pelley's utterances were merely those of a religious prophet or a partisan Republican. The defendant's statements and past activities, including his creation of the paramilitary Silver Shirts, Ewing said, demonstrated his longstanding "devotion to Hitler and Nazi ideals." Addressing what he may have suspected were the ambivalent feelings of some of the jurors, Ewing conceded that "a man can hate Roosevelt, he can hate Great Britain . . . he can admire Germany [and] Japan . . . and still be a loyal American," but, he insisted, "no man can be a loyal American and preach all the themes of Axis propaganda!" Naturally, Ewing said, Pelley did not admit that he was intent on furthering Axis objectives but, he told the jury, the defendants must "be presumed to have intended the normal and natural consequences of their acts."[11]

In early August, Pelley and an associate were found guilty and sentenced to 15 and 5 years imprisonment, respectively.[12] They appealed on the grounds that the indictment did not name anyone who was influenced by the publications, that the government had shown no specific intent on the part of the defendants to influence the armed forces, and that the statements set forth in the indictment were merely opinions and not testable as to their accuracy. In mid-December, the Seventh Circuit Court of Appeals, relying heavily on *Schenck* and other World War I cases upholding convictions under the Espionage Act, rejected their claims, noting that the law required only that the government show intent to do harm, not the harm itself. Accepting the Lasswell analysis, the court concluded that the jury was justified in concluding that Pelley was a retailer of "secondhand Axis propaganda" and in inferring criminal intent from that. The circuit court, consistent with the position it would adopt in three succeeding federal anti-sedition cases,[13] made little of the issue of "clear and present danger," merely alluding to its use to convict Schenck.[14] The Supreme Court refused to grant certiorari.

Anti-fascists were pleased but not satisfied,[15] and Biddle took every opportunity to indicate that his war on domestic fascism had just begun. Nevertheless, following Pelley's conviction, a lack of immediately prosecutable cases forced a pause in this aspect of the campaign against fascism, and Biddle's concerns shifted temporarily to the (interim) resolution of the matter of Harry Bridges.

In September 1941, Charles Sears, the special examiner appointed by Attorney General Robert Jackson to hear Bridges's case for a second time, had found that: (1) the Communist Party advocated the violent overthrow of the government, and that (2) Bridges had been affiliated with the party. The decision as to whether to deport Bridges on the basis of these findings now rested with Attorney General Biddle, subject only to possible appeal to the circuit court of appeals and, perhaps, the Supreme Court. Biddle, who despised the Communist Party and had no sympathy for Bridges,[16] might simply have ratified Sears's conclusions. Instead, he submitted them to a five-person Board of Immigration Appeals, despite warnings from former Attorney General Jackson that the board was prejudiced in favor of Bridges. As Jackson predicted, the board focused on what it concluded was the unreliable testimony of the government's two key witnesses and unanimously recommended that the deportation order be vacated.[17] Biddle was now obliged to render a verdict.

Political considerations naturally entered into his calculations although, disconcertingly, they pointed in different directions. Both deporting Bridges and dismissing Sears's findings held their perils, and neither promised an end to the affair. Since the German assault on the Soviet Union, America's Communists had enthusiastically backed the war effort, and Bridges's own conduct had been exemplary.[18] In December, Senator Sheriden Downey of California wrote FDR urging him to intervene on

Bridges's behalf. Echoing a sentiment heard among shipping executives and many political leaders on the West Coast, Downey insisted that Bridges was making a critically important contribution to labor peace and the efficiency of the defense effort on the coast. The longshoreman's deportation now, Downey warned, would make him a martyr in labor and leftist circles, and would likely undercut the war effort. Despite their hostility toward Communism, administration officials were conscious of the need to discourage Soviet thoughts of a separate peace with Hitler and to keep American Communists behind the war effort. In early March 1942, aware of State Department opposition, Biddle put aside, for the duration of the war at least, plans for the prosecution of the Communist leadership.[19] This decision was symbolically confirmed in mid-May when, in a move he described as a gesture of "international unity," FDR announced that he was commuting the sentence of Communist Party Secretary Earl Browder, who had been sentenced to four years in prison in March 1941 for passport law violations.[20]

On the other hand, the Communist issue was far from dead, and any decision favorable to Bridges was bound to be used against the administration in the fall elections—and ever after. Red-baiting Representative Leland Ford of California, announced that "my people on the Pacific Coast, and many throughout the United States, know that Harry Bridges has been thousands of times more seditious, and committed more treasonable acts, than many of the people [fascists] whom the Attorney General is now prosecuting. . . . Why is this man still protected?" Something was rotten in Washington, he suggested, and he warned Biddle from the floor of the Congress that the whole country was watching to see "whether you have enough red American blood in your body . . . to do your duty."[21] The continuing force of anti-Communism was suggested by the durability of its principal protagonist, Congressman Martin Dies. In March 1942, the House of Representatives voted overwhelmingly to continue funding for Dies's Committee on Un-American Activities.[22] His position assured, Dies revived the Communists-in-government issue by reminding the Justice Department of a list of 1,124 government-employed security risks he had sent the attorney general in October 1941.

The administration wanted no part of Dies's list or the investigations it entailed. In the spring, the president established an informal interdepartmental committee purportedly to facilitate investigation of Dies's allegations, but actually, according to Biddle, to shield the administration from the "heat" generated by the congressman and others.[23] The administration, particularly the president, was far more interested in focusing public interest on Nazis (Bundists) and fascists, than in licensing a fishing expedition among its leftist employees. Indeed, at the end of May (at the same time he pardoned Browder), FDR instructed Biddle to speak to Hoover about the need to readjust his investigative priorities from the Left to the Right.[24]

The administration would continue to duck the issue of Communists in government and put off criminal prosecution of the party, but Biddle, after nearly six months of "deliberation," could no longer avoid addressing the matter of Harry Bridges's deportation. At the end of May, he issued his verdict. In a 30-page opinion, the attorney general reviewed the history of the CPUSA and the evidence bearing on Bridges's alleged membership. He concluded that Bridges had been a member of both the Marine Workers Industrial Union, which had played a key role in the San Francisco general strike, and the CPUSA. Further, noting that the defendant had not contested this point, he ruled that these organizations advocated the "overthrow by force and violence of the Government of the United States." Biddle ordered that "the alien Harry Renton Bridges, be deported to Australia."[25]

Anti-Communists were pleased, and a few local jurisdictions announced plans to use the ruling as the basis for hostile actions against the party.[26] The deportation order produced consternation among many people, particularly on the Left,[27] who worried about its assumed adverse effect on the war effort.[28] They need not have been concerned. Bridges and the party remained calm and continued to support the struggle against fascism. Biddle's action was portentous for the thousands of party members and fellow travelers who might be prosecuted under the Smith Act,[29] but his decision would be appealed; the issue of the applicability of the act to the CPUSA leaders and members was yet to be resolved.

Biddle saw his decision as an act of political courage—at least that is the way he wanted it understood. His accounts of how he told the president about it made this point. In remarks to reporters at the time,[30] and in the memoirs he wrote 20 years later, Biddle insisted that he had not consulted the president, but merely *informed* him of Bridges's fate shortly before announcing it. As he recalled the occasion, the president was stunned. Roosevelt, according to this story, "whistled, drew deeply on his cigarette, and for a moment was concentrated in thought" before collecting himself sufficiently to say that he was "sorry to hear that." A few days later, Biddle, emphasizing that he alone was responsible, told the press that the president had no power to revoke his order.[31]

Biddle sought to create the impression that he had acted on his own, as perhaps he had, but his motive remains unclear. In a letter to Eleanor Roosevelt he explained his action in two ways. The first lady had written the attorney general asking how she could justify his actions to all those (including apparently herself) who would not understand why, with the situation as it was in Russia, the attorney general would act as he did. In his response, Biddle presented himself as the objective executor of the laws, who had simply examined the facts and done his duty. He could not, he suggested, let political considerations shape his judgment. Having said that, however, he went on to claim that his decision served the administration's best interests. It was foolish, he wrote, to attempt to satisfy the Soviet Union, given its notorious inconstancy, but the dictates of domestic politics were clear and of immediate concern. His deportation order had the value of assuring those concerned about Communism "that because we are aiding the Russians . . . it does not follow [as conservative critics had charged] that we are permitting any Communists a free hand in this country."[32] In doing his duty as the nation's chief law enforcement officer, he had also protected the administration's political interests.

The matter was not closed. Bridges was free to appeal Biddle's decision to the courts and, as expected, he promptly did so. While the case made its way through the judicial system, the attorney general turned once again to the struggle against domestic fascism.

The government's effort to imprison the anti-Semitic and fascistic critics of the war got underway on July 23, 1942, when the attorney general proudly announced that a special grand jury in the District of Columbia had returned an indictment charging 28 leading lights of the fascist "movement" with conspiracy to undermine the loyalty, morale, and discipline of the armed forces.[33] The grand jury's action was proof, the attorney general said, that a democracy could move swiftly and effectively against its enemies.[34] Perhaps, but the indictment was a hollow shell—the product of political necessity glued together with a theory born of expedience. It would not hold.

The decision to ask for a single indictment and trial rather than to indict and try the defendants in the locales in which they operated seems to have originated with Biddle's assistant, James Rowe, who was concerned about the prospects for the success of local prosecutions. By the early summer of 1942, the government had failed to secure indictments of fascists in Los Angeles and Chicago,[35] and Rowe feared for the outcome of the government's case against the Reverend Gerald Winrod, one of the most prominent of the fascistic agitators. The preacher, he noted, had a large following in his home state of Kansas,[36] and he wondered if it wouldn't be better "to move the case to Washington?"[37] A week later senior officials began exploring the possibility of pursuing a "theory of over-all conspiracy," and moving all 28 of the contemplated cases to the nation's capital.[38] The move was made possible by the fact that Dillard Stokes, a reporter for the *Washington Post,* in the course of investigating fascist activity, had requested (under an assumed name) that the various fascists send him some of their literature. They had obliged, thus making the District of Columbia a scene of their alleged crimes.

The Washington venue promised more than simply getting the demagogues out of their home territories. It also made it possible to have the cases presented by an experienced, vigorous prosecutor, to a jury likely to favor the government. William Power Maloney, the special prosecutor who would take over the case, had been presenting evidence of Nazi propaganda activities to a Washington grand jury for the past year. In the course of this inquiry (which was accompanied by a steady leak of information to the press), Maloney had become well acquainted with the alleged fascist conspiracy, and the jury pool in the District of Columbia had been primed for an understanding of the government's case.

Most importantly, joining the cases and charging the 28 with seditious conspiracy promised to overcome the prosecution's central problem—the inadequacy of evidence establishing *individual* criminal intent. Through the magic of the law, the illicit purposes of those against whom a case might be made, could be assigned to others against whom it might not.[39] The government need only find one person among the 28 with ties to Berlin. His association with the others could transform a lone San Diego eccentric or Wichita fanatic into a member of an immense conspiracy extending all the way to Berlin.

The case of C. Leon de Aryan, one of those named in the *Life* article, suggested the basis of department concerns and the value of the mass prosecution.[40] De Aryan was the owner and publisher of *The Broom,* a San Diego–based sheet that was consistently anti-administration, anti-Communist, anti-British, anti-Semitic, antiwar, anti–international bankers, and anti–Federal Reserve system. On occasion it was anti-Hitler and anti-Japan as well. By the summer of 1942, De Aryan, who described himself as "Mazdaznan or Sun-Worshipper," had been investigated by California's Un-American Activities (Tenney) Committee and by a federal grand jury in Los Angeles, without result. James Ruffin, a senior department attorney assigned to analyze the case, concluded that (1) de Aryan was a "crack pot" with a persecution complex, who would probably relish prosecution for the sake of the publicity; and that (2) the content of *The Broom* (circulation 1,600) was not seditious. De Aryan, he noted, had made no attempt to get his paper into the hands of servicemen, and in any event "these articles do not advocate the doing by anyone of any acts to impair the Government in any of its activities." If sedition was to be proven, it would have to be established not from what de Aryan had written (the strategy employed in the Pelley case), but "by extrinsic evidence." That is, the government would have to show that de Aryan had done things (such as taking money from Axis agents) that demonstrated that his statements were intended to harm the United States.[41] Wendell Berge, who headed the Criminal Division, agreed.[42]

Complicating the government's task was the anticipated difficulty of convincing a San Diego jury that de Aryan was a threat to the war effort. The fact that de Aryan was a "nut" did not make him a pariah—at least not in San Diego, where he had endorsements from a number of local luminaries, including at least two judges and the district attorney of San Diego county. The result was that de Aryan found himself charged in a Washington indictment along with 27 others, most of whom he did not know and some of whom he probably had never heard of. He finally had the martyrdom he craved, and despite his ordeal he was, as he wrote the attorney general from jail, grateful.[43]

The indictment of the 28 accused fascists in Washington was a bravura performance of prosecutorial legerdemain and a public relations coup, but the government was still faced with confronting the defense in court, and defending its legal theories and procedures on appeal. Time was against the prosecutors. The legal process, especially where the accusation was seditious expression, was influenced by the climate of opinion. Conviction under the anti-sedition statutes was most likely in circumstances in which judges and jurors could conclude that the nation was endangered by the defendants' actions. From this perspective, the ideal time to bring them to trial was in the first months of the war, when the outcome of the struggle was most in doubt. As the threat of defeat faded, so did the likelihood of conviction.

Questionable aspects of the department's program did not escape notice. Some critics focused on the fact that the government seemed to target persons who had resisted United States involvement in the war, and they worried that they might be next. The editors of the liberal, Protestant, and pacifist *Christian Century,* along with Socialist leader Norman Thomas and Joseph Patterson's *New York Daily News* (all of whom had opposed the war, though from very different perspectives) were among the first to express concern that the July indictment treated prewar opposition to the war as evidence of disloyalty.[44] Others focused on the government's tactics.

Arthur Garfield Hays, co-counsel for the ACLU, noted that only nine of the defendants were charged with overt acts of incitement to disaffection, and that the remainder were included in the indictment as co-conspirators merely on the grounds that their views were similar. The charges against all of them, he observed, were vague, and many of the statements complained of had been uttered in substance at one time or another by many other individuals, including some persons on the ACLU board. As "bad as were the cases in the last war," he concluded, none compared with this.[45] Zechariah Chafee, the man who wrote the book on free speech, found it "indefensible" that the government should force persons from all over the country to stand trial in the nation's capital. Even the worst of their ravings, he wrote, was unworthy of the government's time and, he concluded, they could safely have been "left to stew in their own juice."[46]

Although the ACLU board voted by a narrow margin to condemn the indictment in Washington, D.C. of defendants drawn from all over the country, and to offer assistance to defendants who resisted the move, further intervention was precluded by the board's policy of refusing to participate in sedition cases where there was room to believe that the defendants had enemy affiliations. Government assurances on this score seemed sufficient.[47] A number of the defendants turned to Chafee for help. Convinced of the unfairness of the government's treatment of the fascists, he took the issue to the Bill of Rights Committee,[48] but the committee would not act, and Chafee would go no further.[49] He had suffered for his views a generation earlier,[50] but was unwilling to do so now. Perhaps who the defendants were and what they believed in made a difference. Perhaps it was the fact that he was more than 20 years older now than he had been in 1921 when he nearly lost his teaching post at Harvard for his criticism of the Department of Justice of that day. Moreover, ironically, the extent of repression in World War I and after left him a bit callused to the relatively modest scale of repression in 1942. According to his biographer, Chafee accepted the removal of the Japanese Americans as an inevitable incident of war, and, in light of this reaction, it was little wonder that he refused to assist the accused fascists.[51]

While neither the Bill of Rights Committee nor the ACLU would interfere, Roger Baldwin and a few others worked very hard on their own to temper the department's actions. Convinced that the prosecution was a mistake, Baldwin worried that a trial would do more to arouse latent anti-Semitic and other unwholesome attitudes than to put them to rest.[52] The ACLU founder sought to persuade his contacts at the Justice Department that they were off course, and urged them to find a way to postpone the trial indefinitely.[53] His advice was always cordially received, although its effect seems to have been confined to confirming existing official doubts.[54] According to Baldwin, department officials were embarrassed that politics had brought them to this pass, but insisted that "an influential section of the public" backed up by "hundreds of letters from ordinary citizens" was demanding action, and they were determined to pursue the prosecution, if only to save the attorney general.[55] They assured Baldwin, however, that they did not view the Washington indictments as a precedent but as a way to keep antifascist feelings from turning into a "witch hunt."[56]

In fact, prosecution was a long way off, and the delay that Baldwin urged was, de facto, department policy. The wait was occasioned by the difficulties officials encountered in producing a satisfactory case, by their doubts about the appropriateness of the hastily contrived program, and by Biddle's diffident leadership.[57] Slowing matters further was friction between units within the department[58]—between the Criminal Division and the FBI,[59] and between the Criminal Division and the Special War Policies Unit under L. M. C. Smith.[60] Tensions between department personnel and William Powers Maloney, who was in charge of bringing the indictment and preparing the prosecution, were particularly acute.[61] There was, according to one senior official, "no support for the seditious conspiracy case in the Criminal Division," and he predicted that the prosecutor would "get very little help from the Department," which seemed to be looking for a graceful way to delay the trial, at least until the war was over.[62] Meanwhile, the defendants, most on bail, some residing in a District of Columbia jail, awaited news of the government's next move. They would have a long wait.[63]

The disposition to delay, or at least recast, the trial was both encouraged and complicated by an apparent decline in administration popularity in the fall and winter of 1942, and a corresponding boldness on the part of its critics. As more Americans benefited from the economic boom that accompanied the war, many came to resent taxes, government controls, and "wasteful" spending on social experiments. They grumbled about prices, shortages, the "coddling" of labor, and the slowness of the military effort, blaming bureaucratic mismanagement, "politics-as-usual," and the influence of radicals (and Jews) in Washington.[64] In the fall 1942 election, despite the efforts of liberals to rid the Congress of its reactionary and isolationist elements, the Republicans gained 44 seats in the House and 7 in the Senate, and a number of the administration's worst enemies were reelected. On many issues, an alliance of GOP and Southern Democrat conservatives easily controlled the Congress that convened in January 1943.[65]

In February the House would vote overwhelmingly to renew its Committee on Un-American Activities, and Speaker Sam Rayburn would reappoint the administration's arch enemy, Martin Dies, to the chairmanship. Two other House investigations of alleged radicalism among federal employees were authorized at the same time.[66] Critics, emboldened by the administration's weakness, seemed poised to turn a tenuously based prosecution of "American fascism" against the administration, and James Rowe, pointing to "a popular revolt," warned Biddle that it was time for the administration to be "humble and conciliatory."[67]

The prewar isolationists who formed the core of the anti-Roosevelt coalition were convinced that the Washington indictment represented the president's effort to silence opposition to his policies. This conclusion gained credibility from the fact that antifascist rhetoric frequently targeted the isolationist congressmen, and that the July indictment named Capitol Hill propagandists George Sylvester Viereck and Prescott Freese Dennett among the alleged conspirators. Both had been involved in using the franking privileges of various isolationist congressmen to spread antiwar propaganda,[68] and including them could be taken as a sign that Maloney (who had put Viereck in prison) was attempting to include the isolationists in Congress in the Nazi-inspired conspiracy alleged against Reverend Winrod and company. This was also suggested by the fact that the indictment identified the anti-interventionist America First Committee as a distributor of seditionist material and listed the *Congressional Record,* along with *The Broom, The Galilean,* and other fascist sheets, as an outlet for Nazi propaganda.

The isolationists in Congress made it plain that they would not stand by while the administration prepared to put their ideas and associations on trial. Senator Robert A. Taft of Ohio, a first-term Republican who was a prewar isolationist and an administration foe, attacked the prosecution's theory and publicly declared that the case reminded him of the "'witch hunting' of the first war, except that this witch hunt is more dangerous, more calculated and vicious than that of '17."[69] Representative Clare Hoffman, the Michigan Republican whose name was frequently linked by the *Hour* and the liberal press to the accused fascists, delivered an hour-long speech on the floor of the House in which he called for an investigation of the "conspiracy against Congress,"[70] and isolationist stalwart Gerald P. Nye of North Dakota told the Senate that the accused were no more guilty of seditious conspiracy than he, or any of the millions of other Americans who opposed intervention in the war.[71]

The most formidable critic was Burton K. Wheeler, one-time leader of the isolationists in Congress whose wife and son had been active in the

America First Committee. In December, the Montana Democrat wrote to Biddle that, while he scarcely knew the defendants, he was sufficiently conversant with prosecutorial techniques (having served for five years as a federal prosecutor in the Wilson administration) to know a politically motivated governmental prosecution when he saw one. Why, he asked, "was my name, and the names of other [isolationist] Senators dragged in before the Grand Jury, and people asked if they knew me?"[72] The whole affair, Wheeler told Biddle, was reminiscent of the reign of Harry Daugherty, William J. Burns, and Gaston Means,[73] and he warned the attorney general that several members of the Senate agreed with him that an investigation of the department was in order. Since Wheeler had recently secured an appointment to the Senate Judiciary Committee, his threat was not to be taken lightly.[74]

The isolationist-cum-civil-libertarian campaign took an interesting turn in the spring of 1943 when Representative Hamilton Fish introduced an amendment to the Smith Act that would have severely curtailed, if not eliminated, its use against the alleged seditionists. Fish warned that unless the government was prevented from bringing "American citizens, clergymen, editors, writers, and crackpots or cranks from all parts of the Nation" to Washington to try them for expressing their noninterventionist and anti–New Deal views, "half of Congress and 80 percent of the American people could be sent to prison. . . ."[75] Fish's proposal, which did not succeed, constituted belated recognition by the man who pioneered the congressional hunt for "un-Americans," of the pernicious consequences of government condemning persons simply on the basis of their unpopular expressions and associations.

On January 4, 1943, the department announced that a new grand jury impaneled in Washington the previous October had produced an indictment that added five names to the twenty-eight indicted in July. The charges were far more detailed. The government now claimed that the German government, acting through World Service, a distributor of Nazi propaganda headquartered in Erfurt, had since 1933 been using the American conspirators to undermine the morale of the armed services in an attempt to cause the collapse of the U.S. government.[76] In furtherance of this scheme, World Service provided the defendants with anti-Semitic, anti-government propaganda that they, in turn, made available to servicemen as well as other Americans.[77] The case still rested on the theory that the defendants were linked (mainly by the similarity of their views), and that this link made each as guilty of sedition as those few who might be shown to have at some point worked for the Axis. Berge, responding to "numerous charges" of departmental bad faith, insisted that the seditious conspiracy case was soundly based on many months of inquiry and urged critics to withhold judgment until the government had gone to trial.[78] Few appear to have taken his advice.

While the new indictment suggested the department's determination to proceed, an announcement a few weeks later revealed the disarray behind the government's purposeful facade. In early February 1943, the department announced that William Power Maloney, the white knight of the antifascist cause, had been "promoted" to an administrative post within the Criminal Division and would no longer have a direct hand in bringing the fascists to justice. The response was predictable. The following day a *Washington Post* editorial blasted the attorney general for capitulating to the defendants' congressional friends. Maloney, who the *Post* said had not lost a case in eight years, would not have pulled any punches and would have followed the evidence wherever it led. Having encouraged the seditionists by turning them loose after Pearl Harbor, the *Post* wrote, the attorney general was now "in effect, concel[ing] their innocence."[79] Actually, Biddle had little to do with the firing.

Described by a superior as "extremely energetic," Maloney was the kind of prosecutor who got results.[80] But some of his colleagues had the feeling that the man lacked professionalism, and that his careless and flamboyant ways reflected poorly on the department. Chester Lane, who came to the Criminal Division shortly after Maloney had secured the July indictment, recalled talking to him on a number of occasions and coming away with doubts concerning both the case and Maloney's methods. Asked by Biddle to assess the prospects of the October 1942 indictment, Lane confessed that he was unable to get a sense of what evidence the brash young prosecutor had, either because he had little, or because, not wanting to share credit for his anticipated triumph, he refused to tell. No one, Lane noted, not even members of Maloney's own staff, understood the case in its entirety.[81]

Then there was the matter of integrity. James Rowe, to whom Biddle referred an inquiry from FDR as to the reasons for Maloney's firing, noted that in preparing the case against Viereck, Maloney had leaked information to the press suggesting that he was seeking an indictment against Fish and other isolationist congressmen,[82] a circumstance that left those gentlemen understandably aggrieved. Rowe also pointed out that department lawyers, jealous of the agency's good name, were concerned about what the bench and bar were saying about Maloney and that the prosecutor's methods had offended the judges of the Second Circuit and provoked Chief Justice

Harlan Stone to warn that he intended to censure the government for its tactics. Berge and others, Rowe wrote, were worried that the government might lose pending cases as a result of Maloney's misconduct.[83] Officials had tolerated the prosecutor's efforts to this point because his methods, which enjoyed great success, appeared only mildly questionable. But faith and forbearance could stretch only so far, and when Maloney became the legitimate object of criticism from Senator Wheeler and the chief justice, the prosecutor had outlasted his usefulness.

Maloney had to go, but, contrary to speculation, the case was to continue. Rowe dismissed the idea that the change of leadership signaled any abandonment of the prosecution. The case, he said, had to be won "*at all costs,*" and the fact that Rowe replaced Maloney with O. John Rogge testified to his commitment. Rogge, who preceded Wendell Berge as head of the Criminal Division, was a tenacious, some would say ruthless, prosecutor known for his leftist and militantly antifascist views. He had been fired by Attorney General Jackson two years earlier. Ironically, the precipitating event was Rogge's public denunciation of the Smith Act, one of the two statutes under which he was now to pursue the fascists.[84]

Rowe assured Biddle, who passed his observations on to the president, that there would be no delay—Rogge had claimed that he would be ready for trial in a month's time. The prediction was preposterous, as was Rogge's assertion that his prosecution would be based on "actual connections" between the defendants and Axis agents, not on mere expressions of fascistic sentiments.[85] Apparently Rogge was among those who did not understand the case Maloney had developed. He would soon discover that Maloney's files were full of innuendo and suggestive leads, but did not hold the stuff that assured a successful prosecution. Nor would several more months of efforts by the FBI and six department researchers uncover the needed proof. At the end of July a now uncertain prosecutor wrote to William L. Langer, the eminent historian who was chief of the Research and Analysis Branch of OSS, desperately seeking the evidence of the worldwide fascist conspiracy the government should have had when it sought the original indictment a year earlier.[86]

While Rogge searched in vain for evidence to support the indictment, enthusiasm for the antifascist effort waned.[87] During the first half of 1942 popular journals produced on average more than three articles a month urging a crackdown on fascist agitation, but in the weeks thereafter coverage fell to about one article every two months.[88] In May 1943, the *Hour,* the principal voice of the antifascist crusade (and the source of much of the information on fascist activities), abruptly ended publication. A few journalists sought to revive flagging interest in the anti-sedition proceedings, but apathy toward fascism at home seemed the rule.[89]

And there were more setbacks in court. In October 1943, the district court in the District of Columbia voided the amended indictment on the grounds that its charges included references to activities that took place before the Smith Act was enacted.[90] A new grand jury began taking testimony and, on January 3, 1944, it handed down what was for many of the defendants, a third indictment on essentially the same charges. A few of the original defendants, including de Aryan and Court Asher, were dropped from the new indictment, as was mention of the America First Committee and the National Committee to Keep America Out of Foreign Wars (with which Fish was associated). A few new defendants, including Lawrence Dennis, the intellectual advocate for American fascism, and Yorkville fuehrer Joseph McWilliams, were added, along with three former leaders of the now defunct German-American Bund.[91] The Bundists had been included to strengthen the allegations of the co-conspirators' Nazi connections. The third indictment also differed in that its charges rested entirely on the Smith Act. Rogge apparently believed that while the government might not be able to satisfy the Espionage Act's requirement that the government prove the defendants had acted "deliberately and with a specific purpose," he could meet the requirements of the more generally phrased Smith Act.[92]

In April 1944, two years and five months after the Pearl Harbor attack, the leaders of the alleged fascist conspiracy in the United States finally went on trial. The long gestation had done little to improve the government's prospects of success. Its problem was systemic and irremediable—there was no criminal statute that covered the utterances that had given rise to their indictment. The defendants had been targeted because they propagated obnoxious, hate-filled, divisive sentiments. But the law was aimed at those who deliberately sought to incite disaffection in the military, resistance to the draft, or revolution. The gap between what the fascists said and what the law forbade plagued the prosecutors from beginning to end.

The difficulties of making a case was explanation enough for the long delay, but fear of embarrassing failure served to drag out the process. During World War I, officials had been able to present weak cases against radical agitators with some certainty that the government would be sustained by juries, upheld by appellate courts, and applauded by the public. But the political climate now was not nearly as hostile to "fascism" as it had been to socialism, nor quite as insensitive as it had once been to free speech appeals. Legal protections for dissent were now greater, and the department's false steps were more likely to draw criticism from civil libertarians and from congressmen hostile to the administration. Over the whole proceedings hung the shadow of possible rejection of the government's case by a Supreme Court that appeared sympathetic, if only narrowly so, to the minority opinion expressed by Justice Holmes in *Abrams*.

If a lack of enthusiasm and a sense of impending defeat account for departmental delay, Biddle's fear of appearing weak guaranteed that the effort would continue. Both demands from the president and liberal opinion had been crucial in producing the July 1942 indictment. Once Biddle had announced it, turning back was politically impossible. Too many condemnations of the fascist conspiracy had been uttered; too much effort expended in exposing and punishing it. And although every day brought the end of the war closer and made the legal enterprise more anachronistic, the government's law machine was forced to try to squeeze success out of this increasingly pointless enterprise. By the spring of 1944 the process was sustained by a combination of bureaucratic inertia, Rogge's now passionate attachment to the cause, and Biddle's refusal to let go.

Chapter 14

The Great Sedition Trial:
The End of the Campaign Against Disloyalty

The case of the fascistic propagandists dragged on throughout the war, a little-noticed monument to compromised civil libertarian principle and political expediency. The pursuit of the fascist conspirators had taken on a life of its own. Unwanted in the first instance, the prosecution once underway had won Biddle over, although it is not clear what he thought was to be gained beyond peace with the president and a respite from antifascist criticism. Even after FDR's death and the war's end, the case continued to make martyrs of a despicable bunch, who could rightly claim that they were being persecuted for their views.

Indicted in July 1942, the accused, described by constitutional scholar Edward Corwin as a "queer . . . kettle of fish,"[1] were brought to Washington and kept there for two years while the government sought to construct a winnable case against them. By the time their trial began in the spring of 1944, the department had amended its charges twice, and now 33 defendants stood accused of seditious conspiracy in what would be called the Great Sedition Trial (*U.S.* v. *McWilliams*) of World War II. The government's legal objectives (and the case's fundamental flaw) were set forth by prosecutor O. John Rogge in a three-hour opening statement. In a monologue interrupted repeatedly by objections from the defense attorneys (a fitting prelude to the protracted proceedings), Rogge promised to prove that the accused had served as agents of the Nazi propaganda effort in the United States by demonstrating that their words echoed Berlin's propaganda themes. True to his word, he documented in the months that followed the similarities between Nazi propaganda themes and the defendants' words, but produced little evidence establishing any other connection between them or demonstrating, as the indictments asserted, that the alleged conspiracy had created disaffection in the military.[2]

The government had taken on a nearly impossible task.[3] As the trial progressed, the prosecutor seems to have been hoping that his staff would uncover the evidence he needed or, failing that, that jurors would focus on the enormity of the Nazi conspiracy and overlook the government's inability to establish the defendants' involvement in overtly criminal activity. The weakness of the government's case drew out the proceedings, and the large number and obstreperous behavior of the defendants helped turn the trial into a circus that, long in coming, threatened to go on indefinitely.[4] By mid-July, a few of the defendants had been severed from the mass (to be tried separately), and one had died. One was too ill to attend court regularly; another's partial deafness made him unable to follow what was going on. The defendants quarreled among themselves and with the prosecution in open court and in the corridors. Although the trial as theater continued to attract some attention, much of the earlier interest had disappeared.

The Washington prosecution had originated in Biddle's efforts to satisfy the president, assuage an indignant antifascist public, and bolster the department's image. But the public's indignation had turned to indifference, the president was no longer heard from on the issue, and the Justice Department's reputation seemed more threatened by the trial's continuation than by its abandonment. The *Washington Post* had been largely responsible for the indictments in the first place, but after several weeks the editors, while continuing to believe that the defendants were "Nazis" whose suppression was in the nation's best interest, concluded that their conviction was no longer worth the effort to obtain it. Fearing that, whatever its outcome, the trial would "stand as a black mark against American justice for years to come," the *Post* hinted that it might be a good idea to "end this sorry spectacle" and try the individual defendants separately. A few days after issuing this sobering assessment, the paper, which had been giving the trial front-page coverage, suddenly withdrew reporter Dillard Stokes.[5]

Even before the trial the Supreme Court had begun handing down a series of decisions that made it unlikely that convictions, even if obtainable, would be sustained on appeal. The court was divided between a solid core of liberal activists—Hugo Black, William O. Douglas, Frank Murphy, and Wiley Rutledge—who tended to give an expansive meaning to free speech and other civil liberties, and the rest of the Court, who were less protective of individual rights. The civil libertarian foursome were often able to gain the support of one or another of the remaining justices, and during the war years the Court established a remarkably liberal record on First Amendment issues.

Two decisions in 1943, each of which made use of a speech-protective interpretation of the "clear and present danger" formulation, foreshadowed trouble for the government.[6] In *Schneiderman* v. *U.S.*, the denaturalization case discussed earlier, Justice Murphy, speaking for the Court, insisted that the government was required to show that the Communist official was guilty not merely of abstract advocacy, but of "agitation and exhortation," which created a "clear and present danger of public disorder or other substantive evil." In *Taylor* v. *Mississippi,* a far different case involving the allegedly disloyal preaching of Jehovah's Witnesses, the Court affirmed the right of Americans, even in the midst of war, to utter sentiments that might encourage disloyalty and disaffection as long as what they said did not threaten "any clear and present danger to our institutions or our Government." The implications for Bundists and native fascist agitators were clear. In a popular and successful war, disloyalty per se was not necessarily a crime. As Holmes had insisted years earlier, context was critical.[7]

Two months before the sedition trial began, the Court further undercut the government's case. *Baumgartner* v. *United States* involved a German American stripped of his citizenship in 1942 on the basis of remarks that, according to the government, showed that he had not truly renounced his allegiance to Germany. The evidence made it plain that Baumgartner was an enthusiastic supporter of Hitler even before the Nazis came to power in Germany, and that he believed that Nazism was superior to American democracy and rejoiced at Germany's early diplomatic and military victories. Nevertheless, writing for a unanimous Court, Justice Frankfurter pointed out that the government had offered no evidence that Baumgartner recognized that his sympathy with Germany and Nazism were inconsistent with his pledge of fidelity to the United States. The standard for adducing fraudulent intent from the defendant's behavior subsequent to his naturalization was very high, he said, and the government in this case had not met it. Justice Frankfurter (a naturalized American himself) wrote that immigrants were not obliged to abandon a cultural affinity with their native land, and all citizens, naturalized or native born, had the "right to criticize public men and measures—and that means not only informed and responsible criticism, but the freedom to speak foolishly and without moderation." The evidence, he concluded, was "not sufficiently compelling to . . . penalize a naturalized citizen for the expression of silly or even sinister-sounding views which native-born citizens utter with impunity." The decision brought an end to the denaturalization attack on the Bund, and the sentiments it expressed threatened the ultimate success of the Washington sedition prosecution as well.

In another landmark case decided the same day, the Court took on more directly the question of whether fascistic invective was seditious within the meaning of the Espionage Act. The case originated in 1940, before American involvement in the war, when FDR received copies of three anonymous pamphlets consisting of crude and vile diatribes directed against the Jews, the British, and the president himself.[8] The words were as obnoxious as any published during the war, outstripping the filth attributed to the fascists who were on trial in the district court in Washington. They were written and distributed, it turned out, by one Elmer Hartzel, a native-born American who had enlisted in the army in World War I and served honorably overseas. In an apparent effort to emphasize his credentials as an "authentic" American, the Court pointed out that Hartzel was the descendent of people (Scotch, Irish, and German) who had come to this country 120 years earlier.

Hartzel, who had begun his pamphleteering in 1940, had operated with impunity until after the Pearl Harbor attack, when he was arrested and charged with violating the portion of the Espionage Act that prohibited encouraging disaffection in the armed forces or resistance to the draft. Hartzel was tried before a jury, and convicted. His conviction was upheld by the circuit court of appeals, and he appealed to the Supreme Court.

In the only World War II case brought before the Court under the Espionage Act, the justices ruled that for Hartzel's conviction to stand, the government had to prove beyond a reasonable doubt that he had "willfully" sought to injure the military, and that his efforts constituted a "clear and present danger" of doing so. In cases involving freedom of expression, the Court said, the statute's use of the word "willfully" meant that the government must show that the defendant had "deliberately and with a specific purpose" undertaken to do legally proscribed acts. The majority concluded that Hartzel's pamphlets were not direct appeals to insubordination, disloyalty, or refusal to serve, but were merely vicious and unreasoning attacks from which the requisite criminal intent could not be inferred. Having failed to satisfy itself on this point, the Court did not address the issue of clear and present danger.[9] The ruling suggested that the government could not prevail in Espionage Act cases without producing evidence, beyond the defendant's writings, that indicated intent to interfere with the war effort. The five-to-four division and limited scope of the decision made *Hartzel* a less-than-ringing endorsement of free speech. Nevertheless, taken along with the other cases, it suggested that the Court, albeit narrowly, was not inclined to support the government's efforts to suppress merely hateful expression.[10]

In mid-June the defense in the Washington sedition trial, taking note of the recent ruling, moved for a directed acquittal, telling Judge Edward C. Eicher[11] that the *Hartzel* decision made the current proceedings "a waste of time." Rogge replied that he would introduce evidence that the defendants had discussed staging a military coup. Eicher rejected the defense motion, noting that he would reconsider when the prosecution had finished presenting its evidence.[12] This ruling could not have been very encouraging to government lawyers, who were aware of the weakness of their case. In conversations with Baldwin, Rogge confessed that he had only circumstantial evidence that German money played a part in the propaganda activities of two or three of the defendants (before the war) and that he took the activities of only three of the defendants seriously.[13]

While Rogge pressed on, Roger Baldwin pursued his efforts to get attorneys for the government and the defendants, as well as outside interested parties, to agree to some sort of settlement. His chances of success seemed to increase dramatically in early December when the sudden death of trial judge Edward C. Eicher led to a mistrial. The government had the option of retrying the defendants, nine of whom were in prison on other convictions, or dropping the charges. An immediate answer was neither necessary nor expected, and Baldwin hoped that the department would announce that it was studying the issue and then, perhaps after the defeat of Germany, which was not far off, quietly abandon the whole matter.[14]

But the rationale for the trial was no longer (if it ever was) the threat the defendants posed to the war effort. Something, Rogge told Baldwin, had to be done to "stop the spread of racial and religious intolerance" and destroy the fascistic enemies of democracy. He had received considerable mail from individuals and organizations all over country urging that he continue (Baldwin noted that a canvass of newspapers showed no support outside the Communist press),[15] and despite all the objections on legal grounds that he had heard, Rogge insisted that he was seriously considering retrying the case on its original theory.[16]

Such a move was openly opposed in the highest counsels of the department. A long discussion among senior department officials on February 21 found only Rogge favoring a new trial. Solicitor General Fahy and J. Edgar Hoover urged the attorney general to let the effort die. They were vigorously supported by Special Assistant Herbert Wechsler, who attacked the proceedings as a "political trial" that should not have been initiated and could not succeed. Biddle was noncommittal, but seemed to favor trying again.[17] In April, FDR died, and in early May the war in Europe ended, but the attorney general continued to consider resuming the prosecution—albeit against a reduced number of defendants. In June, Wechsler wrote Biddle a long confidential memorandum in which he reviewed the by now familiar fallacies of the prosecution and spoke of the harm the case was doing to the department's reputation, particularly among "decent men."[18]

In mid-June, the department's anti-sedition campaign suffered another setback.[19] In *Keegan* v. *United States,* the Supreme Court overturned the conviction of 24 leaders of the German-American Bund who had been charged with advising members to *evade* the draft. The Court, carefully distinguishing between service (after being drafted) and *evasion* of the draft process itself, concluded "that to counsel mere refusal to serve," as the Bund leaders did, "was not to advise draft evasion or resistance"—the acts made criminal in the Selective Service Act. More importantly, the Court suggested that the trial judge may have abused his discretionary authority in permitting the government to attempt to establish the defendants' criminal intent by reciting "at such inordinate length" evidence of the disloyal character of the Bund in the years before the inception of the alleged conspiracy.[20] The rebuke was particularly significant because Rogge's strategy in the sedition trial was to encourage the jury to infer criminal intent by presenting, at far greater length, evidence of the nature of the worldwide Nazi conspiracy. Should the Washington trial resume, the new judge, having read *Keegan,* might deny the government the use of this strategy.

The same disposition to protect political speech was apparent in the Court's resolution of the government's long-running effort to deport Harry Bridges. Justice Jackson, who doubtless would have decided against Bridges, recused himself because of his earlier connection with the case, and the liberal activists joined Justice Stanley Reed in a five-to-three decision reversing the circuit court of appeals, which a year earlier had upheld Biddle's deportation order.[21] Without deciding whether the CPUSA was a subversive organization within the meaning of the immigration statute, the Court held that the notorious longshoreman was neither affiliated with nor a member of the party, and that the government had denied him the fair hearing to which he was entitled.[22] Justice Murphy, who as attorney general had led a Justice Department prewar campaign against "subversives," wrote a concurring opinion in which he castigated the government (Jackson and Biddle) for a record of persecution of an individual that, he said, would "stand forever as a monument to man's intolerance of man."[23]

"What a windbag," Biddle commented, and Justice Jackson no doubt concurred. The genteel Solicitor General Fahy, who had argued the government's case, was incensed. Privately, and months later publicly, he wrote of the Court's nullification of acts of Congress. In each of the free speech cases, he complained, "the Court finds some defect in proof, or the like, to defeat the litigation." Addressing the likely outcome of a new case designed to test whether past membership in the Communist Party was now a bar to naturalization, he predicted that the "Court would probably find a narrow basis" for deciding against the government.[24] This was likely to be the outcome of the Washington sedition trial as well, should it ever reach the Court on appeal.

Prospects for a renewal of the case declined precipitously with Biddle's departure. In June 1945, six weeks after replacing FDR, President Harry Truman asked the attorney general for his resignation, effective at the end of month. Biddle recalled that he was shocked by the abrupt manner of his firing, but in a statement revealing his view of the office and his idealized view of his association with FDR, he told Truman that he understood perfectly. The new president, he said, would naturally want to appoint "his own man," since the relationship of attorney general to president was "a highly personal one, lawyer to client."[25] Biddle would go on to serve as the American judge on the international tribunal established to try the major German war criminals. Thereafter he retired to write his memoirs and faded into relative obscurity.

Truman appointed Tom Clark, who earlier had succeeded Berge as head of the Criminal Division, to replace Biddle.[26] In August 1945, Japan surrendered. The Second World War was over, but the Great Sedition case remained in suspension. Baldwin had succeeded in gaining the support of the American Jewish Committee and the conditional approval (if the department agreed) of the Anti-Defamation League of B'nai B'rith for dropping the prosecution. Only the Communists, he told Attorney General Clark, insisted that the trial resume.[27] Clark was unmoved. He had no enthusiasm for the case, but the defendants were in no mood to allow the department a graceful retreat,[28] and Clark was reluctant to capitulate unconditionally.

The issue still interested some, and was just controversial enough to ensure official procrastination. Democratic congressman Adolph J. Sabath of Chicago was quoted as saying that if the attorney general did not do something about the fascist defendants, he would.[29] The long-time legislator, who was the chairman of the powerful House Rules Committee, did not say what he would do if Clark did not act, but such threats may have cleared the way for the final stage of Rogge's mission.

In the spring of 1946, Rogge was off to Germany, where amid the rubble he hoped to find the evidence of the seditious conspiracy that had eluded him in the United States. In September, after completing his searches in the Nazi archives and having interviewed German propaganda officials, he submitted his report on the "World-Wide Nazi Movement" to the attorney general. Rogge had by this point given up hope of reopening the trial, concluding that recent Supreme Court decisions had made it almost certain that a conviction, even if obtainable, would not be sustained on appeal.[30] He nevertheless wanted his report made public so that the Nazi conspiracy in America, which he insisted involved former isolationist congressmen, would be fully exposed.[31] When the attorney general chose not to release the report, Rogge revealed his findings to the press. In October, Clark fired him. His departure, and the changing political climate in Washington, ended any chance of reviving the antifascist campaign.[32] By now the Department of Justice was getting ready to use the experience it had gained in the antifascist effort against the agents of the "Worldwide Communist Conspiracy."[33] In December 1946, the indictment against America's Nazis was dismissed.

In the end, the prosecution of the Washington seditionists failed, but not before it and the rest of the campaign against disloyalty had taken its toll. What was lost through the pursuit of the obnoxious dissidents was not the value of their speech (it had little), but the opportunity for the wartime administration to endorse with more than mere rhetoric the principle of free expression that emerged in the aftermath of World War I. As expressed in the Holmes-Brandeis dissents and in a series of Court decisions in the early 1940s, this ideal held that society had an obligation to tolerate political expression regardless of its merits or source, so long as it did not imminently threaten the nation's safety. This principle, which appeared to offer a reasonable standard for checking majoritarian enthusiasms and a government's inclination to silence its critics, was worth affirming in the face of the provocative agitation of the era.

The people who ran the Department of Justice did not always agree on how to approach specific instances of suspected sedition, but by and large they favored a policy of tolerance and restraint. Civil libertarian ideals did matter, and they disposed department officials to turn a blind eye to obnoxious dissent. The inclination, partly a reflection of the general attachment to civil liberties common among liberal minded persons in the late 1930s, was intensified by the desire of officials to overcome the reputation for police state excesses that had come to be associated with the department's performance in World War I and the postwar Red Scare. These dispositions were reinforced by professional concerns. As lawyers, department officials tended to assess their accomplishments by how the courts responded to their initiatives. Intent upon avoiding judicial repudiation, they were moved to deal with disloyalty within the confines of the anti-sedition statutes, narrowly construed and administered in what Jackson called a "lawyerly way." In the end, however, their libertarian convictions and inclinations were not enough to ensure a policy of political tolerance.

The department's problem was not, as it was in World War I, chiefly an aroused public. There were, of course, significant numbers of Americans who were concerned about disloyalty and subversive attitudes, and officials were troubled from time to time by the demands of Martin Dies and company, and later by accusations emanating from antifascist quarters. But on the eve of the war the Justice Department had succeeded in pacifying or preempting local loyalty concerns, and this, together with a propaganda strategy that avoided hysteria-inducing appeals, helped contain chauvinistic enthusiasms. There would be no intense domestic security anxiety, and little demand for indiscriminate repression.

But if violations of civil liberties were not dictated by popular pressures, neither did the department enjoy great support for restraint. Before the war the tolerant inclinations of the attorney generals and their staffs received considerable backing from civil libertarians. Yet doubts about applying the free speech ideals associated with Holmes and Chafee had begun to creep into civil libertarian discourse in the two years before Pearl Harbor. With the coming of the war, support for tolerance was confined to relatively few. Although lawyers could be found to defend individuals accused of violating the anti-sedition statutes, the legal community in general, represented by the American Bar Association's Bill of Rights Committee, did almost nothing to encourage government restraint. The American Civil Liberties Union, badly divided on the issue, took a hands-off attitude, and political pundits in general, and the liberal press in particular, insisted that fascists not be permitted to carry on their divisive propaganda behind the shield of First Amendment protections.

The department might still have been able to shape policy based on libertarian forbearance had the White House been supportive. But the president, while he supported freedom of speech in principle, rarely interpreted it as preventing the executive branch from doing what was necessary to ensure his broadly conceived view of national security. The president's involvement was episodic rather than systematic. Nevertheless, in his communications with the Justice Department and the FBI, his approval of Hoover's activities, and an occasional significant policy initiative, he repeatedly let his attorney generals know his attitude concerning the prerogatives of government in combating disloyalty. Where department policy diverged from what he thought was the national interest, the president intervened directly to make his will felt. In the process he helped define the operative meaning of free speech and other constitutionally protected rights.

FDR's direct interventions in issues bearing on civil liberties were infrequent—but significant. The most important of these, apart from his involvement in the Japanese-American relocation, came not long after the attack on Pearl Harbor, when he demanded that Biddle ignore his libertarian scruples and silence the fascistic agitation. The factors that produced the Justice Department's collaboration in the internment tragedy were also at work in determining its response to the accused seditionists: a narrow but vocal segment of the public demanding action in the name of common sense and national security, the ambiguity of free-speech principles and the adversarial nature of the law, and Biddle's determination to act principally as the President's Lawyer.[34]

Yet despite the department's repeated concessions to pressure from outside and above, the nation's civil liberties record was not as bad as it might have been. In the end, the system worked, though just barely. Much of the credit goes to those department officials who dragged their feet in implementing what the president demanded, a stratagem made effective by the fact that the laws at their disposal were of relatively limited application. Though the administration sought to augment its repressive tools, the legislature, suspicious of the president, denied the attorney general the expanded powers he sought. Thus Congress, improbably and not necessarily for the best of reasons, deserves much of the credit for ensuring that the administration's campaign against dissent did not claim more victims than it did.

Responsibility for limiting the success of the administration's assault on disloyalty is shared as well by the Supreme Court. Congress's refusal to amend the laws to reach those guilty only of disloyal associations, beliefs, and utterances meant that the success of wartime prosecutions would depend on judicial interpretations of criminal intent and "clear and present danger" that favored the government. Concerns that the Court, which had shown increasing sensitivity to free speech, would uphold the First Amendment claims of the defendants no doubt held down the number of prosecutions. Such fears proved well founded when in 1943 and 1944 the Court (albeit, narrowly) repeatedly ruled in favor of freer speech, in effect scuttling the government's loyalty campaign. The Supreme Court turned out to be a bulwark against repression, although the direct effect of its rulings was not apparent until well after the administration campaign had claimed most of its victims.

In the end, the ideas and ideals broached by Holmes and Brandeis, and expanded upon by Chafee and the ACLU, had a significant impact. Though the result was less than civil libertarian purists might have hoped for, their principles, reflected in the limits of the law, the decisions of the Court, and the department's attachment to restraint, helped ensure the obnoxious dissenters of World War II a measure of the exemption from federal repression held out to them by Holmes a quarter of a century earlier.

Note on References

Books and articles are noted with full bibliographic citation on their first appearance in each chapter's notes. Thereafter they are referred to in short form.

Abbreviations

acc.—accession number. This refers to the number by which the Federal Records Center identifies batches of records received from time to time from federal agencies.

AG—Attorney General

CUOHP—Columbia University Oral History Project

DoJ—Department of Justice. Unless otherwise noted, all records designated "DoJ" are from the Criminal Division of that agency. DoJ records may be found in the National Archives (such records are referred to by their record group number, RG 60); those from the Federal Records Center in Suitland, MD, are designated "FRC," and those from the Department of Justice itself, pursuant to Freedom of Information Act requests, are identified as DoJ/FoI.

FBI—Federal Bureau of Investigation. FBI records were obtained under Freedom of Information Act requests (FBI/FoI), or were examined in the FBI Reading Room (FBI/RR) in the FBI building, Washington, DC.

FDRL—Franklin D. Roosevelt Library, Hyde Park, NY

fldr.—folder

FoI—Freedom of Information and Privacy Act

FRC—Federal Records Center, Suitland, MD

NA—National Archives, Washington, DC

NA-NR—National Archives—Northeast Region, New York, NY.

NA-PR—National Archives—Pacific Region, San Bruno, CA.

No. Cal. Br.—Northern California Branch, ACLU

OAG—Office of the Attorney General

OF—Official Files (FDRL)

PPF—President's Personal Files (FDRL)

PSF—President's Secretary's Files (FDRL)

RG—Record Group. Unless otherwise indicated, all records so designated are found in the National Archives in Washington, DC, or in College Park, MD.
RR—Reading Room (FBI Building, Washington, DC)
SAC—Special Agent in Charge (FBI)
Times OHP—New York Times Oral History Program (microfilm)
WPO—War Policy Office [files] (FRC)

Government Records Collections

National Archives:

RG 21	District Courts of the United States
RG 28	Post Office Department
RG 44	Office of Government Reports
RG 59	Department of State
RG 60	Department of Justice
RG 83	Bureau of Agricultural Economics
RG 85	Immigration and Naturalization Service
RG 118	United States Attorneys and Marshals
RG 165	War Department Special and General Staffs (Military Intelligence Division)
RG 208	Office of War Information
RG 226	Office of Strategic Services
RG 262	Foreign Broadcast Intelligence Service
RG 407	Adjutant General's Office

Collections of Private Papers

Baker, Newton D.	Library of Congress, Washington, DC [LC]
Berge, Wendell	LC
Berle, Adolf A., Jr.	Franklin D. Roosevelt Library, Hyde Park, NY [FDRL]
Biddle, Francis	FDRL
Bontecou, Eleanor	Harry S. Truman Library, Independence, MO [HSTL]
Burlingham, Charles	Harvard Law School Library, Cambridge, MA [Harvard Law]
Carter, John Franklin	University of Wyoming Library, Laramie, WY
Chafee, Zechariah, Jr.	Harvard Law
Clark, Tom	HSTL
Corcoran, Thomas	LC
Cox, Oscar	FDRL
Cummings, Homer	University of Virginia Library, Charlottesville, VA
Early, Stephen	FDRL

Ewing, Oscar R.	HSTL
Fahy, Charles	FDRL
Gressman, Eugene	Bentley Historical Library, University of Michigan, Ann Arbor, MI
Hays, Arthur Garfield	Seeley G. Mudd Manuscript Library, Princeton University, Princeton, NJ
Ickes, Harold L.	LC
Jackson, Robert H.	LC
McWilliams, Carey	Special Collections, University of California at Los Angeles
Mellett, Lowell	FDRL
Murphy, Frank	Bentley Historical Library, University of Michigan
Niles, David	HSTL
Norris, George W.	LC
O'Brian, John Lord	Charles B. Sears Law Library, State University of New York at Buffalo, Amherst, NY
Patterson, Robert P.	LC
Roosevelt, Franklin D.	FDRL
Rosenman, Samuel I.	FDRL
Rowe, James	FDRL
Stimson, Henry L.	(microfilm) Sterling Library, Yale University, New Haven, CT
Waldman, Morris	YIVO collection, New York, NY
Wallace, Henry A.	(microfilm) Special Collections Department at the University of Iowa Libraries, Iowa City, IA

Papers of Organizations

American Civil Liberties Union—Seeley G. Mudd Manuscript Library, Princeton University, Princeton, NJ

American Civil Liberties Union—*Records and Publications of the American Civil Liberties Union* [microfilm] (New York: Microfilm Corporation of America, 1975). [Cited as *ACLU, Records and Publications*]

American Committee for the Protection of the Foreign Born—Special Collections Library, University of Michigan, Ann Arbor

American Council for Nationalities Service—Immigration History Research Center, University of Minnesota, St. Paul, MN. This collection contains the papers of the Foreign Language Information Service and Common Council for American Unity.

American Jewish Committee—Blaustein Library, American Jewish Committee, New York, NY

Bill of Rights Committee, American Bar Association—Harvard Law School Library

Columbia University Oral History Project—Butler Library, Columbia University, New York, NY [Cited as CUOHP]

New York Times Oral History Program (Glen Rock, NJ: Microfilm Corporation of America, 1972) [Cited as *Times* OHP]

National Association for the Advancement of Colored Peoples (microfilm)—Library of Congress

Northern California Branch, American Civil Liberties Union—California State Historical Society, San Francisco, CA

Notes

Introduction

1. Of course, the Japanese-American relocation alone makes the nation's wartime record a civil libertarian disaster. Robert Justin Goldstein is one of the few scholars to place this episode in the larger context of the administration's civil liberties record. Goldstein, *Political Repression in Modern America From 1870 to the Present* (Boston: Schenckman Publishing Company, Inc., 1978), 284. The best account of the war against domestic fascism is Leo P. Ribuffo, *The Old Christian Right: The Protestant Far Right From the Great Depression to the Cold War* (Philadelphia: Temple University Press, 1983). Ribuffo agrees with Goldstein and concludes that "Roosevelt personally intervened to curtail far right expressions that were only distantly dangerous or merely obnoxious," noting that these were "routine decisions by a president little concerned about civil liberties." See p. 215. William Preston, Jr. also paints a very negative picture of civil liberties and civil rights during the war but balances it somewhat with a number of positive developments that suggested that "certain anti-libertarian evils were on the wane." See his essay "Shadows of War and Fear" in *The Pulse of Freedom, American Liberties, 1920–1970s,* ed. Alan Reitman (New York: W.W. Norton, 1975), 105–53 (quote on 150). Geoffrey Perrett, *Days of Sadness, Years of Triumph, The American People 1939–1945* (Baltimore: Penguin Books Inc., 1974), 357–67, in a chapter called "The Civil Liberties Disaster," is more critical. Contrast with Samuel Walker, *In Defense of Liberties, A History of the ACLU* (New York: Oxford University Press, 1990), 135, 153. Walker alludes to "the administration's relative tolerance of free speech during the war" and contrasts Roosevelt's counsels of tolerance with President Wilson's efforts to whip up public hysteria. See also John P. Roche, "American Liberty: An Examination of the 'Tradition' of Freedom," in *Aspects of Liberty, Essays Presented to Robert E. Cushman,* ed. Milton R. Konvitz and Clinton Rossiter (Ithaca, NY: Cornell University Press, 1958), 159. Roche calls World War II the good war from the civil liberties standpoint and credits Biddle and FDR. See Patrick S. Washburn, "FDR Versus His Own Attorney General: The Struggle over

Sedition, 1941–42," *Journalism Quarterly* 62 (Winter 1985): 717–24. Washburn credits Biddle with a record of which he could be proud considering he confronted a relentless FDR bent on repression. A recent work, Francis MacDonnell, *Insidious Foes, The Axis Fifth Column and the American Home Front* (New York: Oxford University Press, 1995), 141,143, acknowledges some overreaction but concludes sympathetically that "FDR's concerns were entirely understandable" and that he "met the Trojan Horse menace with considerable equanimity."

2. The following is based on Paul L. Murphy, *World War I and the Origin of Civil Liberties in the United States* (New York: W.W. Norton & Co., 1979).

3. U.S. National Commission on Law Observance and Enforcement [Wickersham Commission], "Report on Prosecution" (Washington: Government Printing Office, 1931), 10–11.

4. Murphy, *World War I and Civil Liberties,* 52.

5. Donald Johnson, *The Challenge to American Freedoms: World War I and the Rise of the American Civil Liberties Union* (University of Kentucky Press, 1963), 64–65.

6. William Preston, Jr., *Aliens and Dissenters, Federal Suppression of Radicals, 1903–1933* (Cambridge: Harvard University Press, 1963), 140.

7. Thomas Gregory, "Suggestions of Attorney-General Gregory to Executive Committee in Relation to the Department of Justice," *American Bar Association Journal* 4 (1918): 313ff.

8. Harry N. Scheiber, *The Wilson Administration and Civil Liberties, 1917–1921* (Ithaca, NY: Cornell University Press, 1960), 57.

9. Zechariah Chafee, "Freedom of Speech in War Time," *Harvard Law Review* 32 (June 1919): 932–73, particularly 965–66. See also David M. Rabban, "The Emergence of Modern First Amendment Doctrine," *The University of Chicago Law Review* 50 (Fall 1983): 1205–1351, particularly 1246–57.

10. Chafee, *Free Speech in the United States* (Cambridge: Harvard University Press, 1941), 27–28, 51–79.

11. Chafee, "Freedom of Speech in War Time," footnote 120, p. 966.

12. Roger M. Smith, *Liberalism and American Constitutional Law* (Cambridge: Harvard University Press, 1985), 96–101.

13. Scheiber, *Wilson and Civil Liberties,* 23.

14. John Lord O'Brian memoir, *New York Times Oral History Program* (Glen Rock, NJ: Microfilm Corporation of America, 1972) [Times OHP], 271.

15. The Postmaster General withheld delivery of the September 14, 1918, issue of the *Nation,* which contained "Civil Liberties Dead," an article that attacked administration policies. See Johnson, *Challenge to American Freedoms,* 78.

16. Richard W. Steele, "Fear of the Mob and Faith in Government in Free Speech Discourse, 1919–1941," *The American Journal of Legal History* 38 (January 1994): 55–83.

17. John Dewey, "The Cult of Irrationality," *New Republic,* 9 Nov. 1918, 34–35.

18. Zechariah Chafee, "Freedom of Speech," *New Republic,* 16 Nov. 1918, 66–69.

19. Chafee, "Freedom of Speech in War Time," 949, 972, 973.

20. Joan Jensen, *The Price of Vigilance* (Chicago: University of Chicago Press, 1968), 293–95.

21. O'Brian memoir, Times OHP, 19–34, 223–48.

22. Ibid., 263, 366.

23. "Regulation of Free Speech," April 25, 1919, box 18, folder 5 [18/5], John Lord O'Brian papers.

24. O'Brian, "Civil Liberty in War Time," *New York State Bar Association, Proceedings of Annual Meeting,* no. 42 (1919): 275–313; U.S. Congress, Senate, "Civil Liberties in War Time," 65th Cong. 3d. sess., 1919, S. doc. 434 [serial set #7469].

25. Donald L. Smith, *Zechariah Chafee, Jr.: Defender of Liberty and Law* (Cambridge: Harvard University Press, 1986), 37–38.

26. Zechariah Chafee, Jr., *Freedom of Speech* (New York: Harcourt, Brace and Howe, 1920).

27. Maguire to O'Brian, January 28, 1920, and Maguire to O'Brian, July 17, 1920, 5/18, Chafee to O'Brian, April 22, 1941, 4/1, O'Brian papers.

28. David M. Rabban, "The First Amendment in Its Forgotten Years," *Yale Law Journal* 90 (1981): 514–95.

29. Quoted in "Palmer Pleads Guilty," *New Republic,* 19 Jan. 1921, 217. See also "A Federal Judge Speaks Up," *New Republic,* 31 March 1920, 135.

30. National Popular Government League, *Illegal Practices of the Department of Justice* (Washington: National Popular Government League, 1920).

31. This account is based on Richard Gid Powers, *Secrecy and Power: The Life of J. Edgar Hoover* (New York: The Free Press, 1987), 63–123.

32. Robert K. Murray, *The Harding Era: Warren G. Harding and His Administration* (Minneapolis: University of Minnesota Press, 1969), 254–56, 296–97, 475–80. Continued involvement in illegal anti-radical activities is discussed in Michal R. Belknap, "The Mechanics of Repression: J. Edgar Hoover, The Bureau of Investigation and the Radicals 1917–1925," *Crime and Social Justice* 7 (spring/summer 1977): 49–58. The testimony is in ACLU, *The Nation-Wide Spy System Centering in the Department of Justice* (New York: ACLU, 1924).

33. Nancy V. Baker, *Conflicting Loyalties: Law and Politics in the Attorney General's Office, 1789–1990* (Lawrence: University of Kansas, 1992), 135–38.

34. Alpheus Thomas Mason, *Harlan Fiske Stone: Pillar of the Law* (New York: The Viking Press, 1956), 145–46, 167.

35. Statement of May 15, 1924, quoted in ACLU, *Nation-Wide Spy System,* 3.

36. Statement of May 23, 1924, in ibid., 4.

37. Powers, *Secrecy and Power,* 123, 128–29.

38. This account relies on Belknap, "J. Edgar Hoover, The Bureau of Investigation," 55–56.

39. Gregory to O'Brian, March 5, 1927, and Gregory to Atty. Gen. John Sargent, May 5, 1927. Both 18/5, O'Brian papers.

40. See Biddle, *Fear of Freedom,* 58.

41. Homer Cummings and Carl McFarland, *Federal Justice, Chapters in the History of Justice and the Federal Executive* (New York: Macmillan Co., 1937), 414–30.

42. Chafee, "Conscription of Public Opinion," *The Journalism Bulletin* 2 (June 1925): 8.

43. Leon Whipple, *Our Ancient Liberties: The Story of the Origins and Meaning of Civil and Religious Liberty in the United States* (New York: H.W. Wilson Company, 1927), 12, 144–45. The interest in civil liberties in the 1920s is fully covered in Paul Murphy, *The Meaning of Freedom of Speech: First Amendment Freedoms from Wilson to FDR* (Westport, CT: Greenwood Publishing Co., 1972).

44. See Steele, "Fear of the Mob and Faith," 57.

45. The definitive work on the ACLU is Samuel Walker, *In Defense of Liberties: A History of the ACLU* (New York: Oxford University Press, 1990).

46. Ibid., 61, 72.

47. Baldwin memoir, Times OHP, 191–92, 180–82; Lucille Milner, *Education of an American Liberal* (New York: Horizon Press, 1954), 157, 179–80, 189, 235–43.

48. Baldwin memoir, Times OHP, 130–31.

49. Ibid., 187–89, 191–92.

50. Kenneth L. Karst, *Law's Promise, Law's Expression: Visions of Power in the Politics of Race, Gender and Religion* (New Haven: Yale University Press, 1993).

51. *Schenck v. United States,* 249 U.S. 47 (1919). "The question in every case is whether the words used are used in such circumstances and are of such a nature as to create a clear and present danger that they will bring about the substantive evils that Congress has a right to prevent."

52. *Abrams v. United States,* 250 U.S. 616 (1919).

53. See L. E., "The Emergence of a Nationalized Bill of Rights: Due Process and a 'Higher Law' of Liberty," *Brooklyn Law Review* 7 (May 1938): 506–7; Robert Cushman, "Constitutional Law in 1930–31," *American Political Science Review* 26 (April 1932), 273–75. Samuel Walker, in *Hate Speech: The History of an American Controversy* (Lincoln: University of Nebraska Press, 1994), 29, calls *Stromberg v. California* (283 U.S. 359 [1931]) the first meaningful expression of the Court's determination to protect expression that the majority deemed "dangerous or offensive."

54. Mark Graber, *Transforming Free Speech: The Ambiguous Legacy of Civil Libertarianism* (Berkeley: University of California Press, 1991).

55. Paul L. Murphy, "Near v. Minnesota in the Context of Historical Developments" *Minnesota Law Review* 66 (1981): 95–160.

56. See Richard W. Steele, *Propaganda in an Open Society: The Media and the Roosevelt Administration, 1933–1941* (Westport, CT: Greenwood Press, 1985), 126–34.

57. Excerpt from "Address 'Justice, Sure and Speedy, For All'. . . . July 29, 1938," in 1/8, records of the Bill of Rights Committee of the American Bar Association.

58. Baldwin memoir, Times OHP, 135.

59. Address, June 11, 1938, and printed as "Conservatism and Civil Liberty," *American Bar Association Journal* 24 (August 1938): 640–44. See also his address before the Chicago Bar Association, "The Prospects for Civil Liberty," in *ABA Journal* 24 (October 1938): 833–36.

60. The Bill of Rights, drafted in 1789, was ratified in 1791.

61. Lewis Wood, "Bar Urged To Help Set up 'Hyde Parks,'" *New York Times,* 12 July 1939, 20.

Chapter 1

1. Murphy's life is told in the excellent multi-volume biography by Sidney Fine. Except as noted, the following is drawn from volume I, *Frank Murphy: The Detroit Years* (Ann Arbor: University of Michigan Press, 1975), 178–79; 119–20; 148–52; 396–98; 401–2; 405–6.

2. Ibid., 179.

3. Ibid., 397–98.

4. Ibid., 451.

5. Michael Schaller, *Douglas MacArthur: The Far Eastern General* (New York: Oxford University Press, 1989), 12.

6. For Cummings' tenure see: George Creel, "The Tall Man," *Collier's,* 4 Jan. 1936, 23ff; Gordon Dean memoir, Columbia University Oral History Project [CUOHP], 88–93; "Hacking to Justice with Cummings," *Nation,* 3 July 1935, 14–16; Peter Irons, *The New Deal Lawyers* (Princeton, NJ: Princeton University Press, 1982), 11–12; Cummings to FDR, January 26, 1934 and March 20, 1935, in "Correspondence with White House" fldr., box 174, Cummings papers; "Jackson vs. Richberg," *Nation,* 29 Jan. 1938, 119–20; Harold Ickes, *The Secret Diaries of Harold Ickes,* II (New York: Simon and Schuster, 1954), 537–38.

7. J. Woodford Howard, Jr., *Mr. Justice Murphy: A Political Biography* (Princeton NJ: Princeton University Press, 1968), 21, 29, 50, 203, 206–8. Comments on his character and his appointment can be found in Oswald G. Villard, "Issues and Men: Recent Appointments," *Nation,* 21 Jan. 1939, 94; "St. Francis," *Time,* 5 June 1939, 16; "Cabinet Appointment," *Time,* 9 Jan. 1939, 13; "Murphy: New Broom . . .," *Newsweek,* 24 April 1939, 14; Raymond Moley, "Mercy and the Big Chance," *Newsweek,* 15 May 1939, 56.

8. Jackson memoir, CUOHP, 788; Dean memoir, CUOHP, 101–4.

9. Sidney Fine, *Frank Murphy: The Washington Years* (Ann Arbor: University of Michigan Press, 1984), 30.

10. Russell Porter, "Our No. 1 Trouble-Shooter," *New York Times Magazine,* 16 April 1939, 3ff.

11. Frank Buckley, "The Department of Justice: Its Origin, Development and Present Day Organization," *Boston University Law Review* 5 (June 1925): 184–85.

12. L. E., "The Emergence of a Nationalized Bill of Rights: Due Process and a 'Higher Law' of Liberty," *Brooklyn Law Review* 7 (May 1938): 506–7.

13. John W. Hevener, *Which Side Are You On? The Harlan County Coal Miners, 1931–39* (Urbana: University of Illinois Press, 1978).

14. In *Harlan Miners Speak: Report on Terrorism in the Kentucky Coal Fields Prepared by Members of the National Committee for the Defense of Political Prisoners* [Theodore Dreiser et al.], orig. published by Harcourt, Brace and Company Inc., 1932. Reprint edition (New York: Da Capo Press, 1970), 345–46.

15. Irving Bernstein, *A History of the American Worker, 1933–41: Turbulent Years* (Boston: Houghton Mifflin Company, 1970), 450–51; and Jerold S. Auerbach, "The La Follette Committee: Labor and Civil Liberties in the New Deal," *The Journal of American History* 51 (December 1964): 435–59.

16. Hevener, *Which Side Are You On?* 150–53; "Washington Notes," *New Republic,* 9 Mar. 1939, 128.

17. "Murphy Weighing Civil Liberty Unit," *New York Times,* 26 Jan. 1939, 13.

18. "Hacking to Justice with Cummings," *Nation,* 3 July 1935, 14–16; John T. Elliff, "Aspects of Federal Civil Rights Enforcement: The Justice Department and the FBI, 1939–1964" in *Law in American History,* vol. 50, *Perspectives in American History* (Cambridge: Charles Warren Center for Studies in American History, Harvard University, 1971), 607.

19. "Civil Rights Unit Set Up by Murphy," *New York Times,* 4 Feb. 1939, 2.

20. Programs for the March "Bill of Rights Symposium" and the October "National Conference on Civil Liberties in the Present Emergency" found in "General Conferences, 1933–45" fldr., subject files, box 16, Records of the American Committee for the Protection of the Foreign Born.

21. Asst. Attorney General [AG] Brien McMahon for the AG, re: "Tentative Proposal for Attorney General's Conference on Civil Liberties," February 23, 1939, "Civil Liberties" fldr., Division of Public Relations, records of the Department of Justice [DoJ], Record Group [RG] 60.

22. Memo for AG. re: "Washington Star's National Radio Forum," March 3, 1939, 59/8, Murphy papers.

23. Norman L. Rosenberg, "Another History of Free Speech: The 1920s and the 1940s," *Law and Inequality* 7 (July 1989), 354–59.

24. Address, March 27, 1939, "Civil Liberties," in *U.S. Law Review* 73 (April 1939): 198–202.

25. Porter, "Our No. 1 Trouble-Shooter," 4; "Address to United States Conference of Mayors," *New York Times,* 16 May 1939, 16; Marshall College address, quoted in "Murphy, In Jersey, Denounces Hague," ibid., 14.

26. "Murphy Demands Law Enforcement," 20 April 1939, 13; and editorial, "Defense of Civil Liberties," 21 April 1939, 22. Both *New York Times.*

27. "Guard Civil Rights, Murphy Asks Cities," *New York Times,* 16 May 1939, 1 (text on 16).

28. Dayton David McKean, *The Boss: The Hague Machine in Action* (New York: Russell & Russell, 1940), 236.

29. *Hague v. C.I.O.,* 307 U.S. 496 (1939).

30. "Murphy in Jersey, Denounces Hague," *New York Times,* 22 June 1939, 14.

31. ACLU "Bulletins" 876 (July 8, 1939) and 880 (August 12, 1939), in *Records and Publications of the American Civil Liberties Union* [microfilm] (New York: Microfilm Corporation of America, 1975).

32. Roger Baldwin memoir, *New York Times Oral History Program* [Times, OHP] (Glen Rock, NJ: Microfilm Corporation of America, 1972), 202–3.

33. "New Civil Liberties Section, . . ." *New Republic,* 8 Mar. 1939, 128–29.

34. "Murphy on Civil Liberties," *New York Times,* 26 Jan. 1939, 20. Actually the unit did little. Dean to L. Danenberg, March 6, 1939, and "Statement of Purposes of Civil Liberties Unit of D.J.," March 13, 1939, both "Civil Liberties" fldr., Division of Public Relations, RG 60. McMahon for AG, February 3, 1939, Re: "Enforcement of Civil Liberties Statute," 1–59, in Murphy papers; Schweinhaut, "The Civil Liberties Section of the Department of Justice," *The Bill of Rights Review,* I (1940), 206–16; Fine, *Murphy, Washington Years,* 82. Baldwin concluded that the unit had been "too inactive and too cautious, . . . however the fact that the federal government was investigating . . . had some effect on improving the situation." Baldwin to Besig, June 26, 1941, vol. 2318, p. 46, American Civil Liberties Union papers.

35. Address, "Civil Liberties," March 27, 1939, *U.S. Law Review* 73 (April 1939): 198–202.

36. See Maurice Isserman, *Which Side Were You On? The American Communist Party During the Second World War* (Middletown, CT: Wesleyan University Press, 1982), 3–4.

37. Harvey Klehr, *The Heyday of Communism: The Depression Decade* (New York: Basic Books, 1984), 186–211.

38. American Institute of Public Opinion (AIPO) poll, November 28, 1939, *Public Opinion Quarterly* 4 (March 1940): 92.

39. The extreme right is discussed generally in Geoffrey S. Smith, *To Save A Nation: American Countersubversives, the New Deal, and the Coming of World War II* (New York: Basic Books, 1973); Leo Ribuffo, *The Old Christian Right: The Protestant Far Right from the Great Depression to the Cold War* (Philadelphia: Temple University Press, 1983). Anti-Semitic themes and uses in Dov Fisch, "The Libel Trial of Robert Edward Edmondson: 1936–1938," *American Jewish History* 71 (1981): 79–102; Hyman Berman, "Political Anti-Semitism in Minnesota During the Great Depression," *Jewish Social Studies* 38 (1976): 247–64.

40. See Alan Brinkley, *Voices of Protest: Huey Long, Father Coughlin and the Great Depression* (New York: Alfred Knopf, 1982), 207–42.

41. Arthur Schlesinger, Jr., *The Age of Roosevelt: The Politics of Upheaval* (Boston: Houghton Mifflin Company, 1960), 15–69, 550–61.

42. Sander A. Diamond, *The Nazi Movement in the United States, 1924–1941* (Ithaca, NY: Cornell University Press, 1974), 101–205.

43. Thomas Maddux argues that many Americans tended to lump the extremes together. Maddux, "Red Fascism, Brown Bolshevism: The American Image of Totalitarianism in the 1930s," *The Historian* XL (1977): 85–103.

44. "The Question of Federal Sedition Legislation," *The Congressional Digest* 14 (October 1935): 225–56; Michal Belknap, *Cold War Political Justice: The Smith Act, the Communist Party, and American Civil Liberties* (Westport, CT: Greenwood Press, 1977), 17–19.

45. See *Freedom of Speech, References and Reprints,* compiled by J. E. Johnson in *The Reference Shelf* 8, no. 10 (New York: The H. W. Wilson Company, 1936); "Federal Sedition Bills: Speech Restriction in Theory and Practice," *Columbia Law Review* 35 (June 1935): 917–27.

46. David Williams, "The Bureau of Investigation and Its Critics, 1919–1921: The Origins of Federal Political Surveillance," *Journal of American History* 68 (Dec. 1981): 561–79.

47. Donner, *Age of Surveillance, The Aims and Methods of America's Political Intelligence System* (New York: Alfred A. Knopf, 1980), 62.

48. An insightful essay on the origins of the national surveillance state is in Norman L. Rosenberg, *Protecting the Best Men: An Interpretive History of the Law of Libel* (Chapel Hill: University of North Carolina Press, 1986), 208–18.

49. Harry Ward, Chairman ACLU et al. to FDR, March 7, 1936, and FDR to Ward, March 23, 1936, in Official File 2111, Roosevelt papers.

50. Discussed in U.S., Congress, Senate, Senate Select Committee to Study Governmental Operations with Respect to Intelligence Activities, *Intelligence Activities and the Rights of Americans,* Book II, 94th Cong., 2d sess., 26 April 1976, Senate Report 94–755 (hereinafter "Senate, *Intelligence Activities*"), 24–25.

51. William W. Keller, *The Liberals and J. Edgar Hoover, Rise and Fall of a Domestic Intelligence State* (Princeton, NJ: Princeton University Press, 1989), 58.

52. Confidential Memorandum, August 24, 25, 1936, in Hoover Official and Confidential file 136, records of the Federal Bureau of Investigation, FBI Reading Room. One may question the reliability of Hoover's account, but historians critical of the director have chosen to accept its authenticity, claiming merely that Hoover stretched FDR's meaning. See Athan Theoharis, *Spying on Americans: Political Surveillance From Hoover to the Huston Plan* (Philadelphia: Temple University Press, 1978), 67–68.

53. Theoharis, *Spying on Americans,* 68–69.

54. Richard W. Steele, "FDR and His Foreign Policy Critics," *Political Science Quarterly* 94 (spring 1979): 15–32.

55. Quoted in Powers, *Secrecy and Power,* 230.

56. David J. Williams, "'Without Understanding': The FBI and Political Surveillance, 1908–1941" (Ph.D. diss., University of New Hampshire: 1981), 345–48.

57. An excellent discussion of this freedom is in Joseph B. Robison, "Protection of Associations from Compulsory Disclosure of Membership," *Columbia Law Review* 58 (1958): 614–49.

58. Powers, *Secrecy and Power,* 233.

59. Draft letter, Murphy to FDR, June 17, 1939; FDR for Secretaries of State [et al.], June 26, 1939, both in "Case Files—Espionage and related material," 58/346, Murphy papers.

60. Senate, "Intelligence Activities," 31.

61. Sidney Fine, *Frank Murphy: The Washington Years* (Ann Arbor: University of Michigan Press, 1984), 116.

62. Eugene C. Gerhart, *America's Advocate: Robert H. Jackson* (Indianapolis: Bobbs-Merrill Company, Inc., 1958), 184.

63. "Diary notes, 1942, of Frank Murphy, includes meetings with Pres. Roosevelt, etc.," Eugene Gressman [Murphy's secretary/assistant] papers.

64. Asked by the Senate to define the scope of executive powers this conferred upon the president, Murphy declined. J. Woodford Howard, *Mr. Justice Murphy* (Princeton: Princeton University Press, 1968), 208.

65. Press conference, September 8, 1939, in *Complete Presidential Press Conferences of Franklin D. Roosevelt,* vol. 14 (New York: Da Capo Press, 1972), 151–55.

66. Senate, *Intelligence Activities,* 29.

67. ACLU, "Report on Prosecutions Allegedly Brought for Political Purposes," March 1940, in "ACLU General, 1940" file, fldr. 408, box 20, records of the Northern California Branch of the ACLU.

Chapter 2

1. Les K. Adler and Thomas G. Patterson, "Red Fascism: The Merger of Nazi Germany and Soviet Russia in the American Image of Totalitarianism, 1930s–1950s," *American Historical Review* 75 (April 1970): 1047–51; Hadley Cantril, ed., *Public Opinion 1935–1946* (Princeton, NJ: Princeton University Press, 1951), 164.

2. "Notes, September 7, 1939, of Cabinet Meeting," in the Eugene Gressman papers.

3. Sidney Fine, *Frank Murphy: The Washington Years* (Ann Arbor: University of Michigan Press, 1984), 119–21.

4. Speeches of September 7 and October 1, 1939, quoted in Frank Donner, *The Age of Surveillance, the Aims and Methods of America's Political Intelligence System* (New York: Alfred A. Knopf, 1980), 59.

5. Address on September 25, 1939, in "Press Releases," 22/58, Frank Murphy papers.

6. Sidney Fine, *Frank Murphy: The Detroit Years* (Ann Arbor: The University of Michigan Press, 1975), 198.

7. In November 1939, FDR told Murphy that 1940 was not his year, but hinted that the presidency was still not beyond his reach. Fine, *Murphy: Washington,* 30–31.

8. Walter Goodman, *The Committee, The Extraordinary Career of the House Committee on Un-American Activities* (New York: Farrar, Straus and Giroux, 1968), 18–24; Richard Polenberg, "Franklin Roosevelt and Civil Liberties: The Case of the Dies Committee," *The Historian* 30 (February 1968): 167.

9. The following discussion is based on Goodman, *The Committee,* 25–61; and Polenberg, "Franklin Roosevelt and Civil Liberties," 165–69.

10. See "Re: Investigation of Un-American Activities," attached to McMahon, "Memorandum for J. Edgar Hoover . . . Re: Dies Committee Investigation," January 3, 1939, file 236377, records of Department of Justice, Record Group [RG] 60.

11. Fine, *Murphy: Washington,* 112.

12. The committee's public support was exaggerated. Lindsay Rogers, "Do the Gallup Polls Measure Opinion?" *Harper's Magazine,* Nov. 1941, 627.

13. Fine, *Murphy: Washington,* 99–100.

14. Don Whitehead, *The FBI Story, A Report to the People* (New York: Random House, 1956), 165.

15. Goodman, *The Committee,* 62–92; Polenberg, "Franklin Roosevelt and Civil Liberties," 170–72.

16. Statement by Dies, October 23, 1939, "Dies" fldr., box 48, Public Relations files, RG 60.

17. Fine, *Murphy: Washington,* 112, 117.

18. File 235343, RG 60, contains a number of complaints and responses.

19. "Heils are Absent at German Camp," *New York Times,* 26 July 1937, 2; "Veterans Defied by Bund On Camp," ibid., 25 July 1937, 9.

20. Joe Starnes, "They're On the Run," *The American Legion Magazine* (April, 1940), 16–17ff. On public preferences about which subversives to investigate (Communists—70 percent, Nazis—30 percent [no opinion—22 percent]), see poll, January 4, 1940, in *Public Opinion Quarterly* 4 (June 1940): 349.

21. Maurice Isserman, *Which Side Were You On? The American Communist Party During the Second World War* (Middletown, CT: Wesleyan University Press, 1982), 36–47. See Edmond Taylor, *Awakening From History* (Boston: Gambit Incorporated, 1969), 256–57.

22. Adler and Patterson, "Red Fascism," 1050; Isserman, *Which Side Were You On?* 44–45.

23. Frank A. Warren, *Liberals and Communism: The "Red Decade" Revisited* (Bloomington: Indiana University Press, 1966), 202, 209.

24. "U.S. Promises 'Sensation' In Spy Inquiry," *Washington Post,* 27 Dec. 1939, 1.
25. "Russian Agent, Fined in Spy Probe, to Leave," *Washington Post,* 28 Dec. 1939, 1.
26. Dillard Stokes, "U.S. Names 8 in Spy Probe Here," *Washington Post,* 3 Jan. 1940, 1.
27. "Notes Re. Press Conference, December 15, 1939," "Murphy Press Conferences" fldr., Subject files, item 132, RG 60.
28. "Notes on Attorney General's Press Conference, December 28, 1939," in ibid.
29. William A. Mueller, "Coughlin and the Nazi Bund" and "Hitler Commands the Bund Obeys," *Look,* 26 Sept. 1939, 10–15, and 10 Oct. 1939, 16–21; J. Wechsler, "The Coughlin Terror," 22 July 1939, 92–97; George Britt, "Poison in the Melting-Pot," 1 April 1939, 374–76. Both in the *Nation.*
30. Fine, *Murphy: The Detroit Years,* 66–67.
31. Fisher for AG, December 5, 1939, file 235343, RG 60.
32. Edward Ryan, "Jury to Probe Sabotage," *Washington Post,* 29 Dec. 1939, 1.
33. Ronald Modras, "Father Coughlin and Anti-Semitism: Fifty Years Later," *Journal of Church and State* 31 (1989): 231–47.
34. See "Notes on Attorney General's Press Conference, December 28, 1939," in "Murphy Press Conferences" fldr., item 132, RG 60.
35. Geoffrey S. Smith, *To Save a Nation: American Countersubversives, the New Deal, and the Coming of World War II* (New York: Basic Books, 1973), 133–34; Dale Kramer, "The American Fascists," *Harper's,* Sept. 1940, 380–93.
36. Fine, *Murphy: Washington,* 121.
37. FBI, "Memorandum," January 22, 1940, in file 235343–10, RG 60.
38. Ibid.
39. "Saboteur Arrests in Boston Likely" and "Philadelphia Inquiry On," 16 Jan. 1940, 3; "Sabotage is Seen as Motive of Plot," 17 Jan. 1940, 14; "17 Held in Plot Against U.S. Jeered, Cheered at Court," 16 Jan. 1940, 1. All *New York Times.*
40. "Sabotage Is Seen As Motive of Plot," 17 Jan. 1940, 14; and "A Thwarted Putsch," 16 Jan. 1940, 22. Both *New York Times.*
41. Hoover for AG, June 27, 1940, "Attorney General—Subversive Activities—Christian Front Sedition Investigation" file, Robert Jackson papers.
42. Jackson memoir, Columbia University Oral History Project [CUOHP], 797.
43. ACLU, "Report on Prosecutions Allegedly Brought for Political Purposes," March 1940, in "ACLU General, 1940," fldr. 408, records of the Northern California Branch, ACLU.
44. Harvey Klehr, John Earl Haynes, and Fridrikh Gorevich Firsov, *The Secret World of American Communism* (New Haven: Yale University Press, 1995), 152–53.
45. Hoover for AG, March 30, 1939, and McMahon for AG, February 9, 1938, both file 71–21–0; McMahon for AG, February 4, 1937, "Neutrality" fldr., Division of Public Relations. All RG 60.

46. Jackson memoir, CUOHP, 793.

47. Hoover for AG, March 30, 1939; Edward Kemp for AG, April 27, 1939, and attachments. All file 71–21–0, RG 60.

48. Murphy for Kemp, May 8, 1939, ibid.

49. Isserman, *Which Side Were You On?* 48–49.

50. Hoover for AG, February 8, 1940, file 71–21–0, RG 60.

51. Fine, *Murphy: Washington,* 123–29 covers the entire episode in detail. Quote on 123.

52. "Statements Made with Regard to Various Charges . . .," March 18, 1940, in file 94–3–4–690–8, records of the FBI, Freedom of Information [FoI] Act request.

53. FDR for secretary of labor and commissioner of immigration, November 18, 1939, Official File 133, Roosevelt papers.

54. Notes on December 19, 1939, cabinet meeting in "Notes Dec. 19 and Dec. 28, 1939 Cabinet Meetings," Gressman papers.

55. Cabinet meeting, January 26, 1940, in Wallace diary (microfilm), Henry Wallace papers.

Chapter 3

1. John T. Elliff, *The U.S. Department of Justice and Individual Rights, 1937–1962* (New York: Garland Publishing Inc., 1987), 98.

2. Jackson's career outlined in Eugene C. Gerhart, *America's Advocate: Robert H. Jackson* (Indianapolis: The Bobbs-Merrill Company, 1958).

3. Karl Schriftgiesser, "Robert Jackson," *North American Review* 248 (winter 1939–40), 334–44.

4. Jackson to Stone, March 14, 1938, "Jackson, Robert H." fldr., Harlan Fiske Stone papers. Jackson memoir, Columbia University Oral History Project [CUOHP], 639–41, 656.

5. Brandeis remark in Gordon Dean memoir, CUOHP, 140–41.

6. Ickes to FDR, September 18, 1939, in President's Secretary's File [PSF]—Interior/Ickes, Franklin D. Roosevelt papers; Dean memoir, CUOHP, 99.

7. "Biddle Reported Choice for Solicitor," *New York Times,* 11 Dec. 1939, 13.

8. Jackson to FDR, December 30, 1939, in Gerhart, *America's Advocate,* 186.

9. "Robert Jackson," *Current Biography,* 1940; Jackson memoir, CUOHP, 786; Dean memoir, CUOHP, 143.

10. Wallace diary, January 18, 1940, Henry Wallace papers.

11. Morgenthau diary, January 15, 1940, Henry Morgenthau papers.

12. Jackson to FDR, December 30, 1939, in Gerhart, *America's Advocate,* 186.

13. Gerhart, *America's Advocate,* 36; Schriftgiesser, "Robert Jackson," 336.

14. Manuscript draft of "America's Advocate," 6, "Biographical File," Robert Jackson papers.

15. "Justice Jackson's Story," manuscript of tape recordings taken by Dr. H. D. Phillips [edited by Jackson], 1952–53, pp. 98–102, in "Biographical File," Jackson papers.

16. Manuscript "America's Advocate," 56, Jackson papers.

17. "Draft Autobiography," fldr. 2, "Biographical file," Jackson papers.

18. Jackson memoir, CUOHP, 640; Dean memoir, CUOHP, 145–46.

19. Nancy V. Baker, *Conflicting Loyalties: Law and Politics in the Attorney General's Office, 1789–1990* (Lawrence: University of Kansas Press, 1992), 35.

20. Jackson memoir, CUOHP, 793.

21. Wallace diary, February 9, 1940.

22. "Draft Autobiography," fldr. 2, "Biographical file," Jackson papers.

23. Hoover to AG, June 27, 1940 in "Attorney General—Subversive Activities—Christian Front Sedition Investigation" fldr., Jackson papers.

24. "Protection of Civil Liberties by Federal Prosecutors, April 1, 1940," item 9, "Pamphlets" file, *Records and Publications of the American Civil Liberties Union* (New York: Microfilm Corporation of America, 1975); Jackson memoir, CUOHP, 1061.

25. "Jackson, The Federal Prosecutor," *Journal of the American Judicature Society* 24 (June 1940): 18–20.

26. Jackson to Chafee, April 25, 1941, "Immigration and Naturalization—Alien Registration" fldr., Jackson papers.

27. "Neutrality laws" in this context referred to laws designed to keep the United States free of propaganda activities aimed at altering the nation's neutral status.

28. This account is by Chester T. Lane, who was later brought in by Smith as his deputy. See Lane memoir, *New York Times Oral History Program* (Glen Rock, NJ: Microfilm Corporation of America, 1972), [hereinafter *NY Times OHP*], 604–5.

29. Smith reviews the unit's work in draft "Report of the Chief of the Special Defense Unit . . . for Fiscal Year Ending June 30, 1941," dated October 20, 1941, in "Inter-Office Memoranda" fldr., box 732, records of the Department of Justice [DoJ], accession 62A47, Federal Records Center [FRC], Suitland, MD.

30. Dean for AG, April 22, 1940, "Work Program Projects and Sources of Materials" fldr.; "Confidential Memo for the Attorney General," May 13, 1940, Re: "Materials on Wartime Justice Problems," in fldr. "R"; and A. Glasser for Smith, May 31, 1940, Re: "Research Materials . . ." in "Work Program, Projects . . . Material" fldr., 148 War Policy Office [WPO] files, DoJ, 62A47, FRC.

31. "Memo of Conference with Carl MacFarland," May 10, 1940, in "R" fldr., 148 WPO files, DoJ, 62A47, FRC.

32. Smith for AG, September 23, 1940, in file 66–6200–100–20X, records of the FBI, obtained through a Freedom of Information Act [FoI] request.

33. Hoover for AG, April 30, 1940, in "Subversive Activities . . . Criticism of FBI" fldr., Jackson papers.

34. "New Unit To Assay Neutrality Cases," *New York Times,* 29 April 1940, 5. Remarks by Presidential Press Secretary Stephen Early suggesting Hoover's eclipse in transcript of his press conference, April 29, 1940, in "Scrapbook," Stephen T. Early papers.

35. "White House Hails Neutrality Unit," *New York Times,* 30 April 1940, 8.

36. Smith, "Memorandum for Attorney General," September 23, 1940, 66–6200–100–20X, FBI/FoI.

37. As reported by Chafee to O'Brian, May 5, 1941, 4/1, John Lord O'Brian papers.

38. Robert H. Jackson, "Messages on the Launching of the 'Bill of Rights Review,'" *Bill of Rights Review* I (summer 1940), 34.

39. O. J. Rogge to Lindemann, June 26, 1940; R. Baldwin to Jackson, July 30, 1940; and Rogge to ACLU, August 12, 1940. All 144–51–0, records of DoJ, Record Group [RG] 60.

40. Jackson, "Messages," op cit.

41. John T. Elliff, *The Reform of FBI Intelligence Operations* (Princeton, NJ: Princeton University Press, 1979), 15, 32–35.

42. "Draft Autobiography," fldr. 2, "Biographical file," Jackson papers.

43. "American Ogpu," *New Republic,* 19 Feb. 1940, 230–31.

44. John Bugas et al., "Statements made with regard to . . . arrests . . ." March 12, 1940, 94–3–4–690–8, FBI/FoI; Hoover for AG, May 1, 1940, 235343–10, RG 60.

45. Richard Lowitt, *George W. Norris: The Triumph of a Progressive, 1933–1944* (Urbana: University of Illinois Press, 1978), 293–98. See also "Bureau of Investigation—Max Lowenthal" fldr., George Norris papers.

46. Dean memoir, CUOHP, 142. Norris to Jackson, February 22 and March 10, 1940, in file 71–21–0, RG 60.

47. Baldwin to Jackson, March 7, 1940, "Attorney General—Subversive Activities & Investigations—General," Jackson papers.

48. "'Plot' Against Hoover," *Nation,* 9 Mar. 1940, 323; and "Investigate the American Ogpu!" *New Republic,* 11 Mar. 1940, 331 provide excerpts from the critics.

49. "Critics Open Fire on Hoover's G-Men," *New York Times,* 17 Mar. 1940, IV, 6.

50. Hoover to Stone, April 23, 1940, and Stone to Hoover, April 26, 1940, in "Hoover, John Edgar" fldr., Harlan Fiske Stone papers.

51. Hoover to Stone, April 23, 1940, ibid.

52. Remarks in Minutes of Special Intelligence Service (SIS) meetings on March 5, 19, and 26, 1940, in Military Intelligence Division (MID) 9794–186A, records of the MID, War Department, RG 165. See Berle diary entries March 21 and April 5, 1940, in Adolf A. Berle, Jr. papers.

53. Richard Gid Powers, *Secrecy and Power, The Life of J. Edgar Hoover* (New York: The Free Press, 1987), 307.

54. Berle diary, March 27 and April 5, 1940, Berle papers.

55. Sen. Resolution 224 (February 1, 1940), 76th Cong., 3d sess.

56. *Olmstead* v. *U.S.* 277 U.S. 438 (1928). Frank C. Hanighen, "Wire-tapping and the Labor Bogey," *Common Sense,* May 1941, 148–49. In *Nardone* v. *U.S.* (302 U.S. 338 [1939]), the Court ruled that information acquired through tapping was not admissible in federal prosecutions.

57. Berle diary, March 21, 1940, Berle papers.

58. Baldwin to Jackson, March 7, 1940, and Jackson to Baldwin (draft) April 6, 1940, in "Attorney General—Subversive Activities and Investigations—General" fldr., Jackson papers.

59. Hoover, "Memorandum for the AG, February 27, 1940, in 71–21–0, RG 60. "Jackson Denies Charges FBI 'Overstepped' Authority," *Washington Post,* 2 Mar. 1940, 7.

60. Jackson to Norris, May 3, 1940, "Subversive Activities and Investigations—Criticism of FBI" fldr., Jackson papers.

61. Jackson memoir, CUOHP, 794.

62. Jackson to John L. Lewis, June 19, 1940; to Philip Murray, February 20, 1941; to Rep. John M. Coffee, May 15, 1941. All "Attorney General Wiretapping Controversy—Legislation" fldr., Jackson papers.

63. Jackson memoir, CUOHP, 967.

64. "Justice Department Bans Wiretapping," *New York Times,* 18 Mar. 1940, 1.

65. "FBI is No OGPU, Jackson Asserts," *New York Times,* 31 Mar. 1940, 19.

66. Conference 629 (March 8, 1940) in *Complete Presidential Press Conferences of Franklin D. Roosevelt* (New York: Da Capo Press, 1972), 192. Press Club encounter described in Powers, *Secrecy and Power,* 236.

67. Jackson memoir, CUOHP, 969.

68. Charles Fahy memoir, CUOHP, 122.

Chapter 4

1. John Dewey, "Our Un-Free Press," *Common Sense* (Nov. 1935), 6–7; George Seldes, *Freedom of the Press* (Indianapolis: Bobbs-Merrill and Co., 1935); J. T. Laprade, "The Freedom of the Press: An Outworn Shibboleth?" *South Atlantic Quarterly* 35 (April 1936): 212–19; M. Whitcomb Hess, "Is Free Speech a Right?" *The Journal of Philosophy* 33 (July 1936): 437–43; Alfred McLung Lee, "Freedom of Press: Services of a Catch Phrase" in *Studies in the Science of Society presented to Albert Galloway Keeler,* George Peter Murdock, ed. (New Haven: Yale University Press, 1937), 255–75; Murdock, "Violations of Press Freedom in America," *Journalism Quarterly* 15 (March 1938): 19–27; Graham J. White, *FDR and the Press* (Chicago: University of Chicago Press, 1979), 49–50, 94, 159–61.

2. Carl Becker, "Freedom of Speech," *Nation,* 24 Jan. 1934, 94.

3. See Robert Westbrook, "Lewis Mumford, John Dewey, and the Pragmatic Acquiescence" in *Lewis Mumford, Public Intellectual,* Thomas P. Hughes and Agatha C. Hughes, ed. (New York: Oxford University Press, 1990), 301–22.

4. See Lewis Mumford, *Men Must Act* (New York: Harcourt Brace and Co., 1939), 116–17; Archibald MacLeish, "The Irresponsibles," *Nation,* 18 May 1940, 618–23; Peter Novick, *That Noble Dream: The 'Objectivity Question' and the American Historical Profession* (New York: Cambridge University Press, 1988), 281–92.

5. Clayton D. Laurie, *The Propaganda Warriors: America's Crusade against Nazi Germany* (Lawrence: University Press of Kansas, 1996), 29–44.

6. Edward A. Purcell, Jr., *The Crisis of Democratic Theory: Scientific Naturalism and the Problem of Value* (Lexington: The University Press of Kentucky, 1973), 158, 161, 167, 172, 209.

7. Karl Loewenstein, "Militant Democracy and Fundamental Rights," *The American Political Science Review* 31 (June 1937): 423–24; Karl Loewenstein, "Legislative Control of Political Extremism in European Democracies I," *Columbia Law Review* 38 (April 1938): 593, 602, 621; and "Legislative Control of Political Extremism in European Democracies II," ibid. (May 1938): 725–74.

8. "Civil Liberties," *New Republic,* 17 Feb. 1941, 248–49.

9. Peggy Lamson, *Roger Baldwin: Founder of the American Civil Liberties Union* (Boston: Houghton Mifflin Company, 1976), 148–50.

10. Samuel Walker, *In Defense of American Liberties: A History of the ACLU* (New York: Oxford University Press, 1990), 115–34.

11. Jackson to Baldwin (draft), April 6, 1940, in "Attorney General—Subversive Activities and Investigations—General" fldr., Robert Jackson papers.

12. *Minersville School Dist.* v. *Gobitis,* 310 U.S. 586 (1940).

13. Frankfurter, in a September 1942 address, quoted in Michal Belknap, "Frankfurter and the Nazi Saboteurs," *Yearbook of the Supreme Court Historical Society Minersville School District v. Gobitis,* 595.(1982): 66–71.

14. *Minersville School Dist. v. Gobitis,* 595. Joseph L. Rauh, Jr., "Felix Frankfurter: Civil Libertarian" (Francis Biddle Memorial Lecture, Harvard Law School, Feb. 26, 1976), *Harvard Civil Rights—Civil Liberties Law Review* II (1976): 496–520.

15. George Gardner and Charles D. Post, "The Constitutional Questions Raised by the Flag Salute and Teachers Oath Acts in Massachusetts," *Boston University Law Review* 16 (November 1936); "The Gobitis Case in Retrospect," *The Bill of Rights Review* (summer 1940): 267–68. Alpheus Thomas Mason, *Harlan Fiske Stone: Pillar of The Law* (New York: The Viking Press, 1982), 525–35.

16. Clark recapitulates Jackson's views in G. Clark to Jackson, April 16, 1940, "Attorney General—Committee on Civil Rights" [AG-CCR] fldr. Solicitor General Francis Biddle, with whom Jackson also shared his concerns, rec-

ommended an *unofficial* advisory group that Jackson could turn to for advice "on borderline cases." Biddle for AG, April 19, 1940, and Elbert M. Barron for Solicitor General, "Subversive Activities . . . General" fldr. Charles Burlingham—Jackson correspondence, May 31 and June 14, 1940, "AG-CCR" fldr. All Jackson papers.

17. Alistair Horne, *To Lose a Battle, France 1940* (New York: Penguin Books, 1979).

18. Louis DeJong, *The German Fifth Column in the Second World War,* trans. C. M Geyl (Chicago: University of Chicago Press, 1956) deals with the phenomenon worldwide. Francis MacDonnell, *Insidious Foes: The Axis Fifth Column and the American Home Front* (New York: Oxford University Press, 1995) surveys the scare in the United States. Nicholas John Cull, *Selling War: The British Propaganda Campaign Against American "Neutrality" in World War II* (New York: Oxford University Press, 1995) 82, 169, suggests the British contribution to American concerns.

19. Horne, *To Lose a Battle,* 520–22.

20. "There Are Signs of Nazi Fifth Columns Everywhere," *Life,* 17 June 1940, 10–11.

21. Stanley High, "Alien Poison," *Saturday Evening Post,* 31 Aug. 1940, 9–11ff.

22. George Britt, *The Fifth Column is Here* (New York: Wilfred Funk, 1940).

23. Quoted in review in *The Bill of Rights Review* I (spring 1941): 254.

24. In "Correspondence, 1935–41," fldr. 361, box 18, records of Northern California Branch [No.Cal Br.], ACLU.

25. "Warning Note," *Time,* 8 July 1940, 38.

26. Berle diary, June 20, 1940, Adolf Berle papers.

27. Norman Alley, *I Witness* (New York: Wilfred Funk, 1941), 326–70.

28. Berle diary, June 26, 1940, Berle papers.

29. J. Edgar Hoover, "The Test of Citizenship," speech to Daughters of the American Revolution, April 18, 1940, in *Vital Speeches of the Day* 6 (October 1939–October 1940): 440–43.

30. Martin Dies, *The Trojan Horse in America* (New York: Dodd, Mead, 1940).

31. "Our Enemies Within" *Nation,* 22 June 1940, 745–46.

32. Collier/Indians in Wallace diary, May 24, June 20 and 24, 1940, Henry Wallace papers; Berle diary, June 26, 1940, Berle papers; "Indians of Both Americas Targets of 'Fifth Columns'," *Science News Letter* 38, August 10, 1940: 94.

33. Message to Congress, May 16, 1940, p. 198; Fireside Chat on National Defense, May 26, 1940, pp. 230, 238–39; Acceptance of Third Term Nomination, July 19, 1940, pp. 296, 298 in Samuel I. Rosenman, comp., *The Public Papers and Addresses of Franklin D. Roosevelt* (13 vols.) (New York: Harper & Brothers, 1950), vol. 9.

34. Ibid., 665, 670.

35. Most chose to "do everything possible to help *except* go to war." The figures for this response in 1940: May 14—67 percent; May 23—65 percent; June

11—73 percent; June 25—67 percent; Sept 17—76 percent. Support for a declaration of war never exceeded 5 percent. *Public Opinion, 1935–1946,* Hadley Cantril, ed. (Princeton: Princeton University Press, 1951), 971.

36. Hoover for AG, May 29, 1940, "National Defense Matters" fldr., Jackson papers. Annual Report of the Attorney General of the United States, 1940 (Washington D.C.: Government Printing Office, 1940), 152.

37. Documented in "Labor Free Speech—Strikes, 1938–43" fldr. (662), box 31, No.Cal.Br., ACLU.

38. "National Affairs," *Time,* 3 June 1940, 12.

39. Cabinet discussion of volunteers in Wallace diary, May 24, 1940, Wallace papers.

40. Berle diary, June 25, 1940. Sampling of volunteer offers in "Citizen Cooperation" and "Citizens Organizations" folders, 148 War Policy Office [WPO] files, records of the Department of Justice [DoJ], in accession 62A47, Federal Records Center [FRC], Suitland, MD.

41. Justice Department, "Press Digest on Sabotage, Espionage and Related Matters," June 17, 1940, "Press Digests" fldr., box 8, Gordon Dean papers, Record Group [RG] 60; B. W. Patch, "Civil Liberties in War Emergencies," *Editorial Research Report* 15 (October 15, 1940): 283–96.

42. See Walter E. Helmke, "Report of the Committee on Civil Liberties of the National Institute of Municipal Law Officers," in *Municipalities and the Law in Action* 5 (1942): 477–95.

43. Memorandum of Notes Taken at a Conference Held in the Office of the Solicitor General . . . August 5, 1940 . . ." in "Reports—L. M. C. Smith—Sedition Section" fldr., box 735, DoJ, 62A47, FRC.

44. Press release, June 5, 1940, "Wartime Civil Liberties, 1940–45," fldr. 678, box 32, No.Cal.Br., ACLU.

45. "Memo of Conference with Carl MacFarland," May 10, 1940, in "R" fldr., 148 WPO files, DoJ, 62A47, FRC.

46. Speech before the New York State Bar Association at Saranac, NY. Quoted in "Roosevelt Signs Alien Registry Bill," Washington *Post,* 30 June 1940, 1; and in New York *Herald Tribune* editorial cited in Justice Department, "Press Digest on Sabotage, Espionage and Related Matters," June 17, 1940, "Press Digests" fldr., box 8, Gordon Dean papers, RG 60.

47. H. Wallace to AG, June 25, 1940; AG to Wallace, July 5, 1940, in "Citizen Cooperation" fldr.; and circular from Office of Attorney General . . ." (June 1940), in "Solicitor General Memos" fldr. Both 148 WPO files, DoJ, 62A47, FRC.

48. Justice Department, "Press Digest on Sabotage, Espionage and Related Matters," June 17, 1940, "Press Digests" fldr., box 8, Dean papers, RG 60.

49. Hoover to L. Milner, November 7, 1939, 2147/81, ACLU papers. "Diametrically opposed" in Conference of Special Intelligence Service [SIS] Representatives, May 31, 1940, SIS file 9794–186A, records of Military Intelligence

Division (MID), War Department, RG 165; Hoover, "Outlaw the Vigilante," *This Week* magazine sec., New York *Herald Tribune,* 18 Aug. 1940, 2.

50. Minutes of the SIS meeting of August 2, 1940 (dated August 4), in SIS file 9794–186A, encl. 1, RG 165.

51. Hoover, "Memorandum for AG," May 31, 1940, in "Subversive Activities . . . General" fldr.; Hoover for AG, June 2, 1940, in "House Committee on Un-American Activities" fldr. Both Jackson papers.

52. Jackson to E. Roosevelt, April 29, 1941, in "Bridges case" fldr., Jackson papers.

53. Jackson memoir, Columbia University Oral History Project [CUOHP], 962.

54. William Pencak, *For God & Country, The American Legion, 1919–1941* (Boston: Northeastern University Press, 1989), 237–317. See also Kenneth O'Reilly, *Hoover and the Un-Americans: The FBI, HUAC, and the Red Menace* (Philadelphia, Temple University Press, 1983), 87.

55. "American Legion" [yellow, legal-size, handwritten notes, no date] in "Aliens Historical Materials" fldr., DoJ, 62A47, FRC.

56. Hoover for Attorney General, June 7, 1940, in "American Legion, Civil Defense Plan" fldr., 148 WPO files, DoJ, 62A47, FRC.

57. Jackson to Raymond J. Kelly, June 27, 1940. Copy found in the Americanism Division files at the American Legion headquarters and supplied to the author by Librarian Joseph J. Hovish. Pencak, *For God & Country,* 312–14, 317.

58. Don Whitehead, *The FBI Story: A Report to the People* (New York: Random House, 1956), 209; Kent Hunter, "To Maintain Law and Order," *The American Legion Magazine,* Oct. 1940, 1.

59. L. M. C. Smith for AG, June 18, 1940, Re: "Conference Called by National Defense Council . . ." in "Neutrality Laws Unit" fldr., Jackson papers.

60. Memorandum, "State and Local Cooperation in National Defense," attached to circular letter from William H. McReynolds, Secretary of the Council of National Defense to Governors, August 2, 1940, in The Council of State Governments, *The Book of the States, 1941–1942,* vol. IV (Chicago: The Council of State Governments, 1941). Chester Lane memoir, CUOHP, 631; Berle for FDR, June 26, 1940, in "Roosevelt, Memos to," Berle papers.

61. For an excellent discussion of the bill see Michal R. Belknap, *Cold War Political Justice: The Smith Act, the Communist Party, and American Civil Liberties* (Westport, CT: Greenwood Press, 1977), 22–27.

62. Helmke, "Report of the Committee on Civil Liberties . . .," 491.

63. Support for the legislation in "Notes on Meeting of June 3, 1940," in MID 9794–186A/3, SIS file, RG 165; Miles, "Memorandum for the Chief of Staff," June 3, 1940, and attachments, G-2/10525–821, Classified Decimal File, 1940–42, AG 014.31, in Records of the Adjutant General's Office, RG 407; Solicitor General for AG, June 13, 1940, "National Defense Matters" fldr., Jackson papers; Francis Biddle, *In Brief Authority* (Garden City, NY: Doubleday & Company, 1962), 111.

64. Zechariah Chafee, *Free Speech in the United States* (Cambridge: Harvard University Press, 1941), 443.

65. U.S., Congress, House, *Congressional Record.* 76 Cong., 3d sess., 1940, 86, pt. 8: 9031–9036.

66. "Sharp Limit is Set on Entry of Aliens," *New York Times,* 15 June 1940, 9; speech to the New York Bar Association in "Jackson Counsels Calm in Nation," ibid., 30 June 1940, 14. Memo, Stephen Early for FDR, June 26, 1940, Official File 133, Roosevelt papers.

67. Chafee, *Free Speech in the US,* 442.

68. Hays to Jackson, July 9, 1940, 2280/162–63, ACLU papers.

69. Baldwin, "Abstract of Speech on National Defense and the Fifth Column," October 6, 1940, 2166/277–79, ibid.

70. Chafee, *Free Speech in US,* 489.

71. Overstreet, "Administration and Civil Liberties."

72. "Remarks at the Federal-State Conference, August 1940," 62/4, John Lord O'Brian papers.

73. Governor Burnet R. Maybank to Attorney General Jackson, June 12, 1940, in "Kane, R. K. (Interoffice Memoranda)," 148 WPO files, DoJ/FRC. "Memorandum for the Attorney General re: Conference Called by National Defense Council . . .," June 18, 1940, "Neutrality Laws Unit" fldr., Jackson papers; "The Purpose and Plan of the Federal-State Conference on Law Enforcement Problems of National Defense," July 10, 1940, in "Smith, Lawrence" fldr., Berle papers.

74. See "Federal-State Conference on Law Enforcement," *Defense* 30 (Aug. 1940): 7.

75. Belknap, *Cold War Justice,* 24; Council of State Governments, *The Book of the States 1941–42,* 44; "State Plans for Civil Protection," *Defense* 25 (Oct. 1940): 4; "Memorandum of Notes Taken at a Conference . . . August 5, 1940 . . .," in "Reports—L. M. C. Smith—Sedition Section" fldr., DoJ, 62A47, FRC.

76. David Kennedy, *Over Here; The First World War and American Society* (New York: Oxford University Press, 1980).

77. R. Baldwin to Friends, April 9, 1940, "Wartime Civil Liberties, 1940–45," fldr. 678, box 32, No.Cal.Br. ACLU papers.

78. Weekly Press Release, November 11, 1941, *Records and Publications of American Civil Liberties Union* (New York: Microfilm Corporation of America, 1975).

79. Ingoldsby for L. M. C. Smith, "Re: State Legislation," May 14, 1941, "Kane, R. K. [Interoffice Memoranda]" fldr., 148 WPO files, DoJ, 62A47, FRC.

80. Remarks reported in Hoover for AG, August 5, 1940, in "National Defense Matters" fldr., Jackson papers.

81. "Clear and Present Danger," *Nation,* 29 June 1940, 772.

82. Clark, "The Limits of Free Expression," *U.S. Law Review* 73 (July 1939): 392–404.

83. Clark, "Free Institutions and the War," *Bill of Rights Review* (summer 1940): 10–15.

84. Mulder, "Changing Concepts of Civil Liberties," ibid. (winter 1941): 95–97.

85. Clark, "Perversions of Civil Liberty," *Bill of Rights Review* (summer 1941): 262–64.

86. [Draft] "Statement on the Subject of Civil Rights . . .," in fldr 2, box 3, records of the Bill of Rights Committee, American Bar Association.

87. Baldwin, "Abstract of Speech on National Defense and the Fifth Column," October 6, 1940, 2166/277, ACLU papers.

88. "Justice Jackson's Story" [transcription with written emendations of tape recording taken by Columbia University Oral History Research Project, 1952–53] in chapter "The War Years," p. 104, box 190, Jackson papers.

89. Francis Biddle, *In Brief Authority* (Garden City, NY: Doubleday & Company, 1962), 129.

90. Charles Malcolmson, "Mr. Jackson's Dilemma," *Nation,* 8 June 1940, 699–700.

Chapter 5

1. John Lord O'Brian memoir, *New York Times Oral History Program* [Times OHP] (Glen Rock, NJ: Microfilm Corporation of America, 1972), 224–27.

2. See for examples Ared White, "Lampposts and Sabotage," *The American Legion Magazine,* July, 1940, 167ff; Sam Bass Warner, "The Model Sabotage Prevention Act," *Harvard Law Review* 54 (February 1941): 624–31.

3. John Hamilton, "One Reason Why Airplanes Crash," *New Republic,* 14 June 1939, 150–51.

4. Press conference 649-A (June 5, 1940), in *Complete Presidential Press Conferences of Franklin D. Roosevelt,* 25 vols., with an intro. by Jonathan Daniels (New York: Da Capo Press, 1972), vol. 15, p. 484; Jackson memoir, Columbia University Oral History Project [CUOHP], 974.

5. Robert R. Mullen, "How the G-Men Guard Industry," *Christian Science Monitor,* 3 May 1941, 5–6.

6. Jackson memoir, CUOHP, 974–75, 982; Stimson diary, September 13, 1940, Henry L. Stimson papers.

7. Jackson memoir, CUOHP, 982.

8. Hoover for AG, June 2, 1940, "House Committee on Un-American Activities . . ." fldr., Jackson papers.

9. "Listing Aliens in Key Plants," *New York Times,* 6 Aug. 1940, 4.

10. "Last of Blast Dead in Kenvil Identified," *New York Times,* 18 Sept. 1940, 25; Hoover for AG, October 21, 1940, Hoover Official and Confidential [O&C] file no. 59, FBI Reading Room [FBI/RR]; Martin Dies, *The Trojan Horse in America* (New York: Dodd, Mead, 1940), 350.

11. Clippings of Dies comments attached to Hoover for AG, November 16, 1940, Hoover O&C 59, FBI/RR.

12. Hoover for AG, October 21, 1940, and November 16, 1940; and L. Nichols for Director, November 26, 1940. Both in O&C 59; Tamm for Director, November 14, 1941, O&C 144. All FBI/RR.

13. Warner, "The Model Sabotage Prevention Act," 624–31.

14. W. P. A[llen] for Smith, Re: "Elimination of Communists and Nazis in National Defense Plants," January 15, 1941, file 146–13–5, sec. 1, records of Department of Justice [DoJ], accession 53A10, Federal Records Center [FRC], Suitland, MD.

15. Lee Pressman, D. William Leider, and Harold I. Cammer, "Sabotage and National Defense," *Harvard Law Review* 54 (1941): 632–46.

16. See Hoover for AG., October 21, 1940, and November 16, 1940; on press campaign, see L. B. Nichols for Director, November 25, 1940. Both O&C 59, FBI/RR.

17. "The President's Conference with Rep. Martin Dies," November 29, 1940, Official File [OF] 320, Roosevelt papers.

18. Jackson for Jerry Voorhis, December 10, 1940, in O&C 59, FBI/RR.

19. Hoover quoted in Pressman, et al., "Sabotage and National Defense," 633. The FBI would contend that though it investigated 19,649 cases, "not a single case of enemy-directed sabotage" was found. Don Whitehead, *The FBI Story: A Report to the People* (New York: Random House, 1956), 206.

20. Mullen, "How the G-Men Guard Industry," 5–6.

21. "Governors Stress Role in Defense," *New York Times,* 22 Jan. 1941, 4; "Jackson Reveals Curbs on Sabotage," ibid., 9 Feb. 1941, 29.

22. Jacob Vander Meulen, *The Politics of Aircraft: Building an American Military Industry* (Lawrence: University Press of Kansas, 1991).

23. Jacob Vander Meulen, "West Cost Labor and the Military Aircraft Industry, 1935–1941," *Pacific Northwest Quarterly* 88 (spring 1997): 82–92.

24. The following, except as noted, is based on Roger Keeran, *The Communist Party and the Auto Workers Unions* (Bloomington: Indiana University Press, 1980), 12, 205, 210–13.

25. Steven Fraser, *Labor Will Rule: Sidney Hillman and the Rise of American Labor* (New York: The Free Press, 1991), 459.

26. Jackson memoir, CUOHP, 946, 949; Keeran, *Communist Party and Auto Workers,* 213; Vander Meulen, "West Coast Labor," 89; Fraser, *Hillman,* 462.

27. Fraser, *Hillman,* 464–65; Keeran, *Communist Party and Auto Workers,* 214.

28. "Jackson Draft Autobiography," p. 30, folder 3, "Biographical file," Jackson papers.

29. FDR for AG, May 21, 1940, "Wiretapping Controversy—Dept. of Justice and Wiretapping," Jackson papers.

30. [Max Lowenthal (?)], "Wire Tapping—1941," December 28, 1940, in "FBI/Department of Justice—Wiretapping" fldr., George Norris papers.

Hoover describes Jackson's modest supervision in "Memorandum for the Confidential Files," May 28, 1940, O&C 163, FBI/RR.

31. Jackson for A. Holtzhoff, December 12, 1940, "Wire Tapping Controversy—Legislation," Jackson papers.

32. "There Are Also Earmarks of Hysteria" *Nation,* 1 Mar. 1941, 227. Labor's response described in "Wire Tapping—1941," December 28, 1940, in "FBI/Department of Justice—Wiretapping" fldr., Norris papers.

33. Walter F. Murphy, *Wiretapping on Trial: A Case Study in the Judicial Process* (New York: Random House, 1967), 137; David M. Helfeld, "A Study of Justice Department Policies on Wire Tapping," *Lawyers Guild Review* 9 (spring 1949): 57–69. Liberal discontent in Rowe for FDR, "H. R. 2266—Wire Tapping," February 13, 1941, "Wiretapping" fldr., James Rowe papers.

34. Rowe for AG, "Wire-Tapping," February 21, 1941, covering draft FDR to Eliot, February 21, 1941, in OF 4326, Roosevelt papers; "President Advocates Limited Wire Tapping, In Defense . . .," *New York Times,* 26 Feb. 1941, 1.

35. "Why Tap Wires?" *Nation,* 8 Mar. 1941, 257–58.

36. "Jackson Requests Wire-tapping Law," *New York Times,* 21 Mar. 1941, 22.

37. Jackson memoir, CUOHP, 973.

38. Fly to FDR, March 27, 1941, and reply, April 1, 1941, OF 4326, Roosevelt papers.

39. "Fly of FCC Opposes Wiretapping Power," *New York Times,* 20 May 1941, 17.

40. Jackson to McCloy, May 16, 1941, in "A G/Wiretapping Controversy, War Department Involvement," Jackson papers; Jackson memoir, CUOHP, 980.

41. "Fund Bills Set Up 33 Billion Record," *New York Times,* 1 July 1941, 1.

42. Robert Justin Goldstein, *Political Repression in Modern America: From 1870 to the Present* (Boston: Schenckman Publishing Company, Inc., 1978), 254. Evidence of taps in Steven Rosswurm, "An FOIA Status Report," *OAH Newsletter,* Feb. 1989, 16. See also Committee on Civil Rights and Liberties, National Lawyers Guild, "Wire Tapping," *Lawyers Guild Review* 1 (1940–41): 32–33; Matthew McGuire, Asst. to the AG, "Memorandum for Mr. Hoover . . .," "Re: Boeing Aircraft . . .," May 5, 1941, 66–62000–100–37, records of the FBI, obtained pursuant to Freedom of Information Act [FoI] request.

43. Prichard for Biddle, March 3, 1941; Biddle for AG, March 5, 1941; and Hoover for AG, April 5, 1941. All in "Bridges" fldr, Jackson papers.

44. AG for Solicitor General, March 7, 1941, ibid.

45. AG to Rep. John M. Coffee, May 15, 1941, "Wire tapping Controversy—Legislation," ibid.

46. AG for Hoover and reply, both June 27, 1940, "Subversive Activities and Investigations . . .," Jackson papers.

47. Bureau Bulletin No. 60, second series 1940, December 2, 1940, 66–6200–100-NR, FBI/FoI.

48. Jackson "To Departments and Agency Heads [draft]," no date, in Hoover O&C 91, FBI/RR.

49. Hoover for the AG, April 1, 1941, and reply, April 4, 1941, ibid.

50. Fraser, *Hillman,* 465.

51. McCloy's role discussed in Kai Bird, *The Chairman: John J. McCloy, The Making of the American Establishment* (New York: Simon & Schuster, 1992), 126–28.

52. McCloy to Hoover, November 18, 1940, "Attorney General—Correspondence with Cabinet Members—War Department," Jackson papers.

53. Hoover for AG, April 26, 1941, in "AG/Wiretapping—War Department" fldr., Jackson papers; McCloy for Secretary of War, Sub: "Proposed Sabotage Investigations," May 1, 1941, in "Labor, 1941," Robert P. Patterson papers.

54. See Keith E. Eiler, *Mobilizing America: Robert P. Patterson and the War Effort, 1940–1945* (Ithaca, NY: Cornell University Press), 164–70.

55. McCloy for Secretary of War, May 1, 1941, in "Labor, 1941," Patterson papers.

56. Jackson "Memorandum for the President," April 29, 1941, ibid. Original of Jackson's memo to FDR found in Patterson's papers.

57. Jackson, "Memorandum for . . . Patterson and . . . McCloy, April 30, 1941, ibid.

58. Stimson diary, May 1, 1941, Stimson papers.

59. Harold Ickes, *The Secret Diary of Harold L. Ickes,* III (New York: Simon and Schuster, 1954), 504; handwritten notes on White House stationary dated May 1 in "Attorney General—Cabinet Meetings, April-May 1941—Jackson's Notes" fldr., Jackson papers.

60. McCloy to AG, May 6, 1941, "AG/Wiretapping, War Department," Jackson papers.

61. Jackson to McCloy, May 16, 1941, and McCloy to Jackson, offering War Department support, May 19, 1941. Both in "AG/Wiretapping, War Department," Jackson papers.

62. Stimson diary, May 23, 27, 28, 1941, Stimson papers.

63. The concern dated back to the Civil War (see W. A. Dunning, "Disloyalty in Two Wars," *American Historical Review* 24 (1919): 625–30), and was a theme of Homer Cummings and Carl McFarland, *Federal Justice, Chapters in the History of Justice and the Federal Executive* (New York: The Macmillan Co., 1937), 204, 424–25.

64. O'Brian and Bettman for AG, "Regulation of Free Speech," April 25, 1919, box 18, fldr 5, O'Brian papers.

65. O'Brian, "The Experience of the Department of Justice in Enforcing War Statutes 1917–1918" (remarks to the State Federal Conference, August 1940), box 18, fldr 5, ibid.

66. Jackson for Solicitor General, March 7, 1941, in "Wire Tapping Controversy—Legislation," Jackson papers.

67. Quoted in "The Attorney General on Civil Liberties," *New Republic,* 19 May 1941, 681.

Chapter 6

1. Stanley I. Kutler's chapter "'If at First . . . : The Trials of Harry Bridges," in *The American Inquisition: Justice and Injustice in the Cold War* (New York: Hill and Wang, 1982) provides an excellent brief treatment of the subject. An early assessment of the literature is found in Harvey Schwartz, "Harry Bridges and the Scholars: Looking at History's Verdict," *California History* 59 (1980): 66–79.

2. Charles P. Larrowe, *Harry Bridges, The Rise and Fall of Radical Labor in the United States* (New York: Lawrence Hill and Co., 1972), 11.

3. Bruce Nelson, *Workers on the Waterfront: Seamen, Longshoremen, and Unionism in the 1930s* (Urbana: University of Illinois Press, 1988), 103–55.

4. The law is set forth in *Kessler v. Strecker,* 307 U.S. 22 (1939), and criticized in Zechariah Chafee, *Freedom of Speech* (New York: Harcourt, Brace and Co., 1920), 230, 232, 237, 241. The rights of aliens in deportation hearings (established by judicial rulings) is in Sidney Kansas, *U.S. Immigration: Exclusion and Deportation and Citizenship of the United States of America,* 2nd ed., (New York: Matthew Bender Co., 1941), 112–20.

5. Robert W. Cherney, "Harry Bridges: Labor, Radicalism, and the State," working paper no. 1 [Oct. 1944] (Center for Labor Studies, University of Washington, Seattle), 11.

6. Steven Fraser, *Labor Will Rule: Sidney Hillman and the Rise of American Labor* (New York: The Free Press, 1991), 416.

7. George Martin, *Madam Secretary: Frances Perkins* (Boston: Houghton Mifflin Company, 1976), 410–17.

8. Lillian Holmen Mohr, *Frances Perkins, "That Woman in FDR's Cabinet"* (North River Press, 1979), 252–59.

9. Ibid., 149.

10. *Kessler* v. *Strecker,* 307 U.S. 22 (1939). Landis quote in "In re: Harry Renton Bridges," January 8, 1940, Bridges case file, records of the Department of Justice [DoJ], Record Group [RG] 60.

11. Larrowe, *Harry Bridges,* 217–19.

12. See *Foreign Language Information Service (FLIS) Legislative News-Letter,* 27 March 1940.

13. *FLIS Legislative News-Letter,* 3 June 1940.

14. AG to Russell, June 18, 1940, Bridges case file.

15. *Congressional Record,* 76 Cong., 3d sess., 1940, 86, pt. 8:9031; AG to Rep. S. Hobbs, March 13, 1941, discussed in Arthur G. Hays to AG, March 19, 1941, 2280/108–09, American Civil Liberties Union [ACLU] papers.

16. ACLU, "Report on Prosecutions Allegedly Brought for Political Purposes," March 1940, in "ACLU-General" file 408, box 20, records of the Northern California Branch [No. Cal. Br.] of the ACLU.

17. Jackson memoir, Columbia University Oral History Project [CUOHP], 1023; Jackson to Chafee, April 25, 1941, "Attorney General—Immigration and Naturalization—Alien Registration" fldr., Jackson papers.

18. Henry Hart, memos for the AG, October 9 and 11, 1940, and Biddle for Holtzhoff, July 12, 1940, in "Attorney General—Immigration and Natural-ization—Deportation of Aliens" fldr., Jackson papers.

19. Jackson memoir, CUOHP, 1031, 1033; Hobbs to AG, July 9, 1940, Bridges case file.

20. Holtzhoff for AG, August 20, 1940, "Re: Harry R. Bridges," ibid.

21. "House Bill to Oust Bridges Softened," *New York Times,* 16 Aug. 1940, 17. Discussed in Holtzhoff for AG, "Re: Bridges Deportation Bill," August 16, 1940, Bridges case file.

22. Holtzhoff for AG, August 14, 1940, "Re: Harry Bridges," ibid.

23. Quoted in Kutler, *American Inquisition,* 136; Larrowe, *Harry Bridges,* 104, 106, 145, 224–25.

24. Justice Department "For Release in Morning Papers . . . August 25, 1940," in Bridges case file; Jackson memoir, CUOHP, 1033–34; "Bridges Inquiry Separate," *New York Times,* 26 Aug. 1940, 10.

25. McGuire for Hugh Clegg (FBI), August 26, 1940; McGuire for Hoover, "Re: Questions Submitted Relative to the Bridges Case," August 27, 1940. Both Bridges case file.

26. Hoover for AG, December 5, 1940, ibid.

27. Smith for Rogge, December 15, 1940, ibid; W.P.A [Allen] for Smith, January 15, 1941, Re: Elimination of Communists and Nazis in National Defense Plants, file 146–13–5–0, records of DoJ, accession [acc.] 62A47, Federal Records Center [FRC], Suitland, MD.

28. *New York Times,* 17 Dec. 1940, 1, quoted in note 12 of "In Re Harry Bridges," *The Yale Law Journal* 52 (December 1942): 108–29.

29. Hoover for AG, December 18, 1940, Bridges case file.

30. Rowe for FDR, April 11, 1941; FDR for Rowe, April 21, 1941. Both in President's Secretary's File [PSF] "Rowe," Roosevelt papers.

31. "Bridges Must Face Deportation Trial, *New York Times,* 13 Feb. 1941, 1.

32. Jackson memoir, CUOHP, 1033.

33. Foster Hailey, "Bridges is Waging a Dramatic Fight," *New York Times,* 6 April 1941, IV, 10.

34. Foster Hailey, "Bridges Witness Changes His Story," ibid., 7 May 1941, 26.

35. Hoover "Memorandum," March 10, 1941, in Bridges case file; Francis Bid-dle, *In Brief Authority* (Garden City, NY: Doubleday & Company, 1962), 304.

36. Stimson diary, June 6, 1941, Henry L. Stimson papers.

37. Bennett Milton Rich, *The Presidents and Civil Disorder* (Washington, DC: The Brookings Institution, 1941), 178–79.

38. Account based on Roger Keeran, *The Communist Party and the Auto Workers* (Bloomington: Indiana University Press, 1980), 215–18; and Bert Cochran, *Labor and Communism: The Conflict that Shaped American Unions* (Princeton: Princeton University Press, 1977), 176–81. See also "President Scored by Bridges Union," *New York Times,* 12 April 1941, 8. The government's perspective on events is in Nichols Official and Confidential files [O&C], "Harry Bridges," 7–9, FBI Reading Room [FBI/RR]. Use of the event at the hearing is described by L. Schofield for AG, June 16, 1941, Bridges case file.

39. "Defense Strikes," IV, 2; Louis Stark, "Labor's Communist Issues Brought Into Open," IV, 5; Turner Catledge, "Administration Seeks Further Strike Curbs," IV, 7. All in *New York Times,* 15 June 1941.

40. George Gallup, "Sympathy for Labor Shows Sharp Drop," ibid., 13 June 1941, 12.

41. Freda Kirchwey, "Keep Cool on Labor," *Nation,* 21 June 1941, 713.

42. "Capital Weighing Plan to Fire Reds," *New York Times,* 13 June 1941, 12.

43. Goodwin, "Opening Statement on Behalf of the Government . . .," March 31, 1941, Bridges case file.

44. Larrowe, *Harry Bridges,* 227.

45. Goodwin to AG, May 9, 1941 and May 14, 1941, Bridges case file.

46. Schofield "Memorandum for the Assistant to the Attorney General," June 17, 1941, Bridges case file.

47. Patterson for President, June 12, 1941, Official File [OF] 407B, Roosevelt papers.

48. Stimson diary, June 12, 1941, Stimson papers.

49. Biddle for President, June 23, 1941, PSF "Justice Department," Roosevelt papers.

50. Harvey Levenstein, *Communism, Anti-Communism and the CIO* (Westport, CT: Greenwood Press, 1981), 150.

51. Rowe for President, June 26, 1941, PSF "Justice Department," Roosevelt papers.

52. Chafee to G. Clark, May 28, 1940, fldr. 1/2, records of the Bill of Rights Committee of the American Bar Association.

53. Chafee to O'Brian, May 5, 1941, box 4, fldr. 1, John Lord O'Brian papers.

54. "Notes [dictated by Murphy to his private secretary], June 4, 1941, of visit with President Roosevelt" fldr., box 1, Eugene Gressman papers. Other occasions were June 18 and July 18, 1941.

55. Robert E. Cushman, in assessing the position of the Justices in non-unanimous personal liberties decisions for the 1941–46 terms, rated Murphy 100 percent pro–civil liberty and 94 percent in favor of personal liberties overall. The comparable figures for Jackson were 33 percent and 30 percent. "Ten

Years of the Supreme Court: 1937–1947, Civil Liberties," *American Political Science Review* 42 (February 1948): 32–67.

Chapter 7

1. Except as noted, the following is based on Francis Biddle, *A Casual Past* (Garden City, NY: Doubleday & Company, Inc., 1961). Quotes on 18, 161, 333.

2. Description of Groton and FDR's experience in Geoffrey C. Ward, *Before the Trumpet, Young Franklin Roosevelt, 1882–1905* (New York: Harper & Row, 1985), 178–83, 189, 191, 193, 206.

3. Peter Irons, *Justice At War: The Story of the Japanese American Internment Cases* (New York: Oxford University Press, 1983), 17.

4. Biddle, *In Brief Authority* (Garden City, NY: Doubleday and Company, Inc., 1962), 6.

5. Biddle, *In Brief Authority,* 4.

6. *U.S.* v. *Darby,* 312 U.S. 100 (1941).

7. 247 U. S. 251 (1918).

8. Quoted in draft of a speech (p. 2) [probably by Thomas Corcoran] covered by note, Biddle to Corcoran, June 30, 1946, in "Biddle, Francis, 1941–1968," Thomas Corcoran papers.

9. Jerre Mangione, *An Ethnic At Large: A Memoir of America in the Thirties and Forties* (New York: G.P. Putnam's Sons, 1978), 288. Biddle, *Casual Life,* 377; *Brief Authority,* 162.

10. *Screws* and *Classic* cases. Irons, *Justice at War,* 17.

11. Berle diary, July 19, 1941, Adolf A. Berle papers. Jackson later said the appointment was not permanent, but a knowledgeable official explains that the circumstances suggesting this were merely the result of clerical error. Jackson memoir, Columbia University Oral History Project [CUOHP], 1096. Boris I. Bittke to Oscar Cox, January 13, 1943, Oscar Cox papers.

12. Biddle, *In Brief Authority,* 169.

13. Ickes diary, May 31, 1942, Harold L. Ickes papers.

14. Jackson memoir, CUOHP, 1095.

15. Baldwin memoir, New York Times Oral History Program [Times OHP] (Glen Rock, NJ: Microfilm Corporation of America, 1972), 203.

16. Rowe for President, October 20, 1941, President's Secretary's File [PSF] "Rowe," Roosevelt papers.

17. Burlingham to Jackson, June 17, 1941, folder 10–6, Charles Burlingham papers; Clark to FDR, August 13, 1941, Official File [OF] 10, Roosevelt papers.

18. Biddle, *In Brief Authority,* 4.

19. Jonathan Daniels, *White House Witness, 1942–1945* (Garden City, NY: Doubleday & Company, Inc., 1975), 177.

20. Biddle, *Casual Life,* 172. See also his comments on the propensity of Americans for mass hysteria and intolerance in Biddle, *The Fear of Freedom* (Garden City, NY: Doubleday & Company, Inc., 1952), 83.

21. Francis Biddle, "Freedom of Speech and Propaganda" [address before the American Bar Association at Philadelphia, September 11, 1940], *American Bar Association Journal* 26 (Oct. 1940): 795–97; and speech to symposium on civil liberties at annual meeting of the Association of American Law Schools [Chicago, December 27, 1940], *American Law School Review* 9 (April 1941): 889–95.

22. Quoted in Richard W. Steele, "Franklin D. Roosevelt and His Foreign Policy Critics," *Political Science Quarterly* 94 (spring 1979): 1640–53.

23. Biddle, "Civil Rights in Times of Stress," speech delivered in Atlantic City, June 2, 1941, in *Bill of Rights Review* 2 (1941): 13–22.

24. See comments by Max Lowenthal, "Solicitor General Biddle's Speech . . . to National Conference of Social Work . . .," in "FBI" file, George Norris papers.

25. An idea he credited to Holmes. Francis Biddle, *Mr. Justice Holmes* (New York: Charles Scribner's Sons, 1942), 57.

26. Nevertheless, at the end of November, the House defeated the Hobbs bill in a surprising move. "By a Vote of 167 to 141," *Nation,* 29 Nov. 1941, 526.

27. Ickes diary, August 3, 1941, Ickes papers.

28. According to Ickes, FDR had told this to Corcoran. Ibid.

29. "Notes June 18, 1941, of Luncheon Conference between President Roosevelt and Frank Murphy," in box 1, Eugene Gressman papers.

30. Attorney General, "Memorandum for the President," no date, "Franklin D. Roosevelt" fldr., Biddle papers.

31. Biddle, *In Brief Authority,* 151.

32. E. A. Tamm for Director, August 16, 1941, August 28, 1941; in Hoover Official and Confidential [O&C] file 30, FBI Reading Room [RR].

33. E. A. Tamm for the Director, October 3, 1941, covering McGuire for Smith and McGuire for Attorney General [AG], both October 2, 1941, all in Hoover O&C 141, FBI/RR. The unit seems to have played no role in the events leading to the prosecution of the Minneapolis Trotskyites.

34. E. A. Tamm for the Director, August 25, 1941, and September 3, 1941, Hoover O&C 85, FBI/RR.

35. "Biddle Approves FBI Wiretapping," *New York Times,* 9 Oct. 1941, 4.

36. Herbert Wechsler memoir, CUOHP, 180.

37. Rowe for the President, October 20, 1941 [supporting his candidacy], PSF Rowe, Roosevelt papers; Tamm for the Director, November 15, 1941, Hoover O&C 107, FBI/RR.

38. M. A. Jones for Nichols, "Supervision of Bureau by Other Than Attorney General," July 3, 1956 [sic], O&C file 30, FBI /RR.

39. "Split Hairs and Tapped Wires," *Nation,* 18 Oct. 1941, 360; T. R. B., "Now It's Up to Hitler," *New Republic,* 22 Sept. 1941, 372.

40. Bridges deposition, August 29, 1941, in O&C 40, FBI/RR. U.S. Senate, "Report of Proceedings: Hearing held before Judiciary Committee on Biddle Nomination," September 3, 1941; Biddle, *In Brief Authority,* 166.

41. Biddle, *In Brief Authority,* 166.

42. Diary entry for January 31, 1942, in Norman M. Littell, *My Roosevelt Years,* ed. Jonathan Dembo (Seattle: University of Washington Press, 1987), 43.

43. U.S. Senate, "Report of Proceedings, Hearings Held Before Judiciary Committee, Biddle Nomination," September 3, 1941; "Biddle Approves FBI Wiretapping," *New York Times,* 9 Oct. 1941, 4; Fahy for AG, October 6, 1941, O&C 164, FBI/RR.

44. "Split Hairs and Tapped Wires," 360.

45. Ickes diary, February 1, 1942, Ickes papers. In *Goldman v. U.S.,* (316 U.S. 129 [1942]) the Court ruled that government wiretapping did not violate the Fourth Amendment.

Chapter 8

1. Zechariah Chafee, Jr., *Free Speech in the United States* (Cambridge, MA: Harvard University Press, 1941), 489, 467; Donald L. Smith, *Zechariah Chafee, Jr., Defender of Liberty and Law* (Cambridge: Harvard University Press, 1986), 14.

2. Irving Bernstein, *A History of the American Worker, 1933–1941: Turbulent Years* (Boston: Houghton Mifflin Co., 1970), 231–33.

3. This material from the "Appellants Brief," 4–5, and "Brief for the United States in Opposition to Petition for Certiorari," 9. Both in *Dunne et al. v. United States,* #12195, U.S. Circuit Court of Appeals, Eighth Circuit [8th CCA] (1943). Victor Riesel estimated the party's membership at 850 in "June–December, 1941," *Twice a Year* (spring/summer 1942): 293.

4. The following account closely follows Bernstein, *Turbulent Years,* 229–52.

5. FBI files on Vincent Raymond Dunne, 100–18341–5; and Farrell Dobbs, 65–12453–5, records of the Federal Bureau of Investigation [FBI], Freedom of Information Act [FoI] request.

6. "Communist Organizations Active in Minneapolis and Communist Leaders Occupying Strategic Positions of Leadership in the Minneapolis Local Labor Movement," September 15, 1936, in 146–1, Department of Justice [DoJ] FoI request.

7. Bernstein, *Turbulent Years,* 780.

8. ACLU, *In the Shadow of War: The Story of Civil Liberties, 1939–1940* (New York: ACLU, 1940), 17, 23. FDR's role in Asst. Attorney General [AG] Henry Schweinhaut for Solicitor General, August 1, 1944, covered by Lyons from Fahy, August 10, 1944, in "Correspondence re Cases—'D'" fldr., Charles Fahy papers.

9. "New Party Formed; To Fight War Plans," *Socialist Appeal,* 8 Jan. 1938, 2. This and a compilation of other party doctrine statements is in DoJ, "Socialist

Workers Party (Trotskyites)," no date [April 1941], pp. 22–23, 146–1–10, DoJ/FoI.

10. Ralph C. James and Estelle James, "The Purge of the Trotskyites From the Teamsters," *The Western Political Quarterly* 19 (March 1966): 5–15.

11. Tel. Tobin to Press Secretary S. Early, June 12, 1941, Official File [OF] 2978, Roosevelt papers.

12. Quoted in ACLU, "Sedition," October 1941, in "Pamphlets" file, *Records and Publications of the American Civil Liberties Union* (New York: Microfilm Corporation of America, 1975) [Cited as ACLU, *Records and Publications*].

13. DoJ Press Release, June 27, 1941, in file 100–16-sub. 44, in FBI/FoI.

14. "The Department of Justice Finds," *Nation*, 12 July 1941, 23; I. F. Stone, "The G-String Conspiracy," *Nation*, 26 July 1941, 66.

15. Thomas L. Pahl, "G-String Conspiracy: Political Reprisal or Armed Revolt? The Minneapolis Trotskyite Trial," *Labor History* 8 (winter 1967): 30–51; Pahl, "The Dilemma of a Civil Libertarian: Francis Biddle and the Smith Act," *Journal of the Minnesota Academy of Science* 34 (1967): 161–64. Subscribing to the conspiracy theory are James, "The Purge of the Trotskyites," 5–15; Robert Justin Goldstein, *Political Repression in Modern America From 1870 to the Present* (Boston: Schenckman Publishing Company, Inc., 1978), 252; William L. O'Neill, *A Better World. The Great Schism: Stalinism and the American Intellectual* (New York: Simon & Schuster, 1982), 44; and Bernstein, *Turbulent Years*, 781.

16. Except as noted, this account is based on DoJ, "Socialist Workers Party," 146–1–10, DoJ/FoI.

17. December 4, 1940, directive described in Hoover to Special Agent in Charge [SAC] St. Paul, "Re: Socialist Workers Party . . . ," March 25, 1941, 100–16–44–4, FBI/FoI.

18. Hoover to M. Watson, June 19, 1941, OF 10b, Roosevelt papers.

19. Steven Fraser, *Labor Will Rule: Sidney Hillman and the Rise of American Labor* (New York: The Free Press, 1991), 466.

20. The warning, undated, in Asst. AG Schweinhaut for AG, August 16, 1941, 146–1–10, DoJ/FoI.

21. See P. E. Foxworth for E. A. Tamm, June 17, 1941, 100–16–44–36; Hoover to SAC St. Paul, May 2, 1941, 100–16–44–17, FBI/FoI; Berge for Hoover, "Re: Socialist Workers Party," April 29, 1941; Berge to Anderson, April 29, 1941; Anderson to AG, "Att. Wendell Berge," May 3, 1941, 141–1–10, DoJ/FoI.

22. Biddle for President, June 23, 1941, covered by Rowe for President, June 26, 1941, in President's Secretary's File [PSF]—Justice, Roosevelt papers.

23. Telegram, Anderson to Berge, June 12, 1941, 146–1–10, Executive Office, US Attorneys files, DoJ/FoI; AG to Stassen, June 19, 1941, 146–1, Office of the Attorney General [OAG] files, DoJ/FoI; Hoover to Edwin Watson, June 9, 1941, OF 10b, Roosevelt papers; "Memorandum For Mr. McGuire," June

16, 1941, OAG, DoJ/FoI; Foxworth for Tamm, June 17, 1941, 100–16–44–36, FBI/FoI; and Berge for Hoover, June 18, 1941, 100–16–44–38, FBI/FoI.

24. Noted in "Dunne Brothers Key Figures in SWP Indictments," *New Leader,* 19 July 1941, 2; Riesel, "June–December, 1941," 293.

25. "Synopsis of Facts," no author or date, 100–1246, FBI/FoI.

26. "In Time of War or Emergency," *Nation,* 6 Sept. 1941, 190; Daniel Eastman, "The Minneapolis 'Sedition' Trial," *New Republic,* 20 Oct. 1941, 503–4.

27. For examples: "Civil Liberties in Minneapolis," *New Republic,* 28 July 1941, 103–4; John Dos Passos, "To a Liberal In Office," *Nation,* 6 Sept. 1941, 195–97.

28. Lucille Milner (ACLU Secretary) to Ernest Besig (No. Cal. Branch), June 26, 1941, 2318/46; Baldwin to Milner, July 7, 1941, 2527/114, ACLU papers.

29. Including James T. Farrell, John Dewey, Waldo Frank, Clement Greenberg, Mark DeWolfe Howe, F. O. Matthiessen, Mary McCarthy, Alexander Meiklejohn, and Edmund Wilson.

30. See letters to Biddle from Carl Raushenbush, Chairman of Workers Defense League (Alfred M. Bingham, George S. Counts, James Farmer, Paul Porter, A. Philip Randolph, James Wechsler), October 24, 1941, and James Loeb, Jr., Exec. Sec. of Union for Democratic Action (Reinhold Neibuhr, Robert Bendiner, Freda Kirchwey, Lewis Corey), November 8, 1941. Both in 146–1–10, OAG, DoJ/FoI.

31. Biddle to John Haynes Holmes, chairman of Board, ACLU, July 10, 1941, 146–1–10, DoJ/FoI.

32. L. B. Nichols for C. Tolson, October 8, 1941, 100–16–44–18, FBI/FoI.

33. Baldwin to Biddle ("Dear Francis"), August 12; Holmes, Hays, Baldwin to AG, August 20; AG to Hays, August 30, 1941, 146–1–10, OAG, DoJ/FoI; ACLU, "Sedition," October 1941, in "Pamphlets" file, ACLU, *Records and Publications.*

34. Bliven to AG, July 23, 1941, and AG to Bliven, July 30, 1941, 146–1–10, DoJ/FoI.

35. Chafee, *Free Speech,* 468, 469, 520, 524.

36. Jackson memoir, Columbia University Oral History Project [CUOHP], 1046.

37. Prichard, "Memo for the Acting AG," July 14, 1941, 146–1–10, DoJ/FoI.

38. Herbert Wechsler, "Symposium on Civil Liberties," speech at meeting of Association of American Law Schools, December 27, 1940, in *American Law School Review 9* (April 1941): 887.

39. *Schenck v. United States,* 249 U.S. 47 (1919).

40. This "puzzling transformation" is discussed in G. Edward White, *Justice Oliver Wendell Holmes: Law and the Inner Self* (New York: Oxford University Press, 1993), 412–36, 607–8.

41. *Abrams v. United States,* 250 U.S. 616 (1919).

42. Smith, *Chafee,* 32.

43. *Gitlow v. New York,* 268 U.S. 652 (1925).

44. Justice Owen Roberts, writing for the five-to-four majority, used the expression in overturning the conviction of an African American Communist organizer charged under an old Georgia law with inciting insurrection. *Herndon v. Lowry,* 301 U.S. 242 (1937).

45. Harry Kalven, Jr., *A Worthy Tradition: Freedom of Speech in America,* ed. (New York: Harper & Row, 1988), 179–80.

46. John P. Diggins, *The American Left in the Twentieth Century* (New York: Harcourt Brace Jovanovich, Inc., 1973), 101, 103.

47. Eastman, "The Limits of Free Speech," *American Mercury* 53 (October 1941): 444–47.

48. Eastman to editor, *New York Times,* 28 Dec. 1941, 7.

49. "Abstract of Record" of *Dunne et al.* v. *U.S.,* 8th CCA (1943), vol. I, 32–33.

50. Berge, "Civil Liberties During National Emergency," October 25, 1941, in *Vital Speeches of the Day,* 1 Nov. 1941, 87–89.

51. Speech by Berge (Jan. 13, 1942) and government's rejection of "clear and present danger" in "Brief for Appellee [U.S.]," in *Dunne et al.* v. *U.S.,* 28. Still later in the war, Berge would declare that "As a statement of policy or general objective [clear and present danger] is still valid. As a guide for determination of action in specific cases, it falls short." Berge, "Civil Liberties After a Year of War," *Ohio Bar Association Report* 15 (March 1, 1943): 625–30.

52. Anderson to AG, October 1, 1941; Berge to Anderson, October 9, 1941, 146–1–10, DoJ/FoI. In 1941 "clear and present danger" had never been used to limit federal authority, and legal scholars generally doubted that the courts would rely on the formula. See: Bernard L. Sheintag, "From Seditious Libel to Freedom of the Press, *Brooklyn Law Review* 11 (April 1942): 125–54; John R. Green, "Liberty Under the Fourteenth Amendment," *Washington University Law Quarterly* 27 (summer 1942): 497–562; Robert E. Cushman, "Some Constitutional Problems of Civil Liberty," *Boston Law Review* 23 (June 1943): 335–78; Edward H. Miller, "The Case of Civil Liberties v. National Security," *Dickinson Law Review* 47 (Jan. 1943): 117–23; Roger S. Hoar, "Subversive Activities Against Government—Two Conflicting Doctrines," *Marquette Law Review* 276 (fall 1943): 72–78.

53. Biddle, *In Brief Authority* (Garden City, NY: Doubleday & Company, Inc., 1962), 152.

54. C. Forster to V. Johnson, October 20, 1941, and attached copy of "U.S. Will Seek Light Terms in Sedition Cases" [*Minneapolis Morning Tribune*], 21 Oct. 1941, 11, 2528/15, ACLU papers.

55. *Abstract of Record, Dunne et al.* v. *U.S.,* 8th CCA (1943), vol. II, 854–55.

56. Bulletin 1001, December 1, 1941, "Weekly Press Releases" file, ACLU, *Records and Publications.*

57. *Abstract of Record, Dunne et al. v. U.S.,* 8th CCA (1943), vol. III, 1130–34, 1143–69

58. Riesel, "June-December 1941," 293.

59. "Radicals: Mice Apprehended," *Time,* 15 Dec. 1941, 29.

60. "Opinion and Sedition," *New Republic,* 8 Dec. 1941, 748; "The Issues at Minneapolis," *Nation,* 13 Dec. 1941, 603.

61. Carl Winter, "Minneapolis Trial Shows Labor Wary of Trotskyites," *Daily Worker,* 19 Dec. 1941, 5.

62. Press Release, December 2, 1941, "Weekly Press Releases" file, ACLU, *Records and Publications.*

63. The defendants' strategy in Grandizo Munis and James P. Cannon, *Defense Policy in the Minneapolis Trial* [1942] reprinted as *What Policy for Revolutionists: Marxism or Ultra-Leftism* (New York: Merit Publishers, 1969), 17.

64. Baldwin for O. Fraenkel and A. Hays, Dec. 16, 1941, 2528/44, ACLU papers.

65. Kalven, *Worthy Tradition,* 151.

66. *Dunne et al. v. U.S.,* 138 F. 2d. 137, 139, 141, 143–45.

67. M. Konvitz for Williams, Re: Press release "NAACP Endorses Bill in Sedition Case," March 28, 1944, doc. 00948, National Association for the Advancement of Colored People papers. Pardon issue in correspondence covered by Fahy for Lyons, August 8, 1944, in "Correspondence re. Cases—'D'" fldr., Fahy papers. Baldwin memoir, *New York Times Oral History Program* (Glen Rock, NJ: Microfilm Corporation of America, 1975), 119.

68. Biddle, *In Brief Authority,* 151.

Chapter 9

1. Geoffrey S. Smith, *To Save a Nation; American Countersubversives, the New Deal, and the Coming of World War II* (New York: Basic Books, 1973), 139–40; Robert Edwin Herzstein, *Roosevelt & Hitler: Prelude to War* (New York: Paragon House, 1989), 270, 284, 362, 372, 403–6. See also Leland V. Bell, "Failure of Nazism in America: The German American Bund 1936–1941," *Political Science Quarterly* 85 (December 1970): 585.

2. Glen Jeansonne, *Women of the Far Right: The Mothers' Movement and World War II* (Chicago: University of Chicago Press, 1996) cites an anti-fascist source as estimating 800 fascistic groups in 1939 (p. 31). I have seen no official estimate in this range.

3. Smith, *To Save a Nation,* 161.

4. "Within the Gates," *Nation,* 11 Jan. 1941, 45.

5. IPA in Walter Goodman, *The Committee; The Extraordinary Career of the House Committee on Un-American Activities* (New York: Farrar, Straus and Giroux, 1968), 124–26.

6. Richard Gid Powers, *Not Without Honor: The History of American Anti-Communism* (New York: The Free Press, 1995), 165.

7. John Roy Carlson, *Under Cover: My Four Years in the Nazi Underworld of America* (New York: E. P. Dutton & Co. 1943).

8. The anti-fascist and democracy lobby is touched on in Richard Steele, *Propaganda in an Open Society: The Roosevelt Administration and the Media, 1933–1941* (Westport, CT: Greenwood Press, 1985), 77–81; and Steele, "The War on Intolerance: The Reformulation of American Nationalism, 1939–1941," in *Journal of American Ethnic History* 9 (fall 1989): 9–35. Friends of Democracy discussed in Wayne S. Cole, *Charles A. Lindbergh and the Battle Against American Intervention in World War II* (New York: Harcourt Brace Jovanovich, 1974), 139–40. Subventions from the American Jewish Committee from 1939 through 1942 are mentioned in "Friends of Democracy" fldr., Morris Waldman papers.

9. Material on *The Hour* is from Robert Soble's introductory notes to the reprint edition of *The Hour* (Westport, CT: Greenwood Reprint Corporation, 1970).

10. Outlined in "Activities of the American Jewish Committee," (about) October 24, 1944, in "Program and Policy, 1943–49" file, Waldman papers. The ADL also supplied the FBI and the Justice Department with information on native fascists. See Hoover for AG, November 20, 1940, "House Un-American Activities Committee," fldr., Robert Jackson papers; "Anti-Defamation League (Miles Goldberg)" fldr., 148 War Policy Office [WPO] files, records of the Department of Justice [DoJ], accession 62A47, Federal Records Center [FRC], Suitland, MD.

11. On British perception of U.S. indifference, see *Washington Despatches 1941–1945: Weekly Political Reports from the British Embassy,* ed. H. G. Nicholas (Chicago: University of Chicago Press, 1981), entry for April 8, 1942, p. 31. On information, see H. Montgomery Hyde, *Room 3603: The Story of the British Intelligence Center in New York During World War II* (New York: Farrar, Straus and Co., 1962), 197; and Susan A. Brewer, *To Win the Peace: British Propaganda in the United States During World War II* (Ithaca, NY: Cornell University Press, 1997), 40–44.

12. Most of the material he gathered, he noted, went directly to government agencies, including the FBI and Department of Justice. Alfred Bernheim to Alan M. Stroock, January 12, 1944, Subj.: "Legal Committee," in "Legal Committee" fldr., Waldman papers.

13. Ellen Herman, *The Romance of American Psychology: Political Culture in the Age of Experts* (Berkeley: University of California Press, 1995), 57. The influence can be seen in the thinking of Freda Kirchwey, editor of the antifascist liberal weekly, *The Nation.* See Sara Alpern, *Freda Kirchwey; A Woman of the Nation* (Cambridge: Harvard University Press, 1987), 99ff. For a socio-psychological explanation of liberal attitudes, see Bruno Bettelheim

and Morris Janowitz, *Social Change and Prejudice* (New York: Free Press of Glencoe, 1950), 60.

14. John Higham, "American Anti-Semitism Historically Reconsidered," in Charles H. Stember et al., *Jews in the Mind of America* (New York: Basic Books, 1966), 240–41.

15. According to one study, while increasing numbers of Americans from 1937 to 1950 believed anti-Semitism was on the rise, hostility toward Jews showed no steady growth during this period. Charles Herbert Stember, "The Recent History of Public Attitudes," in Stember et al., *Jews in the Mind of America*, 78.

16. Baldwin to Elizabeth Allen (National Council for Civil Liberties), March 20, 1944, 2582/14, ACLU papers.

17. Kirchwey, "Curb the Fascist Press!" 28 March 1942, 357–58; and letters by Baldwin and editors, 444. All in *Nation*.

18. See Stephen J. Sniegoski, "Unified Democracy: An Aspect of American World War II Interventionist Thought, 1939–1941," *Maryland Historian* 9 (1978): 33–48.

19. See memo, Presidential Assistant David Niles for Press Secretary Stephen Early, September 2, 1940, in President's Personal File [PPF] 1 ("Whispering Campaign") and material covered by Secretary to the President M. H. McIntyre for J. Edgar Hoover, September 21, 1942, Official File [OF] 4230, both Franklin D. Roosevelt papers.

20. See FDR for Jim Rowe, April 24, 1941, and attached in President's Secretary's File [PSF] "Justice," Roosevelt papers.

21. For fate of the author of the "Diseased Spinal Cord" (Elmer Hartzell), see chapter 14.

22. This account is drawn from a large body of documentation in 148 WPO files, DoJ, 62A47, FRC. Also see Francis Shea et al. for Attorney General [AG] "Recommendations of Representatives of War . . . and Justice . . . for Cooperation . . . ," May 29, 1941, "Internment of Alien Enemies" fldr., Jackson papers; Berge for Sol. Gen. Charles Fahy, June 2, 1942, "Official Correspondence," Wendell Berge papers; Rowe for AG, "Special War Policies Unit," February 1, 1943, "Special War Policies" fldr., James Rowe papers.

23. The list contained the names of about 14,000 persons, more than half of whom were citizens. About a third of the total number listed were native born, 80 percent of them alleged Communists. The rest were Nazi or fascist connected. Joseph Prendergast to AG, December 17, 1941, and Prendergast for L. M. C. Smith, "Re: Proposed Program for the Control of . . . Aliens and . . . Citizens," December 31, 1941. Both in 148–0 "General Correspondence on Special Cases Affecting National Security," sec. 3, DoJ, 62A47, FRC. The list was unreliable and Biddle would later order it destroyed. See AG for Asst. AG Hugh B. Cox and Hoover, July 16, 1943, 100–12876-NS, DoJ, Freedom of Information [FoI] Act request.

24. Charles Fahy memoir, Columbia University Oral History Project [CUOHP], 151–52.

25. FBI, "General Intelligence Survey in the United States," January 1942, in OF 10b, Roosevelt papers.

26. Alan Brinkley, *Voices of Protest, Huey Long, Father Coughlin and the Great Depression* (New York: Alfred A. Knopf, 1982), 185.

27. "Ellis O. Jones, 93, A Radical, Is Dead," *New York Times,* 2 August 1967.

28. A. L. Wirin to C. Forster, December 16, 1941, 2497/130–31, ACLU papers.

29. Account of the meeting in "Voices of Defeat," *Life,* 13 April 1942, 86; and Foster Hailey, "Los Angeles Sets Blackout Rules," *New York Times,* 13 Dec. 1941, 13.

30. Biddle gave this order at a meeting with senior department officials on December 20, 1941. A brief account of the meeting is in handwritten note in margin of Prendergast to AG, December 17, 1941, in 148–0 "General Correspondence on Special Cases Affecting National Security," sec. 3, DoJ, 62A47, FRC.

31. McInerny for Berge, December 19, 1941; Berge to US Attorney William Fleet Palmer, December 20, 1941; Press Release, December 21, 1941. All in file 146–28–2, DoJ/FoI.

32. Zechariah Chafee, Jr., *The Blessings of Liberty* (Philadelphia: J.B. Lippincott Company, 1956), 70.

33. Francis Biddle, *Mr. Justice Holmes* (New York: Charles Scribner's Sons, 1942), 163.

34. See Patrick Washburn, "FDR vs. His Attorney General: The Struggle Over Sedition, 1941–42," *Journalism Quarterly* 62 (winter 1985); 717–24; Cabell Phillips, "'No Witch Hunts'" *New York Times Magazine,* 21 Sept. 1941, 8.

35. Biddle, "Taking No Chances," *Collier's,* 21 Mar. 1942, 41.

36. Biddle, speech delivered in February to American Bar Association, "A War Message to the Bar," *Pennsylvania Bar Association Quarterly* 13 (April 1942): 138–49.

37. DoJ, "Circular No. 3356, Supplement No. 2," April 4, 1942, in OF 1581, Roosevelt papers.

38. Roscoe Drummond, "'Defeatist Bund' Stabs U.S. War Effort . . .," *Christian Science Monitor,* 10 Mar. 1942, 1.

39. Harvey Wolf, "West Coast's Fear of Sabotage . . . Native Pro-Nazis Meet Openly," *New Leader,* 21 Feb. 1942, 5

40. Thompson, "The Firing of the Normandie," 11 Feb. 1942, 15; "More About the Fifth Column, 27 Feb. 1942, 12; "The Nation and the State—3," 6 Mar. 1942, 16. All *New York Post.*

41. Drummond, "Defeatist Bund Stabs U. S. War Effort," 10 Mar. 1942, 1; "Can Nothing Be Done," 12 Mar. 1942, 11. Both in *Christian Science Monitor.* Lippmann, "Our Hidden Allies," *Washington Post,* 21 Mar. 1942, 11.

42. Peter Irons, *Justice At War: The Story of the Japanese American Internment Cases* (New York: Oxford University Press, 1983), 33–39.

43. "Pelley Boosts Japan's Cause," *Hour,* 17 Jan. 1942, 3–4; FDR for Hoover, January 21, 1942, in PSF "Justice—J. E. Hoover," Roosevelt papers.

44. FBI, "General Intelligence Survey in the United States," January 1942, in OF 10b, Roosevelt papers.

45. Early for President, March 20, 1942, PSF "Justice," Roosevelt papers.

46. Francis Biddle, *In Brief Authority* (Garden City, NY: Doubleday & Company, Inc., 1962), 238.

47. See Richard P. Fenno, Jr., *The President's Cabinet: An Analysis in the Period from Wilson to Eisenhower* (Cambridge: Harvard University Press, 1959), 125.

48. Rowe for AG, March 23, 1942, "Rowe, James H. Jr." fldr., Biddle papers. Liberal anti-fascist journalists William L. Shirer and Ralph Ingersoll both told Vice President Henry Wallace that Biddle was "too soft" and "exceedingly weak." Wallace diary, April 29 and May 1, 1942, Henry Wallace papers.

49. At the end of May, Marshall brought this complaint to FDR, who immediately summoned Solicitor General Fahy (acting attorney general in Biddle's absence) and FBI official Edward Tamm. Fahy tried to explain the department's policy, while Tamm noted that the FBI had long opposed it. FDR, without consulting Biddle, ordered Fahy to authorize immediate detention of dangerous persons, and offered to use his confidential fund to obtain a large resort hotel to house the internees, citizens as well as aliens. Tamm for the Director, June 1, 1942, 66–6200–100–146, FBI/FoI.

50. Robert Jackson explained the inadequacies of the Smith Act in Chafee to John Lord O'Brian, May 5, 1941, box 4, fldr. 1, "Personal Correspondence and Subject file 'C' (1941–1959)," John Lord O'Brian papers.

51. Special Assistant AG Franklin S. Pollak for L. M. C. Smith, March 17, 1942, in "Reports L. M. C. Smith, Sedition Section"; J. Prendergast for Smith, April 29, 1942, "Legislation—Misc. Memos" fldr. Both in 148 WPO files, DoJ, 62A47, FRC. Berge for the AG, March 11, 1942, General Correspondence, 1942, Berge papers.

52. Biddle diary, March 20, 1942, in "Cabinet Meetings, 1942," Biddle papers; Ickes diary, March 22, 1942 [sic.], Harold Ickes papers; Paul L. Murphy, *World War I and the Origin of Civil Liberties in the United States* (New York: W. W. Norton & Company, Inc., 1979), 83.

53. Richard W. Steele, "American Popular Opinion and the War Against Germany: The Issue of Negotiated Peace, 1942," *Journal of American History* 65 (December 1978): 704–23.

54. Editorial, "Undemocratic Bill," Washington *Post,* 20 Feb. 1942, 10.

55. E. T. Folliard, "Washington a Rumor Factory Spreading Lies, President Says," Washington *Post,* 18 Feb. 1942, 1; W. H. Lawrence, "'Sixth Column' Seen by the President," *New York Times,* 25 Mar. 1942, 1.

56. Henry Hoke, *It's a Secret* (New York: Reynal & Hitchcock, 1946). For assessment see Richard Kay Hanks, "Hamilton Fish and American Isolationism, 1920–1944" (Ph.D. diss., University of California, Riverside, 1971), 339–59.

57. Fish called Biddle to say that he had heard he was going to be indicted. Biddle denied it. Biddle for Berge, April 16, 1942, "Social Justice" fldr., Berge papers. Actually when the case was being presented to the grand jury in late

1941 Biddle ordered that the Viereck indictments eliminate any mention of congressmen, including Fish. See L. M. C. Smith for the AG, October 21, 1941, "U.S. Government—Francis Biddle" fldr., DoJ, 62A47, FRC.

58. Michael Sayers and Albert E. Kahn, *Sabotage! The Secret War Against America* (New York: Harper & Brothers Publishers, 1942); "In the Wind," *Nation,* 31 Jan. 1942, 116.

59. Littell, *My Roosevelt Years,* 39–40, 44. Opposition by the CIO probably contributed to the defeats.

60. [Notes on conference] "Mr. James Rowe," March 21, 1942, "Denaturalization" fldr., Rowe papers.

61. "FBI to Act on Sedition," *PM,* 26 Mar. 1942, 15.

62. Lewis Wood, "G.W. Christians Accused of Sedition After Writings to Army Camps," *New York Times,* 28 Mar. 1942, 1; "Nation Starts Cracking Down on the 5th and 6th Columnists," *Newsweek,* 6 April 1942, 27. In June, Fahl was acquitted by a jury after 35 minutes; Christians was sentenced to five years in prison.

63. Moley to Biddle, April 17, 1942, in "Cabinet Meetings, Jan.-June 1942," Biddle papers.

64. "Accused of Libel on General MacArthur," 1 April 1942; "Noble, Jones Face 3 Sets of Charges," 2 April 1942. Both *New York Times.* Noble, Jones, and seven others were convicted of violating California's "subversive organizations" act, but in May 1945 the California court of appeals overturned the convictions. "Free Speech Wins in California Decision," *Civil Liberties Quarterly* (June 1945): 4.

65. "Pelley Held By FBI for Sedition," *PM,* 5 April 1942, 11; "Tarnished Silver Shirt," *Newsweek,* 13 April 1942, 30; Arthur Garfield Hays, "Civil Liberties in War Time," *Bill of Rights Review* 2 (winter 1942): 170–82

66. "Milquetoast Gets Muscles," *Time,* 13 April 1942, 20.

67. Cecil Brown, "Do You Know What You're Fighting?" *Collier's,* 11 Dec. 1943, 14–15. Almost half of the people polled thought the nation was threatened by a "group of dangerous native fascists," but 70 percent of this group could not identify who the fascists were. "The Fortune Survey," *Fortune,* Nov. 1943, 10–11ff.

68. Edmond Taylor, in *Awakening from History* (Boston: Gambit Incorporated, 1969), 310–12, suggests the antifascist temper in some quarters.

69. Other goals in Geoffrey S. Smith, "Isolationism, The Devil and the Advent of the Second World War: Variations on a Theme," *International History Review* 4 (February 1982): 76–77; Richard Gid Powers, *Not Without Honor: The History of American Anticommunism* (New York: The Free Press, 1995), 159.

70. Baldwin, "On Freedom of Expression," *Nation,* 25 April 1942, 499; "Free Speech for Native Fascists" *New Republic,* 27 April 1942, 574–75; Baldwin to Hays, March 26, 1942, 2439/46, ACLU papers.

71. ACLU release, March 25, 1942, in Daily Press Releases series, *Records and Publications of the American Civil Liberties Union* (New York: Microfilm Corporation of America, 1975) [ACLU Records and Publications].

72. ACLU release, April 10, 1942, in Daily Press Releases, op cit.

73. A. W. Brian Simpson, *In the Highest Degree Odious: Detention without Trial in Wartime Britain* (Oxford: Oxford University Press, 1992), 1, 409. Sir Oswald Mosley, head of the British fascists, was held in preventive detention in England from 1940 through the end of 1943. Maximilian St. George and Lawrence Dennis, *A Trial on Trial—The Great Sedition Trial of 1944* (no place: National Civil Rights Committee, 1946), 44–48.

74. Baldwin to Hays, March 26, 1942, 2439/46, ACLU papers.

75. Herbert Ehrmann to Hays, April 14, 1942, "Correspondence re. ACLU," Arthur Garfield Hays papers.

76. Kirchwey, "Curb the Fascist Press!"

77. Baldwin to Dale Pontius, August 6, 1942, 2387/126, ACLU papers.

78. DeVoto, "Sedition's General Staff," *Harpers Magazine,* June 1942, 109–12; "Abraham Lincoln Established America's Right To Protect Itself . . .," *PM,* 30 Mar. 1942, 8.

79. See "Civil Liberties In A Period of Transition," *Public Policy* 3 (1942): 33–97. Also, "The Politics of Persecution," *Public Opinion Quarterly* 6 (March 1942): 41–56; "Democracy and Defamation: Fair Game and Fair Comment, II" *Columbia Law Review* 42 (November 1942): 1282–1318.

80. "Civil Liberties in Transition," 53.

81. Ibid., 88.

82. Ibid., 52, 58.

83. Norman L. Rosenberg, "Another History of Free Speech: The 1920s and the 1940s," *Law and Inequality* 7 (July 1989): 355.

84. Riesman, *Individualism Reconsidered and Other Essays* (Glencoe, IL: The Free Press, 1954), 9.

85. See Peggy Lamson, *Roger Baldwin: Founder of American Civil Liberties Union* (Boston: Houghton, Mifflin and Co., 1976), 239; and Dwight MacDonald, "Profiles: The Defense of Everybody, II" *New Yorker,* 18 July 1953, 50–52.

86. Samuel Walker, *In Defense of American Liberties: A History of the ACLU* (New York: Oxford University Press, 1990), 155.

87. Secretary Lucille Milner resigned over the continued efforts of Baldwin and a few others on behalf of fascists. Minutes of the Board, April 30, 1942, in "Minutes" file, ACLU, *Records and Publications.*

88. ACLU, "The Federal Espionage Act Prosecutions: Summary of Report . . . adopted by Board, July 6, 1942," 2501/23, ACLU papers.

Chapter 10

1. See J. H. T., Jr., "The Postal Power and Its Limitations on Freedom of the Press," *Virginia Law Review* 28 (March 1942): 634–48; Eberhard P. Deutsch, "Freedom of the Press and of the Mails," *Michigan Law Review* 36 (March

1938): 703–51; Zechariah Chafee, *Government and Mass Communications,* 2 vols. (Chicago: University of Chicago Press, 1947), 277–307.

2. G. T. Washington for L. M. C. Smith, "Control of Seditious Publications through the Postal Laws," March 21, 1942, "German Saboteurs" fldr., Oscar Cox papers. From the beginning of the war until April 15, 1942, postal officials refused to deliver about 35 pieces of literature they had ruled seditious. Smith for Charles Fahy, Director, War Division, Re: "Status of Sedition Cases—December 7, 1941 to September 30, 1942," October 8, 1942, in "Reports on Sedition to the Attorney General," and "List Ruled Unmailable Under Espionage Act from December 7 to May 15," covered by Miles to Smith, May 20, 1942, "Procedure—PO-Sedition Section" fldr., in records of the Department of Justice [DoJ], accession 62A47, Federal Records Center [FRC], Suitland, MD.

3. Entry for March 20, 1942, in "Cabinet Meetings," Francis Biddle papers; memo, "Mr. James Rowe," March 21, 1942, in "Denaturalization" fldr., Rowe papers.

4. Sheldon Marcus, *Father Coughlin: The Tumultuous Life of the Priest of the Little Flower* (Boston: Little, Brown and Company, 1973), 198–205.

5. Donald Warren, *Radio Priest: Charles Coughlin, the Father of Hate Radio* (New York: The Free Press, 1996), 232–68.

6. A. W. Schwartz for Francis A. Mahony (Re: "Utterances of Social Justice . . ."), April 11, 1942, file 146–28–10, DoJ, Freedom of Information Act Request [FoI]. I am indebted to Professor Patrick Washburn for sharing this and related DoJ documents with me.

7. *New Republic,* 5 Jan. 1942, 7–8.

8. Assistant Attorney General [AG] Wendell Berge for James McInerney [Special Assistant to the AG], January 5, 1942, 146–28–10, DoJ/FoI.

9. Berge to J. Edgar Hoover, January 8, 1942, 146–28–10, DoJ/FoI.

10. Berge, "Confidential Memorandum for Social Justice Staff," April 15, 1942, "Social Justice" fldr., Berge papers.

11. McInerny for Berge, January 15, 1942, DoJ/FoI.

12. Berle to Hoover, January 22, 1942, 62–41602–31; Hoover for Berge (attached to Berge memo, January 8, 1942), "Father Coughlin Internal Security—G, Special Inquiry State Department;" Hoover to Special Agent in Charge [SAC] Detroit, March 27, 1942, 62–41602–7. All records of the Federal Bureau of Investigation, FBI Reading Room [FBI/RR].

13. Hoover to SAC-Detroit, April 15, 1942, 146–28–10, DoJ/FoI; SAC Detroit to Hoover, April 30, 1942, Detroit file 100–4716 (3), FBI/RR.

14. Conclusion reached by FBI officials, April 22, 1942, in Warren, *Radio Priest,* 258–59.

15. Several studies were done. See particularly Francis A. Mahony for L. M. C. Smith, "Social Justice," April 7, 1942; A. Schwartz for Mahony, April 2, 1942; and Schwartz to Mahony, April 10, 1942. All 146–28–10, DoJ/FoI.

16. Warren, *Radio Priest,* 248. Miles to Postmaster General, April 14, 1942, in 103, 777-E-108, records of the Post Office Department [RG 28].

17. The publisher of the magazine was Social Justice Publishing Company, which was owned by Coughlin's parents. The editor was one E. Perrin Schwartz. Memorandum Re: "Social Justice . . .," March 27, 1942, 146–28–10, DoJ/FoI.

18. Post Office Department Press Release, April 15, 1942, in 146–28–10, DoJ/FoI.

19. Quoted in Donald Johnson, *The Challenge to American Freedoms: World War I and the Rise of the American Civil Liberties Union* (Lexington: University of Kentucky Press, 1963), 60.

20. Harry N. Scheiber, *The Wilson Administration and Civil Liberties, 1917–1921* (Ithaca, NY: Cornell University Press, 1960), 29.

21. Lippmann to House, October 17, 1917, in reel 1, microfilm, Newton D. Baker papers.

22. O'Brian and Alfred Bettman for Attorney General, April 25, 1919, box 18, fldr. 5, John Lord O'Brian papers.

23. Paul Murphy, *World War I and the Origin of Civil Liberties in the United States* (New York: W.W. Norton & Co., 1979), 102.

24. According to an associate of Berger's, the postmaster general went further, refusing to deliver letters addressed to the *Milwaukee Leader,* stopping delivery by express companies, pressuring advertisers, and even refusing to deliver mail sent *by* the *Leader.* Oscar Ameringer, "Patriotism, Ltd.," *Common Sense* 9 (March 1940), 5–7.

25. *United States ex rel. Milwaukee Social Democratic Publishing Co.* v. *Burleson,* 255 U.S. 407 (1921).

26. "Mailing Ban Put on *Social Justice,*" 15 April 1942, 1; "Grand Jury to Act on Social Justice," 18 April 1942, 17. Both *New York Times.*

27. D. Newcomb Barco, Jr. for Mahony, April 16, 1942, 146–28–10, DoJ/FoI. On doubts concerning suspension of mailing privilege see Franklin S. Pollak to Smith, April 18, 1942, Re: "Social Justice—Post Office hearing," 146–28–10, DoJ/FoI. See also Assistant Solicitor General Oscar Cox for AG, "Social Justice and the Mailing Privilege," April 28, 1942, "Subversive Activities, Espionage, Sabotage" file, Cox papers.

28. Biddle diary, May 7, 1942, in "Cabinet Meetings, 1942," Francis Biddle papers.

29. Press reaction in Harold C. Field, "The Fascist Press in America," *Contemporary Jewish Record* 5 (June 1942): 291–98. Criticism in Baldwin to Hays, March 26, 1942, 2439/46, ACLU papers; editorial, "The Case of 'Social Justice,'" *New York Times,* 16 April 1942, 20; editorial, "Is Coughlin the Target, or Press Freedom?" *Los Angeles Times,* 16 April 1942; Oswald Garrison Villard, "Are We Going Fascist," *The Progressive,* 9 May 1942, 8; editorial, "No Witch-Hunts Please," ibid., 18 April 1942, 12. Foreign language press anxi-

ety reported in entry for April 23, 1942, in H. B. Nicholas, ed., *Washington Despatches, 1941–1945: Weekly Political Reports from the British Embassy* (Chicago: University of Chicago Press, 1981), 33.

30. Entry for May 7, 1942, in "Cabinet Meetings 1942," Biddle papers. Negotiations covered in Warren, *Radio Priest,* 262–67.

31. Samuel I. Rosenman, comp., *The Public Papers and Addresses of Franklin D. Roosevelt,* vol. 10 (New York: Harper & Brothers, 1950), 234.

32. This is well covered in Richard Norton Smith, *The Colonel: The Life and Legend of Robert R. McCormick, 1880–1955* (Boston: Houghton Mifflin Company, 1997), 319–456.

33. See Bruno Bettelheim and Morris Janowitz, *Dynamics of Prejudice: A Psychological and Sociological Study of Veterans* (New York: Harper & Brothers, 1950), 55.

34. Davis comment in FDR to Russell C. Leffingwell, March 16, 1942, in *FDR: His Personal Letters, 1928–1945,* vol. II, ed. Elliot Roosevelt (New York: Duel, Sloan and Pearce, 1946), 1298–99.

35. Ibid., 415–19, 430–40.

36. Ickes diary, April 11, 1942, Harold L. Ickes papers.

37. "Conference with President," April 22, 1942, "Franklin D. Roosevelt" fldr., Biddle papers.

38. Rowe for AG, April 29, 1942, "Rowe" fldr., Biddle papers.

39. British Intelligence and Friends of Democracy analyses in H. Montgomery Hyde, *Room 3603: The Story of the British Intelligence Center in New York During World War II* (New York: Farrar, Straus and Co., 1962), 196. Library of Jewish Information, "Report for April 1942," May 26, 1942, reports on a study of the *New York Journal American* [Hearst], the *Chicago Tribune,* the *New York Daily News,* and the *Washington Times-Herald.* "Chronology file, 1942–44," American Jewish Committee papers. Special report prepared by Bureau of Liaison for Kenneth Crawford, May 18, 1942, "Sources Division, May 18, 1942" fldr., entry 171, Records of the Office of Government Reports [RG 44].

40. Copy of FDR, "Memorandum for the Attorney General," May 7, 1942, and précis of accompanying material in Official File [OF] 4866, Roosevelt papers.

41. FDR for Under Secretary of State [Welles], May 19, 1942, President's Secretary's File [PSF], "Eleanor Roosevelt," Roosevelt papers.

42. Comparison of early OFF and Justice studies in Ralph O. Nafsiger [Chief, Media Division, OFF] to R. Keith Kane [Chief, Bureau of Intelligence, OFF], "Statement Coding for the Nazi Line in Chicago *Tribune* . . . ," July 15, 1942, in "Media Division, July 15, 1942, "Statement Coding . . ." fldr., entry 171, RG 44.

43. At least four separate analyses had been made of the *Tribune* by November 1942. Edward H. Hickey for Rowe, "Chicago Tribune," October 10, 1942; Smith for AG, Re: Chicago Tribune [et al.], November 19, 1942, 146–7–23–25, DoJ/FoI.

44. Doyle for O'Brien, June 16, 1942, 103, 777-E-111, RG 28; Chester T. Lane, Acting Chief of Special War Policies Unit, to Calvin W. Hassell [Asst. Solicitor, Post Office], August 24, 1942, 146–7–23–25; Asst. AG Tom C. Clark to Hassell, October 1, 1943, 146–7–23–25, DoJ/FoI.

45. George Roudebush [Chief, Sedition Section, Special War Policies Unit], "Control of Propaganda Amounting to Sedition," a talk during Consultative Visit [of Latin American officials] to the United States, July-August 1943, in envelope 2, box 2, War Division/Latin American section, RG 60.

46. Miles to Chief Inspector, April 18, 1942, 103, 777-E-45, RG 28.

47. Smith to Miles, April 22, 1942, ibid.

48. John Roy Carlson, "Our Fascist Enemies Within," *American Mercury* 54 (Mar. 1942): 306–17.

49. Quoted in "Voices of Defeat," *Life,* 13 April 1942, 86ff, and in "Hitler's American Stooges," *Look,* 2 June 1942, 24.

50. Postmaster General to Postmaster, Muncie, Indiana, May 1, 1942, 103, 777-E-50-A, RG 28

51. The opposition to censorship was apparent in the remarks of Chester T. Lane, who joined Smith as associate chief of the Special War Policies Unit in early August 1942. Lane memoir, Columbia University Oral History Project, 616, 633–35,

52. See Harold D. Lasswell, "Detection: Propaganda Detection and the Courts," in Lasswell, Nathan Leites, and Associates, *Language of Politics; Studies in Quantitative Semantics* (Cambridge, MA: The M.I.T Press, 1949), 173–232; Eleanor Bontecou, *The Federal Loyalty-Security Program* (Ithaca, NY: Cornell University Press, 1953), 163.

53. Michael Kazin, *The Populist Persuasion* (New York: Basic Books, 1995).

54. "Memorandum to Mr. Hassell," May 15, 1942, 103, 777-E-50-A, RG 28.

55. Daniel M. Kidney, "'Weighted Average' Plan Checks Nazi Propaganda," *Washington Daily News,* 20 May 1942, 21, in 103,777-E-50-A, RG 28. The second-class mailing privilege was suspended. Doyle for O'Brien, June 9, 1943, 103, 777-E-55, RG 28. By the end of 1943, *X-Ray's* mailing privilege had been restored. See Adele Bernstein, "Laws Held Too Weak to Stop Flow of Seditious Press," *Washington Post,* 1 Sept. 1943, 10.

56. Smith for Fahy, October 8, 1942, Sub: "Status of Sedition Cases—December 7, 1941 to September 30, 1942," "Reports on Sedition to the Attorney General," in DoJ, 62 A 47, FRC. Figures for the year from "Memorandum on the Post Office Censorship," January 18, 1943, 2440/17–20, ACLU papers.

57. David Lawrence, "Mailing Rule Sets Perilous Precedent," *Washington Evening Star,* 27 June 1942, in "Newspaper Clippings Pertaining to Espionage Matters," 103, 777-E-46, RG 28.

58. Hassell for Ironside, May 23, 1942, 103, 777-E-505; W. C. O'Brien, "Memorandum," December 1, 1942, 103, 777-E-326, RG 28.

59. ACLU, "Memorandum on the Post Office Censorship," January 18, 1943, 2440/17–20, ACLU papers.

60. Francis Biddle, *In Brief Authority* (Garden City, NY: Doubleday & Company, Inc., 1962), 176.

61. See warning, Morris Ernst to FDR, January 17, 1944, PSF "Ernst," Roosevelt papers.

62. See "Censorship Matters—Legislation," November 2, 1944, 2608/111, ACLU papers. After the war the Supreme Court decided that the post office had exceeded its authority in this case. See Chafee, *Government and Mass Communications,* 297–304.

63. The April 18, 1942, issue was declared unmailable because of an article by Dr. Felix Morley entitled "For What Are We Fighting?" The article, said the analyst, "follows in a remarkable way and to a remarkable degree the Nazi Radio Themes" supplied by the Department of Justice, particularly in regard to its characterization of the president and his leadership. The issue was mailed. Apparently the *Post* was warned. O'Brien for Miles, May 1, 1942, 103, 777–51, RG 28.

64. *The Progressive,* a populist journal founded by Sen. Robert La Follette, had followed an isolationist line on the eve of war and criticized profiteering and "selfish jockeying for economic advantage and . . . lack of unified planning" during the war. The journal had been on Smith's list of publications to watch. The post office found a number of issues non-mailable, but was overruled by the Justice Department. See Doyle for O'Brien, August 21, 1942, and rest of file 103, 777-E-87, RG 28.

65. The post office ruled that a number of issues of *Christian Century,* as well as literature mailed by the Commission on World Peace of the Methodist Church, were "unmailable." These decisions were overruled by L. M. C. Smith. See Smith to Miles, July 6, 1942, and rest of file 103, 777-E-131. On Commission on World Peace, see Doyle for O'Brien, August 10, 1942, and Lane to Hassel, August 24, 1943, in 103, 777-E-199. All RG 28.

66. Carlson, "Our Fascist Enemies Within," 316. The reference to "Middletown" is an allusion to the fact that Muncie, where *X-Ray* was published, had been the subject of Robert and Helen Lynd's sociological study, *Middletown: A Study in Contemporary American Culture* (New York: Harcourt, Brace, and Company, 1929).

67. Daniel Bell argued that American culture and traditions made it the home of spontaneous mass anti-Semitism. "The Face of Tomorrow," *Jewish Frontier* 11 (June 1944): 15–20. Gordon Allport estimated that 5 to 10 percent of the population was "violently anti-Semitic" with perhaps 45 percent more "mildly bigoted." One-fifth were "implacable Anglophobes." He concluded that "we have, then, a large nucleus of people who are aggressive antis." "The Bigot in Our Midst," *Commonweal,* 6 Oct. 1944, 582–84.

Chapter 11

1. The total number of black nationalists convicted of sedition is difficult to determine. The ACLU, working from Justice Department figures, estimated 21. Approximately 95 blacks, including some of those in the sedition cases, were also convicted of draft evasion (there is some overlap between the two categories). The ACLU lists 28 federal prosecutions for sedition (black and white) between December 7, 1941, and July 1945, involving a total of 123 persons, of whom 75 were convicted. ACLU, "War-Time Prosecutions for Speech and Publication, . . . July 1945," addendum 2, "General Correspondence, 1946," ACLU Publications, 1945, American Civil Liberties Union papers. Robert A. Hill, working from FBI and other sources, concludes that there were 18 convictions of blacks for sedition and approximately two hundred convictions for selective service violations. Hill, introduction to *The FBI's RACON: Racial Conditions in the United States During World War II,* comp. and ed. Robert A. Hill (Boston: Northeastern University Press, 1997), 17.

2. The only significant treatment of the black nationalist phenomenon in World War II is Robert Hill's introduction to *The FBI's RACON,* 1–72.

3. Harvard Sitkoff, *A New Deal for Blacks, The Emergence of Civil Rights as a National Issue: The Depression Decade* (New York: Oxford University Press, Inc., 1978), 326–35.

4. Claude Andrew Clegg, III, *An Original Man: The Life and Times of Elijah Muhammad* (New York: St. Martin's Press, 1997), 4–73.

5. Theodore Kornweibel, *Seeing Red: Federal Campaigns Against Black Militancy, 1915–1925* (Bloomington, Indiana University Press, 1998), 100–31.

6. Richard Gid Powers, *Secrecy and Power: The Life of J. Edgar Hoover* (New York: The Free Press, 1987), 127; Kornweibel, *Seeing Red,* 174–82.

7. Kenneth O'Reilly, "The Roosevelt Administration and Black America: Federal Surveillance Policy and Civil Rights During the New Deal and World War II Years," *Phylon* 48 (1987): 12–25. Estimates of the size of the black fifth column ran as high as 100,000. "The Negro Problem and Its Factors," November 9, 1942, MID 291.2 "Negroes," pp. 6–13, in Regional File, US, 2500–3500, in records of the War Department General and Special Staffs [MID], Record Group [RG] 165.

8. Merl E. Reed, "The FBI, MOWM, and CORE, 1941–1946," *Journal of Black Studies* 21 (June 1991): 465–79.

9. A. Cranston to Read Lewis (head of Common Council), January 9, 1942, "Office of Facts and Figures, 1941–42" fldr., records of the American Council for Nationalities Services.

10. "Recent Negro Reactions Toward the War," [spring 1942] in "Negro Study" fldr., box 5, records of the Bureau of Agricultural Economics, RG 83.

11. Ickes diary, May 24, 1942, Harold L. Ickes papers.

12. Foreign Broadcast Intelligence Service, "Radio Tokyo: Racial Propaganda to the United States," May 25, 1942, in box 1, records of the Foreign Broadcast Intelligence Service, RG 262; "Harlem Nazi Planned Murders," *New York Times,* 17 December 1942, 22. Remarks of Stokely Delmar Hart on May 22, 1942, in the indictment of Hart and others in document 00875, series A, legal files, group II, box B-147, records of the National Association for the Advancement of Colored People (NAACP). Statement by Elijah Muhammed in FBI report, "Allah Temple of Islam," September 30, 1942, file 100–6582–68, FBI Reading Room [RR].

13. Patrick Washburn, *A Question of Sedition: The Federal Government's Investigation of the Black Press During World War II* (New York: Oxford University Press, 1986), 137ff.

14. Ernest Allen, Jr., "Waiting for Tojo: The Pro-Japan Vigil of Black Missourians, 1932–1943," *Gateway Heritage* 15 (fall 1994): 16–33.

15. Clegg, *Original Man,* 28, 42–48, 65.

16. Allen, "Waiting for Tojo," 20.

17. Takahashi spent the war years in prison, mental institutions, and internment camps. FBI, "Gulam Bogans, with aliases, et al.," August 6, 1942, 100–6582–36, FBI/RR. Also *RACON,* 516–17.

18. Allen, "Waiting for Tojo," 18–19.

19. Benjamin E. Mays, "Why Negroes Are Loyal to U.S." (originally appearing in *Crisis*) reprinted in *Des Moines Register,* 20 May 1942, 00956, NAACP papers; Louis Martin, "Fifth Column Among Negroes," *Opportunity* [published by National Urban league] 12 (December 1942): 358–59.

20. Hill, introduction to *RACON,* 6–7, 10.

21. Affidavit by Asst. U.S. Attorney Keith Brown in *U.S.* v. *Lester Holness,* Criminal Case 113–40, in U.S. District Court, Southern District of New York, records of the District Courts of the United States [RG 21], National Archives—Northeast Region (NY) [NA/NER].

22. Dominic J. Capeci, Jr., "The Lynching of Cleo Wright: Federal Protection of Constitutional Rights during World War II," *Journal of American History* 72 (1986): 859–87.

23. Allen, "Waiting for Tojo," 16–33.

24. Joseph Hanlon, "'Fifth Column' Propaganda Among Negroes in St. Louis Area Traced to Japanese," *St. Louis Post-Dispatch,* 5 Mar. 1942, 1.

25. "FBI Hunts Two Japs in Exposé of 5th Column Activity in St. Louis," *Chicago Defender,* 14 Mar. 1942, 00955, NAACP papers.

26. *Butler et al.* v. *United States,* 138 F.2d 977 (1943).

27. Norman M. Littell, *My Roosevelt Years,* ed. Jonathan Dembo (New York: University of Washington Press, 1987), 61.

28. Milton Starr (Negro Morale Section, OWI) for Ulric Bell, June 23, 1942, "Subversive Activities" fldr., entry 1, records of the Office of War Information, RG 208.

29. Capeci, "Lynching of Cleo Wright," 878–81.

30. Allen, "Waiting for Tojo," 27.

31. In late December 1941 the FBI had learned that organizers for the Moorish Science Temple in Mound City, not far from Sikeston, were advising blacks that when "the Japs take over this country, those belonging to the organization would not be molested." FBI report, "The Moorish Science Temple . . .," January 28, 1942, 62–25889–6, FBI/RR. The group would escape prosecution for sedition, but seven were convicted of violations of the Selective Service Act. Berge for Hoover, January 22, 1943, in 146–7–4221, records of the Department of Justice, Freedom of Information request [DoJ/FoI]; *RACON,* 541. The area was the locale of black antiwar, anti-draft activity during World War I. See Theodore Kornweibel, Jr., "The Story of the Church of God in Christ," in *Proclaim Peace: Christian Pacifism from Unexpected Quarters,* ed. Theron F. Schlabach and Richard T. Hughes (Urbana: University of Illinois Press, 1997), 58–81.

32. "The Moorish Temple of Science . . .," May 26, 1942, 62–25889–8, FBI/RR; RACON, 294.

33. See John T. Elliff, *The U.S. Department of Justice and Individual Rights, 1937–1962* (New York: Garland Publishing Inc., 1987), 194–95.

34. General grand jury probes in Pittsburgh and Detroit reported no evidence of recent Japanese activity. L. M. Hopping [U.S. Attorney, Detroit] to AG, April 30, 1943, 146–7–4221, DoJ/FoI. Elliff concludes that the Civil Rights Unit was overzealous in instituting the grand jury investigations, but "succeeded in keeping prosecutions to a minimum." Elliff, *Department of Justice and Individual Rights,* 196.

35. The Espionage Act (1917) criminalized willful obstruction of recruiting or enlistment, and the Selective Training and Service Act (1940) made it a crime for any person to counsel draft evasion or to fail to comply with draft regulations.

36. "Indictment Names 'Black Dragon' Ilk," *New York Times,* 28 Jan. 1943, 12.

37. Elliff, *Department of Justice and Individual Rights,* 194–95

38. Baldwin/Martin correspondence, December 16 and 24, 1942, 2505/173–75, ACLU papers.

39. Baldwin, "Memorandum for the Sedition Committee," March 31, 1943, 00909, NAACP papers.

40. Baldwin to Berge and Marshall to Berge, both April 21, 1943, 00910–00911; Baldwin to Rotnem, April 27, 1943, 00915, NAACP papers.

41. Telegram, Baldwin to Sidney Redmond (Erwin's lawyer), May 7, 1943, 00926, NAACP papers.

42. "Policies Adopted by the Board of Directors, 1942," December 21, 1942, in pamphlet file, *Records and Publications of the American Civil Liberties Union* [microfilm] (New York: Microfilm Corp. of America, 1975).

43. Marshall to C. Foster (ACLU), July 24, 1943, 00936, NAACP papers.

44. John Roy Carlson, *Under Cover: My Four Years in the Nazi Underworld of America* (New York: E. P. Dutton & Company, 1943), 154–58.
45. Hill, introduction to *RACON*, 10.
46. *RACON*, 532
47. Quoted from the indictment, exhibit 1, Criminal Case 113–40 (*U.S.* v. *Lester Holness*), RG 21, NA/NER.
48. "Statement of Mr. Williams," (in interview with Asst. U.S. Attorney Keith Brown, September 16, 1942), exhibit 4, ibid.
49. "Sedition Charged to Five in Harlem," *New York Times*, 15 Sept. 1942, 1.
50. Carlson, *Under Cover*, 154–58.
51. "3 Years for Ashima Takis," 2 Oct. 1942, 6; "Agent For Japan Turns on Jordan," 10 Dec. 1942, 6; "Says Harlem Nazi Planned Murders," 17 Dec. 1942, 22; "Filipino Witness Accuses Jordan," 18 Dec. 1942, 20. All *New York Times*.
52. See affidavit, dated April 15, 1946, by Keith Brown in *U.S.* v. *Holness*, in Criminal 113–40, RG 21, NA/NER.
53. Marshall for Redmond, March 3, 1943, 00905, NAACP papers.
54. "Seize 84 Negroes in Sedition Raids," *New York Times*, 22 Sept. 1942, 22.
55. "Sedition Jury Indicts 12 Heads of Negro Cults," *Chicago Daily News*, 23 Oct. 1942, 00958, NAACP papers. The case against Elijah Muhammed and a number of his followers was eventually dropped, but Muhammed and others were convicted in November 1942 of failing to register. See Clegg, *Original Man*, 92.
56. "The government has had the strongest type of affirmative proof of their charges." Thurgood Marshall for Redmond, March 3, 1943, 00905, NAACP papers.
57. *RACON*, 516–17, 531.
58. *RACON*, 512.
59. Robb and Stokely Delmar Hart, Charles Newby, James Graves and Mrs. Annabelle Goree Robb were associated with both the Brotherhood of Liberty for Black Men of America and the Colored American National Organization.
60. William H. Temple (chairman, Chicago Branch of NAACP Legal Redress Committee) to Marshall, December 8, 1942, 00889, NAACP papers.
61. Copy of the indictment of Hart et al. in 00875, ibid.
62. William Green Gordon, Seon Emmanuel Jones, and David James Logan.
63. She and two of her associates were found guilty. *United States* v. *Gordon et al.*, 138 F.2d 174 (1943).
64. Correspondence between Foster and Rotnem, and Forster and Berge in March-July 1943 in 2505/156–57, 177–79; 2506/11, ACLU papers. "Seven in Cult Seized As Draft Evaders," 14 Jan. 1942, 23; "Draft Evasion Plot Charged," 17 Dec. 1942, 22. Both *New York Times*. Also see *RACON*, 548–49.
65. Information on the House of Israel in 100–168963, FBI/FoI.

66. "Guilty of Sedition Backed by Japanese," *New York Times,* 16 June 1942, 10.

67. *Butler* v. *United States* 138 F.2d 977; *United States* v. *Gordon et al.* 138 F.2d 174. Both Seventh Circuit decisions.

68. Baldwin, "Memorandum on the Clear and Present Danger Test for the Board of Directors . . . (April 30 meeting)," April 28, 1942, 2501/100–101, ACLU papers.

69. Ira Latimer (head of Chicago branch, ACLU) to Baldwin, January 6, 1942, 2506/34, ibid.

70. See Marshall to Temple, December 10, 1942, 2505/132–33, ibid.

71. Baldwin to Walter White, March 31, 1943, 00907, NAACP papers.

72. Baldwin to Frederick Allen, March 5, 1943, 00906, ibid.

Chapter 12

1. The size and character of the membership is covered by Sander A. Diamond, *The Nazi Movement in the United States 1924–1941* (Ithaca, NY: Cornell University Press, 1974). Figures on the size of the organization range from 25,000 (Diamond, 21), to approximately 8,500 members and 5,000 to 6,000 anonymous sympathizers. Leland Bell, "The Failure of Nazism in America: The German-American Bund, 1936–1941," *Political Science Quarterly* 85 (December 1970): 585–99. See also Susan Canedy, *America's Nazis: A Democratic Dilemma, A History of the German-American Bund* (Menlo Park, CA.: Markgraf Publications Group, 1990), 86. She argues that the membership's attitudes were misunderstood. At the grassroots level it was merely a fraternal-social organization that gave German-American immigrants a sense of community and a source of support. The negative aspects she attributes mostly to Fritz Kuhn who was not representative of rank-and-file thinking.

2. Canedy, *America's Nazis,* 196. Bell, "The Failure of Nazism," 593.

3. The foregoing account is based on Bell, "The Failure of Nazism."

4. See Joseph Prendergast, "Notes," April 6, 1942, in "Special War Policies" fldr., James Rowe papers; Jackson for [Immigration and Naturalization Director] Lemuel B. Schofield, December 20, 1940, "Misc. Immigration Matters," fldr., Robert Jackson papers.

5. L. M. C. Smith for Asst. AG Rogge (head of Criminal Division), September 27, 1940, "Nazi Activities in the United States," "Nazi Activities" fldr. in records of the Department of Justice [DoJ], accession 62A47, Federal Records Center [FRC], Suitland, MD.

6. Carr to Brien McMahon, January 28, 1938, file 235343, records of the DoJ, Record Group [RG] 60.

7. Dewey Balch, who was assistant to the attorney general in charge of the Denaturalization Program, later noted that the program was undertaken with the "recognition that the legal theory had received but limited acceptance,

with a statute so general in its terms as to leave many questions in doubt as to its meaning, and with a dearth of judicial precedents and those sharply conflicting." D.E. Balch, "Denaturalization Based on Disloyalty and Disbelief in Constitutional Principles," *Minnesota Law Review* 29 (June 1945): 405–35, quote on 408.

8. Marcia V. Maylott, "Schneiderman v. United States: Nullification of Naturalization Laws?" *George Washington Law Review* 12 (February 1944): 215–22.

9. Forrest R. Black, "Disloyalty and Denaturalization," *Kentucky Law Journal* 29 (January 1941): 143–71.

10. Walter Goodman, *The Committee: The Extraordinary Career of the House Committee on Un-American Activities* (New York: Farrar, Straus & Giroux, 1968), 3, 10–11.

11. Fish's hostility seemed to moderate during the debate. See "Re: H.R. 6250," January 5, 1942, 2431/108, American Civil Liberties Union [ACLU] papers.

12. U.S. Congress, House, *Congressional Record,* 77th Cong., 2d sess., 1942, 88, pt.1: 292–307. Analysis of the bill in ACLU, "Brief of American Civil Liberties Union With Regard to H. R. 6250," 2431/90–98, ACLU papers. The ACLU opposed the measure but Common Council for National Unity (the chief foreign-born support group) supported it, seeing in it a way of protecting the innocent foreign born from the stigma Bund activities attached to the whole group. See Harry Scheiderman and Lawrence Goldsmith, "Joint Conference on Alien Legislation," January 19, 1942, "Immigration-Aliens" fldr., Morris Waldman papers.

13. American Committee for Protection of Foreign Born, "Memorandum on Denaturalization," no date, in "Aliens—Drive Against (1)" fldr., box 1, Carey McWilliams papers.

14. See Arthur Garfield Hays to Senator Joseph H. Ball, February 6, 1942, 2431/130, ACLU papers. Discussion of Senate Immigration Committee hearings in "[Alan] Cranston Reports," February 18, 1942, in shipment 5, box 4, records of the Common Council for American Unity, in American Council for Nationalities Service collection. Department doubts are noted in A. G. Hays to Douglas Arant, February 6, 1942, 2431/202, ACLU papers; Assistant Solicitor General Oscar Cox for AG, October 13, 1942, "Attorney General (Chronological Memoranda)," Oscar Cox papers.

15. U.S. Attorney Mathias F. Correa charged that the Bund, "although formally dissolved, always has been and still remains an agency and tool of Hitler Germany. . . ." See "29 Bund Leaders Indicted As Correa Calls it Nazi Unit," *New York Times,* 8 July 1942, 1.

16. In August 1942, Gerhard Wilhelm Kunze, who succeeded Fritz Kuhn (already serving time in prison on a state charge) as leader of the Bund, would be convicted, along with four others, of conspiracy to commit espionage. In October, 24 others, including Kunze's successor August Klapprott, would be given long jail sentences for participating in a prewar conspiracy aimed at

encouraging members not to register for the draft. A year later, 27 leaders of the German-American Vocational League, a 40-year-old fraternal organization operating in 11 cities, were charged with failing to register as propagandists for the Nazi government. See "29 Bund Leaders Indicted As Correa Calls it Nazi Unit," 8 July 1942, 1; "Bund Round-ups Continued by FBI," 10 July 1942, 9; "Molzahn Convicted As Spy; Kunze Gets 15 Year Sentence," 22 August 1942, 1; "24 Bundists Guilty of Anti-Draft Plot," 20 Oct. 1942, 1; "27 Indicted by U.S. As 5th Columnists," 6 Oct. 1943, 17. All *New York Times.*

17. Pegler, "Fair Enough," *Los Angeles Times,* 1 Jan. 1942, 2.

18. Rowe for AG, March 11, 1942, "Denaturalization" fldr., Rowe papers.

19. Berge for AG, March 16, 1942, "General Correspondence" file, Wendell Berge papers.

20. Speed emphasized in Smith for Rowe, March 18, 1942, and March 20, 1942; Prendergast for Rowe, March 18, 1942, and memo ["Mr. James Rowe," dated March 21, 1942] on conference held in Attorney General's office on March 21. All in "Denaturalization" fldr., Rowe papers.

21. See L. M. C. Smith, "Memorandum Of Conference With Mr. John Lord O'Brian," May 2, 1941, in "Inter-Office Memoranda" fldr., DoJ, 62A47, FRC.

22. Peter Irons, *Justice At War: The Story of the Japanese American Internment Cases* (New York: Oxford University Press, 1983), 61–64. Also troubling was martial law in Hawaii, which continued unnecessarily until 1944. See Harry N. Scheiber and Jane L. Scheiber, "Constitutional Liberty in World War II: Army Rule and Martial Law in Hawaii, 1941–1946," *Western Legal History* 3 (summer/fall 1990): 341–78.

23. John Burling, "Group and Individual Exclusions from Military Areas," 30 July 1942, statement to "Official Press Consulative Visit [of Latin American law enforcement officials]," envelope 1, box 1, War Division/Latin American Section records, RG 60.

24. James Rowe for AG, October 31, 1942, "Correspondence re: Cases—D" fldr., Charles Fahy papers.

25. Rowe was probably referring to the fact that Rogge's leftist views, problematic in other circumstances, would be acceptable in dealing with the Bund. Rowe for AG, March 21, 1941, "Denaturalization Cases," "Denaturalization" fldr., Rowe papers. Also Rowe for AG ["Dear Francis"], March 23, 1942, "Rowe, James H. Jr." fldr., Francis Biddle papers.

26. "Department of Justice" release, March 26, 1942, 2443/207–09, ACLU papers.

27. In one denaturalization case brought by the government, the subject had been naturalized in 1900. His first act of alleged disloyalty was 14 years later. He appealed, and the denaturalization order issued in 1942 was overturned. See *Orth et al.* v. *U.S.,* 142 F. 2d 969 (1944).

28. Joseph Prendergast warned Biddle that charging the Bund with fraud was a questionable practice subject to considerable criticism both for being based

on "an artificial legal theory" and for "opening the way to the indiscriminate and wholesale revocation of citizenship." Prendergast for AG [draft], January 28, 1942, "General Correspondence on Special Cases . . .," section 3, 148–0, War Policy Office files, DoJ, 62A47, FRC. See Prendergast for Smith, March 18, 1942, Re: "Proposed Program of the Criminal Division for the Revocation of the Citizenship of Certain Persons," in "Denaturalization" fldr., Rowe papers.

29. "Naturalized Foes to Lose Citizenship," 26 Mar. 1942, 25; "30 Disloyal Cases Ready," 27 Mar. 1942, 25; "Plan Action Against Kuhn," 1 April 1942, 9; "Citizenship Trials By U.S. To Be Fair," 2 April 1942, 23. All in *New York Times*.

30. Hays et al. to Biddle, April 2, 1942, 2446/21, ACLU papers.

31. Chafee to Baldwin, April 10, 1942, 2431/148, ACLU papers.

32. Telegram, Rowe to Frank Hennesey [U.S. Attorney, San Francisco], December 11, 1942, Criminal Division" fldr., Rowe papers.

33. T. Henry Walnut (a Philadelphia lawyer who defended some of the accused) told Clifford Forster of the ACLU that he had been told by the U.S. attorney that "Washington is anxious to have 40 to 60 additional petitions filed in this district." Walnut to Forster, December 19, 1942, 2443/180–82, ACLU papers.

34. See Joseph Prendergast, "Notes," April 16, 1942, "Special War Policies" fldr., Rowe papers.

35. "64 German Aliens Seized by FBI," *New York Times*, 12 April 1942, 31. The government's case is described briefly in Ralph S. Boyd, "Memorandum for Mr. L. M. C. Smith . . .," "Committee for Political Defense—Control of Organizations and Propaganda . . ." fldr., War Division/Latin American Section, RG 60.

36. "Department of Justice" release, July 7, 1942, "German Saboteurs" fldr., Cox papers.

37. Twenty-five members went on trial in September and twenty-four of them were convicted in mid-October 1942. The Supreme Court would later overturn the conviction. *Keegan* v. *United States* 325 U.S. 478 (1945).

38. "Bundist Round-Up Nets 72 More Here," *New York Times*, 9 July 1942, 1.

39. "Bund Round-Ups Continued by FBI," *New York Times*, 10 July 1942, 9.

40. Twenty-seven members were indicted in late 1943 and early 1944, and on May 28, 1944, nine were convicted. Morris Schonbach, "Native Fascism During the 1930s and 1940s: A Study of its Roots, Its Growth and Its Decline" (Ph.D. Dissertation, UCLA, 1958), 402. The ACLU's Arthur Garfield Hays wrote to Judge Thomas Meaney complimenting him on his fair handling of the case, June 2, 1944, "Thomas Meaney" fldr., Tom Clark papers.

41. "158 More Nazis Are Seized Here In largest Single Haul of War," *New York Times*, 12 July 1942, 1. The records of this case are in case 2017-C, records of the United States Attorneys and Marshals, RG 118, National Archives—Northeast Region (New York City).

42. "4 Leaders of Bund Lose Citizenship" [65 aliens rounded up], 18 July 1942, 4; "Molzahn Convicted as Spy; Kunze Gets 15-Year Sentence," 22 Aug. 1942, 1; "13 of German Origin Lose U.S. Citizenship," 9 Sept. 1942, 13; "Bund Leaders Face Loss of Citizenship," 4 Oct. 1942, 28; "24 Bundists Guilty of Anti-Draft Plot," 20 Oct. 1942, 1; "Mass Bund Trials Now in Prospect—Move Toward Revocation of Citizenship on a Large Scale is Revealed," 21 Oct. 1942, 12; "Jersey Bundsmen Face Wind-Up Suit," 24 October 1942, 7. All *New York Times.*

43. The preoccupation with numbers is suggested by the summary of Justice Department accomplishments and future action in regard to subversion supplied to Biddle (in July 1942). "Justice Department Reports" fldr., Biddle papers.

44. Rowe for AG, August 26, 1942, "Denaturalization" fldr., Rowe papers.

45. Baldwin, "Memorandum—Denaturalization Cases," December 11, 1942, 2443/178, ACLU papers.

46. Berge for Rowe, August 26, 1942, "Denaturalization" fldr., Rowe papers. So that their current activities could more readily be used against them, Berge urged the FBI to get suspects to declare that their attitudes at the time of their naturalization were the same as their attitudes at the time of questioning. Berge for Director, August 28, 1942, 66–6200–100–203, records of the FBI, Freedom of Information request [FBI/FoI].

47. "F.B.I. Net Spread for Foes in Nation," *New York Times,* 6 Dec. 1942, 59.

48. "Memorandum Opinion, Findings and Conclusion, Decree" in *U.S.* v. *Baumgartner* [Western District of Missouri, Western Division], attached to Biddle to all U.S. Attorneys, circular 3663, supplement #2, November 21, 1942, 66–6200–100–241, FBI/FoI.

49. "Decree and Order" in *U.S.* v. *Frank Seraph Fischer,* December 16, 1942, attached to Biddle to all U.S. Attorneys, circular 3663, supplement #4, January 25, 1943, ibid.

50. Hoover identified the following groups: Federation of Italian World War Veterans in the United States, Inc.; the Dante Alighieri Society; and Circolo Mario Morgantini.

51. See, for example, Philip V. Cannistraro, "Luigi Antonini and the Italian Anti-Fascist Movement in the United States, 1940–1943," *Journal of American Ethnic History* 5 (fall 1985): 21–40.

52. Asked to identify the alien groups in the United States that were most dangerous, 42 percent identified Germans, 35 percent Japanese, and only 2 percent Italians. L. M. C. Smith, commenting on these poll results, suggested that a similar distinction "may be valid in governmental handling of the three alien groups." "Distinctions Among Alien Groups," attached to L. M. C. Smith for Fahy, Shea et al., May 7, 1942, 66–6200–96–56, FBI/FoI.

53. Edward J. Ennis (Director, Alien Enemy Control Unit) for Rowe, October 27, 1942, Re: "Italian Fascists"; Chester Lane for Charles Fay, March 4, 1943, Re: "Italian Fascists." Both in "Fascist Organizations and Activities—Sharp" fldr., DoJ, 62A47, FRC; Rowe for Berge, December 12, 1942, "Denaturalization"

fldr., Rowe papers; Smith for Fahy, February 13, 1942 (particularly attached memo Marcel Grilli for L. M. C. Smith, February 8, 1943, Re "Statement of Problem in the Italian Field"), "Special War Policies" fldr., Rowe papers. Note on meeting May 12, 1943, in "Council Meetings" fldr., Biddle papers.

54. "Kuhn, Ten Others Lose Citizenship," *New York Times,* 19 March 1942, 21; Baldwin to Members of the Sedition Committee," August 16, 1943, 2454/183, ACLU papers.

55. Berge for AG, February 3, 1943, "General Correspondence" file, Berge papers. Eventually, the department did pursue Nowak—and it lost. *Nowak* v. *United States,* 356 U.S. 660 (1958).

56. Dewey Balch commented that the decision in effect meant that it would no longer be sufficient to demonstrate a disloyal state of mind in order to secure denaturalization; it would henceforth require the government to prove disloyal behavior. Balch, "Denaturalization Program," 429. Solicitor General Fahy, in later condemning this controversial decision, noted that it had "imposed an extremely burdensome weight of proof upon the Government in denaturalization cases." Charles Fahy, "Notes on Developments in Constitutional Law, 1936–1949," *Georgetown Law Journal* 38 (November 1949): 1–25.

57. *Schneiderman* v. *United States,* 320 U.S. 118. The case is discussed at length against the background of other Supreme Court denaturalization cases in Harry Kalven, Jr., *A Worthy Tradition: Freedom Speech in America,* ed. Jamie Kalven (New York: Harper & Row, Publishers, 1988), 426–31. See also Marcia Maylott and Daniel Crystal, "The Schneiderman Case: Two Views," *George Washington Law Review* 12 (February 1944): 215–37.

58. American Civil Liberties Union, "Weekly News Bulletin," October 11, 1943, *Records and Publications of the American Civil Liberties Union* [microfilm] (New York: Microfilm Corporation of America, 1975), reel 10. The announcement was based on a Department of Justice compilation. See Clifford Forster to Balch, April 20, 1944, 2572/103, ACLU papers. Balch, writing of the entire program, says that of the 11,000 cases examined: 1,000 were pursued; 543 complaints were filed; 169 were awaiting trial; 165 had been denaturalized; 45 had been decided in favor of the defendant; 81 others had been tried and the decision was pending; 83 had been withdrawn by the government. Balch, "Denaturalization Program," 407.

59. Hartmann described in "Ex-Bund Leader is Cited," *New York Times,* 3 July 1942, 2. Dismissal in ACLU, "Weekly News Bulletin," August 30, 1943, ACLU, *Records and Publications,* reel 10.

Chapter 13

1. "Voices of Defeat," *Life,* 13 April 1942, 86ff. Help in putting together the article came from postal authorities, some of whom were impatient with Justice Department policy. Walter K. Belknap (*Life*) to Calvin Hassell (Asst.

Solicitor for the Post Office), April 14, 1942, "Life Magazine" fldr. (E-47), records of the Post Office Department, Record Group [RG] 28.

2. Berge for Rowe, April 15, 1942, "Official Correspondence," Wendell Berge papers.

3. Berge for the AG, April 20, 1942, "General Correspondence," Berge papers; "Biddle to Push Sedition Inquiries, Beginning in Chicago, Then Here," *New York Times,* 23 April 1942.

4. Diary entry, April 24, 1942, "Cabinet Meetings, 1942," Francis Biddle papers.

5. Leo Ribuffo, *The Old Christian Right: The Protestant Far Right From the Great Depression to the Cold War* (Philadelphia: Temple University Press, 1983), 76–77.

6. "Milquetoast Gets Muscles," *Time,* 13 April 1942, 20.

7. "Pelley Boosts Japan's Cause," *Hour,* 17 January 1942, 3–4.

8. The total run of *The Galilean* was between 3,500 and 4,000. Apparently Pelley continued to send out a mimeographed sheet by first-class mail. See Pelley to "Dear Colleague," February 20, 1942, and W.W. McBroom (Post Office Inspector) to Inspector-in-Charge, Cincinnati, September 1, 1942, both in 103, 777-E-5, RG 28.

9. Pelley to "Dear Colleague," February 20, 1942, ibid.

10. Leo Egan, "Axis 'Line' Traced in Pelley Opinions," *New York Times,* 1 Aug. 1942, 3.

11. "United States v. Pelley, et al. (Excerpts from Summation of Oscar R. Ewing . . .)" (press release with handwritten emendations, no date), in fldr. 1, "Political Memos—General, 1940–46," Oscar R. Ewing papers.

12. "Pelley is Convicted on Eleven Counts," *New York Times,* 6 Aug. 1942, 1.

13. *Butler* v. *United States,* 138 F.2d, 977; *United States* v. *Gordon et al.* 138 F.2d 174; and *United States* v. *Hartzel,* 138 F.2d 169. All Seventh Circuit decisions (1943).

14. *United States* v. *Pelley,* 132 Fed Rep., 2d, 170.

15. "Pelley and the Prosecution," *New Republic,* 17 Aug. 1942, 189; "Seditious Publications Still Flourish in the United States, *Hour,* 11 July 1942, 1

16. *Washington Despatches 1941–1945: Weekly Political Reports from the British Embassy,* ed. H. G. Nicholas (Chicago: University of Chicago Press, 1981), entry for June 4, 1942, p. 43; Francis Biddle, *In Brief Authority* (Garden City, NY: Doubleday & Company, Inc., 1962), 297–99.

17. Stanley I. Kutler, *The American Inquisition: Justice and Injustice in the Cold War* (New York: Hill and Wang, 1982), 137.

18. Ibid., 139.

19. The policy is described in L. M. C. Smith for AG, March 2, 1942, attached to Biddle to Under Secretary of State Sumner Welles, March 4, 1942, 811.00B/2059; Welles to Biddle, March 16, 1942; Berle for Welles, "Memorandum Regarding Proposed Prosecution of Communists, March 12, 1942, 811.00B/2061. All in records of the Department of State, Record Group [RG] 59. Unsigned memo for L. M. C. Smith, April 1, 1942, "Re: Special

Cases of Native Born Citizens," in "Special Cases" fldr., DoJ, February 20, 1942, 62A47, Federal Records Center [FRC], Suitland, MD.; Ralph S. Boyd, Chief, Voorhis Administration (Spec. War Policies Unit) for L. M. C. Smith, July 7, 1942, "Report on Organizations," "Committee for Political Defense—Control of Organizations and Propaganda . . .," War Division/Latin American Section, records of Department of Justice [RG 60].

20. Biddle rejected FDR's explanation. Biddle, *Brief Authority,* 303. On Browder's problems, see Earl Latham, *The Communist Controversy in Washington, From the New Deal to McCarthy* (Cambridge: Harvard University Press, 1966), 155–56.

21. Downey to FDR, December 23, 1941; Leland, "Why 'Biddle' While The Country Burns?" and other messages. All in 39–11–254, sec. 4 [Bridges Case file], RG 60.

22. This account drawn from Walter Goodman, *The Committee, The Extraordinary Career of the House Committee on Un-American Activities* (New York: Farrar, Straus and Giroux, 1968), 131–43; August Raymond Ogden, *The Dies Committee: A Study of the Special House Committee for the Investigation of Un-American Activities, 1938–1944* (Washington DC: The Catholic University of America Press, 1945), 245–65; Eleanor Bontecou, *The Federal Loyalty-Security Program* (Ithaca, NY: Cornell University Press, 1953), 165–67.

23. Entry, February 13, 1942, in "Cabinet Meetings, 1942," Biddle papers.

24. Biddle to Hoover, May 29, 1942, 66–6200–100–145; Hoover for AG, June 1, 1942, 66–6200–100–149. Both FBI/ Freedom of Information Act [FoI] request.

25. "In re: Harry Bridges. Before the Attorney General in Deportation Proceedings," May 28, 1942, 39–11–254, sec. 4, Bridges Case file, RG 60.

26. See Thomas Whelan [District Attorney, San Diego] to Department of Justice, April 18, 1944, in sec. 3; "Oklahoma Prosecutor Files Brief Against Robert Wood—Uses Biddle-Bridges as Basis," *International Labor Defense News,* June 27, 1942, sec. 5. Both Bridges case file, RG 60.

27. See sec. 4, Bridges case file, RG 60.

28. Editorial, "The Bridges Case," 8 June 1942, 782–83; T.R.B., "Biddle, Bridges and Browder," 8 June 1942, 796. Both in the *New Republic.* I. F. Stone, "Biddle and the Facts," 13 June 1942, 674–77; Freda Kirchwey, "Biddle and Bridges," 6 June 1942, 646. Both in the *Nation.* Editorial, *New York Herald Tribune,* 30 May 1942, quoted in National Federation for Constitutional Liberties, "The Case of Harry Bridges," July 11, 1942, in C-6405274-E, records of the Immigration and Naturalization Service [RG 85], National Archives-Pacific Region (San Francisco) [NA-PR].

29. Edward J. Ennis "Memorandum for the Attorney General," May 29, 1942, "Ennis" fldr., Rowe papers.

30. T.R.B, "Biddle, Bridges and Browder," *New Republic,* 8 June 1942, 796.

31. Francis Biddle, *A Casual Past* (Garden City, NY: Doubleday & Company, Inc., 1961), 302. Harold Ickes says that Robert Jackson told him at the time

that Biddle had discussed the Bridges decision with the president, who approved of the deportation order as an offset to his pardon of Browder. Ickes diary entry, July 5, 1942, Ickes papers.

32. Eleanor Roosevelt for AG, May 30, 1942; AG for Mrs. Roosevelt, June 8, 1942. Both in Bridges case file, RG 60. For another contemporary explanation see James M. Landis memoir, Columbia University Oral History Project [CUOHP], 59–60.

33. The government charged violations of both the Smith Act (covering acts since June 1940) and the Espionage Act (covering only wartime acts). Department of Justice [press release], July 23, 1942, "Indictment by Federal Grand Jury: Copy of," in file 103,777-E-226, RG 28.

34. "Action is Speeded to Crush Treason," *New York Times,* 30 Aug. 1942, 7. Many commentators noted that the list was not complete. "Crackpots' Roundup," *Time,* 3 Aug. 1942, 16; "Twenty-Eight Petty Troublemakers, *Nation,* 1 Aug. 1942, 82; "Small-Shot Conspiracy," *New Republic,* 3 Aug. 1942, 135.

35. Roger Baldwin, "Confidential Memorandum—Seditious Conspiracy Cases, Washington D.C.," August 21, 1942, 2508/124, ACLU papers. Baldwin noted that officials reported failing to secure indictments in Los Angeles and Chicago, and expecting that none would be forthcoming.

36. On Winrod's popularity in Kansas, see Ribuffo, *Old Christian Right,* 119.

37. Rowe to Berge, April 22, 1942, "Criminal Division" fldr., Rowe papers.

38. Frank W. Crocker, "Memorandum of Meeting, Wednesday, April 29, 1942," in "Special War Policies" fldr., ibid.

39. Confidential analysis of the case in Asst. AG Herbert Wechsler for AG, June 16, 1945, "Propaganda Domestic" fldr., Biddle papers.

40. De Aryan's case was among the weaker ones. When the July 1942 indictment was later re-written, de Aryan was dropped from the list of co-conspirators.

41. James E. Ruffin, Head Attorney, for Mr. Fisher, June 2, 1942, 146–28–107, DoJ/FoI.

42. Berge for L. M. C. Smith, June 5, 1942, Re: "The Broom," ibid.

43. A. L. Wirin (ACLU) to Berge, October 28, 1942; de Aryan to AG, March 25, 1943. Both in ibid.

44. *Daily News* quoted in "Indictments and New Spy Hunt Point to Subversion Crackdown," *Newsweek,* 3 Aug. 1942, 26–27. "Have We Descended to Propaganda Trials?" *Christian Century,* 5 Aug. 1942, 948.

45. "Analysis of Indictment Handed Down in the District Court of the United States for the District of Columbia July 1942 . . ." in "Sedition Cases—Winrod," Arthur Garfield Hays papers.

46. Chafee to A. L. Wirin, October 13, 1942, box 9, fldr. 2, Zechariah Chafee, Jr., papers.

47. Baldwin to John H. Holmes, August 17, 1942, 2355/198, ACLU papers.

48. "Minutes of Meeting of Special Committee on the Bill of Rights," April 17, 18, 1942, in 9–1 Chafee papers. This file has a number of appeals from the seditionists.

49. Chafee to Wirin, October 13, 1942, 9–2, ibid.

50. Donald L. Smith, *Zechariah Chafee, Jr., Defender of Liberty and Law* (Cambridge: Harvard University Press, 1986), 36–57.

51. Ibid., 217, 220. This book only briefly discusses Chafee and the war.

52. A Gallup poll published in September 1942 concluded that "German ideas of racial superiority find their counterpart in our own theories of racial and cultural superiority," and that isolationism was still alive. American Institute of Public Opinion (Gallup) poll, September 10, 1942, in President's Personal File [PPF] 4721, Roosevelt papers. *Fortune* poll in *Public Opinion Quarterly,* 7 (winter 1943): 757.

53. Baldwin to George Dession, December 15, 1942, 2508/107, ACLU papers.

54. Eugene F. Roth for L. M. C. Smith, September 9, 1942, "Reports, L. M. C. Smith-Sedition Section," DoJ, 62A47, FRC.

55. See Baldwin. "Confidential Memorandum—Seditious Conspiracy Cases, Washington D.C.," August 21, 1942, 2508/124 and "Confidential Memorandum of Conversations with Officials at Washington on August 20, 1942," August 26, 1942, 2501/31–33, ACLU papers.

56. "Confidential Memorandum on Conferences in Washington by Dr. Alexander Meiklejohn and Roger N. Baldwin, September 15 and 16, 1942," 2356/53, ibid.

57. Prendergast, "Memorandum for the Attorney General," Re: "Program on Sedition Cases" [draft of April 23, 1942], "Guide for the Analysis of Writings" fldr., DoJ, 67A47, FRC. Biddle's indifference is reflected generally in correspondence and specifically in the comment of Chester Lane. Lane memoir, CUOHP, 640–41.

58. Smith for Rowe, April 28, 1942, in "Special War Policies" fldr., Rowe papers.

59. Berge complaints about FBI in Berge for AG, July 3, 1943, "General Correspondence" file, Berge papers.

60. Smith for Berge, March 28, 1942, Re "Authorization of National Defense Cases"; Berge for Smith, April 1, 1942. Both in "General Correspondence" files, Berge papers. Prendergast, "Notes," April 16, 1942, "Special War Policies" fldr., Rowe papers.

61. Prendergast, ibid. See also Baldwin, "From CForster," November 30, 1942, 3501/104, ACLU papers.

62. Baldwin "From CForster," ibid., confirmed in Baldwin to Howard LeRoy, December 28, 1942, 2498/134, where he writes of a disposition to delay as long as possible. Both in ACLU papers.

63. Ralph Townsend to Z. Chafee, September 11, 1943, 31/9, Chafee papers.

64. Gallup poll dated September 10, 1942, PPF 4721, Roosevelt papers.

65. John Morton Blum, *V Was For Victory* (New York: Harcourt Brace Jovanovich, 1976), 228–34.

66. "House Allots Dies 75,000 for Inquiry," *New York Times,* 19 Feb. 1943, 38.

67. Rowe for AG, Subject: "Baltimore Speech," January 16, 1943, "Attorney General Memos" fldr., Rowe papers.

68. Henry Hoke, *Black Mail* (New York: Reader's Book Service, Inc., 1944), 51. Hoke (who appears to have been the beneficiary of prosecution leaks) identified seven senators and thirteen representatives involved in the use of the frank for the distribution of propaganda (Hoke, 44).

69. Taft to Biddle, September 26, 1942; Taft quote from *Washington Times Herald* (August 17, 1942) in William Power Maloney for AG, Re: "United States v. Gerald B. Winrod et al.," December 1, 1942. Both in 146–28–124, DoJ/FoI.

70. "America Firsters Plot New Campaign," *Hour,* 24 Dec. 1942, 1–2.

71. "Nye Defends Sedition," *New York Times,* 15 Jan. 1943, 11.

72. Copy of Wheeler to AG, December 16, 1942 in 31–10, Chafee papers.

73. The officials who had tried to frame Wheeler in 1924 because of his hand in exposing the Teapot Dome scandal. See Richard Gid Powers, *Secrecy and Power: The Life of J. Edgar Hoover* (New York: The Free Press, 1987), 140–41

74. The Judiciary Committee had censured the Justice Department in 1921 for its anti-Red activities. Powers, *Secrecy and Power,* 123.

75. House, "Extension of Remarks of Hon. Hamilton Fish," 78 Cong., 1st sess., *Congressional Record* (6 April 1943), 89: A1651–53.

76. Heinz H. F. Eulau, "Sedition Trials: 1944," *New Republic,* 13 March 1944, 337–39.

77. O. John Rogge, *The Official German Report: Nazi Penetration 1924–1942, Pan-Arabism 1939-Today* (New York: Thomas Yoseloff, 1961), 77–78.

78. Wendell Berge, "Civil Liberties After A Year of War" [January 23, 1943], *Ohio Bar Association Report* (March 1, 1943): 627.

79. "Appeasement Is Folly," *Washington Post,* 8 Feb. 1942, 16; "Dies and the Backbone Shortage," *Nation,* 13 Feb. 1943, 223–24.

80. Henry Hoke, *It's A Secret* (New York: Reynal & Hitchcock, 1946), 13–14.

81. Lane memoir, CUOHP, 619–22.

82. This course was specifically rejected by Biddle. See L. M. C. Smith for AG, October 21, 1941, in "U.S. Government—Francis Biddle" fldr., DoJ, 62A47, FRC.

83. Two weeks after Maloney was fired, Stone, writing for the Court, called "attention to the conduct of the prosecution attorney [Maloney] which we think prejudiced petitioner's right to a fair trial. . . ." *Viereck* v. *United States,* 318 U.S. 236.

84. "Confidential Not for the Files," Rowe for AG, February 25, 1943, covered by Rowe for AG, March 1, 1943, PSF "Francis Biddle," Roosevelt papers.

85. Baldwin to Rogge, April 1, 1942, 2508/114, ACLU papers.

86. Rogge to Langer, July 31, 1943, "Justice" fldr., entry 1, records of the Office of Strategic Services, RG 226.

87. Vice President Wallace tried to rally liberals with a speech declaring war on "American Fascism," but the public reaction was lukewarm and "middle opinion" seemed "profoundly bored" with Wallace and New Deal ideals. Nicholas, ed., *Washington Despatches,* entry August 1, 1943, 226.

88. Based on a survey of the articles listed in the *Reader's Guide to Periodical Literature.*

89. See series of articles by Peter Edson, August 9–12, 1943, in the *Washington News;* Adele Bernstein, "33 Sedition Suspects Still Operating," *Washington Post,* 3 Sept. 1943. Clippings in 103,777-E-46, RG 28. Walter Winchell broadcast, July 25, 1943 in "Memo for Mr. Ladd," [author blacked out], July 25, 143, in 62–31615–351, FBI/RR.

90. ACLU press release, October 11, 1943, in "Weekly News Bulletins," reel 10, ACLU, *Records and Publications.*

91. The names of those listed in each of the three indictments are found in Hoke, *It's A Secret,* 48.

92. See the analysis in Maximilian St. George and Lawrence Dennis, *A Trial on Trial: The Great Sedition Trial of 1944* (no place: National Civil Rights Committee, 1946), 91. Also, Baldwin to Frederick L. Schuman, March 18, 1944, 2679/114, ACLU papers.

Chapter 14

1. Edward Corwin, *Total War and the Constitution* (1947; reprint ed., Freeport, NY: Books for Libraries Press, 1970), 112.

2. Frederick R. Barkley, "Sedition Trials Go On Amid Heat and Clamor," *New York Times,* 11 June 1944, IV, 7.

3. The proceedings are analyzed fully in Maximilian St. George and Lawrence Dennis, *A Trial on Trial: The Great Sedition Trial of 1944* (no place: National Civil Rights Committee, 1946). See also the excellent account in Leo Ribuffo, *The Old Christian Right: The Protestant Far Right From the Great Depression to the Cold War* (Philadelphia: Temple University Press, 1983), 189–212.

4. "The Sedition Trial: A Study in Delay and Obstruction," *University of Chicago Law Review* 15 (1948): 691–702.

5. *Washington Post* editorials "Mass Trial," 16 July 1944, and "Courtroom Farce," 28 July 1944. Both in "Sedition Cases—Winrod" fldr., Arthur Garfield Hays papers. "Trial By Exhaustion," *Newsweek,* 13 Nov. 1944, 33.

6. See the discussion of the following cases in Harry Kalven, Jr., *A Worthy Tradition: Freedom of Speech in America,* ed. Jamie Kalven (New York: Harper & Row, Publishers, 1988), 179–87, 426–31.

7. To the above should be added another Jehovah's Witnesses case, *West Virginia Board of Education* v. *Barnette,* in which Justice Jackson noted that it was "now

a commonplace" that suppression of expression is tolerated only when it "presents a clear and present danger of action of a kind the State is empowered to prevent and punish." Jackson observed further that "if there is any fixed star in our constitutional constellation, it is that no official, high or petty, can prescribe what shall be orthodox in politics, nationalism, religion, or other matters of opinion." 319 U.S. 624 (1943).

8. "The British: An Inferior Breed;" "The Jew Makes a Sacrifice: Forthcoming Collapse of America;" and "The Diseased Spinal Cord." Copious excerpts from these pamphlets are found in *United States* v. *Hartzel,* 133 F.2d 169.

9. *Hartzel* v. *United States* 322 U.S. 680 (1944).

10. Kalven, *Worthy Tradition,* 185–87.

11. Melvin Gingerich, "Edwin C. Eicher and the Sedition Trial of 1944," *Palimpsest* 61 (Jan./Feb. 1980): 18–24

12. "Army Plot Hinted in Sedition Trial," 20 June 1944, 11; "Refuses to Quash Sedition Cases," 20 June 1944, 9. Both *New York Times.*

13. The three added to the indictment in January 1944 were George E. Deatherage, the leader of the Knights of the White Camellia; fascist intellectual Lawrence Dennis; and Joseph McWilliams, head of the Christian Mobilizers and the premier anti-Semite in the New York City area. Baldwin, "Memorandum on Seditious Conspiracy Trial," December 28, 1944, 2686/28 American Civil Liberties Union [ACLU] papers. O. John Rogge, *The Official German Report: Nazi Penetration 1924–1942: Pan-Arabism 1939-Today* (New York: Thomas Yoseloff, 1961), 174, 195–201.

14. Frederick R. Barkley, "Sedition Trial's Wrangles Come to An Abrupt Close," *New York Times,* 10 Dec. 1944, IV, 10.

15. Baldwin to Rogge, January 12, 1998, 2686/56, ACLU papers.

16. Baldwin, "Memorandum on Seditious Conspiracy Trial," December 28, 1944, 2686/41, ibid.

17. Summary of Sixty-Seventh Meeting, February 21, 1945, in "Council Meetings," Francis Biddle papers.

18. Wechsler for AG, Re: District of Columbia Sedition Cases, June 16, 1945, "Propaganda Domestic" file, Biddle papers.

19. Fahy for Ugo Carusi, Commissioner of Immigration and Naturalization, July 7, 1945, in "Solicitor General Office—Legal Memos," Charles Fahy papers.

20. *Keegan* v. *United States,* 325 U.S. 478 (1945).

21. *Bridges* v. *Wixon,* 326 U.S. 135 (1945).

22. Kalven, *Worthy Tradition,* 407.

23. The decision and the postwar pursuit of Bridges is in Stanley I. Kutler, *The American Inquisition: Justice and Injustice in the Cold War* (New York: Hill & Wang, 1982), 141ff.

24. Fahy for Carusi, July 7, 1945, in "Solicitor General Office—Legal Memos," Fahy papers.

25. Francis Biddle, *In Brief Authority* (Garden City, NY: Doubleday & Company, Inc., 1962), 365.

26. Ibid., 364–66.

27. Baldwin to Clark, July 13, 1945, 2686/46; and July 30, 1945, 2686/48–49, ibid.

28. Lawrence Dennis to Baldwin, October 9, 1945, 2679/148–49, ACLU papers.

29. James E. Chinn, "Sabath Insists Clark Revive Sedition Trial," *Washington Post,* 7 Oct. 1945, 11.

30. "Recommendations and Conclusions From the Report to the Attorney General, September 1946," in Rogge, *Official German Report,* 408.

31. This is apparent in Rogge and in the public controversy following his firing. See the collection of clippings and reports in file 62–54144-A, records of the Federal Bureau of Investigation [FBI] Freedom of Information [FoI] request. I am indebted to the late Richard Ruetten for this material.

32. Rogge, *Official German Report,* 447.

33. Both William Preston, Jr., "Shadows of War and Fear," in *The Pulse of Freedom: American Liberties, 1920–1970s,* ed. Alan Reitman (New York: W.W. Norton, 1975), 114, and Ribuffo, *The Old Christian Right,* 226–27 suggest the continuity between wartime repressive efforts and the postwar Red Scare.

34. See excellent discussion in Peter Irons, *Justice at War: The Story of the Japanese American Internment Cases* (New York: Oxford University Press, 1983), particularly 8, 363–65.

Index